Second Edition

Communication in Question

Competing Perspectives on Controversial Issues in Communication Studies

Second Edition

Communication in Question

Competing Perspectives on Controversial Issues in Communication Studies

Joshua Greenberg
Carleton University

Charlene Elliott
University of Calgary

NELSON / EDUCATION

NELSON / EDUCATION

Communication in Question: Competing Perspectives on Controversial Issues in Communication Studies, Second Edition

by Joshua Greenberg and Charlene Elliott

Vice President, Editorial Higher Education:
Anne Williams

Executive Editor:
Laura Macleod

Marketing Manager:
Terry Fedorkiw

Developmental Editor:
Jessica Freedman

Photo Researcher/Permissions Coordinator:
Daniela Glass

Senior Content Production Manager:
Imoinda Romain

Production Service:
Cenveo Publisher Services

Copy Editor:
Marcia Gallego

Proofreader:
Jitendra Kumar Das

Senior Production Coordinator:
Ferial Suleman

Design Director:
Ken Phipps

Managing Designer:
Franca Amore

Interior Design:
Dianna Little

Cover Design:
Peter Papayanakis

Cover Image:
© Science Photo Library/Alamy

Compositor:
Cenveo Publisher Services

Printer:
R.R. Donnelley

Library and Archives Canada Cataloguing in Publication

Communication in Question: Competing perspectives on controversial issues in Communication Studies / [edited by] Josh Greenberg, Charlene Elliott. — 2nd ed.

Includes bibliographical references.
ISBN 978-0-17-650359-8

1. Mass media—Textbooks.
2. Communication—Textbooks.
I. Greenberg, Joshua, 1973–
II. Elliott, Charlene

P91.25.C64 2012
302.23   C2012-903330-8

ISBN-13: 978-0-17-650359-8
ISBN-10: 0-17-650359-5

TABLE OF CONTENTS

INTRODUCTION

In a seminal essay, communications theorist John Durham Peters (1986) provocatively asks why the discipline of communication has failed to offer a coherent vision of itself in relation to other social sciences. To encourage debate about the field's past, present, and future, Peters suggests that as an institution, communication studies suffers from an identity crisis born out of the myriad "conceptual confusions" regarding its central intellectual tasks. More than twenty-five years have passed since Peters's influential paper, although his argument continues to resonate. Book-length studies (Katz, Peters, Liebes, & Orloff, 2002) and conferences have been devoted to the questions of what makes up communication's vision and central intellectual tasks, but no definitive answers exist. It is disputable whether there are definitive answers at all, and whether all the hand-wringing that sometimes accompanies these debates is even worth it. Intellectual exercises such as those Peters advocates are not unique to communication studies—similar debates remain unresolved within other social science disciplines as well (in the case of sociology see, for example, Brady, 2004; Burawoy, 2004; and Gans, 1989). In the end, Peters modestly proposes that the task of communication studies should be to create the "conditions that help foster a higher quality of mind" (1986, p. 552).

Goal of comm.

We agree with this objective, but a fundamental question for us remains: In what ways might communication studies actually go about doing this? Or, more to the point, how might we, as teachers and researchers, encourage our students to think differently about the central place of communication in their lives and to reflect critically on how it informs their actions in the world? Peters does not identify which steps ought to be taken, preferring instead to "pose questions that need to be asked," and to provide "a sense of how to answer them" (1986, p. 528). His questions are important for students in communication and media studies to think about: What is the discipline's position within the broader university structure and how does communication differ from other fields? What is the status of communication as a profession? What are the intellectual consequences of not taking these questions seriously? To Peters's list we might also add: How can we mobilize our knowledge and understanding of communication to encourage more thoughtful and inclusive discourse, more responsive policy, and more equitable technologies and practices?[1] How can we encourage students to apply communication theories and methods to solving the key social problems of our time? Although no singular answer or approach exists to deal with these questions, we suggest there is opportunity to forge a vision for communication by presenting the field as an open, fluid assemblage of approaches that allow us to explore both the extraordinary and the mundane aspects of everyday life.

American sociologist C. Wright Mills, an important figure in the history of critical communication studies, offers valuable insight into these questions and themes. Mills was the most widely read social scientist in North America at the time of his death in 1962 (Keen, 1999). He was a visionary, an uncompromising dissenter, and a renegade intellectual who believed that critique—the imminent questioning and challenging of assumptions and arguments—was a fundamental prerequisite to the development of a truly democratic society.[2] Drawing inspiration from a number of classical thinkers (including Karl Marx, Max Weber, Thorstein Veblen, and John Dewey), Mills believed that academic work should be seen not as a science per se, but as an intellectual craft. Intellectuals should endeavour not to separate their life from their work, but rather to integrate personal experience with professional interest in order to enrich understanding of both. As a craft, communication research should be critical and reflective, as well as dealing with the substantive problems and experiences of everyday life. And in terms that anticipate Peters's argument almost thirty years later, Mills suggests that what is needed "is a *quality of mind* that will help [citizens] use information and to develop reason in order to achieve lucid summations of what is going on in the world and what may be happening within themselves" (1959, p. 6).

crucial to understand in media

We find much value in Mills's vision for research and argue that it is as crucial for students today as it was for students in Mills's era. Mills believed that all individuals have the capacity to be intellectuals, whether they are professors, students, or people outside the formal institutions of higher learning. He developed the "sociological imagination" as a concept that could apply well beyond the discipline that bore its name to encourage within citizens a capacity for critical thinking and analysis of the personal problems and societal issues that constitute their lives. We heed Mills's wisdom and encourage students to develop a *communicative imagination* to establish connections between their everyday experiences and encounters with communications media and the broader policies, social structures, and historical forces that condition the emergence of these media, the ways in which they are used, and how they transform our lives.

Key Controversies in Communication

Envisaging the relationship between critical inquiry and everyday life is the coordinating theme of *Communication in Question*, Second Edition. Indeed, the genesis of this book came from our informal conversations about the challenges we face in engaging undergraduate students to think critically about the richness of issues and topics they can pursue within the field of communication, or to think about the communicative dimensions of issues and topics with which they are already familiar. Our universitities (like others, we assume) boasts no shortage of students who enroll in communication courses because they want to learn about the latest innovations in new media technology. Yet, when it comes to establishing connections between, for example, the rising popularity of social networking sites with policies that enable the development of digital technology and the increasing tendency toward privatization of information dissemination, retrieval, and storage, student interest often wanes. Many university professors also face increased interest from students in their communication courses who want to know what it takes to succeed in the world of advertising, public relations, or other professions. The challenge, for those of us who don't *do* advertising or PR in the purely instrumental or commercial sense, is to harness this interest by introducing students to the social, historical, and economic conditions from which their favourite ads or PR campaigns for the iPad, Volkswagen, the Gap, Breast Cancer Awareness, or the Government of Canada have emerged.

Our goal with this book is to confront this pedagogical challenge head on. The approach we take here is novel in terms of both content and style. Featuring short, engaging position papers by leading Canadian academics, journalists, and policy advocates, *Communication in Question*, Second Edition, is designed as a tool for generating small-group discussions and debates. Building on the first edition with revised and new debates about cutting-edge issues, the book presents twenty topics that feature competing perspectives from prominent researchers, activists, and journalists. The topics are organized to address a cross-section of five key themes, ranging from the general to the particular: Classical Debates in Canadian Communication Studies, Media and Social Issues, Technology and Everyday Life, Culture and Regulation, and Entertainment and Popular Culture. While these themes and their related topics are not exhaustive, we feel they represent a broad spectrum of interests and capture the diversity of research projects and programs that are ongoing within the field.

Communication in Question, Second Edition, presents students with an issue-oriented, topical reader that can serve as a locus for small-group discussion and debate and generate points of departure that can help students develop their own perspectives. We hope that the engaging prose of the papers and their connections to everyday issues will motivate students to formulate informed perspectives on topics with which they have either limited familiarity (e.g., media ownership, telecommunications regulation) or for which they may lack sufficient critical distance (e.g., the impact of social networking on activism and politics). The "competing perspectives" format of the reader also provides material for students to chew on and consider in relation to the more general overview of the field their instructor or other communication textbooks provide. Even if they disagree with one or both perspectives, students can use each essay as a starting position for asking more probing questions and challenging the assumptions and arguments they have been presented. The book illustrates that there are always at least two clear and reasonable positions to take regarding a contentious question about communication, through which students can develop their own positions and perspectives. Indeed, the cultivation of a more nuanced and arguably sophisticated position entails blending the strengths of each argument, recognizing that we are best served by understanding these issues in ways that are not limited to an either-or perspective.

Finally, the book is designed to provide an alternative to the innumerable American readers of this sort on the market. We have used such books in our own courses and are excited to provide an option that doesn't require the student to spend time unpacking why, for example, Canadian media companies are not bound by FCC regulations, and instead focuses on discussing and debating actual issues in Canadian media regulation. With this in mind, *Communication in Question*, Second Edition, provides valuable Canadian content that we hope will expose readers to the richness and diversity of issues and perspectives that inform communication studies in this country and encourage them to think and act in a more reflective, critically informed way. The fact that almost all the contributors are Canadian and/or currently work in a Canadian university or media institution also reveals the wealth of domestic expertise on issues that transcend national borders and concerns.

Given our interest in encouraging our students to develop a communicative imagination, it seems appropriate to return to the advice of C. Wright Mills. A firm believer in the importance of education, Mills suggested that in a classroom the teacher ought to try to show others how men and women think, and at the same time reveal what "a fine feeling she gets when she does it well." As professors we strive to inspire in our students an interest in and commitment to seeing their everyday lives not as manifestations of individual will or as the effects of powers acting on them from above, but as complex configurations of biography, history, and social structures that they have the capacity not only to understand but also to change. We hope this book embodies this critical ethos.

Josh Greenberg
Charlene Elliott

Notes

[1] Paula Mathieu (2005) advocates a similar pedagogical strategy for students in English.

[2] Mills was especially critical of the "abstract empiricism" that defined both social science and communication research in the early post–World War II era, represented in the works of communication scholars such as Paul Lazarsfeld and Robert K. Merton. However, Mills's own involvement with the Bureau for Social Research (the locus of abstract, empirical scholarship to which he pithily refers) and his proclivity for survey and quantitative methods where it suited him suggest a contradiction at the heart of his radicalism. Jonathan Sterne's (2005) important article speaks to these points.

References

Brady, D. (2004). Why public sociology may fail. *Social Forces, 82*(4), 1629–1638.

Burawoy, M. (2004). Public sociologies: Contradictions, dilemmas, and possibilities. *Social Forces, 82*(4), 1603–1618.

Gans, H. (1989). Sociology in America: The discipline and the public. *American Sociological Review, 54*, 1–16.

Katz, E., Peters, J. D., Liebes, T., & Orloff, A. (Eds.). (2002). *Canonical texts in media research: Are there any? Should there be any? How about these?* Cambridge, UK: Polity Press.

Keen, M. F. (1999). *Stalking the sociological imagination: J. Edgar Hoover's FBI surveillance of American sociology.* Westport, CT: Greenwood Press.

Mathieu, P. (2005). *Tactics of hope: The public turn in English composition.* Portsmouth, NH: Boynton/Cook.

Mills, C. W. (1959). *The sociological imagination.* New York: Oxford University Press.

Peters, J. D. (1986). Institutional sources of intellectual poverty. *Communication Research, 13*(4), 527–560.

Sterne, J. (2005). C. Wright Mills, the Bureau for Applied Social Research, and the meaning of critical scholarship. *Cultural Studies—Critical Methodologies, 5*(1), 65–94.

ACKNOWLEDGMENTS

The genesis of this text was a conversation between the co-editors about the challenges of encouraging undergraduate students to see how their everyday lives are deeply shaped by communication issues, technologies, policies, and practices. While each of us had created patchworks of readings and assembled teaching materials to make communication meaningful in a way that registers with the everyday lives of our students, we wondered why a reader that could meet this need had not yet been produced. Our hope is that this updated volume will not only help to fill this gap, but also present some compelling arguments about the most current issues and challenges facing society and our field. We wish to thank our students (past and present) who have always challenged us to think differently about how to present interesting material that encourages critical thinking and debate. We also wish to thank Jessica Freedman at Nelson, who was an excellent developmental editor. And our biggest expression of thanks goes to all of our authors, whose time, energy, and contributions made this book a reality.

Josh Greenberg
Charlene Elliott

PART 1 Classic Debates in Canadian Communication Studies

One defining debate in Canadian communication studies is the relationship between mass media, democracy, and national identity. Is there something about being "Canadian" that sets citizens in this country apart from other nationalities, especially our neighbours to the south? And if there is such a thing as Canadian identity, what role do television, radio, newspapers, magazines, and other media play in helping to shape, promote, or contest it? These questions have sparked others. Canada has benefited from a public broadcasting system that provides uniquely Canadian perspectives on the world, promotes a Canadian perspective on democracy, and delivers Canadian content that is seen as fundamental to the formation of Canadian identity. Yet for some critics, public broadcasting is not only unnecessary to democracy but irrelevant to the articulation of our collective sense of what it means to be Canadian.

Communication scholars in this country have grappled with these issues and questions for as long as Canada has existed, and certainly since the invention of radio and then television. They have also struggled with the question of what it means to study communication from a Canadian perspective. Do Canadian scholars approach communication and mass media from a distinct perspective? Is there a defining approach to Canadian communication studies? Should there be one?

The issues in this section deal with these questions, albeit in slightly different ways. The section begins with one of the most persistent debates in Canadian communication studies, and that's the question of whether Canada needs a public broadcaster to enhance democracy. David Taras argues that public broadcasting plays a crucial democratic role in reflecting and fostering democratic discourse by engaging citizens in the life of their nation in ways that private broadcasters do not. He argues that because the Canadian mediascape is more tightly controlled by fewer massive corporations than it has ever been, and because "private broadcasters have increasingly abandoned their obligations to the country by gorging on vast amounts of American programming and spending far less on news and

pay attention to argumentive points

public affairs," a vibrant public broadcaster is a necessary democratic force. Taras also challenges the argument that public broadcasting is irrelevant in an era of digital technology, in which Canadians have access to a "vast cornucopia of choices" in media content. In fact, he argues that it is because of this glut in global information that public broadcasting is so important.

Paul Attallah's chapter, republished in its original form from the book's first edition, challenges the theoretical premises of this argument. For him, democratic development has proceeded for millennia without the aid of public broadcasting. And if the objective of public broadcasting is to provide Canadians with content that speaks to their needs, aspirations, and cultural identity, who gets to decide what should be placed on the public broadcast agenda? Attallah argues that public broadcasting operates on the basis of ensuring "simultaneous exposure of all people to the same news, entertainment, drama, sports, and so on." Yet, he claims, not everyone agrees on the topics that we should all be discussing. In a country as diverse as Canada, there is a danger that decision making about what is in the public interest will be left to people who are inherently distrustful of popular tastes and preferences. In fact, Attallah contends, "an unrepresentative elite" has become the primary beneficiary of "a public subsidy in pursuit of its particularistic interests." And this situation, he argues, is not democratic at all.

It's a favourite cultural pastime of Canadians to mock the tone of U.S. news, in particular right-wing television and talk radio. A long-standing view of Canada's cultural elite—and many Canadians who espouse a shared perspective—is that where American news can be defined by its emphasis on titillation and sensationalism, a bombastic tenor, and an emphasis on content that aggressively promotes a consumerist agenda, Canadian news is more serious and highbrow, more polite, and more oriented to progressive politics. Thus, it shouldn't be a surprise that when the Canadian media company

Quebecor announced it was establishing Sun TV News, a right-wing television network to provide a conservative antidote to Canada's "elite liberal" media establishment, cultural commentators recoiled at the prospect of a "Fox News North."

The second issue in this section considers the impact of American media culture and asks whether U.S.-style news is bad for Canada. *Toronto Star* columnist Heather Mallick presents a pointed critique that focuses on the Quebecor case in particular, and argues that Fox News North is a dangerous idea that will erode Canadian public discourse and threaten civility. If the real Fox News is "packed with lies and a racism that ... has turned the U.S. into a contest between the horrified sane and the furious hyperventilators," it doesn't bode well for Canadians to have a maple-infused version on our menu of media offerings.

Chris Dornan challenges the argument that U.S.-style news is bad for Canadians. He accepts the premise that much of the U.S. news media is qualitatively different from what we watch, read, and listen to in Canada. But he disputes the suggestion that the vast output of American media content will somehow "captivate the attention of Canadians" such that the view Canadians have of the world will change, for the worse. More importantly, Dornan argues that even if it were possible to shield Canadians from U.S. news because of its content and tone, to do so would not be healthy for Canadian democracy. Ultimately, Dornan argues that American news is not bad for Canadians because Canadians themselves have shown time and again that when they need a window to the world, they will always defer to CTV or the CBC rather than CNN and Fox.

The third debate speaks less to the alleged effects of foreign media content than to the patterns and principles of media ownership. One of the proactive policies that Canadian governments have taken to preserve Canadian culture is to limit foreign ownership of Canadian media properties. Richard Schultz argues that existing policies that prevent foreign corporations from owning Canadian media "are based on a misreading of Canadian history [and] an undocumented claim that foreign ownership is intrinsically bad." More importantly, these restrictions are "dangerously contagious for others sectors" of the economy, such as telecommunications, where there is a desperate shortage of industry competition. The problem with Canada's foreign ownership policy, Schultz argues, has to do with the claims of its proponents that foreign media ownership will threaten the ability of Canadian media to help shape national identity. He sees in the cultural nationalist project "a gloomy, undefined foreboding of the unknown" that fails to appreciate the strengths of Canada's media industry because it is based on an assumption that Canadian culture is unable to stand for itself against the influence of other (primarily American) cultures. Schultz argues that it should not matter whether the owners of Canadian media are Canadians themselves because Canadian audiences will ultimately determine the flavour of media programming, and no media magnate would ignore this fact.

Kyle Asquith and Valerie Scatamburlo-D'Annibale challenge the argument that foreign ownership restrictions should be lifted and point to strong support from Canadians for policies that ensure Canadian media properties will remain primarily in Canadian hands. They argue that increasing the rates of foreign ownership in Canadian media properties will be a threat not because it will challenge our sense of national identity per se (although they acknowledge the currency of this argument) but because it will ensure that corporate interests are privileged over the public interest, regardless of whether those corporate interests are Canadian, American, or Saudi Arabian. What we need, they argue, is a critical rethinking of Canadian policy about foreign media ownership to ensure that Canada's media industries remain committed to advancing public interests and goals ahead of private profits.

The final debate explores the issue of Canadian communication studies itself and the question of its philosophical and political positioning. At the crux of this debate is the question of why we study communication and mass media. Is it to provide empirically grounded research in service of some kind of administrative function or problem (e.g., opinion polls to influence voting behaviour or to improve product marketing)? Or is it to examine the media system itself, and to bring critical analysis to bear on its cultural, social, and economic foundations and interests? Terry Flynn and Alex Sévigny argue that Canadian communication studies departments have overwhelming emphasized the critical tradition while keeping students "in the dark" about the merits and value of administrative research. They identify an "exploding demand" among undergraduates in communication programs for applied, professional studies (e.g., public relations, market research) and argue that administrative scholarship offers the strategies and tools necessary for success in professional practice. Flynn and Sévigny argue that students who want to pursue a degree and career in professional communication should have the strategic and tactical knowledge that the administrative tradition emphasizes; but to be ethical and reflexive, they must also possess a critical attitude and perspective that recognizes how communication practices are always embedded in relations of power. They argue that a balance between the two traditions is possible, but only if we treat the administrative perspective more seriously.

Sheryl Hamilton argues that the critical tradition is not only a more desirable approach to the study of communication, but given the range of problematic policy directions taking root (e.g., increased surveillance of the Internet by governments and corporations), it's more necessary than it has ever been. For Hamilton, critical research is not only about engaging in critique about the present; it is also about envisioning possibilities for a more just and democratic future. She provides a valuable conceptual foundation for understanding where critical communication research came from and what critical scholarship means, recognizing that the term is often used loosely and (ironically) uncritically. Hamilton provides a detailed account of how the critical tradition arrived to Canada, and the limitations of critical Canadian communication research. She concludes her chapter by arguing, provocatively, that we "need to stop congratulating ourselves on being critical and starting doing critical work."

ISSUE 1

Constructing Canada:
Do we need a public broadcaster to enhance democracy?

✔ YES

The CBC and the Future of the Canadian Media
David Taras

David Taras is professor of communication studies and holds the Ralph Klein Chair in Media Studies at Mount Royal University. He served as an expert advisor to the House of Commons Standing Committee on Canadian Heritage and is on the board of Friends of Canadian Broadcasting. He is the co-author most recently of *The Last Word: Media Coverage of the Supreme Court of Canada* and co-editor of *How Canadians Communicate IV: Media and Politics.*

Since the first edition of *Communication in Question* the very structures of the media have changed. While most commentators tend to concentrate on the rise of social media and the vast participatory culture that it has spawned, fewer media analysts discuss the degree to which much of the media is now controlled by just a handful of giant conglomerates. These behemoths dominate entire stretches of the media landscape, act as toll booths controlling access to other media, and sell information about their users as a product. In Canada, corporate concentration in the media has never been greater. A small number of conglomerates—Bell Media, Quebecor, Rogers, and Shaw—have giant wing spans that stretch across virtually all media, and these companies are vertically integrating their platforms so that they control everything from TV content to Internet service, from cable to smart phones. While people may believe that they have a vast array of media choices at their disposal, and in some ways they do, in other ways they have fewer choices than ever before.

Interestingly, the web has proven to be a winner-take-all environment with a few giant whales such as Google, Facebook, Amazon, iTunes, Zynga, Groupon, Netflix, Skype, PayPal, eBay, YouTube, and craigslist dominating much of the ocean while tens of millions of smaller fish lie in their wake. In the area of news and information, for instance, just a few sites garner much of the traffic.

What has also changed since the first edition of the book is the degree to which every medium is merging with every other medium and every medium is *becoming* every other medium. Where television broadcasting was once a distinct industry, television is now merging with the computer and indeed with social media. Conventional over-the-air broadcasters are now threatened by a phalanx of powerful rivals such as Apple TV, Hulu, Boxee, TV Everywhere, Netflix, and Google TV that specialize in online streaming. Not only do these online broadcasters threaten to destabilize the supremacy of traditional Canadian broadcasters, but as foreign media they threaten the entire broadcasting system. Where Canadian broadcasters have to deal with Canadian regulators and meet Canadian content regulations, these new players have no obligations to Canada and can play by their own rules. For instance, broadcast distributors—cable and satellite providers—contributed $368 million to Canadian content development in 2010 as part of their obligations to the Canada Media Fund. Netflix didn't contribute anything (Doyle, 2011).

I will argue that precisely because of these changes, public service broadcasters (PSBs) such as the Canadian Broadcasting Corporation/Radio-Canada (CBC) are more important than ever. In a country that spans a quarter of the world's time zones, has sharp regional and linguistic divisions, has absorbed more immigrants per capita from more countries than virtually any country in the world, and is deeply penetrated by American popular culture, the public broadcaster has been an essential platform for producing, chronicling, and celebrating Canadian public and cultural life. While private broadcasters have also played a critical role, the CBC has done much of the heavy lifting with regard to public affairs broadcasting and invests more in Canadian programming than all the other over-the-air broadcasters combined. In fact, one can argue that private broadcasters have increasingly abandoned their obligations to the country by gorging on vast amounts of American programming and spending far less on news and public affairs than was the case at the beginning of the century, a point that I will return to later.

Public broadcasters also play a crucial role by reinforcing the system of **checks and balances** that make democracy work. The goal of democratic constitutions is to create checks and balances in order to ensure democratic deliberation and to prevent the arbitrary use of power. The press is part of this series of counterweights. The power of a prime minister, for instance, is challenged and limited to varying degrees by Opposition parties, provincial premiers, and the Charter and the Supreme Court, among other forces and institutions. Prime ministers are also locked into "framing battles" with the press over whose interpretation of events will be conveyed to the public. But checks and balances exist within the media system, as well. PSBs act as a counterweight to the growing power of media conglomerates. They provide citizens with different programming choices, choices that do not treat viewers and listeners only as consumers but address their needs as citizens.

While some critics might dismiss the need for public broadcasting because of the proverbial endless sea of websites, blogs, tweets, cable channels, and videos now available to users, and hence the ready availability of Canadian media options as well as access to diverse opinions, I will argue that the existence of such a vast cornucopia of choices makes the case for public service broadcasting stronger than ever. This is because the need for countries and communities to be able to communicate with their citizens amid so many choices and indeed clutter is also greater than ever. As philosopher John Ralston Saul has described the situation that now confronts so many countries, "Everybody who is smart in bureaucracies and governments around the western world now knows that public broadcasting is one of the most important remaining levers that a nation state has to communicate with itself" (quoted in Cobb, 2001, p. A10).

What is often forgotten is that despite the explosive energy and vitality of web-based media, studies show that the vast majority of what we see, read, redact, and discuss online is still the product of the traditional media. Indeed, one recent study showed that 95 percent of the original information that appears on the web comes from the traditional media (Lohr, 2009; Pew Research Center Project for Excellence in Journalism, 2010). Hence, PSBs remain crucial content providers in the information food chain. Moreover, while online users have an incredible kaleidoscope of options to choose from, evidence from a number of studies suggests that people tend to be drawn into self-enclosed information "ghettos" or "gated communities" where they are increasingly exposed to views that they already hold. As Eli Pariser, president of MoveOn.org, has expressed the problem, "By definition, a world constructed from the familiar is a world in which there's nothing to learn" (2011, pp. 15–16). The danger is that "you can get stuck in a static ever-narrowing version of yourself, an endless you-loop" or, to put it another way, "the user becoming the content" (Pariser, 2011). Author and futurist Don Tapscott (2011) explained the problem in Canadian terms:

> There is a fragmentation of all media, and we've gone from mass media to what I call "molecular media." One upshot is that increasingly any Canadian can be awash in any particular narrow point of view. They can listen to, read or watch the views they support or hold. That means there is a real danger of balkanizing our society—we all may end up in self-reinforcing echo-chambers where all we hear is our own point of view.

This essay will describe **public service broadcasting** in Canada. My argument is that public service broadcasting is now in grave jeopardy and, as a result, our national and democratic spaces are eroding, along with our ability to see and come to terms with ourselves. My focus will be on the CBC and the challenges that it faces. My view is that Canada will have to reimagine public service broadcasting if it hopes to retain a vigorous, creative, and reliable communication infrastructure in the future. In this case the past is not necessarily a guide to the future. There is much at stake.

PUBLIC BROADCASTING AND THE DEMOCRATIC IMPERATIVE

Although the CBC is the most prominent PSB in Canada, there are a host of other public broadcasting services. These include Vision TV, an inspiring religious broadcaster that produces a rich stock of its own original programming; the Aboriginal People's Television Network (APTN), which has spawned a number of Aboriginal TV production companies; educational broadcasters such as TV Ontario and Tele-Quebec; and arguably nonprofit broadcasters such as the Cable Public Affairs Channel (CPAC), a service supported by the cable industry.

Public service broadcasting originally had a paternalistic, top-down quality. The early mandates of the CBC and more famously of the BBC in the United Kingdom, ARD and ADF in Germany, and the NOS in the Netherlands, to name some of the more prominent examples, all stressed the need to defend national sovereignty and traditional values. A stern broadcasting father used radio and eventually TV to teach high culture and social responsibility to the masses. Today the spirit that guides PSBs is entirely different. In the wake of what supporters believe is the failure of private broadcasters to produce anything but glitzy commercial products, the new goal of public broadcasting is to build **social capital** by "bridging," "witnessing," and "connecting," but most of all by treating audiences as citizens rather than as consumers or worse still as "products" whose characteristics are assembled, categorized using sophisticated algorithms, packaged, and sold to third parties.

Much of the case for public service broadcasting is predicated on the need to defend Canada's democratic space against a series of threats. The first is the fear that giant media conglomerates such as Google, Disney, News Corporation, and Comcast in the United States or Bell Media and

Quebecor in Canada are now so large and all-embracing that they threaten to smother alternative voices and viewpoints. Although nominally in competition with each other, media giants coordinate TV, film, and sports schedules, come together to lobby governments, and often act as partners in joint ventures. Competition is now so limited that a single company, Google, controls 80 percent of "search" in Canada, three companies account for the lion's share of global music revenues, six film producers account for over 90 percent of world revenues, and the seemingly multi-headed world of cable TV is dominated both in the United States and Canada by just a handful of owners. While these global media conglomerates arguably produce much of value, they offer little to Canadians in terms of instilling a spirit of community, producing native talent, telling Canadian stories, or stirring citizen participation in Canadian civic life—the very raison d'être of PSBs. At the very least, public service broadcasters allow people to figuratively "cross the street," to have another place to go to for information and ideas.

A second worry is that English-language private over-the-air broadcasters seem to be abandoning many of their civic responsibilities. Between 2006 and 2010, the amount spent on news fell significantly, investments in prime-time Canadian dramatic productions plateaued, and a lot more money was spent on sports. Most critically, by 2011 almost 60 percent of budgets were spent buying the rights to Hollywood shows—an all-time high (Canadian Radio-television and Telecommunications Commission, 2012). The policy of "Canadianizing by Americanizing," which allows Canadian private broadcasters to load up their schedules with American programs in order to become profitable in the hope that they would then invest in Canadian programming, has become laughable. The lack of commitment is especially glaring when one thinks of the amount of financial support that private broadcasters receive. While the CBC is often perceived to be the sole beneficiary of taxpayers' dollars, private broadcasters receive generous subsidies and tax breaks for the Canadian content programs that they do produce, are protected against direct American competition for Canadian advertising dollars by simultaneous substitution, and never have to worry about licence renewals regardless of how little they spend on local programming or on news and public affairs.

PSBs are a resounding success in most advanced democracies. They produce the most popular and innovative programming and largely set the agenda of public debate. The reasons for this success are hardly a mystery. There is a strong correlation between levels of funding and investments in programming, and hence audience numbers. Unfortunately, funding for the CBC compared to PSBs in other advanced countries is shockingly low. Where Germans spent close to $150 (Cdn.) per capita on public broadcasting in 2009, the British $111, and the French $78, Canadians spent $34 only (Nordicity, 2011). Only two countries, the United States and New Zealand, countries that have little to worry about in terms of national unity or the domination of foreign cultures, spent lower amounts than Canada.

The method of funding PSBs can also be critical to their success. PSBs that depend on an annual licence fee (each TV owner is assessed an annual fee), as is the case in Germany, the United Kingdom, and the Netherlands, tend to be more successful than broadcasters that rely on annual allocations from governments. The annual licence fee in the UK is a little over $300 (Cdn.). Stable funding, and hence the ability to undertake long-term planning, allows broadcasters to take greater risks and be more competitive. After all, from the germ of a first idea, to putting partnerships and financing in place, to preparing scripts, to entering into production, and finally going to air can take two to three years or longer, a process that is made far more difficult when you are dependent on the vagaries of annual funding. Arguably, secure funding also makes PSBs less likely to bend to the latest gusts of public opinion or fear offending those in power.

In some countries, PSBs are funded by what is in effect a tax on private media companies, a measure that would be difficult, if not impossible, to implement in Canada.

THE CBC'S BATTLE FOR SURVIVAL

The cruel reality is that many observers believe that the CBC has strayed far from its original ideals and that it has become a shadow of what it once was. Many also believe that it has suffered too many wounds and faces too many obstacles to survive. In a scathing indictment, for instance, John Doyle, *The Globe and Mail*'s über–television columnist, wrote in 2012 that the CBC's English-language TV network in particular needs "a new seriousness." As Doyle lamented, "Oh, the ingredients brought to the CBC schedule by *Republic of Doyle* and *Heartland* and *Arctic Air* are fine. But a blinding sheen of lightweight nonsense covers the schedule. Its executives are addicted to ratings bumps for gimmicky TV such as *Battle of the Blades*. There isn't a single serious-minded cable-quality drama on CBC. There isn't a single searing comedy" (Doyle, 2012, p. R1). His most brutal words, however, were saved for CBC's flagship news program *The National*. According to Doyle, "*The National* is sometimes a disgrace, a meandering journey through the mind of a flibberti-gibbet who spent the day garnering news bits from a hodgepodge of online sources. Bizarrely, it treats Ottawa politics with grave and tedious seriousness, failing to see the theatre that is obvious to everyone else." While his portrait is overdrawn and mercilessly unsympathetic, English-language television's fall from grace has been painful and shocking.

But here are a few points that Doyle conveniently forgot to mention. English-language radio, particularly its morning drive-time shows, remains highly popular with listeners and adds immensely to the social and cultural lives of communities. Radio-Canada's French-language television programming is edgy and popular and often goes where others fear to tread; this is true of its TV dramas as well as its investigative journalism. Its *Tout le monde en parle* has become the new meeting place for Quebec society and a "must" stop for prominent thinkers, actors, musicians, and politicians. Radio-Canada's Tou.tv service offers a well-stocked library of past and current shows and is arguably the most popular such service in Canada next to Netflix.

Moreover, the CBC is a leader in children's programming and produces and airs long-form documentaries and news stories that while sometimes searing and difficult to watch, place an intense spotlight on current affairs. The public broadcaster also provides live coverage of the great events of public life—the swearing in of a new government, the handing down of a federal budget, Remembrance Day ceremonies, and so forth—something that private broadcasters are reluctant to do if it means a loss of revenue. The CBC has become a primary source for health care reporting, as well, a subject in which it has excelled.

Most critically, aside from a QMI agency office in Toronto, the public broadcaster is the only news organization in the country that has French-language journalists regularly stationed in English-speaking Canada (excluding Ottawa), maintaining a vital bridge between the two linguistic communities.[1] The public broadcaster also does Herculean work in covering the vast expanse of the Canadian North, broadcasting in scores of native languages.

The CBC, despite the odds, also remains remarkably popular with its audiences. A Polara poll taken in the fall of 2011 found that 83 percent of Canadians used the CBC each week; 76 percent rated the job that the CBC was doing as excellent, very good, or good; and close to 80 percent favoured either maintaining or increasing government funding (Morrison, 2011). Another poll conducted at the same time, before the Harper government administered yet another sharp cut to the CBC's funding, revealed strong opposition to the budget cuts that were about to be made (Ditchburn, 2011). Support for the CBC tended to be highest among women, in Atlantic Canada, and among people with higher incomes.

There is no question, however, that the CBC is now in a life-threatening situation. Multiple storms are gathering over its future. First, the public broadcaster has been repeatedly bludgeoned by budget cuts since the early 1990s. Taking inflation into account, the CBC's parliamentary appropriation has been cut by more than 50 percent over the last fifteen years. A 10 percent cut announced in the 2012 federal budget has meant even more bleeding. To make matters worse, the Canadian Media Fund, which administers subsidies to help fund Canadian productions, has rejigged its criteria so that funding is geared to audience ratings rather than to producing distinctive, original, or high-value Canadian programming. Under these rules, flaky infotainment and corny reality shows are likely to win over arts, documentary, or public affairs programs.

This slow financial death spiral has deprived the CBC of the capacity to invest in the most crucial areas of programming. The number of lost opportunities has been staggering. The corporation didn't have the resources or political clout needed to win lucrative cable licences when they were first being awarded in the late 1980s and 1990s. While it did gain a valuable foothold with CBC Newsnet and its French-language sister station RDI, its future would have been very different had it been able to add music, children's, or sports channels to its arsenal. Had the CBC won any of these licences it would have enjoyed increased and more dependable revenues and greater economies of scale. Interestingly, cable expansion in countries such Germany and the United Kingdom has been on the public as well as the private side. In Canada, the promised land of cable TV was essentially handed over lock, stock, and barrel to private broadcasters. To make matters worse, the corporation has also had to stage a dramatic retreat from local programming. It closed local stations and curtailed news broadcasts in major centres only to have to restore them later. In the meantime, the damage was done. The CBC had jeopardized its position in Canada's burgeoning cities and could only watch helplessly as audiences and advertisers drifted elsewhere.

Budget cuts have also meant that programs are repeated several times in an evening or during the week and that for a while at least popular U.S. shows such as *Wheel of Fortune* and *Jeopardy* were purchased in order to keep ratings from falling below sea level. These moves can be seen only as acts of desperation.

Second, the CBC may no longer has the financial resources to compete in sports broadcasting. It famously lost the rights to broadcast the 2010 Vancouver Olympic Games as well as the 2012 Games from London, although it did regain them for the 2014 and 2016 Olympic Games. It lost the rights to broadcast the CFL to CTV, as well as the rights to broadcast curling, once one of the mainstays of its sports schedule. A more dismal prospect is that the CBC may be unable to continue broadcasting *Hockey Night in Canada* when its deal with the NHL set to expire in 2014. Given that Rogers and Bell Media, which respectively own Citytv and Rogers Sportsnet and CTV and TSN, have combined forces to buy Maple Leaf Sports and Entertainment, which owns the Toronto Maple Leafs, the Raptors of the NBA, and Toronto FC, among other properties and franchises, along with a host of other broadcasting rights, the CBC is very likely to be cut out of the action. Even if it wins these rights, the amount that it would have to spend might mean that budgets for other programming areas would have to be shredded. To add insult to injury, the CBC lost the rights to the *Hockey Night in Canada* theme song to CTV. Although the CBC has been reluctant to disclose how much revenue it generates from sports, some reports suggest that it may be as much as half of all its advertising.

Third, at the very time that the CBC is the most vulnerable, its competitors have never been stronger, never more unassailable. The CBC now has to compete against giant conglomerates that enjoy the advantage of "vertical integration" and multiple platforms. Bell Media (CTV), Rogers (Citytv), Quebecor (TVA), and Shaw (Global) are not only over-the-air and cable broadcasters but also Internet service providers, cable operators, and phone companies. They own the entire distribution staircase and with it the capacity to promote and distribute their content in ways that that the CBC can't hope to compete with.

REIMAGINING PUBLIC BROADCASTING

People's natural tendency is to judge the CBC by what they watch and listen to today, rather than by what the broadcaster could be if it were given greater resources and a new bolder mandate. As Ira Wagman has put it, "It's better to think of it in a different way. Because it's a public broadcaster, the CBC has to imagine what the country should be. What it needs is to imagine again" (quoted in Taylor, 2011).

Redesigning the CBC has become a kind of cottage industry, with members of the public, commentators, and experts proposing different visions and ideas. Some believe that radio and television should be separated and run as different companies. Others argue that the public broadcaster should reverse its current strategy of being a national broadcaster with weak local roots by reinvesting in local communities and maintaining only a thin national presence. Still others want the CBC to sell off its transmitters and stations and become a "public content" company that develops programming that can be made available anywhere. Another suggestion is that the CBC abandon sports and advertising entirely in exchange for which private broadcasters would pay compensation to the CBC for no longer being a competitor. Still others would like to see a tighter fit between the public broadcaster and the country's educational institutions with specialized programs turned into courseware.

The Lincoln Report, the product of a two-year review of Canadian broadcasting undertaken by the House of Commons Standing Committee on Canadian Heritage (2003), made a number of recommendations that might strengthen the CBC. The report envisioned a new management system where the president would be elected by the board rather than appointed by the government and stressed the need for multiyear funding. It also suggested that the corporation could adopt an asymmetrical model that would allow it to assume different shapes and responsibilities in different parts of the country. It might dispense with local news shows in Toronto or Vancouver, markets well served by private broadcasters and other PSBs, but play a larger role in cities like Regina or Waterloo, in the Canadian North, or in Newfoundland and Labrador, where citizens have fewer choices.

In the end, however, no vision can work unless there is a willingness by governments and citizens to fund the CBC. One can only imagine how strong the CBC might have become had, as had been proposed by a special mandate review committee in 1996, the GST been replaced by a tax on the sale of communication services. Under such a system, every purchase of an app, a cable package, an iPod, or a smart phone would have left the equivalent of the GST on the table for Canadian productions. Needless to say, the private broadcasters strongly opposed the idea. While the proposal was sharply rejected at the time, in retrospect virtually all of the CBC's current problems and dilemmas would have been solved.

Those who advocate less funding for the CBC believe that the costs of funding are simply too great for taxpayers to bear. Interestingly, this is not the case in almost all other democratic countries where taxpayer support for public broadcasting is much higher than in Canada. But few calculate the costs of not funding the CBC. Think of all the stories about government corruption and spending, the loss of manufacturing jobs, the financial system, education, or health care that were underreported or not reported at all; think of great Canadian programs that were never made; think of the talent that was lost to Hollywood; think of the money that could have been made from exporting programs overseas; and think of how little our young people know about the country in which they live. While some of these losses are difficult to quantify financially because they are in some ways amorphous and intangible, in the end they have amounted to a great deal. The question is whether the country can continue to suffer these losses.

Note
[1] Conversation with Florian Sauvageau, April 4, 2012.

References

Canadian Radio-television and Telecommunications Commission. (2012, April 4). CRTC releases 2011 financial results for Canadian conventional television stations [News release]. Retrieved from http://www.crtc.gc.ca/eng/com100/2012/r120404b.htm

Cobb, C. (2001, January 30). Saul enters CBC debate. *National Post*, p. A10.

Ditchburn, J. (2011, November 11). Majority backs public funding for CBC, poll finds. *The Globe and Mail*. Retrieved from http://www.theglobeandmail.com/news/politics/majority-backs-public-funding-for-cbc-poll-finds/article2232586/

Doyle, J. (2012, March 29). Memo to the CBC: Suck it up. *The Globe and Mail*, p. R1.

Doyle, S. (2011, November). High noon at the CRTC. *Literary Review of Canada*, 24.

Lohr, S. (2009, July 13). Study measures the chatter of the news cycle. *The New York Times*. Retrieved from http://www.nytimes.com/2009/07/13/technology/internet/13influence.html

Morrison. I. (2011, October 27). Presentation to the Standing Committee on Access to Information, Privacy and Ethics, House of Commons. Retrieved from http://www.friends.ca/brief/10399

Nordicity. (2011, April). *Analysis of government support for public broadcasting and other culture in Canada.* Retrieved from http://www.nordicity.com/reports/Nordicity%20Analysis-Public%20Broadcasting%20(2011-04).pdf

Pariser, E. (2011). *The filter bubble.* New York: Penguin.

Pew Research Center Project for Excellence in Journalism. (2010, May 23). *New media, old media: How blogs and social media agendas relate and differ from traditional press.* Retrieved from http://pewresearch.org/pubs/1602/new-media-review-differences-from-traditional-press

Tapscott, D. (2011, July 30). A new reason to support the CBC. *Toronto Star*. Retrieved from http://www.thestar.com/opinion/editorialopinion/article/1032448--a-new-reason-to-support-the-cbc Taylor, K. (2011, August 15). Still a happy gang: How the CBC can give Canada what it needs. *The Globe and Mail*, p. A7.

ISSUE 1

Constructing Canada: Do we need a public broadcaster to enhance democracy?

✘ NO

What Is the Public in Public Broadcasting?
Paul Attallah

Paul Attallah taught at l'Université de Montréal and l'Université du Québec, and later in the School of Journalism and Communication at Carleton University. He was the author of several books and articles on communication history and theory.

Public broadcasting serves many excellent purposes. This, however, does not link it intrinsically to democracy any more than to the promotion of industry, world peace, or healthy diets. We must distinguish between *how we use* public broadcasting and *what it is* in itself.

Indeed, most observers agree that democracy predates all forms of broadcasting by approximately 2500 years. Of course, the democratic forms of the past were not always consistent with our contemporary version. Nonetheless, the notion of a self-reflexive, normative structure rooted in a civil society engaged in rational reflection flowered and evolved for millennia entirely without the aid of public broadcasting. Democracy needed free speech, a public sphere, confidence in human reason, articulate individuals, respect for an independent judiciary, deliberative bodies, and so on. But it didn't need broadcasting, public or otherwise.

The alleged benefits of public broadcasting are suspiciously recent.

Furthermore, the very idea that public broadcasting enhances democracy marks a breathtaking shift in attitudes toward the media. Indeed, ever since their first broadcasts to the public, radio and television have been the object of an unending stream of invective and vilification.

Television, in particular, stands accused of numerous crimes. First, it is accused of having ushered in the age of image politics, which displaced substantive political debate with image management, spin doctoring, photo ops, and manipulation. Second, it denatured political discourse by reducing everything to glib sound bites. Third, it transformed election coverage into horse races, thereby replacing knowledge of arguments with the mere spectacle of jockeying for advantage. Fourth, television inserted *itself* into the political process such that much news coverage now concerns the performance of the media in covering politics. Fifth, and most damagingly, television turned all politics into entertainment. Politicians became actors upon its stage and eventually adopted the tricks of the actor's trade. They sought to please rather than to lead. They became consumed by the trivialities of appearance, the cut of their clothes, or the sound of their voice. Worse yet, they began to parade across the small screen pouring out their emotions instead of their ideas.

Television, then, according to the accusations, forces politics to conform to its own peculiar rhythms (the scheduling of press conferences, important announcements, meetings, etc.), to its need for striking images and facile commentary, to its inexhaustible appetite for engaging personalities, and to its unerring instinct for entertainment. The end result is the 24-hour news channel, which, precisely because it needs to fill 24 hours every day, elevates the private lives of politicians to the same status as news about war or terrorism. It flattens everything into triviality and congratulates itself for being so friendly.

It is remarkable, therefore, that we should now call upon broadcasting, the very technology that has debased and corrupted democracy, to enhance it. Furthermore, it is often those who most vociferously denounce broadcasting who also clamour most loudly for public broadcasting.

However, if broadcasting is so bad for democratic life, why is public broadcasting so beneficial? The argument runs as follows. Private or corporate broadcasting is driven by commercial or industrial interests, not by the public interest. These interests draw it ineluctably toward the entertaining, the conventional, the uncontroversial, the mildly amusing, and the slightly bland. Hence, private broadcasting neglects the substantive concerns of citizenship and drives out all noncommercial, unprofitable, or unconventional voices. Therefore, we need public broadcasting, which alone can represent the entire range of public opinion. Only public broadcasting can air unconventional, controversial, or challenging material. Only public broadcasting can speak for those who are disenfranchised, marginalized, or ignored by private broadcasting. Only public broadcasting can treat viewers as citizens rather than as consumers, because only public broadcasting is committed to the public interest rather than the corporate interest.

It's a noble argument, and no one would want a broadcasting system devoid of such sentiments. Unfortunately, it's also inaccurate.

WHY ONLY BROADCASTING?

Public broadcasting rests on the notion that in all societies there exists a general or collective interest that is superior to all private or individual interests and can never be fully or adequately expressed by private media. However, if such an interest really does exist, why should broadcasting alone be required to give it voice? If it is so important, why not have *public* newspapers, *public* novels, *public* movies, *public* magazines and songs, *public* stage plays and nursery rhymes, *public* pamphlets, *public* billboards, and *public* websites?

It would of course be laughable—indeed dangerous—to propose that newspapers be required to express the overarching public interest. However, newspapers *are* unregulated and owned by private interests. Should the state, therefore, intervene to regulate them or launch its own newspaper that would achieve in print what public broadcasting does electronically?

Such a course of action seems ill-advised and should incite us to reconsider the flawed notion that public broadcasting is required to enhance democracy.

WHAT IS THE PUBLIC INTEREST?

But this raises the most difficult question of all. What *is* the public interest, and how does public broadcasting defend it? Broadcasting basically ensures the simultaneous exposure of all people to the same news, entertainment, drama, sports, and so on. Should *that* be our definition of public interest? One might have thought that public interest consisted not in narrowing the range of information and entertainment but in guaranteeing its maximum diversity; not in ensuring uniformity of exposure but in multiplying the opportunities for unique and individualized thought; not in ensuring the centralized production and dissemination of unitary content but in maximizing the possibilities for decentralized production and distribution.

Nonetheless, if we assume that the public interest is best served through the type of homogeneous exposure that broadcasting favours, then another uncomfortable question arises. Who gets to decide the nature of the programming, who gets to choose the specific news, sports, drama, and entertainment to which all will be exposed? After all, our differences in age, sex, income level, general interests, life experience, and so on, might lead us to make very different choices. And that's a problem with the notion of a *public* interest. The definition always emanates from a particular point of view and only pretends to be a general, universal, public interest.

The main reason for simultaneous mass exposure to content is to ensure collective orientation, meaning everyone agrees that the same topics are important and should be on the public agenda. Unfortunately, different people from different backgrounds often disagree. Some think the public agenda should focus on the decriminalization of drugs, others on universal daycare, and still others on increased military expenditure. Who gets to decide which of those, which mixture of those, which emphasis upon those is right? In the world of newspapers, each newspaper decides for itself and seeks out whatever readers it can. In the world of public broadcasting, we view such plurality of viewpoints with suspicion and seek instead to create consensus.

So far, we've examined the problem of public interest in relationship to news. But what happens if we look at entertainment? Typically, public broadcasting has viewed mass appeal entertainment as an opportunity to circulate content that exhibits approved social norms and attitudes; that highlights issues and attitudes deemed politically or socially relevant; that is most aesthetic, challenging, or difficult; and that speaks to minority audiences.

Again, none of these goals is hateful in itself. The issue is whether such goals can lay claim to the enhancement of democracy. They cannot because they assume that even entertainment should serve a consensus-building function by circulating the approved views of those who get to define public interest.

Public broadcasting, therefore, is distrustful of public taste, fearing that if left to their own devices, people will choose unapproved content. Consequently, public broadcasting has long insisted that we aspire to something higher, that public taste in itself is unworthy and in need of improvement. It seeks, therefore, to elevate and educate public taste. Indeed, the world's first public broadcaster, the BBC, was specifically intended to wean its audience from the merely popular content of BBC One toward the loftier and more valuable content of BBC Two. It was, quite simply, based on a deep prejudice against popular taste and the enduring conviction that only the higher tastes of the higher classes were truly worthy of mass dissemination.

CBC television was constructed on a similar paternalistic pattern. It looked down upon American broadcasting as merely popular and set itself the task of enlightenment and education. Now, such a task can be accomplished with greater or lesser talent, and, in all fairness, the CBC has enjoyed some notable successes. But the point is not to attack the CBC for the mere fact of being a public broadcaster or to anoint private broadcasters for the mere fact of *not* being public broadcasters. It is to highlight the fact that prejudices against public taste eventually undermine the very rationale for public broadcasting by digging a chasm between the broadcaster and its audience. To be truly public, broadcasting should have the same regard for all tastes. It cannot be content with just a fraction of the audience. However, by condemning popular taste, it alienates large segments of the public. As a result, CBC television shares have dwindled to approximately 5 percent of the total population, and CBC radio is smaller yet. These low numbers, in turn, generate demands for the dismantling of the CBC on the grounds that serves not the public interest but only an unrepresentative elite, which enjoys a public subsidy in pursuit of its particularistic interests.

There are no easy answers to these problems. But it might be useful to acknowledge that the shaping of collective attitudes and the enforcement of cultural choices are not the expression of public interest; they are the expression of particular interests masquerading as public.

THE FUNCTIONS OF PUBLIC BROADCASTING

We also need to challenge the notion that public broadcasting accomplishes important social functions that private broadcasters can never meet. Private channels such as the Discovery Channel, the History Channel, and National Geographic clearly fulfill a classic public broadcasting agenda. There has never been so much educational and documentary programming, and most of it emanates from private broadcasters.

The same is true of such private outlets as the Independent Film Channel, Bravo, ARTV, and CoolTV. As for minority audiences, private specialty channels cater to gays and lesbians, science fiction fans, lovers of drive-in movies, NFL aficionados, game show fans, book lovers, news junkies, horror fans, cartoon watchers, and so on.

Consequently, if the claim is that public broadcasting enhances democracy by serving marginalized or disenfranchised audiences, by airing unconventional or aesthetically important content, by treating viewers as citizens with appetites for information, knowledge, and opinion, then we must conclude that private broadcasters also accomplish virtually all of these goals.

Public broadcasting has no monopoly on the enhancement of democracy, just as private broadcasting has no monopoly on mass appeal programming. Indeed, internationally, several large private broadcasters—Channel 4 in Britain, STV in Sweden, SBS in Australia—act for all intents and purposes just like public broadcasters. And the audiovisual landscape of North America is littered with private specialty channels that serve the same function.

Conversely, in Canada, the national public broadcaster, the CBC, provides some services—Newsworld, Sirius radio—available only on a private pay model. Indeed, the public BBC is available in Canada only to paying cable and satellite subscribers. Hence, in our impure reality, private broadcasters espouse public objectives and public broadcasters use classically private business models. This underscores the need to unlink notions of public interest and democracy from the structures that we are accustomed to and that may prevent us from thinking anew.

Perhaps, then, the public interest is better served not by creating a public broadcaster, with its attendant bureaucracy and internecine struggles, but by encouraging the development of numerous voices from all sectors of society. But to do so requires us to abandon the illusion that only public broadcasting can enhance democracy.

If we look only to Canada, who can argue that *Corner Gas*, which aired on the private CTV network, was less successful, less Canadian, and less important than any of the sitcoms that have aired on the public CBC? Would it be useful to argue that the privately produced *W5* is less of a news program than the publicly produced *the fifth estate*? Can it be claimed that sports coverage on a private network lacks some essential quality that it would suddenly possess if only it were aired on a public network?

Of course, this does not mean that in the absence of public broadcasting, private broadcasters would suddenly be more respectful of the public interest. It means that the public interest can assert itself in unanticipated ways and that neither public nor private broadcasting has an intrinsic link to democracy.

CIVIL SOCIETY

Democracy is more robust than just public broadcasting. Furthermore, numerous other institutions and social factors such as laws, an independent judiciary, literacy, relative social stability and wealth, free speech, and deliberative assemblies play an infinitely more important role in enhancing democracy. And to them may be added sociocultural habits such as individualism, reason, and the transmission of our heritage to the future. All of these factors hugely predate and will outlast the transitory phenomenon of public broadcasting.

The desperate urgency with which so many in Canada pine for public broadcasting really has nothing to do with the imaginary virtues of public broadcasting. It has to do with their uneasy sense that Canadian civil society is weak and incapable of shouldering its burden. Historically, **civil society** has been the realm of spontaneous or elective social relations ungoverned by the authority of the state. It is the social space that gives rise to aspirations of autonomy and democracy, that allows rational discourse to be exercised and honed, that fosters spontaneous and humane social and individual arrangements. The impulses of civil society—the civil rights movement, the women's movement, the movement of gays and lesbians, the anti-war movement, the environmental movement, the anti-globalization movement—can certainly cross over into the political sphere, but they do not depend on it and are not driven by it. Indeed, civil society frequently stands opposed to the political order and has fought it in the name of norms and values that have been only slowly accepted. On the other hand, some civil society phenomena—bowling leagues, a preference for white over red wine, dog owners' associations—are extremely unlikely ever to cross over into the political realm but nonetheless contribute to the texture of our collective life.

Alas, as innumerable observers have noted, Canadian civil society is weak. Spontaneous citizens' organizations are just as likely to turn to the state for funding or official sanction as they are to stand opposed to it. Indeed, many civil society groups—dance groups, legal reform associations, various rights-seekers—would barely exist without direct government subsidy.

The hope, therefore, is that public broadcasting will somehow stand in for our weak civil society, somehow strengthen it by finally putting us all in touch with each other. That is where the linking of public broadcasting to democracy comes from: public broadcasting will somehow play the role that civil society cannot. Unfortunately, we can neither rescue nor repair civil society through public broadcasting. Its problems need to be addressed in civil society itself. This does not mean that public broadcasting can never make a contribution to civil society; it means that public broadcasting has no privileged link to the defence of democracy. Civil society is made up of the vastest possible range of groups and interests and associative forms. Public broadcasting is only one among them—not the most important, not the singular focus of our hopes and aspirations, not the thing that should absorb all of our energies.

Indeed, as the Canadian example shows, public broadcasting very easily falls prey to special interests rather than to the public interest. For example, when was the last time public broadcasting offered a program that you looked forward to with fevered anticipation? Or that captured perfectly the mood of your time or generation? That generated a star whose name was on everyone's lips? The point is not that these absolutely never happen but that they happen so infrequently as to be almost invisible. If the public interest means that, occasionally, the public is interested, then our implementation of public broadcasting has not been very successful, as evidenced by the modesty of audiences, the lacklustre performance of programming, and the overwhelming preference for American television.

A NEW DISPOSITION

We now stand at the brink of the biggest media shakeup since broadcasting itself. Traditional over-the-air network broadcasting in which the flow of content is centrally produced and disseminated is disappearing before our very eyes. It is being replaced by file sharing and downloading, online streaming, video blogging, location-free viewing, and so on. People increasingly watch TV over the Internet via BitTorrent or YouTube.com, on PVRs and DVDs. Indeed, networks now deliberately make their content available online. And user-generated content is at least as compelling as centrally produced programming. Broadcasting is yesterday's technology.

These new technologies detach individuals from network programming and encourage them to associate based on their elective affinities. Any one of them is closer to civil society than broadcasting ever was, and any one of them is as likely to generate autonomous feelings of citizenship or selfhood as public broadcasting ever could.

In this context, the argument over public broadcasting is simply quaint. Not just because of new technologies but also because the technological shift points to a new definition of the public interest. The public interest is no longer the synthesized culture and opinion shaping of the past—it is the interest of individuals to make their own culture as they wish, to sample and use collective culture on their own terms, to be heard above and beyond the structures and strictures of existing media. This does not mean that the future is a nirvana in which all will turn out well. There will be mistakes, abuses, and false starts. But it does point to a fundamentally **new media disposition** in which the production and dissemination of content are no longer the exclusive purview of centralized producers and distributors.

In an age of increasingly decentralized technologies that disconnect citizens from uniform schedules and program menus, democracy is no longer coterminous with broadcasting's mass transmission of uniform content. Democracy comes instead from freedom of speech and mutual respect and the attendant institutional arrangements that enshrine and honour those values. Of course, public broadcasting can contribute to democracy, but it is only one contributor among many. Indeed, the sensible approach might be to look beyond the media altogether and toward a reinvigorated public sphere.

Discussion Questions

1. What are the main arguments usually made against broadcasting?
2. What argument is usually made in favour of public broadcasting specifically, despite the arguments against broadcasting generally?

3. What is "the public," and how is it defined by (a) the defenders of public broadcasting and (b) those who point to new television technologies? How are debates about the value of public broadcasting essentially debates about the concept of the public and the public interest?

4. What is civil society, how does it manifest itself, who can participate in it, and why is it weak in Canada?

5. If you could turn back the clock and were given the chance to construct the Canadian broadcasting system from scratch, what would you keep, what would you change, and how would you build a better system than the one that exists today?

6. Do you think the CBC is doomed to extinction? Why or why not?

7. Some observers believe that the old broadcasting models are breaking down. Describe the forces that are bringing about this change. Do you agree with their predictions?

ISSUE 2

Not neighbourly:
Is American news bad for Canadians?

✔ YES

Fox News North Is a Rancid Idea*
Heather Mallick

Heather Mallick is a staff columnist for the *Toronto Star*, writing on politics, feminism, economics, and many other subjects. She has written for *The Globe and Mail*, the *Financial Post*, *The Guardian*'s Comment Is Free website, and CBC.ca. The author of two books of essays, *Pearls in Vinegar* (2004) and *Cake or Death* (2007), she has a master's degree in English literature from the University of Toronto and a journalism diploma from Ryerson.

Fox News and I have a history, a painful sordid history with rancour on their side and disgust on mine. Now their rumoured-to-be illegitimate child, something called Sun TV News— "Fair and Balanced Eh" would be their slogan, I guess—wants to set up camp in Canada and I will have none of it.

Of course I may have to have all of it, given that their business plan is said by many to include the Harper government pressuring the CRTC to give Sun TV News a "mandatory" cable deal, which is an almost unheard-of status, particularly for a new specialty channel in the digital age.

It means that it must be included in at least one tier, or cable package, that you're probably buying for other reasons. It's the kind of deal other corporations, fighting for every viewer and every dollar, would bleed themselves with leeches to win. Quebecor, which owns the *Sun*, says if it doesn't get this special CRTC-granted status, the channel will collapse.

Everyone has assumed that if CRTC chair Konrad von Finckenstein does the legal, ethical thing and tells Sun TV News to run the same gauntlet as every other channel, he will have his fragile head crushed between leathery Conservative fingertips. Von Finckenstein has publicly said he has not been approached and that the standard public hearings will be held this fall. He thinks he won't be targeted.

He is naïve, which is odd for a former judge and public servant of such experience. Konrad, if I can place us on a first-name basis, watch out.

The argument that Fox News North will be fair and balanced, a hard-right antidote to the allegedly liberal CBC, is nonsense. A privately owned propaganda channel is not the equivalent of an underfunded non-profit public broadcaster stuck with the legal requirement to inform a huge fractured country on a factually immaculate basis. The CBC's disastrous recent effort to make itself young, populist, and silly notwithstanding, it really does try hard. But its new style of hard-hitting

---

*Reprinted with permission - Torstar Syndication Services

investigative reporting—that down market coffee shops are crusted with dirt or that people should avoid fire and flood—is the equivalent of the ponderous *Washington Post*'s absurd offshoot, Slate. com, which has a male reporter on the uterine beat and runs articles headlined "A history of quicksand in the movies."

Canadians may not be familiar with Fox News except as a running gag on *The Daily Show with Jon Stewart* and *The Colbert Report*, run late at night on CTV's The Comedy Network (brilliant shows that you must PVR right now. Go on, do it. I'll wait.)

Fox celebrates ignorance and fosters hate, it's your weasel heart, that chunk of you that spurts endorphins when a hated rival crashes his car on Ambien or is caught with a gerbil where a gerbil shouldn't be. It's a poison tree. Weirdly transfixing as Glenn Beck is, when you eat the Fox apple, it eats away at you.

And it's a news cartoon. When real journalists make a mistake, we feel a sickness in our soul. It's humiliating, it should, and will be, publicly corrected, and co-workers avert their eyes. Fox isn't like that. They seemingly make up numbers, flying unburdened through their fenced-in no-fact zone.

I know Fox because, kindly liberal caricature that I am, I went on Bill O'Reilly's show in 2004. I didn't see why Fox viewers should be deprived of an alternative view though I bet they'd never seen a Canadian before. (I remember once being told by the New York Times Syndication Service that Canada couldn't possibly have two left-wing women commentators, and getting a grovelling apology from the editor after Naomi Klein called him and, well, crushed his little head.)

The O'Reilly appearance was a disaster. Trying to be kind and rational, I kept sending wide-eyed moral reproaches into the black monitor of a Toronto TV studio while O'Reilly invented wildly incorrect stats from non-existent publications about the alleged U.S. boycott of France for not trotting off obediently to Iraq. Readers later joyously sent me "Paris Business Review" coffee mugs with "beellions of dollars" over a photo of a baguette (O'Reilly's sex scandal involved an intern and phallic bread and yes, I laughed).

The fallout was more troubling, hundreds of emails from enraged men who wanted me dismembered. Fox, I contend, and an apparently large contingent of its viewers actively dislike women (and blacks, Muslims, Mexicans, people who get more sex than they do, i.e., everyone, latte, cranberry bogs, cities, passports, chicken living outdoors, etc.). It hates Canada. It eggs on its women-hating fanbase which is, like the subsequent SwiftBoaters and TeaBaggers, a malign force bubbling with rage.

Weirdly, I worked for the Toronto Sunday *Sun*, both before and after it was sold to Quebecor. The *Sun* fancied itself much as I imagine the Fox News North people do now, iconoclasts speaking up for regular people (or "folks," the patronizing word George W. Bush popularized), non-unionized and crushed by government. But Quebecor did the crushing. Now the paper is thin and tubercular, its staff sparse and ghostly pale.

An editor there, a kind man I liked, used to rail against the "elites." This is the centrepiece of Pierre Karl Péladeau's Sun News TV strategy. (Péladeau, an erratic heir to wealth, has always seemed perfectly Parisian. His political outlook is puzzling.) Which was fine, but this editor pronounced it "elights." I am a slave to my natural courtesy and when someone mispronounces a word, the only decent thing is to go along with it. Yes, "Frood" was wrong, psychoanalysis so silly.

But I could never bring myself to say "elights." Everyone has a line they won't cross, and I was unwilling to mock what Harper has always resented since some ancient slight: the wine-sipping book-reading types who snubbed him when he first came to Ottawa. I grew up in small northern towns, with the allegedly stupid people who allegedly vote for Harper, and books were my ticket to what Harper calls élitism, which is plain old city living and he's wrong to fear it.

Goodness, we have travelled far. Let's get back to Sun TV News, owned by Péladeau, still only a concept, to be run by the young permanently enraged Kory Teneycke (a thin Beck) and modelled after Fox News. Fox, owned by Rupert Murdoch's News Corp., is a malevolent presence in American life. Packed with lies and a racism that would shame Jesse Helms, it has turned the U.S. into a contest between the horrified sane and the furious hyperventilators.

Although there is no corporate connection between Fox and Sun, there is a visceral one. In March 2009, CP has reported, Prime Minister Stephen Harper lunched in New York City with Murdoch, accompanied by Fox news president Roger Ailes and then-Harper communications director Tenycke.

The great British TV dramatist Dennis Potter said it best when he excoriated Murdoch's effect on British life in a BBC TV interview in 1994. Potter was dying of pancreatic cancer—he had a bottle of liquid morphine by his side during the program—and he named his cancer "Rupert."

"I would shoot the bugger if I could," Potter said on-air. "There is no one person more responsible for the pollution of what was already a fairly polluted press, and the pollution of the British press is an important part of the pollution of British political life, and it's an important part of the cynicism, and misperception of our own realities, that is destroying so much of our political discourse."

Murdoch, who admittedly rescued the British press by destroying hidebound printers unions in Wapping in the 1980s, started Fox News in 1985. He was exporting "evil," as Sen. Al Franken put it, long before Potter reviled him.

The weird thing is that Fox has an influence far beyond its actual reach in fragmented U.S. TVland. (On Friday of last week, for example, it had only 1.7 million viewers in prime time, reports TVbythenumbers.com.) I know this to my cost.

When Sarah Palin appeared at the Republican convention in 2008, I wrote about her honestly, an online CBC.ca column that would have disappeared into the ether as usual, except Fox News found out about it. I said Palin was a dangerous idiot. It made me the target of the worst Americans and Canadians, men with a violent hatred of (see list above). The attack was organized, as all Internet attacks are. And online anonymous hate is like a poison gas.

It was the same as my previous experience with Fox, but hotter and filthier. I'm happy to be called a pig by Greta Van Susteren, whatever. But this time people really were hunting not just me, but friends, which made me frantic with guilt and fear. They were trying to find out where I lived. I'm only writing this now because I'm in a building with security guards. Here's a typical email from a Fox viewer … minus the x-rated words I've beeped out.

"So you don't like Sarah Palin you ugly slut? Beep you, you liberal piece of shit. I'll bet your beep smells like rotten meat. You are one ugly beep. I'd love to punch you right in your chops and knock every tooth out of your head. Come see me beep! I have something for you. Something all liberal pieces of shit need. Beep off and die you beeping beep!"

Being the target of Internet swarming is paranoia-producing and lonely-making. I got no sympathy from girlfriends—they eat for comfort like normal people—for my subsequent weight loss. I spent the winter not eating and thinking gloomy thoughts. My favourite TV show was a Brit comedy called *Human Remains*. I lost so much weight that my feet and fingers shrank. I asked my doctor if I was underweight, and he said grimly, pointing to my breasts, "Not if those are real," (they are), which I still think is a funny line. I laughed, unwillingly, and went out to buy a smaller wedding ring and new shoes plus insoles for my pumps.

Fox targets women. And racial groups. But most worryingly, it targets individuals in the same way the Harper government does. Tom Flanagan, who has helped guide Harper since he met him in 1990 at the University of Calgary, laid out his game plan for the conservative takeover in his book *Harper's Team*. What matters is the cleansing of alleged liberals from the actual governance of the country. Once you get elected, Flanagan wrote, "you choose judges, appoint the senior civil service, fund or de-fund advocacy groups." This is the Fox agenda and certainly the Harper agenda we see now.

And you are free to approve of the Harper agenda but it is very wrong to trash the telecommunications regulation process—which regards the airwaves as precious to Canadians—to bring in a northern version of what has turned the U.S. into a nation where fact-based people are scorned and tormented by screamers. Fox did this.

Here's the thing. Fox won't succeed here. It is only viable, as *Globe* TV critic John Doyle has written, "if it is shoved down our throats" by Péladeau seeking mandatory access. Now viewers are happy to see new channels, but they notoriously hate to pay for them. You wouldn't be able to avoid buying Fox without giving up huge TV slices. I buy Rogers' fancy package just so I can get *Mad Men*. But I chose that. The money isn't extracted from me with forceps.

I can't even see Sun News TV succeeding here, mainly because Canada has never even been able to sustain an evening talk show, much less 24 hours of political ranting. When it comes to interesting people, we have a shallow talent pool, partly because our star performers move to the States and partly because we are civilized and decent, which doesn't set an interview alight. When someone says something godawful dumb, we wince but we don't say, "I hate you and I'm going to crush your head."

We say, "You may have a point there."

A nation that thinks *Corner Gas* is funny because it is us is a nation that won't go for full-bore mean stupidity. We like underdogs because Canada is an underdog. I adore *Corner Gas*.

Fox/Sun will be boring. But it's still wrong.

ISSUE 2

Not neighbourly:
Is American news bad for Canadians?

✖ NO

Voice of America
Christopher Dornan

Christopher Dornan is director of the Arthur Kroeger College of Public Affairs at Carleton University and an associate professor in the School of Journalism and Communication. He is the co-editor of *The Canadian Federal Election of 2011,* as well as four previous volumes in the series. A selection of his essays and criticism can be found at http://www.educatedguesses.ca.

Is American news bad for Canada? What exactly do we mean by the question? Do we mean that the output of U.S. networks, newspapers, magazines, and news sites somehow comes to captivate the attention of Canadians such that the view of the world Canadians inevitably adopt is an American view?

Or do we mean something different? Do we mean that there is something noxious about the discursive heat of American journalism, particularly its "all-news" cable and satellite channels? Is the fear that Canadian media outlets will come to emulate a form of "news" that is hysterical, ideologically driven, and socially divisive, with poisonous results for a peaceable dominion that prides itself on its calm and tolerance for opposing political viewpoints?

Either way, the question is a variation on a larger, deeper, and much older question—one that has troubled British North America since before Confederation—namely, Is America bad for Canada? Without doubt, Canada has enjoyed immense advantages from being adjacent to and allied with our southern cousins, not least economically. And there are myriad aspects of the United States that we can only envy and admire. But throughout the history of the two nations, Canadians have watched—sometimes uneasily, sometimes aghast—as the United States has inflicted injury upon itself or on other nations, from the nightmare of its Civil War to its imperial adventurism, from its war on its Aboriginal peoples to the Jim Crow laws of the American South, from the folly of Vietnam to the race riots of the 1960s. Particularly of late, it has been worrisome to watch our neighbours across the border. The America of the Bush–Cheney years prosecuted a needless war under false pretences and behaved with such reckless abandon on Wall Street that the country's financial and credit markets immolated themselves. It behaved with contempt toward its staunchest allies; suspended the civil liberties on which it was founded; condoned, outsourced, and indeed practised torture. The result is a deeply riven country, at war with itself over what it stands for. From a Canadian perspective, the civil discourse of the United States has become a cauldron of animosity.

But even if one worries about the conduct (not to say the sanity) of the contemporary United States, does this mean that news of and from America is bad for Canada?

If it is, then presumably we should want less of it. By that reasoning, ideally we should want none of it at all. We should want a border impermeably sealed against reportage from our nearest neighbour, a country walled off from journalism issuing from the most powerful nation on the planet.

Absurd and grotesque as it may be, there are actually countries in the world that have pursued just such a policy, but you would not want to live there. Know where they don't get much American news? North Korea, that barrel of laughs. Even in Tehran, the mullahs may despise American journalism as much as they despise American geopolitics, but they do not make the mistake of ignoring either, because the first is the fastest way to keep up with the second. To be attentive to the world at all is necessarily to be attentive to the United States.

The result is that, apart from isolated pockets of despotism, the world is awash in American news, from Helsinki to the Honduras.

There are those who argue that this amounts to a form of information imperialism, a means by which the United States forces itself on the rest of the globe. In the 1960s and 1970s, this theory established itself as a truism, to the point that UNESCO—the United Nations Educational, Scientific and Cultural Organization—insisted that what was necessary was nothing less than a massive readjustment of the global television set. What it saw as the international information imbalance—in which the rest of the world was subject to torrents of U.S. news while the United States, in turn, ethnocentrically ignored the world beyond its borders—was so pernicious that it simply had to be redressed. UNESCO called for a grandiose **New World Information and Communication Order** (**NWICO**), in which the global news diet would be bureaucratically re-engineered.[1] How exactly this was to be accomplished was murky at best, especially since it was proposed at about the same time as entire families from Antigua to Zimbabwe were transfixed by the same primetime soap opera, all wondering who shot J.R. The world might well resent the brash American dominance of the airwaves, but if pulling the plug means no more *Dallas* or *Dexter*, it is always going to be a hard sell.

The proposals for a NWICO came to nothing, not because the U.S. government and big media corporations became apoplectic at the mere suggestion, but because the premise on which it was founded was simply false. The NWICO doctrine held that the hypnotic lure of American media content was a sure route to the extermination of other forms of nationalism and identity. Drenched in Hollywood sitcoms and locked into a news agenda dictated by New York and Washington, the world could not help but become vassal to the United States. It would lose the ability to think outside a box stamped "Made in the U.S.A."

In fact, U.S. media content did not extinguish other nationalisms or identities—it stoked them. It made American priorities vivid and palpable, something to embrace or resist as one chose. Even something to detest. What it did not do is narcotize the world into thinking like Americans. The Palestinians who cheered in the streets when the World Trade Center towers collapsed had been reared on *Friends* and *Frasier*, pulling them in on the satellite dishes that carpet the rooftops of the Third World. They liked the sitcoms just fine, but this did not make them love America.

Canada is likely the global citizen that has the greatest affection for the United States. Nestled against it for as long as both countries have existed and sharing a common language, we know America best. We admire its virtues, are impressed by its strengths, imitate its finest features, and do all we can to avoid its faults. We are also the country that has had the longest experience with exposure to U.S. cultural products and therefore the country that has been longest troubled by it.

Blessed by safety, prosperity, and civility, Canada is by any measure an enviable dominion. But it is also a nation whose political preoccupation, and particular neurosis, is whether it can continue to exist as a nation. We have always been taught to believe that Canadian **cultural sovereignty** is a fragile thing perpetually threatened on two fronts, the first of which is internal—the aspirations of those Quebecers who would rather go it alone under their own flag—while the second runs along the 49th parallel. The external danger is no longer annexation but assimilation. Foreign and domestic policy might become so attuned to that of our muscular neighbour as to become indistinguishable. The two economies could become so integrated that Canada risks ending up as a mere comprador subsidiary of America, Inc. Were that to happen, the nation of Canada would cease to exist in all but name. We might keep our own flag, but it would not amount to much beyond a separate team at the Olympics and a vote at the United Nations, which would be handily in the pocket of the United States.

The concern over cultural assimilation may seem misplaced and dated in the early twenty-first century, but it was keenly and prominently felt in Canada throughout the twentieth century. The fifth column that would supposedly soften our resistance and ease the way for assimilation was something as seemingly innocuous as information. The Yanks were coming with their wire services and their network news divisions, their glossy magazines and their dazzling celebrity culture. Slavishly attentive to all things American, even our own television channels and newspapers would be little more than conduits for U.S. content—so cheap to acquire and so much more tantalizing than the drab domestic equivalent.2 After a while, we would simply forget who we were. We would be welcomed into the hive.

It is a decidedly Canadian anxiety, as old as Canada itself. It is as if we need to tell ourselves this cautionary tale even though, deep down, no one truly believes it, the way children like to be frightened by stories of monsters in the basement they know are not real. In 1902 Sir Sanford Fleming, then the chancellor of Queen's University, became so alarmed at what he saw as the unsavoury influence of the newfangled mass-circulation newspaper that he commissioned a $250-prize essay competition on the subject "How can Canadian universities best benefit the profession of journalism, as a means of moulding and elevating public opinion?" The following year the winning entries were anthologized by the editors of *Queen's Quarterly* in a volume published by Copp Clark. One by one, they itemized the by-now familiar sins of a populist press: the undue influence of advertising, the unseemly invasions of privacy, the literary bankruptcy of journalistic prose, and the pursuit of sensation at the expense of civic duty. Prominent among these was the complaint that Canadian newspapers featured all too much news from and about the United States.

Almost seventy years later, even after the creation of the CBC and CTV, the complaint was still extant and even more inflamed. In 1970 a special Senate committee, under the chairmanship of Keith Davey, delivered a report on the mass media, ruefully concluding in its very first pages that Canada had become "a cultural as well as economic satellite of the United States. And nowhere is this trend more pronounced than in the media" (Senate of Canada, 1970, p. 11). The fifth column was in our midst, and our own media corporations had become its eager quislings. "What we *are* suggesting," the report continued, "is that the Canadian media—especially the broadcast media—have an interest and obligation to promote our *apartness* from the American reality. For all our similarities, for all our sharing, for all our friendships, we *are* somebody else" (p. 11).

It therefore became all but established in Canada that a nation that laps up another's media products imperils itself as a nation. The only problem with this axiom is that, like the NWICO doctrine, it is not true. And the proof of that is all around us. Anyone who believes that Canada is a pale excuse for a nation, a junior doppelganger of the United States, simply has not lived in the United States for any length of time, or anywhere else for that matter. The apprehension over how Canadian identity is smothered by U.S. cultural exports—as though a nation's sense of what it is about can be expressed only through situation comedies and junk journalism—is tiresome, misplaced, and mystifying to an outsider. And sometimes it takes an outsider to state plainly what should be evident to all. In 1990 a British academic, Richard Collins, published *Culture, Communication and National Identity: The Case of Canadian Television*, in which he demolished the argument that Canada was diminished as a nation by its appetite for American media content. Collins makes the simple and devastating point that it is more than possible to foster a separate society while still gorging on the Oprah Winfrey Network, *American Idol*, and *iCarly*, because a nation's sense of purpose and its centre of gravity depend on robust civic institutions that transcend the ephemera of the media. Put it this way: Canada has its problems, no question, but it remains a less violent society than the United States by a truly remarkable margin. If the two nations share essentially the same media content, why should this be? Perhaps it has nothing to do with what's on television.

To argue, then, that American news is bad for Canada, one would have to show that Canadians attend to American news at the expense of the affairs of their own community; or that the practices of American journalism have somehow sullied a purer Canadian strain; or that Canadians are simply poorer for the wealth of choice of American journalism we have at our disposal. But all of these contentions are, in a word, nonsense.

First of all, Canadians do not ignore their own news in preference for American news. Far from it. They might seek out U.S. news *in addition to* news of Canada, but not instead of it. Viewership of U.S. news is negligible in English Canada compared to CTV, CBC, and Global, whose national newscasts together draw more than three million viewers a night. All-day viewership figures for CNN, the most popular U.S. news network in Canada, typically amount to some 0.9 percent of audience share, only slightly above the viewership share for CP24, the Toronto all-news station, at 0.8 percent. CNN Headline News commands 0.4 percent of audience share, while CBC and CTV's news networks together command 2.2 percent of viewership (Bureau of Broadcast Measurement [BBM], 2012).

It is possible to buy *USA Today* in Canada, but it sells in minuscule numbers and even then largely to U.S. business people passing through, as opposed to the almost four million copies of Canadian daily newspapers sold each day (Newspapers Canada, 2010). In 2006 the Canadian edition of *Time* magazine closed up shop, its parent company judging that it was no longer worth the expense of maintaining it.

So, there are simply no grounds to worry that news from the United States eclipses Canadians' attention to their own domestic news outlets or to their own political, cultural, or economic affairs. Canadians may well still overwhelmingly watch U.S. movies and sitcoms rather than Canadian, but by the same token they clearly prefer their own news and journalism to the American product.

What of the worry that the form and content of Canadian journalism risk being corrupted by the model of its American counterpart? Certainly, the United States produces genres of journalism that make one's jaw drop. For decades now, local U.S. television news has been a parade of grisly car crashes, blood-soaked murder scenes, nightly drug busts, and smoking arson sites. The reflection they offer to their own cities seems to be of a society in near-apocalyptic ruin. Canadian local newscasts will pay attention to crime and catastrophe, certainly, but it is not their raison d'être. They are just as likely to report on hundredth birthdays and diamond wedding anniversaries, school science fairs and ethnic community festivals. It may be hokey, but better the benign than the malign.

Further, it appears that Canadians are more than capable of distinguishing between the tone of U.S. news sources and that of their domestic equivalents, and of valuing the latter over the former. In 2010 CBC commissioned Ipsos-Reid to conduct a study of English Canadian news consumers' attitudes toward fairness and balance in news sources. While those surveyed had their complaints about Canadian journalism, the overwhelming majority of respondents thought that in the main Canadian news outlets were fair (i.e., they represented issues in a way that corresponded to the facts) and balanced (i.e., they represented different perspectives on issues). In the case of CTV, 87 percent of respondents rated the network excellent, very good, or good in its coverage, and only 3 percent judged it poor or very poor. The equivalent figures for CBC were 84 percent and 5 percent. Global also rated 84 percent excellent, very good, or good and only 4 percent poor or very poor.

The figures for the U.S. all-news networks were significantly different. Only 65 percent of Canadians rated CNN in the excellent–good range, while 13 percent thought it poor or very poor. And only 47 percent of Canadian respondents judged Fox News excellent–good, while 29 percent rated it poor or very poor (Ipsos Reid, 2010, p. 25). It may be that Canadians place less trust in U.S. news sources, but this does not appear to have diminished their trust in domestic news outlets.

True, the advent of the Quebecor-owned Sun News Network in Canada, on April 18, 2011, triggered a wave of anticipation and concern. Those on the right welcomed what they saw as an unapologetically conservative perspective on the airwaves. Others fretted that the virus had arrived at last: a national network explicitly modelled on the U.S. Fox News, where opposing viewpoints are entertained not in debate but only to be brayed at, mocked, and vilified. Clearly, Fox News did not create the political divisions that cleave the United States, but the network has certainly done everything it can to goad them into outright hostility. Was this what Canadians had to look forward to: a news channel determined to put an end to polite civil discourse in favour of scorched-earth demagoguery?

In fact, so far Sun News has not proven to be the serpent in the garden its critics feared. First, it is nowhere near as extreme in either its politics or its comportment as Fox News. One may think that Ezra Levant—perhaps Sun News's best-known personality—is wrong-headed, but he is not wrong in the head. Long-time Fox News fixture Glenn Beck, by comparison, with his bug-eyed mixture of paranoia and delusions of grandeur, would have been under observation in the Clarke Institute of Psychiatry in Canada. In the United States he had a messianic following until even Fox News dumped him.

Second, neither Fox News nor Sun News has been fulsomely embraced by the Canadian public. In Canada, Fox News garners some 0.1 percent of audience share, or a quarter of the viewership of the Game Show Network (Bureau of Broadcast Measurement, 2012). As to Sun News, nine months after its debut the network reported proudly that its marquee names (Ezra Levant, David Akin, Charles Adler, and others) were drawing an average of 25 400 viewers per night ("Sun Shines," 2011), but failed to mention that in comparable time slots CBC News Network draws 263 000 viewers and even CNN attracts more Canadian viewers (some 38 000) in the evenings ("Sun News Drawing," 2011). BBM figures show Sun News capturing between 0.1 and 0.2 percent of audience share, or about one-tenth of the viewership of CBC News Network.

Third, Canadians have not reacted positively to instances in which Sun News has indulged in Fox-like mauling of interview subjects whose politics the network abhors. Most famously, on June 1, 2011, Sun host Krista Erickson interviewed interpretive dancer Margie Gillis on the topic of public funding for the arts. Erickson berated and belittled Gillis, shouting at her, interrupting her, while Gillis attempted to defend herself and the arts with grace ("Sun News 'Interview,'" 2011). To their credit, most Canadians who saw the exchange were appalled, and the Canadian Broadcast Standards Council would receive some 6676 complaints about it, three times the number of complaints the CBSC normally receives in a year (CBSC, 2012; Krashinsky, 2011).

Finally, we should remind ourselves that while Fox News may be odious, it is not emblematic of American journalism as a whole. The United States has given us a range of splendid journalistic outlets we should count ourselves lucky to have: *The New Yorker, The New Republic, The Nation, Harper's, The Atlantic Monthly, Scientific American, Lapham's Quarterly, The Smithsonian,* PBS's *Frontline* and *Nova* documentary series, *Wired, Esquire, The Wall Street Journal, The Utne Reader, Forbes, Fortune,* and even (perhaps especially) *The Daily Show* and *The Colbert Report.* The availability of all of these and more are a boon to Canada, not a liability.

That is one of Canada's singular advantages over the United States: we have the full range of their media content and our own besides. They, by contrast, pay almost no attention to any media content other than their own. One might think, for example, that in the wake of 9/11, the wars in Iraq and Afghanistan, and the tumult of the Arab Spring, Americans would be keenly, pointedly interested in knowing all they can about the politics and perspectives of those in the Arab world. And yet Al-Jazeera English is all but unavailable over U.S. cable and satellite carriers, while in Canada it is carried by almost all of ours. Perversely, in this regard the United States has something in common with North Korea: a deafness and blindness to the media beyond its borders. If only for this reason, Canadians should welcome the availability of American news in all its varieties. We may not want to be like them, but we should want to know all we can about them.

Know your enemies, says the adage. We should know our friends just as well.

Notes

[1] The United States, the United Kingdom, and the major Western news agencies such as Reuters and the Associated Press saw the NWICO proposals as a pretext to infringe on the free flow of information. Authoritarian governments, they argued, would use the provisions to control what information their populations might have access to. In the wake of the MacBride Report, the UNESCO (1980) document that first proposed a New World Information and Communication Order, both the United States and the United Kingdom withdrew from UNESCO in protest—the former in 1984 and the latter in 1985. Britain rejoined in 1997 and the United States in 2003.

For a clear, contemporaneous account of the NWICO debate, see Anthony Smith (1980). Most academic studies have taken the side of UNESCO against Western **cultural imperialism**, but there have been those who unapologetically champion U.S. dominance of global culture. See, for example, David Rothkop (1997), who argues that "globalization is a vital step toward both a more stable world and better lives for the people in it. Furthermore, these issues have serious implications for American foreign policy. For the United States, a central objective of an Information Age foreign policy must be to win the battle of the world's information flows, dominating the airwaves as Great Britain once ruled the seas."

[2] This is an argument that has long enjoyed currency in Canadian academic circles. While the national mythos invites Canadians to be proud of our innovations in communication (the world's first domestic communication satellite, a robust continent-wide telecommunications system, etc.) because these have helped to stitch together a sparse population spread over a vast geographic expanse, contrarians have been at pains to point out that this elaborate technical apparatus has actually been an aqueduct system sluicing American content into Canadian households. See, for example, Hardin (1986) and Babe (1990).

References

Babe, R. (1990). Telecommunications in Canada: Technology, industry and government. Toronto: University of Toronto Press.

Bureau of Broadcast Measurement. (2012). Audience share of English-language TV station groups; all persons 2+; all day 2 a.m.–2 a.m.; August 29, 2011–January 1, 2012.

Canadian Broadcast Standards Council. (2012). Aggressive interview style is acceptable, says Canadian Broadcast Standards Council [News release]. Retrieved from http://www.cbsc.ca/english/documents/prs/2012/120203.php

Collins, R. (1990). Culture, communication and national identity: The case of Canadian television. Toronto: University of Toronto Press.

The Editors of Queen's Quarterly (Eds.). (1903). How can Canadian universities best benefit the profession of journalism, as a means of moulding and elevating public opinion? Toronto: Copp Clark.

Hardin, H. (1986). Closed circuits: The sellout of Canadian television. Vancouver: Douglas & McIntyre.

Ipsos Reid. (2010, September). The news fairness and balance report: What Canadian news consumers think about fairness and balance in news. Report prepared for CBC English Services. Retrieved from http://www.cbc.ca/news/pdf/public-opinionreportengexecsumm-oct1_10.pdf

Krashinsky, S. (2011, June 28). Complaints over Sun News interview overwhelm watchdog. The Globe and Mail. Retrieved from http://www.theglobeandmail.com/news/politics/complaints-over-sun-news-interview-overwhelm-watchdog/article557302/

Newspapers Canada. (2010). Daily newspaper paid circulation data. Retrieved from http://www.newspaperscanada.ca/daily-newspaper-paid-circulation-data

Rothkop, D. (1997, June 22). In praise of cultural imperialism? Effects of globalization on culture. Foreign Policy. Retrieved from http://www.globalpolicy.org/globaliz/cultural/globcult.htm

Senate of Canada. (1970). Special Senate Committee on the Mass Media: The Davey Committee report. Ottawa: Queen's Printer.

Smith, A. (1980). The geopolitics of information: How Western culture dominates the world. New York: Faber & Faber.

Sun News drawing as little as 4,000 viewers during some time slots. (2011). Marketing. Retrieved from http://www.marketingmag.ca/news/media-news/sun-news-drawing-as-little-as-4000-viewers-during-some-time-slots-26636

Sun News "interview" with Margie Gillis [YouTube video]. (2011). Retrieved from http://www.youtube.com/watch?v=LrUfKrQpQbg

Sun shines on SaskTel. (2011, Sept. 29). Sun News. Retrieved from http://www.sunnewsnetwork.ca/sunnews/business/archives/2011/09/20110929-112408.html

UNESCO. (1980). Many voices, one world: The MacBride report. Paris: Author.

Discussion Questions

1. If the world loves U.S. entertainment, why does the world not love America?

2. Most American media products are freely available to Canadian consumers, from *Newsweek* to *Hustler*. A few, however, are prohibited. One can receive CNN in Canada but not Comedy Central, Fox News but not Nickelodeon. On what grounds? Compile a list of U.S. media outlets and products that cannot be legally purchased in Canada. Why have these been banned to us? Argue either in favour or against.

3. Canadians overwhelmingly watch American movies, read American magazines, listen to American music, and prefer American TV dramas and comedies. But they pay far more attention to Canadian journalism in all its guises than to U.S. news. Canadians read Canadian newspapers, watch Canadian nightly news, listen to Canadian call-in shows. Why should this be so? What are the implications?

4. Although Canadians largely rely on Canadian sources of news, how are they still affected by U.S. news styles and techniques?

5. How were American attitudes about going to war in Iraq reflective of the kind of news Americans choose to believe?

6. What kinds of interests do local TV stations have in ad-driven U.S. political campaigns?

ISSUE 3

Evil empires:
Should limits to foreign ownership of
Canadian media be lifted?

✔ YES

Evil Empires? Nonsense: A Case for Eliminating Restrictions on Foreign Ownership of Canadian Media Properties
Richard Schultz

Richard Schultz is James McGill Professor and former chair of the Department of Political Science at McGill University. He is the author or co-editor of eight books and more than fifty articles and book chapters, including Changing the Rules: Canadian Regulatory Regimes and Institutions, "From Master to Partner to Bit Player: The Diminishing Role of Government Policy in Communications," and "Canadian Communications and the Spectre of Globalization: Just Another Word.... " His current project is a book entitled Contested Networks: The Bureaucratic Transformation of Canadian Telecommunications 1976–1993. In 2005 he was a visiting fellow at the Shorenstein Center on Press, Politics and Public Policy at the Kennedy School of Government at Harvard University, where his research concentrated on the links among media diversity, concentration, and cross-ownership.

INTRODUCTION

In the garden of Canadian media policy there are many sacred totems. These include the notions embedded in the *Broadcasting Act, 1991*, that broadcasting is a "single system"; that broadcasting is "a public service essential to the maintenance and enhancement of national identity and cultural sovereignty"; that "the Canadian broadcasting system should serve to safeguard, enrich, and strengthen the cultural, political, social, and economic fabric of Canada"; and that "the programming ... should be of high standard." Undoubtedly the most sacred, and consequently the most powerful, totem is that the Canadian broadcasting system, and arguably the media system more generally, "shall be effectively owned and controlled by Canadians."[1]

Anyone who dares challenge these totems, especially that of Canadian ownership, risks being branded a heretic, or worse, a follower of a false god—the market—or a member of the "economic right" with a "crabbed critique of cultural products" (Grant & Wood, 2004, p. 8). There is no question that government can play an important role, through the use of tax and subsidy policies and especially a well-funded public broadcaster, in supporting Canadian media to further cultural, as opposed to industrial, policy objectives. However, the existing mix of foreign ownership restrictions is neither necessary nor helpful in pursuing these objectives. Canada's current media foreign ownership policies are based on a misreading of Canadian history, on an undocumented claim that foreign ownership is intrinsically bad, and on simplistic assumptions. These policies have resulted in unintended yet profoundly negative consequences for media ownership and are proving to be dangerously contagious for other sectors. And although they will shortly become irrelevant, their continuance will prove to be costly without any demonstrable benefit.

Before developing these arguments, it is important that we understand what the current foreign ownership policies are and the assumptions upon which they are based. In the following section, I provide a summary overview of the policies for both broadcasting and media generally. In the subsequent sections I will discuss the assumptions and the rationale for such policies and then go on to my critique of them and why I think they should be eliminated.

CANADA'S MEDIA FOREIGN OWNERSHIP POLICIES

There are two types of foreign ownership restrictions. The first, found in both the broadcasting and telecommunications sectors, limits direct foreign ownership to 20 percent and indirect ownership by a holding company to 33 percent. This limitation is combined with a requirement in both sectors that non-Canadians cannot exercise control over either a licensed broadcaster, including cable companies, or a telecommunications company. Moreover, 80 percent of the directors of broadcasting licensees and telecommunications carriers must be Canadian.

A number of commentators, including the House of Commons Standing Committee on Canadian Heritage in its 2003 report, *Our Cultural Sovereignty*, defend the restrictions on the grounds that the actual limitations are not 20 percent and 33 percent respectively but combined amount to 46.7 percent (p. 389). This is accounting hocus-pocus. There is not, and has not been, a single case since the restrictions were introduced of a non-Canadian interest owning 46.7 percent of a Canadian broadcasting licensee. It simply would not make economic sense for a non-Canadian interest to invest this heavily in a company where it could not exercise any degree of control. Given the large number of family-controlled corporations in the broadcasting sector (e.g., Rogers, CHUM, and Shaw), where differential shareholder voting rights are common, why would any foreign shareholder consider making a large investment if it knew that a single Canadian shareholder with perhaps a minority of preferred shares could exercise near total control? It is quite simply intellectually dishonest to claim that 46.7 percent is the upper limit of foreign ownership when the actual effective percentage is only 20 percent.

The second form of ownership restrictions applies to various publishing media. The *Income Tax Act* is employed as an indirect means of keeping publishing firms Canadian owned by limiting deductions for advertising expenses to newspapers and magazines that are 75 percent or more Canadian owned. In the 1990s Canada also attempted to supplement this form of restriction by imposing an 80 percent excise tax on foreign periodicals that contained advertisements directed at Canadians.[2] The conflict that this caused, and the subsequent setback for Canada's policies, played a major role in the Canadian push for an international treaty to restrict the impact of international trade agreements on cultural products.

RATIONALE FOR CURRENT OWNERSHIP RESTRICTIONS

Before critiquing the current restrictions it is worthwhile to spend some time on the major arguments and reasons advanced in their defence. Defenders of the status quo have a much-distorted understanding of the history of Canadian policies. The Heritage Committee, for example, claims that "the philosophy of Canadian ownership and control has always been central to Canada's cultural industries" (2003, p. 385). The fact is these policies, and their underlying philosophy, are of relatively recent vintage, dating primarily from the 1960s and 1970s. Prior to these years, and it is worth remembering that broadcasting dates from the 1920s, there were no foreign ownership restrictions in the individual media sectors. More importantly, when the prohibitions on foreign ownership were introduced in the broadcasting sector in 1969, no attempt was made to justify the new policy on the grounds that foreign owners had acted against Canadian public policy interests or that their behaviour had somehow been deleterious compared to that of Canadian owners.[3]

In the 1993 *Telecommunications Act*, the current restrictions were established for telecommunications companies. Again, no specific explanation was provided justifying the restrictions. This was indeed unfortunate because for most of the last century, the Canadian telecommunications sector was a laboratory that could have been used to establish if foreign ownership truly poses a public policy problem. From the 1920s, the second-largest telephone company in Canada, BC Telephone, as well as a regional operator in Quebec, had been foreign controlled by the same American parent. At no time in the history of that ownership was a credible case made that BC Telephone's service record was deficient because of its foreign ownership.

In terms of specific arguments invoked to justify foreign ownership restrictions, most are not particularly persuasive. One, in fact, is risible. In their submission to the Commons Heritage Committee, the Canadian Conference of the Arts claimed that television program scheduling would be negatively affected. They argued that "the creation of a program schedule should be based on appealing to a Canadian audience—not as an afterthought to an international schedule but as the primary focus" (2002, p. 4) As anyone who can read a television schedule will know, since the advent of simultaneous substitution thirty years ago, Canadian private television schedules in prime time are largely based on American schedules so that broadcasters can capture the substantial indirect subsidy in advertising revenues that results. Of course, given the popularity of these shows, their placing does satisfy the premise of the Conference of the Arts argument: appealing to a Canadian audience.

A second argument, which has been advanced by Raboy and Taras (2004), is that foreign-owned as opposed to Canadian-owned companies would either not respect Canadian laws and regulations or introduce serious obstacles to their implementation. Surely this argument cannot be taken seriously. In almost every sector of the Canadian economy there are major non-Canadian firms. Yet no one would argue that these firms violate applicable Canadian laws, such as those dealing with occupational health and safety, consumer protection, or environmental standards. Nor could they argue that these firms act with impunity or impose extra costs and delays through foot-dragging, legal action, or American government lobbying sufficient to eviscerate Canadian public policies. If the Canadian media industry is somehow different from other industrial sectors and the state and its regulators are so weak that, without ownership prohibitions and stringent restrictions of the kind now in place, non-Canadian firms will operate untrammelled by public laws, then our national problems go much deeper than simply protecting Canada's cultural industries.

Raboy and Taras also argue that "to imagine that Viacom, or News Corporation or Sony would become major producers of Canadian programming is to live in a fantasy world" (p. 64).

This is undoubtedly true, but as every official study since the 1970s has shown, it is fantasy to imagine that Canadian broadcast companies have or will become major producers of Canadian programming. As Grant and Wood have noted, "strict caps on local ownership would seem to ensure local control. But do they? Experience suggests that in this, as in the evasion of content and spending requirements, much ingenuity can be expended to make this reality depart from the experience" (2004, p. 242). They go on to argue that the proposition that domestic broadcasters "will reliably support local expression … cannot be relied upon" (p. 260). Anyone with the slightest familiarity with the history of Canadian content rules can only agree. This should be obvious because, notwithstanding the totem of the public service role that is assigned to broadcasting, Canadian private broadcasting is, as the editor of *Canadian Business* has noted, "a business first and foremost" (Chidley, 2003, p. 8).

If the preceding arguments can be debated on factual grounds, the larger overarching reason for Canada's foreign ownership restrictions is much more difficult to debate or refute—not because it is a particularly strong argument based on persuasive facts and logic, but just the opposite. It is a quasi-religious, almost apocalyptic argument for which no rational evidence, as opposed to fears, can be adduced. Most of the defence of current ownership restrictions is based on deep-seated, long-standing emotional fears and/or dislike of American popular culture. Defenders of the current policies have always been consumed by what I would describe as a "gloomy, undefined foreboding of the unknown" (Stewart, 1975, p. 1813), and they appear to believe that just invoking the presumed threat is a sufficient defence.

Defenders of the restrictions routinely point to the size of the American market and its cultural industries and the economies of scale that characterize them, compared to the small Canadian market and industries. They contend that removing the restrictions would lead to the swamping of the Canadian cultural sectors by imported products. From these arguments, they then go on to argue that, absent foreign ownership restrictions, Canada's cultural space would be eradicated, and ultimately Canadian culture in all its manifestations would be lost (White, 2005). While the first part of these arguments is true, there is no way of assessing the conclusion since we cannot prove a negative.

Canadian cultural nationalists in many respects are the mirror image of Quebec language nationalists. They invoke similar arguments about the need to protect their identity from a menacing sea of foreign challengers. They have little confidence in the vibrancy of their communities—linguistic or cultural—but see them as fragile, intrinsically weak, and constantly threatened. In the case of the cultural nationalists, they are not prepared to concede, or even recognize, that their fears may be grossly exaggerated or that the restrictions they support may be unnecessary. Two arguments can be advanced to support this assessment.

The first, that foreign ownership restrictions fail to serve their putative purposes, is offered by Grant and Wood. They conclude their review of such policies by arguing that "statutory limits on foreign ownership *may* be of value to the extent that they preserve a greater number of local gatekeepers able to bring new cultural expression before their domestic publics. But in contrast to other available measures … they are surely not the sharpest or surest tools in the kit" (2004, p. 262).

The second, that the Canadian cultural character is stronger than the cultural nationalists would have us believe, is argued by Michael Adams in his book *Fire and Ice: The United States, Canada and the Myth of Converging Values* (2003). Adams finds strong and growing cultural divergence rather than the unidirectional convergence called Americanization that the nationalists fear most. Using longitudinal public opinion studies, Adams concludes that "at the most basic level—the level of our values, the feelings and beliefs that inform our understanding of and interaction with the world around us—Canadians and Americans are markedly different, and becoming more so" (p. 4). In short, Canadians are not what they watch or read, and therefore the threatened loss of Canadian culture is grossly exaggerated.

The fact that cultural nationalists have been unable to make a strong, empirically based case that Americanization is occurring suggests that they exhibit what has been labelled the "third-person effect."[4] This hypothesis was first formulated in 1983 by W. Phillips Davison, a professor of journalism and sociology, who noted,

> In its broadest formulation, this hypothesis predicts that people will tend to overestimate the influence mass communications have on the attitudes and behavior of others. More specifically, individuals who are members of an audience that is exposed to a persuasive communication (whether or not this communication is intended to be persuasive) will expect the communication to have a greater effect on others than on themselves. (p. 3)

Cultural nationalists, sophisticates that they are, of course, do not consider themselves to be susceptible to Americanization but worry about the rest of us, who presumably do not have sufficient defensive skills. Therefore, we must be protected through such measures as foreign ownership restrictions.

THE CASE FOR REMOVAL

Although the rationales for the current restrictions are weak, the case for their removal is stronger when one considers three significant arguments against them. The first is the impact of the restrictions on media concentration; the second is the unfortunate and costly contagion the current restrictions may have on a related sector, telecommunications; and the third is the growing irrelevance of the restrictions in the face of technological changes that may result in an excessively costly burden being imposed without any commensurate benefits. We shall examine each in turn.

One of the great ironies in the current debate over foreign ownership restrictions is the widespread failure to appreciate the fundamental link between those restrictions and the degree of concentrated media ownership in Canada. The House of Commons Heritage Committee, for example, devoted a chapter of its report *Our Cultural Sovereignty* to two ownership issues: **media concentration** (both within and across different forms of media) and foreign ownership. The conclusion—debatable, in my opinion—of the committee is that Canadian media are concentrated and something should be done about it. Yet in its report the committee appears to be completely unaware that the high degree of media ownership concentration in Canada is a direct consequence of the foreign ownership restrictions.

The size of Canada's media conglomerates is a product of our foreign ownership policies. Who were the alternative purchasers when CanWest Global bought Southam from Hollinger? Who were the alternative purchasers of CHUM? According to newspaper accounts, the only possible alternatives in the latter case were other, already large, Canadian media conglomerates. Had the restrictions on foreign ownership not been in place, a much wider pool of potential purchasers could have been found. This is simple common sense: widen the pool of potential buyers and you decrease concentration; narrow it, as we inevitably do with our restrictions, and you encourage greater concentration.

The second reason for removing the restrictions is that they risk infecting the telecommunications sector, where large infusions of investment are required if Canada is to establish the necessary infrastructure to enjoy the promises of the information age. The contagion from the cultural sector was exemplified after the House of Commons Standing Committee on Industry, Science and Technology concluded that the existing restrictions in the telecommunications sector "compromise, among other important economic contributions, the diffusion of new communications technologies and Canadians' access to modern telecommunications services" (2003, p. 55). Consequently, the committee recommended the complete removal of foreign ownership restrictions for telecommunications carriers.

For the cultural nationalists, as well as some of the companies that benefit from the existing restrictions, the Industry Committee's recommendations were sacrilege. The House Heritage Committee stated that it "strongly disagrees" with its Industry counterpart. It rejected Industry's emphasis on economic factors and called its recommendations "extremely simplistic … to a complex set of issues" (2003, p. 421). It consequently recommended that the existing foreign ownership restrictions in both the broadcasting and telecommunications sectors be maintained without change.

Raboy and Taras (2004) described the Heritage Committee's recommendation as a "no-brainer," and although they did not mean it this way, it certainly was that: a mindless, knee-jerk reaction that, if acted upon, could have serious negative consequences for the Canadian telecommunications sector and consequently for Canadian society and economy. No industrial sector has flourished in this country without access to considerable foreign capital. No sector has gone through the profound transformation that telecommunications is experiencing. We simply do not have enough domestic capital to finance the growth and technological changes that are required. While the larger companies have adequate access to meet their capital needs under the current regime, it is the small, newer companies, the future Research in Motions (the makers of the BlackBerry) of this world who need access. Regrettably, the domestic venture capital sector in Canada is neither large enough nor adventurous enough to satisfy their needs.

Although it may appear initially to contradict the second, the third reason for removing restrictions is that increasingly, with technological changes that are currently under way, foreign ownership restrictions will become irrelevant. The reason that this argument is *not* contradictory is that the restrictions will impose significant costs without any commensurate benefits on domestic companies.

In the United States, where there is significantly less media concentration and cross-ownership than in Canada, a ferocious debate has been waged over the past few years over attempts by the FCC to relax existing ownership rules and restrictions. As a result of court challenges, opponents of the new rules successfully derailed the original proposals, and the FCC is currently holding a new proceeding to develop regulatory changes. Unlike the earlier period when communications companies were driving the move for relaxation of the rules, in the current debates the media companies, according to one report, "may take little advantage of changes this time" (Ahrens, 2006,

p. D1). Why? Because they have found ways through technology, if not to reinvent themselves, to get around the barriers that exist between them and their potential audiences.

"Big media" in the United States are exploiting the rollout of higher broadband speeds and the Internet as well as handheld devices such as iPods and cellular telephones to download video signals, to attain "greater reach and potentially more influence, than it would have had, were companies allowed to buy a few more television stations" (Ahrens, 2006, p. D1). Ahrens notes in the case of CBS, "the company sees its future not in owning more television stations but in expanding a revenue stream that was an afterthought in 2003: the Internet and its various iterations of digital downloading and streaming, channels that give CBS a far bigger footprint than local television stations" (p. D1). Various American industry players, from NewsCorp to Clear Channel, are also reducing their stakes in traditional broadcasting, both television and radio, and substituting Internet companies, such as MySpace, to gain direct, immediate, and financially rewarding access to consumers.

Notice the use of the word "consumers." Just as the concept of a "telephone subscriber" has disappeared to be replaced by "telecommunications consumer," the technological wave is having the same consequences for the concept of broadcasting audiences. What is most important in this wave is the empowering of the consumer of the broadcasting service at the expense, but not the fortune, of the service provider. Canada's "old media," now "protected" by regulation and foreign ownership, risk being deregulated not by the wish of corporations or the decisions of state regulators but by those who are the real deregulators—customers exercising choice. What transformed the Canadian rail and air sectors and is now underway in telecommunications is about to hit, like a tsunami, the broadcasting sector (Schultz, 1995). In the words of Jerry Brown, PriceWaterhouseCoopers executive responsible for the firm's Canadian entertainment and media advisory practice, "media consumption is being driven more and more by consumers' desire to have access to the news, music, TV and videos they want, when they want it, and in a format that suits the situation they are in at the time" (Adams, 2006, p. R3).

Pressures for removal or relaxing the current Canadian foreign ownership restrictions are mounting. Some of these come from corporate interests such as Postmedia, the owner of the former Black and then Asper newspapers, who are desperately short of capital (Ladurantaye 2012) or from new entrants in the mobile telephone sector. The Conservative government has indicated that it is sympathetic to the removal or at least the relaxation of the restrictions and indeed has gone so far as to overturn a CRTC decision that a new entrant was "not controlled in fact" by Canadians and therefore ineligible to operate in Canada (Schultz, 2011). Thus there has been a major breach in the foreign ownership barriers, and other carriers and media outlets are demanding equal treatment.

More importantly, technological developments are increasingly providing opportunities for Canadian viewers and media subscribers to "exit" the current regime and thus undermine the foreign ownership restrictions. As any astute undergraduate student can attest, where once "exit" was reasonably easy through pirating and the use of proxy servers, today such exit is now available wholesale, as it were. Netflix, for example, operates in Canada, although with a much restricted set of offerings. Most significantly, the CRTC has ruled that the Internet-based movie and television company will not be regulated and subject to the requirements of the *Broadcasting Act*, especially regarding content, despite pleas from its Canadian-owned competitors such as BCE and Astral.

Netflix is, however, only the thin edge of change coming to the broadcasting and larger media sectors. To see the future of the media one needs only to be familiar with Internet provisioning of newspapers and radio. In the former case, not only are there aggregators such as Google, Yahoo, and Fluent News, but full subscription services are available such as PressReader, not to mention direct subscriptions with non-Canadian journals and magazines. In radio, not only do you have Apple's iTunes, Pandora, Aluratek, and Spotify, but literally thousands of individual stations from around the world are freely accessible on computers and mobile devices. Where there are limitations on the offerings, such as in Netflix or Pandora, they are copyright based and not government determined. Moreover, when international content providers decide that they should sell the Internet streaming of their wares separately rather than as is the custom today as part of a package with the original versions, even copyright will be diminished as a tool. Finally, if Steve Jobs's last dream of Apple TV comes true, and it surely will, it will render hollow existing restrictive access regimes.

CONCLUSION

In 1999 President Bill Clinton, speaking to a conference on federalism, turned from his text to address a number of Quebec separatists who were in the audience, including then-premier Lucien Bouchard, and urged them to set aside their "fear of the other." His admonition, I believe, can be justly directed at Canada's cultural nationalists and in particular their support for the current foreign ownership restrictions. These policies have never been rationally based but are premised on a fear that, notwithstanding its potency among certain elite circles, simply does not resonate with the Canadian public. The current policies are costly, are not particularly effective in promoting the ends desired, and are becoming irrelevant in the new media world. The Canadian government has many other instruments, from subsidies to the public broadcaster, to foster Canadian voices and to ensure that Canadian stories are told. Foreign ownership restrictions are a tool best discarded.

Notes

[1] These are all extracts from the statement of broadcasting policy in Section 3 of the *Broadcasting Act, 1991.*

[2] See Acheson & Maule, 1999, pp. 186–205.

[3] There was no claim, for example, that foreign owners had ignored long-standing regulatory prohibitions on the formation of radio networks other than that allowed by the CBC. Nor was there evidence adduced to support the claim that foreign owners were worse than Canadian owners in respecting and fulfilling the first attempts by the Board of Broadcast Governors to impose Canadian content regulations. See Stewart and Hull, 2004.

[4] I am grateful to Adam Thierer, author of *Media Myths: Making Sense of the Debate over Media Ownership* (Progress and Freedom Foundation, 2005) for drawing this hypothesis to my attention.

References

Acheson, K., & Maule, C. (1999). *Much ado about culture: North American trade disputes.* Ann Arbor: University of Michigan Press.

Adams, A. (2006, July 25). A good news, bad news issue. *The Globe and Mail,* p. R3.

Adams, M. (2003). *Fire and ice: The United States, Canada and the myth of converging values.* Toronto: Penguin.

Ahrens, F. (2006, June 29). As FCC digs into ownership, big media no longer cares. *The Washington Post,* p. D1.

Canadian Conference of the Arts. (2002, December 10). *Safeguard, strengthen and enrich: Review of the Canadian broadcasting system, cross-media ownership and foreign ownership.* Retrieved from http://www.ccarts.ca/en/advocacy/publications

Chidley, J. (2003, October 26). What made Izzy so smart. *Canadian Business,* p. 8.

Grant, P., & Wood, C. (2004). *Blockbusters and trade wars: Popular culture in a globalized world.* Vancouver: Douglas & McIntyre.

House of Commons Standing Committee on Canadian Heritage. (2003). *Our cultural sovereignty.* Ottawa: Public Works and Government Services Canada.

House of Commons Standing Committee on Industry, Science and Technology. (2003). *Opening Canadian communications to the world.* Ottawa: Public Works and Government Services Canada.

Ladurantaye, S. (2012, January 11). Postmedia calls for new ownership rules. *The Globe and Mail.*

Phillips Davison, W. (1983). The third-person effect in communication. *Public Opinion Quarterly, 47*(1), 1–16.

Raboy, M., & Taras, D. (2004, March). The politics of neglect of Canadian broadcasting policy. *Policy Options,* 64.

Schultz, R. (1995). Paradigm lost: Explaining the politics of deregulation. In C. E. S. Franks, J. E. Hodgetts, O. P. Dwivedi, D. Williams, & V. S. Wilson (Eds.), *Governance in a mature society* (pp. 259–277). Montreal: McGill-Queen's University Press.

Schultz, R. (2011). Industry Canada as economic regulator: Globalive and the lessons of political licensing. In G. B. Doern & C. Smiley (Eds.), *How Ottawa spends: 2011–2012.* Montreal: McGill-Queen's University Press.

Stewart, A., & Hull, W. H. N. (2004). *Canadian television policy and the Board of Broadcast Governors.* Edmonton: University of Alberta Press.

Stewart, R. B. (1975). *The reformation of American administrative law, 88,* 1667–1813.

White, J. (2005, October 31). Losing Canadian culture. *Briefing paper: Trade and investment series* (Vol. 6, No. 3). Ottawa: Canadian Centre for Policy Alternatives.

ISSUE 3

Evil empires: Should limits to foreign ownership of Canadian media be lifted?

✘ NO

Opening the Floodgates: Foreign Ownership, Neoliberal Ideology, and the Threat to Democratic Media Culture
Kyle Asquith and Valerie Scatamburlo-D'Annibale

Kyle Asquith has a Ph.D. in media studies from the University of Western Ontario and is currently an assistant professor in the Department of Communication, Media and Film Studies at the University of Windsor. He is the recipient of several undergraduate teaching awards, in addition to a Social Sciences and Humanities Research Council of Canada (SSHRC) Doctoral Canada Graduate Scholarship. His research interests encompass the complementary fields of advertising and consumer culture, media history, and the political economy of communication.

Dr. Valerie Scatamburlo-D'Annibale is an associate professor and current head of the Department of Communication, Media and Film Studies at the University of Windsor. She is the author of two books—*Cold Breezes and Idiot Winds: Patriotic Correctness and the Post-9/11 Assault on Academe* (2011) and *Soldiers of Misfortune: The New Right's Culture War and the Politics of Political Correctness* (1998), which earned her an American Educational Studies Association's Critic's Choice Award in 2000. She has published more than thirty book chapters and journal articles in venues including *Cultural Studies/Critical Methodologies* and the *International Journal of Progressive Education*, and her work has been translated into many languages. She is the recipient of numerous teaching accolades including the University of Windsor Faculty of Arts and Social Sciences Teaching Award.

INTRODUCTION

Let the air remain as the prerogative of commercial interests and subject to commercial control, and how free will be the voice, the heart of democracy.... There can be no liberty, no democracy supreme, if the commercial interests dominate the vast, majestic resource of broadcasting. (Spry, cited in Raboy, 1990, p. 36)

In 1930 Graham Spry, often referred to as the father of Canadian public broadcasting, co-founded the Canadian Radio League (CRL), which was committed to establishing a media system based on the recommendations of the 1929 Aird Royal Commission. Spry also sought to counter a burgeoning campaign spearheaded by American corporations to bring commercial radio broadcasting to Canada. The CRL argued against viewing radio primarily as a business enterprise; instead, it maintained that the public should control radio. Radio was to be used as an instrument for cultivating an informed citizenry and promoting the public interest, rather than serving merely as a conduit for American advertising. As Spry put it, to trust radio to "advertising agents and interested corporations" represented the "uttermost folly" (cited in McChesney, 1999). Despite pressure from American broadcasters and Conservative prime minister R. B. Bennett's pronouncement to cut federal expenditures in order to balance the budget, Spry's persistence "won the day" (Lorimer, Gasher, & Skinner, 2008, p. 158). After nearly two years of intense lobbying, Spry's CRL succeeded in convincing the government to establish the Canadian Radio Broadcasting Commission (predecessor of the Canadian Broadcasting Corporation) in 1932.

We invoke this history because we believe that Spry's struggle can inform the present as "new" debates unfold about foreign ownership in this age of "globalization." At the current historical juncture, dominated as it is by talk of a "borderless world," Spry's concerns about Americanization may appear to be anachronistic. However, there was much more to his arguments than fear of a foreign "other" threatening Canadian culture. Spry also counselled citizens to be cautious of relying on free market forces as a proxy for serving the common good. Time and circumstances have changed, yet the core of his arguments is still with us today (Lorimer et al., 2008, p. 158). And, as McChesney (1999) states, democratic principles, rather than Canadian nationalism, motivated Spry, for he believed that a system beholden to corporate interests "disenfranchised the public and empowered big business, regardless of nationality."

This is primarily why we are opposed to opening the floodgates to foreign ownership; doing so would further serve large corporations instead of Canadian citizens. Our argument is not rooted in cultural nationalism; rather, it is animated by a concern with public interests being pitted against corporate interests.

In recent years, several government committees and reports have suggested loosening or removing the foreign ownership restrictions prescribed by both the *Broadcasting Act* and *Telecommunications Act*. In 2003 the House of Commons Standing Committee on Industry, Science and Technology (SCIST) released a report entitled *Opening Canadian Communications to the World*. Of particular importance for us is SCIST's (2003, p. 34) advocacy of a "free entry" approach that would entail the complete removal of foreign ownership restrictions for both telecommunications carriers and broadcasting distributors, including cable, wireless, and satellite. Similar arguments about the benefits of "liberalizing [telecommunications] foreign investment restrictions" appeared five years later in a report entitled *Compete to Win* (Competition Policy Review Panel, 2008, p. 47).

These reports do not explicitly identify their underlying neoliberal assumptions, yet the imprint of that ideology permeates through references to the imperatives of "globalization" and its conceptual partner, "free trade." Like globalization, free trade has an aura of virtue; both concepts connote a sense of internationalism and an air of inevitability. For this reason, we believe **neoliberalism** is a far superior term in describing the political-economic paradigm that informs calls to remove foreign ownership restrictions. Whereas the term "globalization" tends to signify some uncontrollable and unchallengeable order presumably engendered by the "technological revolution" and devoid of human agency, "neoliberalism" better epitomizes the deliberate, calculated promulgation of a corporate-controlled agenda. Neoliberalism is neither uncontrollable nor unchallengeable; rather, it is best understood as "the set of national and international policies that call for business domination of all social affairs with minimal countervailing force" (McChesney, 2001, p. 2). The basic rules of neoliberal ideology are to "liberalize trade and finance" and abolish "outdated" government regulation that constrains "competition" (Chomsky, 1999, p. 20).

We argue that the removal of foreign ownership restrictions, consistent with neoliberal principles, is an example of *re-regulation* to serve business interests. Specifically, we (1) question whether the removal of foreign ownership restrictions will actually change the telecommunications marketplace, (2) outline the problems of trying to separate telecommunications from broadcasting, and (3) argue against those who frame regulation as inherently negative.

WILL FOREIGN INVESTMENT HELP WITH CANADIAN CONSUMER WOES?

Canadians are increasingly more conscious (and rightly concerned) about the fact that they pay more for telecommunication services than consumers in some other nations. Canadian mobile users pay a heavy premium to profitable corporations like Bell, Rogers, and Telus—companies that create an illusion of competition through their subsidiary mobile brands: Virgin, Fido, Chatr, and Koodo. Nonetheless, Canadians must question whether opening telecommunications markets to foreign ownership will rectify this problem.

A truly competitive market, we are told, "offers the promise of the best combination of product selection, service quality and prices" (SCIST, 2003, p. 32). Doing away with foreign ownership restrictions would allegedly allow ambitious new entrants to compete as never before. In turn, consumers would be offered a treasure trove of exciting possibilities in a new telecommunications nirvana. Such arguments must be carefully dissected.

The notion that foreign investment will benefit consumers rests on blind faith, not empirical conditions. McChesney (2000, p. 8) reminds us that the claim that the market is a fair and rational allocator of resources is premised on the notion that the "market is based on competition." However, a small number of providers dominate the Canadian telecommunications industry; these providers, in turn, are often connected to larger media conglomerates. Such concentrated control amounts to an **oligopolistic** communications regime in Canada. But removing the barriers to foreign capital is unlikely to ameliorate the situation. The notion that eliminating ownership regulations would benefit upstart companies, increase competition, and offer more choices to consumers is the sort of rhetoric that is served up to disguise what is really at issue: the increasing consolidation of media power in fewer and fewer hands. Allowing increased foreign ownership does not necessarily mean new entrants. Rather, foreign ownership simply means *foreign investment*. There is no guarantee that foreign investors will support or launch upstart companies; instead, without effective regulation, foreign investors could simply provide additional financial resources to existing telecommunications behemoths such as Bell, Rogers, or Telus— giving them even more market strength.

While "opening the floodgate to foreign investment in Canada's media seems a sure way to raise share prices, history illustrates that it will *not* [italics added] increase the range of diversity in media" (Skinner, 2006, p. 46). In a true free market, relaxing regulations may lead to new entrants; but in oligopolistic markets, **deregulation** often leads to consolidation and "far less market competition" (McChesney, 2007, p. 142). History also demonstrates that new firms, when they are actually created by foreign owners, are ill-equipped to challenge the oligopolistic control of industry giants. The recent case of Wind Mobile provides an example.

In 2008 Industry Canada allocated spectrum space to Egypt-based Globalive to set up Wind, a new mobile provider. However, in October 2009 the Canadian Radio-television and

Telecommunications Commission (CRTC) ruled that Globalive did not satisfy all criteria for Canadian ownership. Industry Minister Tony Clement reviewed the CRTC's assessment and, in December 2009, overturned the ruling in the apparent interest of increasing "competition." Interestingly, while Clement reviewed the decision, Telus heavily lobbied Ottawa policymakers to respect the CRTC's ruling and not allow Wind to operate in Canada. Although Wind has made some inroads on the mobile scene in some Canadian cities, the big three—Bell, Telus, and Rogers—still control "over 90% of the market" (Dampier, 2011).

Even Naguib Sawiris, the billionaire who financially backed Wind Mobile's Canadian launch, acknowledges how the big three telecommunication companies quash new entrants. In a CBC interview, Sawiris characterized Wind's Canadian launch as an investment mistake ("Wind Mobile," 2011), and although he complained about Canada's strict, inconsistent, and confusing foreign investment rules, he also pointed to a larger problem: the regulatory and market abuses of Rogers, Bell, and Telus that allow them to be inefficient and expensive, and to effectively prevent competition. Furthermore, when asked about an upcoming wireless spectrum auction, Sawiris indicated he had no interest in investing further in the Canadian market. Some proponents of removing foreign ownership restrictions cite Wind as an example of how competition from "new entrants" helps consumers; it is revealing, then, that the company's financial backer describes his experience in Canada in such a negative light.

It is also vital to consider the ramifications of greater foreign control of Canadian telecommunications. Across the spectrum of industries, "some 64% of foreign direct investments have been attributed to American firms" since Investment Canada began keeping track of them in 1985; therefore, in the Canadian context, "talk about foreign ownership and control" essentially means American control (Hurtig, 2006, pp. 2–3). With foreign investment in, or ownership of, telecommunications providers, Canadians may, at best, not garner any consumer benefits. But there are potentially disturbing consequences; American ownership of telecommunications, for example, could force Canadians to cede privacy rights and subject them to the stipulations of the United States *Patriot Act*.[1]

CAN TELECOMMUNICATIONS BE SEPARATED FROM BROADCASTING?

Because broadcasters control the content of their transmissions, for policy purposes, broadcasting is treated separately from telecommunications and is subject to the *Broadcasting Act*. Recent discussions about relaxing foreign ownership rules have most often been within the realm of telecommunications, not broadcasting. For Canadian policymakers, loosening foreign ownership barriers in telecommunications is a less sticky issue, because telecommunications providers are thought to offer services that do not have significant bearing on Canadian culture.

The problem is that telecommunications and broadcasting companies are not separate entities. Over the last decade, the Canadian media landscape has witnessed a barrage of horizontal and vertical acquisitions. As of 2011, three cable or telecommunications companies control Canada's private English broadcast networks: Rogers (Citytv), Shaw (Global), and Bell (CTV). This unprecedented concentration caused the CRTC to hold hearings about the problems of vertical integration in Canadian media industries. The relationship between content and carriage concerned the CRTC— for example, whether a company such as Bell could offer its mobile subscribers exclusive CTV content that other mobile users would not access. Given the vertically integrated nature of the broadcasting and telecommunications industries, it would be virtually impossible to permit foreign ownership in telecommunications without affecting the broadcasting sector.

Those in favour of greater foreign ownership would have us believe that such concerns reflect an old-fashioned nationalistic mindset. Citing a representative of CanWest Global, the SCIST (2003, p. 50) report states that the "nationality of the owner of a programming undertaking has no measurable impact on the programming that the undertaking carries." However, the argument that "carriage and content are distinct entities, and that distribution can be separated from programming undertakings" (p. 52) is misleading:

> [The] system and structure of media distribution has everything to do with what gets produced and circulated—especially when ... the same companies own subsidiaries in virtually every corner of the media industry.... There is no longer a sharp divide between broadcasting and telecommunications, hardware and content. (Raboy & Taras, 2004, p. 64)

The ties between telecommunications and broadcasting are significant, and to suggest that deregulating telecommunications will not affect Canadian media content and culture is, arguably, disingenuous. Likewise, it is naive to think that mammoth corporations functioning in any market economy can or would benevolently serve the public interest. Hence, the issue of foreign ownership must be treated as a political, cultural, and social issue. This debate must not be framed in purely economic terms.

REGULATION IN THE PUBLIC INTEREST

The Canadian regulatory regime is outdated and does not effectively protect the interests of our citizens. On this point, we agree with those who want to relax or remove foreign ownership barriers. However, we depart on the solutions. Those in favour of increased foreign ownership believe that all regulations are inherently restricting. For example, the Telecommunication Policy Review Panel (2006, p. 4) claimed that deregulation should become a default, because "competitive forces can be relied on to ensure that Canadians receive a wide range of services at prices and on conditions that are among the best in the world." We disagree; eliminating regulations will benefit only the largest companies, domestic and foreign. The solution to a rapidly changing communications environment is rethinking policies and the way in which policy deliberations are conducted. Hackett and Carroll (2006, p. 9) rightfully argue that one of the more glaring "democratic deficits" of our current media system is the "elitist process" of policymaking that is usually conducted "behind closed doors" without adequate public input.

We are not alone in our call to reassert the importance of domestic regulation. In May 2010 former CRTC chair Konrad von Finckenstein emphasized that foreign investment must be "properly regulated." Echoing our position, he claimed that even in a world "where digital information doesn't recognize national borders," the "controlling minds of a company" must be Canadian. Similarly, the World Bank has said that domestic governments must effectively regulate foreign capital investment in telecommunications. Both von Finckenstein and the World Bank can be criticized for favouring corporate interests, so it is all the more remarkable that they both stressed domestic regulation.

The Public Interest Advocacy Centre (PIAC), a nonprofit consumer protection organization, notes that removing foreign ownership limits is an ill-conceived panacea for previous telecommunications (de)regulatory failures. PIAC claims that dominant domestic telecommunications companies use the mantra of deregulation as a "cudgel" to "bludgeon new entrants"; moreover, the fundamental error committed by government and regulators has been equating the "implementation of deregulation with the onset of real competition" (2010, pp. 12–13). Finally, PIAC concludes that Canadian consumers would benefit most from consistent and stronger regulations of our existing communications providers, because "new entrant competition … can be easily negated by a pattern of mergers that would effectively re-concentrate the market" (p. 19).

In late 2011 Canadian media circulated rumours that a federal cabinet committee considered allowing total foreign ownership of a telecommunications firm, as long as that firm had less than 10 percent market share.[2] A Rogers senior vice-president responded immediately, claiming "if the government wants to change the foreign ownership rules, they should change them for all players" (cited in Trichur & Chase, 2011). On the issue of foreign ownership, Rogers, Bell, and Telus favour whatever policies benefit their oligopolies. When the industry minister reviewed Wind Mobile's ownership structure in 2009, some major players asked the government to respect Canada's regulations and not allow Wind to operate in Canada. Two years later, Rogers claimed to support foreign ownership deregulation *as long as it benefited them as well*.

Although current regulators have created, in Canada, one of the most concentrated media markets in the world wherein only a few large companies profit, this does not mean we should dismiss all talk of regulation. It is worth repeating that our communication woes are not the consequences of regulation per se, but rather regulation dominated by big business interests. Deregulation is not the solution, since deregulation usually means, "*re-regulating* purely to service powerful corporate interests with no concern for the general public" (McChesney, 2007, p. 142).

CONCLUSION

We acknowledge that the rhetoric of "consumer choice" so central to the larger discourse of neoliberalism is seductive. On the surface, the promises of more products and improved services sound appealing. But there are far greater issues at stake.

The current debate over ownership restrictions on Canadian media is, at its very core, a debate about competing interests: the interests of the Canadian public and those of a few media corporations, including Canadian cable and telecommunications empires and other global conglomerates. This struggle is a microcosm of the broader struggle between neoliberalism espoused by big business interests and a substantive and viable critical democracy. Among the defining characteristics of neoliberalism are a disdain for public values and the public good (Giroux, 2011; McChesney, 2001). We should, therefore, be wary about neoliberalism being operationalized within the realm of communication policy. The oligopolistic market in Canada cannot be corrected by merely opening the floodgates to foreign ownership/investment; if existing barriers are removed, the chances of Canadians ever reclaiming that vital space will be small indeed. Canadians seem to understand this and overwhelmingly support current restrictions on foreign ownership. Polling conducted by Harris/Decima (2010) found that most Canadians (68 percent) believe broadcasting and communications are too important to our national security and cultural sovereignty to allow foreign control over Canadian companies. Why, then, is the current Harper government poised to relax such restrictions? The answer is disturbingly simple: in an era of corporate power run amok, there is often a gap "between public preferences and public policy" (Chomsky, 1999, p. 5). Too often, governments are beholden to moneyed corporate interests at the expense of citizens' interests.

Canadians must push back. We must listen to the ghost of Spry and harness his passion; we must demand that our government representatives uphold their obligation to the public interest. In democratic societies, the way in which the communication landscape is structured is of paramount political importance. Control over, and access to, the means of communication is a fundamental aspect of economic, social, and cultural power. The debates over communication policies require informed, spirited, and *public* debate. They should not be left to the machination of corporate moguls, their political bedfellows, and academic cheerleaders of neoliberalism.

Notes

[1] In this regard, one may recall the 2005 scandal, which revealed that AT&T, a major American mobile provider, was helping the national security agency with illegal, warrantless spying.

[2] In March 2012, the minister of industry announced that foreign ownership requirements, as per the *Telecommunications Act*, will no longer apply to telecommunications companies with less than 10 percent market share. How this policy change will affect the next round of spectrum auctions, to be conducted in 2013, or whether or not it ultimately contributes to the public interest, remains to be seen.

References

Wind Mobile backer regrets Canadian launch. (2011, November 17). *CBC News*. Retrieved from http://www.cbc.ca/news/technology/story/2011/11/17/f-naguib-sawiris.html

Chomsky, N. (1999). *Profit over people: Neoliberalism and the global order*. New York: Seven Stories Press.

Competition Policy Review Panel. (2008). *Compete to win*. Ottawa: Industry Canada. Retrieved from http://www.ic.gc.ca/eic/site/cprp-gepmc.nsf/vwapj/Compete_to_Win.pdf/$FILE/Compete_to_Win.pdf

Dampier, P. (2011, January 3). Telecom deregulation fails Canadian consumers. Retrieved from http://stopthecap.com/2011/01/03/telecom-deregulation-fails-canadian-consumers-mediocre-broadband-now-comes-with-limits/

Giroux, H. (2011). The crisis of public values in the age of new media. *Critical Studies in Media Communication, 28*(1), 8–29.

Hackett, R., & Carroll, W. (2006). *Remaking media: The struggle to democratize public communication*. New York: Routledge.

Harris/Decima. (2010). *Foreign ownership of Canadian broadcasting and telephone companies*. Toronto: Author. Retrieved from http://www.friends.ca/files/PDF/strategyproject-fcb-summary.pdf

House of Commons Standing Committee on Industry, Science and Technology. (2003). *Opening Canadian communications to the world*. Ottawa: Public Works and Government Services Canada.

Hurtig, M. (2006). *Selling off our country: Takeovers place key Canadian industries in foreign hands*. Ottawa: Canadian Centre for Policy Alternatives. Retrieved from http://www.policyalternatives.ca/publications/monitor/april-2006-selling-our-country

Lorimer, R., Gasher, M., & Skinner, D. (2008). *Mass communication in Canada* (6th ed.). Don Mills, ON: Oxford University Press.

McChesney, R. (1999). Graham Spry and the future of public broadcasting: The 1997 Spry Memorial Lecture. *Canadian Journal of Communication, 24*(1), 25–47.

McChesney, R. (2000). So much for the magic of technology and the free market. In A. Herman & T. Swiss (Eds.), *The World Wide Web and contemporary cultural theory* (pp. 5–35). New York: Routledge.

McChesney, R. (2001). Global media, neoliberalism, and imperialism. *Monthly Review, 52*(10), 1–19.

McChesney, R. (2007). *Communication revolution: Critical junctures and the future of media.* New York: New Press.

Public Interest Advocacy Centre. (2010). *Opening Canada's doors to foreign investment in telecommunications: Options for reform.* Ottawa: Author. Retrieved from http://www.piac.ca/files/piac_comments_foreign_ownership_telecom.pdf

Raboy, M. (1990). *Missed opportunities: The story of Canada's broadcasting policy.* Montreal: McGill-Queen's University Press.

Raboy, M., & Taras, D. (2004). The politics of neglect of Canadian broadcasting policy. *Policy Options, 25*(3), 63–68.

Skinner, D. (2006). Media democracy in Canada. *Culture Front Relay, 11,* 44–46. Retrieved from http://www.socialistproject.ca/relay/r11_media.pdf

Telecommunications Policy Review Panel. (2006). *Final report.* Ottawa: Author.

Trichur, R., & Chase, S. (2011, November 24). Open big telecoms to foreign ownership: Rogers. *The Globe and Mail.* Retrieved from http://www.theglobeandmail.com/globe-investor/open-big-telecoms-to-foreign-ownership-rogers/article2248435/

von Finckenstein, K. (2010, May 6). *Speech delivered to telecom in Canada panel.* Ottawa: CRTC. Retrieved from http://www.crtc.gc.ca/eng/com200/2010/s100506.htm

Discussion Questions

1. Identify the competing interests that emerge in debates over the foreign ownership of Canadian media corporations.

2. What are the two types of foreign ownership restrictions within Canada?

3. Explain the flaws inherent in restricting industry ownership in Canada.

4. How does the history of Graham Spry's Canadian Radio League, and the ensuing birth of Canadian public broadcasting in the 1930s, relate to contemporary debates about foreign ownership of Canadian media?

5. What is wrong with the assumption that deregulation will lead to a more competitive telecommunications marketplace?

6. Why, in the Canadian media landscape, is it difficult to regulate broadcasters independently of telecommunications service providers?

ISSUE 4

Administrative vs. critical:
Where should we stake our claim?

Administrative

A Fool's Errand: Separating Critical and Administrative Communication Studies in Canada
Terry Flynn and Alex Sévigny

Dr. Terence (Terry) Flynn is currently an assistant professor of communications management in the Department of Communication Studies and Multimedia at McMaster University. He previously held a faculty appointment in the DeGroote School of Business at McMaster, where he founded the master of communications management (MCM) degree program, in partnership with Syracuse University. In 2010 he was awarded the BASU Teaching Award for Best MBA Professor, and in 2011 he was awarded the MBA Student Choice for Best Professor. Prior to obtaining his Ph.D. from the S.I. Newhouse School of Public Communications at Syracuse University, he was president and CEO of Frontline Corporate Communications—a North American consulting company with offices in Kitchener, Ontario, and Memphis, Tennessee. He is currently the senior associate editor of the *Journal of Professional Communication,* and his research has been published in academic and professional journals. Dr. Flynn is an accredited member (APR) of the Canadian Public Relations Society and an elected member of the CPRS College of Fellows (FCPRS), and in 2009 he was elected the national president of the CPRS.

Dr. Alex Sévigny is director of the master of communications management program and an associate professor of communication studies and communication management at McMaster University. He co-founded the communication studies program in 2001. He is co-founder and executive director of the COMM-LAB: McMaster Communication Metrics Lab. He is also the co-founder and editor-in-chief of the new *Journal of Professional Communication,* and the co-founder of the international graduate STUDENT journal *The McMaster Journal of Communication,* of which he has been faculty editor for eight years. He won a McMaster Students Union Teaching Merit Award in 2003 and the Petro-Canada Young Researcher Award in 2006. His areas of interest are media content measurement, social media strategy, community building and fundraising, communications management, and political communication. He maintains an active consulting and public speaking practice outside the university alongside his academic work and has served as communications counsel on several nonprofit boards. He is also a member of the Canadian Public Relations Society National Education Council and its Public Relations Knowledge Exam Subcommittee.

Students in most Canadian communication studies departments have only been hearing half the story about their chosen field of study—the critical half. There is another tradition, rich in explanatory power and useful to professional practice, about which they are being kept in the dark—administrative communication theory. We argue that Canadian critical scholars ignore the practical side of communication studies at the risk of becoming irrelevant and marginalized as students will choose programs focused both on criticizing *and* doing, rather than exclusively criticizing. Furthermore, we propose that there can be an acceptable compromise between critical-cultural and administrative approaches that both satisfies exploding student demand for professional training and enables research into the new social, economic, political, and cultural realities being created by the rapidly expanding communications industry, without sacrificing Canada's rich critical-cultural tradition in research and teaching.

In the West, the scholarly study of communication can be traced back to Antiquity (Ellul, 1976), while systematic scholarship concerning the influence and effects of communication is less than a century old. Over the last seventy years, the discipline—much like others in the humanities, arts, and social sciences—has seen a growing separation and splintering of the field along critical and administrative lines. It is our contention, supported by the stated views of other scholars in the field such as Abramson, Shtern, and Taylor (2008), that the time has come to end the either-or paradigm of administrative versus critical scholarship. Why now? Our answer is simple: we live in a world in which information and communication are as present as the air we breathe, and those messages are being shaped by communicators in an industry that is rapidly professionalizing. To be effective, that industry requires data and a practical-functional understanding of how communication works between people, between organizations, and in social media. This means that students who want to succeed will need the administrative tools required to understand communication in a professional context. While we don't question the legitimacy of purely critical research, we do contend that the purely critical approach is taken less seriously in policy and industry circles, which tend to favour quantitative data. Up to now, only a few Canadian institutions of higher learning have provided programs that attempt to address this latest challenge. Simply put, we contend that it's time for the rest of the Canadian communications academy to catch up to today's communicative realities.

We are not arguing that **critical theory** should be replaced by **administrative theory** in communication departments across Canada. In fact, we argue that in the context of rapid change in the practice, it no longer makes sense to have programs that focus on either side of the critical–administrative divide. Rather, we contend that the emerging set of professional practices imposes a necessary blending of the two approaches: administrative knowledge and critical reflection and ethics, so that we might offer students the education and skills training that will enable them to be wise practitioners who work effectively for their clients while always bearing in mind the public interest.

HEADS IN THE SAND

Today, everyone faces a bewildering new mediascape that surrounds and engulfs them, frames their perceptions, and influences what they feel it is important to think about. The situation is even more serious for communication practitioners, who not only have to be able to navigate this roiling sea of information successfully, but have to interpret trends and then craft messages that will have a serious impact on people's social, political, and cultural lives. To be effective, practitioners must have strategic and tactical knowledge of communication; to be ethical and reflexive, they must take a critical attitude and perspective.

Administrative theory provides strategic and tactical knowledge of media and communication. It looks for facts and conducts experiments, using the social scientific techniques, and asks the "how" and the "what" questions, like "How do I do effective market research before writing a communications plan?" or "What do I need to learn about the theory of persuasion before planning this political campaign?" Critical theory aims to understand the power relations inherent to communication in a historical context, and asks the "when," "why," and "who" questions, like "When did it become important for everyone to wear branded clothes?" or "Why do children privilege certain gender stereotypes?" or "Who benefits from the latest government campaign to spend our way out of the recession?" It seems obvious that a professional communication practitioner must seek answers to all of these questions—administrative and critical—to be effective and ethical.

The critical theory perspective is amply represented in Canadian communication departments, but the administrative perspective is scarce. This gap must be addressed because the lifeblood of **professional communication** practice is administrative research. Without a steady stream of academic research into Canadian communications from an administrative perspective, the practice of professional communication in Canada remains hobbled, having to rely on American, British, and Oceanic (New Zealand, Australia, and South Africa) data that are only applicable by analogy to the Canadian context. Without Canadian administrative research it becomes almost impossible to develop standards of practice, accreditation programs, and best practices that cater to a specific Canadian context. If the research is not being produced, then students are not learning about it. This, in turn, means that there is a gaping hole in the centre of Canadian research and teaching in communication departments—a hole that represents a disconnect between the academy and the profession.

The problem is that the academy hasn't been paying attention. Complacent in the midst of the information and communication revolution taking place around them, Canada's communications academy has remained focused on "Marxist analysis of how media corporations captured the leisure time and the minds-at-leisure of the populace and induced audience members to work (by consuming media products and ads), thereby transforming them into complete consumers" (Lorimer, 2000, para 2), while setting aside the study and research of micro-level influences of policy and practice within a Canadian context (Abramson et al., 2008). This situation must be viewed as irresponsible if communication departments in Canadian universities are to provide administrative perspectives alongside critical ones so that students have the tools to succeed as professionals. Academics, who have tenure and the comforting support of like-minded, critical colleagues, don't have to face the reality of the marketplace the way their students do, and yet students are expected to have graduated with the tools required for success in the professional communications world, where they simply do not have the luxury to pursue an exclusively critical approach.

A quick glance through the list of scholarly papers related to the various Canadian professions of communication provides conclusive evidence of the lack of interest in the Canadian academy: it is a sparse literature, at best (Gombita, 2008; Likely, 2009). Apart from these few examples, professional communication has been left to the colleges.[1] This is largely a historical accident given that Canadian departments of communication were heavily influenced by the "Toronto School of Communication," popular in the mid-twentieth century, whose most famous members were Harold Innis and Marshall McLuhan.

This is not to say that Canadian communication departments have universally neglected to offer students administrative course options. A few departments[2] have recognized the importance of this emerging professional arena and are starting programs in professional communication, although mostly at the master's level.[3] These few universities have recognized what the practice has been experiencing since the onset of the Internet—rapid change and a trend toward professionalization, prompted by the ascension of the communications function into the executive suite of many public, nonprofit, and private organizations. Indeed, the communication function in organizations is becoming increasingly strategic, with professional communicators taking a seat at the executive table, making decisions, and shaping organizational policy. At the same time, professional organizations, such as the Canadian Public Relations Society (CPRS), the International Association of Business Communicators (IABC), and the Marketing Research and Intelligence Association (MRIA), are introducing professional accreditation programs, creating knowledge exams, and defining official standards for pathways into the professional communications industry.

However, the unfortunate reality is that Canadian university students are emerging from communication studies programs across the country with a limited understanding of how these systems operate and with even less understanding of how they might utilize their critical perspectives to ultimately change or improve the functioning of these industries. The need to respond to these challenges is real, it is urgent, its time frame is now. The Canadian communications academy has kept its head, and the heads of its students, in the sand for too long.

SOME BACKGROUND ON ADMINISTRATIVE THEORY

Perhaps a little background on the nature of administrative theory is in order. Administrative theory has also been called American empiricism. In 1938 Paul Lazarsfeld, one of the founding thinkers behind administrative theory, brought Theodor Adorno, one of the founding thinkers in the critical tradition, to Princeton to discuss whether convergence between critical and administrative approaches could be envisaged. Adorno didn't think so, given what he felt was a lack of reflexivity in administrative research, that is to say, that administrative research didn't systematically take a phenomenon under investigation in its socio-cultural context.

This binary way of thinking about the relationship between administrative and critical research is taken up by Dallas Smythe and Tran Van Dinh (1983), who argue that all researchers fall into two categories: those who wish to change the status quo and those who wish to preserve it. They claim that many of the models used by administrative researchers are positivist and behaviouralist in nature, while critical theory encompasses a broad range of qualitative approaches drawn from across the humanities and social sciences.

Stewart Ewen (1983) provides an example of the rejection of numbers- and model-based research: "Data are collected and translated into manageable units of analysis. These, in turn, contribute to the development of models. The voice of people who make up an audience is heard, but only insofar as it translates into a scientific, analytical model" (p. 221). The problem with this criticism of administrative research is that it oversimplifies what the scientific method does. It also implies that someone who is following an opinion-based or critical paradigm is not effecting the same reductivism. This is patently untrue. Given its use of measurement parameters, a scientific article is often better equipped to represent the range of opinions in a population than is a critical approach since the latter relies on qualitative research methods that can sometimes incorporate significant research bias and and yet lack the means needed to control such bias in any systematic way. This often reduces the ability of critical scholarship to represent the feelings and perspectives of a population, a gap that can be systematically met by the approach underlying an equivalent scientific article based on administrative theory.

THE MOVEMENT TOWARD PROFESSIONAL COMMUNICATION

This is an important moment of change in the professions of communication. Once proudly independent professions are experiencing a new self-awareness and beginning to recognize that their interconnections and common concerns outweigh their differences (Sévigny & Flynn, 2011). The practice of journalism has been affected by failing traditional media outlets and shrinking job prospects. As well, the rise of in-house and social journalism has meant that many journalists work for organizations that provide content to news outlets as well as to public relations offices. Indeed, it could even be said that, given the shrinking pool of journalists employed by traditional media, in-house and citizen journalists are writing the first draft of what will eventually be worked over and perfected by journalists working for news organizations. Annexed to this is the rise of the public opinion and communications measurement industry—infographics are beginning to dominate the news and allowing readers the freedom to play with data in interactive charts is becoming a *sine qua non* in many major papers.[4]

At the same time, public relations professionals and communications managers are facing new challenges, as organizations grow in size and face an ever more complex media, social media, and regulatory environment, putting a greater focus on measuring and evaluating their efforts to build mutually beneficial relationships with their diverse publics. Organizational leaders are also looking to their chief communicators to build, manage, and protect the reputation of the enterprise while at the same time ensuring that the voice of their stakeholders is effectively represented and defended during the strategic management and decision-making process.

All of this tumult has signalled a moment of self-definition and redefinition for the various professions of communication. In fact, several industries are realizing their commonalities and coming together in a series of self-organizing moments. A discourse of intersection, accountability, and ethical responsibility is being developed, guided by principles of fairness, duty to clients, and the public interest. This definitional process isn't just about the professional societies defining their own mandates. In fact, professional organizations are beginning to define what they require from academic programs. The standards for accreditation, as outlined by the Public Relations Society of America, demand a strong liberal arts background, as well as the requisite professional courses (PRSA, 2011a). The requirements set out by the Chartered Institute of Public Relations (CIPR, 2011) and Canadian Public Relations Society (CPRS, 2011) are very similar.

Unfortunately, Canadian communication departments are mostly choosing (1) to ignore the emergence of a coherent set of professional standards and (2) not to teach students administrative theory—because their faculty prefer to teach a set of theories and perspectives that seem vital to academia but have little or no currency in the world of professional communication practice, when they are considered in isolation of administrative theory. In fact, students and recent graduates whom we meet in professional circles often complain that they feel as though they are taking the same course several times during their B.A. or that classes privilege a particular ideological perspective. This is admittedly anecdotal evidence, but Canadian communications scholars should take it under advisement—students who enter the workforce don't feel well prepared by an exclusively critical education.

There is a serious informational gap, especially given that another tradition exists, rich and vast and full of explanatory power—the administrative tradition—to which Canadian students are not being exposed. When students hear a discussion of the powerful forces that have the potential to influence the production and dissemination of communicative messages in Canada, they hear it from only one point of view—critical theory. Besides representing an impoverishment of undergraduate education in Canadian communications, this also has meant that the Canadian professions of communication cannot rely on university-educated graduates having the administrative research and skills background necessary for success in the field.

The fact that Canadian universities decided to privilege one theoretical perspective has meant that research in the area of administrative communications has been seriously, if not completely, neglected, and yet administrative communications research is the lifeblood of professional communication practice. This unfortunate situation has set the public relations industry back in Canada significantly and put the onus to develop a useful body of scholarship on professional associations. This disconnect between the academy and the professions isn't healthy for either group. To remedy the situation, the professional associations have been actively reaching out since the mid-2000s, but to no avail. To date, with a few notable exceptions, there have been few official gestures toward convergence between the academic and professional worlds on the part of university communication studies programs.

We contend that things don't have to be this way.

A THIRD, VERY CANADIAN WAY: CRITICAL PROFESSIONAL COMMUNICATION STUDIES

Just as the distinctive Canadian critical approach achieved international attention and influence in the 1960s, Canada is now uniquely positioned to take international leadership in establishing a unique progressive example in the globally emerging field of professional communication. It is time for the Canadian critical communication studies establishment to open a space for professional communication studies programs in universities across the country and desegregate its departments, allowing professional communication to expand beyond the colleges and participate as an equal partner in university life. This shouldn't mean two solitudes, but rather integration, where a new critical–professional consensus is achieved. There is ample evidence that the Canadian professions of communication are eager for this consensus and have moved proactively to begin implementing it on their own.

It is impossible to teach professional communication without giving the students a solid grounding in administrative research in areas such as strategic management, financial literacy, basic numeracy, marketing, market research, opinion polling, citizen and in-house journalism, and advertising. These are the tools that will give the graduates of professional communication studies programs the skills and competencies they need to be effective in the workforce. A critical perspective will provide them with a historically contextualized understanding of the great movements of the arts, history, philosophy, politics, and social life so that they will be able to develop the necessary macroscopic perspective to become wise leaders in their industries. Educated, wise leaders can make positive change not only because they know how their organizations function, but also because they have insight into the human condition, understand historical precedent, and are able to foresee the impact of their choices on their fellow citizens, their country, and the world.

One example of the critical–professional consensus on the part of the Canadian professional associations is the recent development of a distinctly Canadian definition of public relations.[5] In the past, Canadian public relations scholarship and pedagogy has been overshadowed by a powerful and expansive American body of knowledge that is generally characterized by a more neoliberal, corporatist, and functionalist approach to the study of the practice. This dominant American paradigm was neither an adequate reflection of the state of the practice in Canada nor representative of the prevailing attitudes among Canadian practitioners toward their profession.

In late 2008, a research team comprising two academics and a professional communicator examined current definitions in use in Canadian public relations programs with a view to creating a uniquely Canadian definition of professional communication, one that reflects Canadian values of peace, order, and good government. After considering a number of potential theoretical frameworks, the research team proposed the following definition for the practice of public relations in Canada[6]: "Public relations is the strategic management of relationships between an organization and its diverse publics, through the use of communication, to achieve mutual understanding, realize organizational goals and serve the public interest" (Flynn, Gregory, & Valin, 2009).

The uniqueness of the Canadian definition was highlighted recently. In a recent social media discussion initiated by the Public Relations Society of America (2011b) called "Public Relations Defined," many voices proposed that the official Canadian definition could be a model for the rest of the world. Debate raged online for several weeks, and many Canadian participants were surprised to find the clause pertaining to the public interest in their national professional society's definition become the most hotly contested part of the discussion (Flynn, 2011). This was in stark contrast to the Canadian process, where including the public interest as a part of the official definition of public relations was accepted without question.

Given the built-in critical perspective (viz. the "public interest") in the CPRS definition cited above, it is only natural that professional communication studies should develop in a close relationship with critical communication studies. Common concerns in ethics, mass media, political economy, cultural practices and norms, law, and policy (Babe, 2000) should not be arbitrarily separated between the two approaches: the critical and the professional. The alternative model we propose would see critical communication and professional communication studies curricula interwoven so that students are not subject to any one theoretical perspective, but rather understand the breadth of influence and impact that their eventual practice as professional communicators will have on our culture, society, politics, and economy.

We think that Canadian communication studies programs need not face the grim, sterile future of an exclusively critical approach. In fact, given the progressive turn that Canadian public relations practitioners have taken in their official definition, the emergence of a uniquely Canadian approach to critical professional communication studies is inevitable. This could make Canada a progressive global leader in the field, forging a new path that enshrines the concepts of social justice and the public interest and influences professional associations in other countries to take the same high road. To keep critical and administrative perspectives apart in an interconnected world where the practice of professional communication is growing so rapidly appears to be a fool's errand.

Notes

[1] This is especially true in Ontario.

[2] These universities include Royal Roads, Victoria, Mount Saint Vincent, Mount Royal, Ottawa, Ryerson, and McMaster.

[3] There are no Ph.D.-level programs in professional communication in Canada, with one exception: McMaster has proposed a Ph.D. in communication and new media practice, which offers a specialization in professional communication.

[4] *The Guardian* and *The New York Times* are at the forefront of this.

[5] Another example is the development of the Public Relations Knowledge examination (PRK), which includes, at the request of the industry, a serious focus on ethics, history, and policy.

[6] See Flynn, 2011, for a more thorough discussion of the process.

References

Abramson, B. D., Shtern, J., & Taylor, G. (2008). "More and better" research? Critical communication studies and the problem of policy relevance. *Canadian Journal of Communication, 33*(2), 303–317.

Babe, R. (2000). *Canadian communication thought: Ten foundational writers.* Toronto: University of Toronto Press.

Canadian Public Relations Society. (2011). Pathways to the profession: A report of the National Education Counci. *Journal of Professional Communication, 1*(1), 211–241.

Chartered Institute of Public Relations. (2011b). *A new membership structure.* Retrieved from http://www.cipr.co.uk/content/about-us/new-membership-structure

Ellul, J. (1976). *L'histoire de la propagande* (2nd ed.). Paris: Presses Universitaires de France.

Ewen, S. (1983). The implications of empiricism. *Journal of Communication, 33*(3), 219–225.

Flynn, T. (2006). A delicate equilibrium: Balancing theory, practice and outcomes. *Journal of Public Relations Research, 18*(2), 191–201.

Flynn, T. (2011, December 7). A defining moment for public relations. Retrieved from http://www.prconversations.com/index.php/2011/12/a-defining-moment-for-public-relations/

Flynn, T., Gregory, F., & Valin, J. (2009). Defining Public Relations Project. Retrieved from http://defining-publicrelations.wikispaces.com/

Gombita, J. (2008). PR resources, about or by, Canada and Canadians. *PR Conversations* [Blog]. Retrieved from http://www.prconversations.com/index.php/2008/08/pr-resources-about-or-by-canada-and-canadians/

Likely, F. (2009). A different country, a different public relations: Canadian PR in the North American context. In K. Sriramesh & D. Verčič (Eds.), *The global public relations handbook: Theory, research and practice* (2nd ed., pp. 654–675). New York: Routledge.

Lorimer, R. (2000). Introduction: Communications teaching and research—Looking forward from 2000. *Canadian Journal of Communication, 25*(1). Retrieved from http://www.cjc-online.ca.libaccess.lib.mcmaster.ca/index.php/journal/article/view/1136/1055

Public Relations Society of America. (2011a). Guidelines 2011: Certification in Education for Public Relations (CEPR). Retrieved from http://www.prsa.org/conferences/internationalconference/program/sessions/details/441/certification_in_education_for_public_relations_be

Public Relations Society of America. (2011b). Submissions open for "Public Relations Defined" initiative. Retrieved from http://prdefinition.prsa.org/index.php/2011/10/30/public-relations-defined/

Sévigny, A., & Flynn, T. (2011). A reflection on the future of the field of professional communication. *Journal of Professional Communication, 1*(1), 3–14.

Smythe, D. W., & Van Dinh, T. (1983). On critical and administrative research: A new critical analysis. *Journal of Communication, 33*(3), 117–127.

ISSUE 4

Administrative vs. critical:
Where should we stake our claim?

Critical

Why Critical Communication Study Is Still Relevant, and Even Necessary, in Our Contemporary Mediascape
Sheryl N. Hamilton

Sheryl N. Hamilton is the Canada Research Chair in Communication, Law and Governance and an associate professor in the School of Journalism and Communication and the Department of Law and Legal Studies at Carleton University. She is the author of *Impersonations: Troubling the Person in Law and Culture* (2009), *Law's Expression: Communication, Law and Media in Canada* (2009), and numerous articles and book chapters on media studies, intellectual property, science and media, and gender and technology. She is also a co-author of *Becoming Biosubjects: Bodies. Systems. Technologies* (2011). Her current research examines the cultural life of law and the emotional publics it generates in Canada.

When the Canadian government tables "lawful access" legislation requiring Internet service providers (ISPs) to turn over to police detailed user information without a warrant, and to implement technology enabling real-time surveillance of users by police, should we just sit back and be comforted that our government is getting "tough on crime"? When Google owns 65 to 70 percent of the search market in the United States, controls 95 percent of the mobile search market, and is before a Senate antitrust committee charged with privileging its own services and products in searches and using its monopoly position to disadvantage its business competitors, should we even worry about it? After all, we use Google every day and it seems to work just fine. When the Chinese government denies its citizens access to Facebook, Twitter, YouTube, Wikipedia, and Foursquare, blocks over 100 million articles per day, and shuts down over a million websites annually, producing what has been nicknamed the "Great Firewall of China," should we be concerned? Really, isn't that business as usual in a Communist dictatorship? What does it have to do with us here in North America?

Some might argue that the time has passed for a critical approach to communication studies, that it is outdated. Others might suggest that "critical" has become so ubiquitous an adjective to describe research that it no longer means anything (see Chang, 2011). However, the above examples of governments trampling the privacy rights of citizens through the cooperation of policing and technology, abuses of power stemming from corporate dominance of a media market, and citizens being denied free speech by a fearful state are unfortunately not exceptional in our contemporary communicative environment. They are increasingly the norm. The stakes are therefore high and complacency on our part as scholars of communication, and as citizens, is not enough. The contemporary mediascape demands of us that we think (again or still) about issues of media ownership, state and corporate structures of power, communication rights, technological possibilities (for resistance and control), security and surveillance, and more. In other words, we need to think about the kind of society in which we would like to live—we need to think critically.

But what we mean by "critical" is not self-evident. As Kent A. Ono notes, "at this particular moment in the field of communication, putting a finer edge on the meaning of the word 'critical' seems like a good idea" (2011, p. 93). In this chapter, I explore how the notion of critical communication came to be a term of art in American communication studies and outline its major tenets. Next, I examine how Canadian communication studies uncritically adopted a notion of critical communication as its dominant paradigm. Finally, I suggest some ways that we can still benefit from thinking critically about communication today.

AMERICAN CRITICAL COMMUNICATION STUDIES

When linked to communication research, "critical" is often contrasted either latently or expressly with "administrative." I suggest three significant intellectual events entrenched that frame, a frame that continues to structure discussions to this day: Paul Lazarsfeld's 1941 article entitled "Remarks on **Administrative** and **Critical Communication Research**," Todd Gitlin's 1978 article entitled "Media Sociology: The Dominant Paradigm," and the 1983 special issue of the *Journal of Communication.*

Lazarsfeld, one of the "founding fathers" of the field of communication, perhaps best known to students of communication as one of the authors of the two-step flow theory of media influence, was grappling with the conflict between his own approach, which he labelled "administrative," and that of his Frankfurt School colleagues, which he labelled "critical."[1] Administrative research, he suggested, pursued questions useful to corporations or government, focused on the effects of media on individuals, and deployed scientific methodologies and statistical methods. It privileged questions about people's exposure to media, their preferences, and the varying effects of different delivery systems of media content (Lazarsfeld, 1941, p. 3). Critical scholarship, on the other hand, was theoretically rather than empirically driven, understood communication in a much broader social and historical context, and was concerned with human alienation and social values (Lazarsfeld, 1941, pp. 9–10).

Lazarsfeld's distinction was taken up by Todd Gitlin in 1978 to condemn the state of communication research in the United States. Gitlin carefully situates the historical emergence of the administrative paradigm and then systematically demolishes its underlying theory of behaviourism, its marketing orientation, its empirical failings, and its pluralist view of power. He defines administrative research as that which "poses questions from the vantage point of the command-posts of institutions that seek to improve or rationalize their control over social sectors in social functions" (Gitlin, 1978, p. 225). Against this, he situates critical research as the alternative with a more hierarchically structured notion of power, asking questions about the organization of media and its relationship to politics, and taking up the larger social meanings of communicative practices.

The intellectual and academic gauntlet thrown down by Gitlin was taken up in the 1983 special issue of the *Journal of Communication* entitled "Ferment in the Field."[2] Editor George Gerbner was seeking an interrogation of the "state of the field," and "administrative versus critical" became a primary axis of the ensuing debate. I suggest that six generalizable attributes of critical communication studies emerge from this history.[3]

First, critical communication studies takes as its primary question the relationship between communication and social power. Critical scholarship might explore the ways that communications giants such as Yahoo!, Google, Microsoft, Skype, and Cisco, in their efforts to access China's 450 million+ Internet users, find themselves walking a delicate line between "collusion and collision" with the authoritarian regime in that country (see SecDev Group, 2011).

Second, critical scholars reject a liberal pluralist understanding of social power, holding that power is unequally distributed. "Critical communication scholarship is rooted in the assumption that social institutions and human relations are relations of history, power and struggle" (Bailie, 1997, p. 33). Therefore, the increasing concentration of the Canadian telecommunications and broadcasting industries in the hands of a very small number of conglomerates and what that means for the range of voices in media is of concern to critical researchers (see Winseck, 2010).

Much of the debate in "Ferment in the Field" played out over issues of methodology—the third key attribute used in distinguishing administrative from critical approaches. The traditional view assumed that administrative research was empirical and critical research was not. Numerous scholars contested this, and some continue to do so, suggesting that critical research often uses empirical methods (Allen, 1999; Elasmar, 1999; Gerbner, 1964; Habermas 2006; Halloran, 1983; Mosco, 1983; Rogers, 1982). I have argued elsewhere that this was an unproductive line of debate (Hamilton, 2009), and concern to classify critical research by means of its methodology seems to have ebbed over time.

A fourth element of critical communication research is the self-reflexive way in which values shape the research (Blumler, 1983; Mosco, 1983, 1996; Smythe & Van Dinh, 1983; Straw, 1985). Research questions do not shy away from normative value statements and/or the political orientation of the researcher. Typical values might include a belief in democratic participation in media, universal access to communication technology, state regulation to control monopolistic tendencies in media markets, state support for the cultural industries, or an embrace of diversity in representational practices.

A fifth attribute that has historically united critical scholars in communication studies is the influence of Continental critical theory, and Marxist thought in particular. However, as Ono (2011) effectively argues, the field is increasingly more complicated as scholars draw upon a wide range of post-structuralist, critical race, feminist, queer, post-colonial, diaspora, social movement, and other more contemporary theories.[4]

The sixth shared attribute that continues to be identified with critical communications scholarship focuses on the knowledge claims that it makes. Critical communications both critically analyzes and seeks to disrupt or change existing social relations and configurations of power (Halloran, 1983; Mosco, 1983). A key objective of research is thus "the production of intellectual and political resources for social transformation and individual and collective emancipation" (Bailie, 1997; see also Gerbner, 1964; Haight, 1983; Jansen, 1983; and Splichal, 2008). This focus has meant, for example, that numerous communication scholars working within the critical tradition incorporate activism into their practice (e.g., McLeod, 2011; Napoli & Aslama, 2011; Shade, 2011).

The concern with the role that a critical orientation plays within American communications scholarship continues today in the repeated revisiting of what critical communication means.[5] The enduring concern with "being critical" has emerged, I suggest, as a central element in defining the character of American communication studies.

CRITICAL COMMUNICATION STUDIES IN CANADA

Canadian communication scholars have been just as obsessed with "critical" as their American colleagues, albeit in a different way. Communication studies in Canada has long been proud of its critical orientation, deploying it as a tool to distinguish itself from the American "dominant paradigm"—administrative research—particularly as the field institutionalized in the 1960s and 1970s. And it seems that the label of critical persists, at least in our origin stories. Robert Babe, in his intellectual history of Canadian communication thought, cites its critical-ness as a defining characteristic (2000a) and others generally agree (Acland & Buxton, 1999; Carey, 1975, 1983; Grosswiler, 1996; Hardt, 1992; Kroker, 1984; Robinson & Theall, 1975).[6] Babe suggests that work in the Canadian critical tradition is "evaluative research presuming enduring criteria for judging policies, activities, events, human relations, institutions, and so forth, and as well enduring goals towards which we should strive" (2000a, p. 16).

To a significant degree, the six attributes of American critical communication studies discussed above resonate with Canadian perspectives. The claim of a critical orientation in Canada has been grounded in a dialectical understanding of power, where history is produced through the encounter of contradictory social forces (Babe, 2000a, 2000b; Kroker, 1984; Theall, 1975; Tremblay, 1981), and a focus on the relationship between technology, communication, and society (Carey, 1983; Kroker, 1984). As well, Canadian scholarship is held to place a commitment to human emancipation and exploring the conditions of a better life at the centre of its inquiry (Babe, 2000a, 2000b; Kroker, 1984). While not denying the rich intellectual legacy of Harold Innis, Marshall McLuhan, C. B. Macpherson, or George Grant, Canadian communications' claim to be always, already critical reproduces three problems, I suggest.

First, critical-ness is assumed rather than demonstrated. Our position as critical is seen to flow *naturally* from our economic, political, social, and geographical marginality, almost always constituted in relation to the United States (Babe, 2000a, 2000b; Carey, 1975; Robinson & Theall, 1975; Theall, 1975). Arthur Kroker (1984) argues, for example, that Canadian communication thought is an oppositional mode between European and Canadian thinking, characterized by its "in-betweeness." This discourse of marginalization requires updating for a globalized world. Further, if a critical orientation is to be effective in its engagement with social power, then it must be a *process* in which we are continually engaged, rather than an *outcome* inevitably produced by structural forces outside of our control. We must be critical agents in the mediascape.

The second critique of the story of Canadian critical communication studies is that "critical" operates too frequently as an identity claim framed in a discourse of national distinction. Our field has been plagued by the same questions that have dogged the cultural industries, scholars, and policymakers since Confederation: What makes Canadian communication studies unique? What makes it Canadian? (See, for example, Babe, 2000a, 2000b; Kroker, 1984; and Robinson & Theall, 1975.) Of course, the "other" to which we are inevitably comparing ourselves is again the United States, and so the easy answer becomes that we are critical in contrast to American communication studies, which is administrative. This claim is certainly now dated but has always been problematic. It flattens much diversity and complexity in the American instance (see Meehan, 2004) and too often operates as a smug statement of superiority. It further prevents us from reflecting on our own potential "dominant paradigms" and the place of administrative research in our own history.[7]

A third critique of Canadian critical communication studies is that "critical" has been too narrowly interpreted, often being conflated with a narrow political economy orientation (Lorimer, 2000). As result, we have not recognized the diversity of approaches that can fall under the umbrella of "critical," including critical race work, feminist research, queer theory, post-colonial analyses, institutional study, globalization studies, social movement theory, and even the multiplicity of approaches to political economy.

So how do we respond in the face of such critiques? Should we abandon critical thinking in Canadian communication studies? Absolutely not! I argue that critical communication study is more essential than ever.

DOING CRITICAL COMMUNICATION STUDIES IN THE TWENTY-FIRST CENTURY

A report of the Organisation for Economic Co-operation and Development (2011) found that Canadians pay the highest roaming fees in the world, and among the highest rates for their cellphones. BCE, Rogers, and Telus own 94 percent of the wireless market in Canada. In 2010 BCE presented arguments to the Canadian Radio-television and Telecommunication Commission (CRTC) that it should be allowed to bill Internet resellers according to bandwidth used. Usage-based billing on the model that BCE was proposing would have sorely disadvantaged small service providers and resulted in dramatically increased costs for any consumers engaged in prolific downloading.[8] While adopting a rhetoric of greater consumer choice, Canadian copyright reform legislation simultaneously legitimizes the technological measures that copyright owners are putting into place to lock up content and criminalizes anyone who attempts to circumvent those digital locks, even if their intended use of the content is fully legal. Five Canadian companies own 75 percent of all the private television stations in the country, and three companies own 60 percent of the newspapers. What happens to a diversity of voices in that context?

It is long past time to stand up and say these practices are not acceptable. We clearly still need to be concerned about structures of social subordination and the ways in which our communication practices and technologies are integral to them. We need to take up Slavko Splichal's exhortation to think critically, to "broaden the horizons of what is *relevant* today and *possible* in the future, identify the seeds of what may stimulate social transformation and trace its direction" (2008, p. 20). Doing communications critically continues to mean, as it has since Lazarsfeld's time, that "power has to be integrally constitutive of the scholarly questions and the political goals of scholarship" (Ono, 2011, p. 95). We need to ask what the impact is of a lack of competition for service in media markets; how technology can be used for surveillance or for limiting access to content; how we can ensure that all voices are heard in our media; how we can ensure that globally citizens have the right to access information critical of their governments.

In doing so, however, I suggest that we need to stop congratulating ourselves on being critical and starting *doing* critical work. I suggest that we need to be more self-reflexive—always thinking about how each of us plays a part in the reproduction of the very systems of power with which we want to engage. This means making critical thinking a process and not an outcome. Critical communications is something we do, not something we are. I suggest that we recognize the myriad theoretical resources available to us, many produced out of the lived experiences of women, people of colour, marginalized communities, and people identifying as LGBTQ. In this way, we can work to make critical communication studies an orientation toward research and not a rulebook. Finally, if we are going to be effective critical communications scholars in the twenty-first century, we will have to be part of what Hardt called a more "combative agenda of democratization" (in McLuskie et al., 2004, p. 228). We will have to think about creative ways to talk back to power, to imagine other possible communications frameworks, to share information with various publics.

Fortunately, there are many examples of ways in which critical communications work is having an impact right now. Intellectual property scholar Michael Geist has effectively used Facebook, online publishing, blogging, and newspaper commentary to have a visible pro-user impact on the copyright reform process in Canada and to mobilize thousands of Canadians to think about how copyright issues implicate them. A grassroots organization, Openmedia.ca, featuring a number of communications scholars, is circulating an online petition requesting the government intervene to protect competition in Canada's wireless market; 30 000 Canadians signed it within a week. South of the border, widespread grassroots and ISP mobilization (on and offline) against the *Stop Online Piracy Act* (widely held to trample users' rights and radically increase state control of the Internet in an effort to curb illegal downloading) is being credited with the seeming permanent delay of that legislation. After Wikipedia went offline for twenty-four hours, eight million visitors to the site sought information to contact their politicians.

These examples are all instances where alliances of communications academics, activists, everyday citizens, and media actors have taken seriously the work of "unraveling communication (in)equalities among individuals and social groups and impediments to the civil right to communicate" (Splichal, 2008, p. 27). They use new and old media and diverse knowledge tactics to engage with our social conditions of communication, to imagine and then demand or make more democratic alternatives. They are doing some of the essential work of critical communication studies in our contemporary mediascape.

Notes

[1] The Frankfurt School was the name given to a group of émigré Jewish scholars who fled Nazi Germany to settle in the United States. Trained in Continental schools of thought, and heavily influenced by Marxism, scholars such as Max Horkheimer, Theodor Adorno, and Herbert Marcuse worked with, but also came into conflict with, Lazarsfeld and his colleagues at the Princeton Office of Radio Research and later Columbia University's Bureau of Applied Social Research.

[2] Following directly on the heels of the "Ferment" issue, the *Canadian Journal of Communication* published a special issue in 1985 focusing on the teaching of critical communication studies and in 1984, *Media, Culture and Society* offered an issue focused on critical communication research.

[3] Different scholars obviously emphasize different elements of the six attributes. For a fuller discussion of this argument see Hamilton, 2009.

[4] He sees this as a positive intellectual turn likely to engender "a more inclusive conception of critical scholarship" (Ono, 2011, p. 95). It must be noted that this is still a contested terrain, with scholars like Christian Fuchs arguing for a return to "the Marxian roots of this field" (2009, p. 6) as a way of delimiting critical communication studies.

[5] To note but a few examples, the *Journal of Communication* dedicated another special issue to "The Future of the Field—Between Fragmentation and Cohesion" in 1993 featuring the section "Rethinking the Critical Tradition." A *Festschrift* in honour of Hanno Hardt organized in 2003 took up the question "A Conversation

with Hanno Hardt on the Future of Critical Communication Studies" (see McLuskie, Hegbloom, & Woodfin, 2004). The discussion persists in a 2011 forum "Being Critical" in the journal *Communication & Critical/ Cultural Studies.*

[6] In particular, the role of Harold Innis in our field's critical identity is emphasized.

[7] See de la Garde, 1987; Robinson, 2000; Salter, 1987; and Tate, Osler, Fouts, and Segal, 2000, for a recognition of the relationship between the rise of communication studies as a discipline in Canada and the needs of multiple Royal Commissions studying media.

[8] For a close and nuanced analysis of the CRTC's ultimate decision, see Winseck, 2011.

References

Acland, C. R., & Buxton, W. J. (1999). *Harold Innis in the new century: Reflections and refractions.* Montreal and Kingston: Queen's University Press.

Allen, M. (1999). The role of meta-analysis for connecting critical and scientific approaches: The need to develop a sense of collaboration. *Critical Studies in Mass Communication, 16,* 373–379.

Babe, R. E. (2000a). *Canadian communication thought: Ten foundational writers.* Toronto: University of Toronto Press.

Babe, R. E. (2000b). Foundations of Canadian communication thought. *Canadian Journal of Communication, 26,* 19–37.

Bailie, M. (1997). Critical communication pedagogy: Teaching and learning for democratic life in democratizing communication? In M. Bailie & D. Winseck (Eds.), *Democratizing communication? Comparative perspectives on information and power* (pp. 33–56). Creskill, NJ: Hampton Press.

Blumler, J. G. (1983). Communication and democracy: The crisis beyond and the ferment within. *Journal of Communication, 33*(3), 166–173.

Carey, J. (1975). Canadian communication theory: Extensions and interpretations of Harold Innis. In G. J. Robinson & D. F. Theall (Eds.), *Studies in Canadian communications* (pp. 27–60). Montreal: Graduate Program in Communications.

Carey, J. (1982). The mass media and critical theory: An American view. In M. Burgoon (Ed.), *Communication Yearbook 6* (pp. 18–34). Beverly Hills, CA: Sage.

Carey, J. (1983). The origins of the radical discourse on cultural studies in the United States. *Journal of Communication, 33*(3), 311–313.

Chang, B. G. (2011). Introduction: Sixteen and a half questions on "being critical." *Communication and Critical/Cultural Studies, 8*(1), 85–87.

de la Garde, R. (1987). The 1987 Southam lecture: Mr. Innis, is there life after the "American Empire"? *Canadian Journal of Communication,* 7–21.

Elasmar, M. G. (1999). Opportunities and challenges of using meta-analysis in the field of international communication in critical studies. *Mass Communication, 16,* 379–384.

Fuchs, C. (2009). A contribution to theoretical foundations of critical media and communication studies. *Javnost—The Public, 16*(2), 5–24.

Gerbner, G. (1964). On content analysis and critical research in mass communication. In L. A. Dexter & D. Manning (Eds.), *People, society and mass communication* (pp. 476–500). New York: Free Press.

Gitlin, T. (1978). Media sociology: The dominant paradigm. *Theory and Society, 6*(2), 205–253.

Grosswiler, P. (1996). The dialectical methods of Marshall McLuhan, Marxism, and critical theory. *Canadian Journal of Communication, 21*(1), 95–124.

Habermas, J. (2006). Political communication in media society: Does democracy still enjoy and epistemic dimension? The impact of normative theory on empirical research. *Communication Theory, 16,* 411–426.

Haight, T. R. (1983). The critical researcher's dilemma. *Journal of Communication, 33*(3), 226–236.

Halloran, J. D. (1983). A case for critical eclecticism. *Journal of Communication, 33*(3), 270–278.

Hamilton, S. (2009). Considering critical communication studies in Canada. In L. Regan Shade (Ed.), *Mediascapes* (pp. 9–27). Scarborough, ON: Nelson.

Hardt, H. (1992). *Critical communication studies: Communication, history and theory in America.* London and New York: Routledge.

Jansen, S. C. (1983). Power and knowledge: Toward a new critical synthesis. *Journal of Communication, 33*(3), 342–354.

Kroker, A. (1984). *Technology and the Canadian mind: Innis/McLuhan/Grant.* Montreal: New World Perspectives.

Lazarsfeld, P. F. (1941). Remarks on administrative and critical communication research. *Studies in Philosophy and Social Science, 9*(1), 2–16.

Lorimer, R. (2000). Introduction: Communications teaching and research—Looking forward. *Canadian Journal of Communication, 25,* 9–17.

McLeod, K. (2011). On pranks. *Communication and Critical/Cultural Studies, 8*(1), 97–102.

McLuskie, E., Hegbloom, M., & Woodfin, F. (2004). In the company of Hanno Hardt: A *Festschrift* on the future of critical communication studies. *Journalism, 5*(2), 227–241.

Meehan, E. R. (2004). Moving forward on the left: Some observations of critical communications research in the United States. *The Public, 11*(3), 19–30.

Mosco, V. (1983). Critical research and the role of labour. *Journal of Communication, 33*(3), 237–248.

Mosco, V. (1996). *The political economy of communication: Rethinking and renewal.* London and Thousand Oaks, CA: Sage.

Napoli, P. M., & Aslama, M. (Eds.). (2011). *Communication research in action: Scholar activist collaborations for a democratic public sphere.* New York: Fordham University Press.

Ono, K. A. (2011). Critical: A finer edge. *Communication and Critical/Cultural Studies, 8*(1), 93–96.

Organisation for Economic Co-operation and Development. (2011). *International mobile data roaming.* Retrieved from http://www.oecd.org/dataoecd/57/62/48127892.pdf

Robinson, G. J. (2000). Remembering our past: Reconstructing the field of Canadian communication studies. *Canadian Journal of Communication, 25,* 105–125.

Robinson, G. J., & Theall, D. F. (1975). Introduction. *Studies in Canadian Communications* (pp. 1–6). Montreal: Graduate Program in Communication.

Rogers, E. M. (1982). The empirical and critical schools of communication research. In M. Burgoon (Ed.), *Communication Yearbook 5.* New Brunswick, NJ: Transaction Books.

Salter, L. (1987, Winter). Taking stock: Communication studies in 1987. *Canadian Journal of Communication,* 23–45.

SecDev Group. (2011, September 20). *Collusion and collision: Searching for guidance in Chinese cyberspace.* Retrieved from http://www.Scribd.com/doc/65531793/Collusion-Collision

Shade, L. R. (2011). Media reform in the United States and Canada: Activism and advocacy for media policies in the public interest. In R. Mansell & M. Raboy (Eds.), *The handbook on global media and communication policy* (pp. 147–165). London: Blackwell.

Smythe, D. W., & Van Dinh, T. (1983). On critical and administrative research: A new critical analysis. *Journal of Communication, 33*(3), 117–127.

Splichal, S. (2008). Why be critical. *Communication, Culture and Critique, 1,* 20–30.

Sjovaag, H., & Hallvard, M. (2009). From fermentation to maturity? Reflections on media and communication studies: An interview with Todd Gitlin, Jostein Gripsrud and Michael Schudson. *International Journal of Communication, 3,* 130–139.

Straw, W. (1985). Teaching critical media analysis. *Canadian Journal of Communication, 11*(1), 5–16.

Tate, E. D., Osler, A., Fouts, G., & Segal, A. (2000). The beginnings of communication studies in Canada: Remembering and narrating the past. *Canadian Journal of Communication, 25*, 61–103.

Theall, D. F. (1975). Communication theory and the marginal culture: The socio-aesthetic dimensions of communication study. In G. J. Robinson & D. F. Theall (Eds.), *Studies in Canadian communications* (pp. 7–26). Montreal: Graduate Program in Communications.

Tremblay, G. (1981). Préface. In L. Salter (Ed.), *Communication studies in Canada/Études Canadiennes en communication* (pp. vii–x). Toronto: Butterworths.

Winseck, D. (2010). Financialization and the "crisis of the media": The rise and fall of (some) media conglomerates in Canada. *Canadian Journal of Communication, 35*, 365–393.

Winseck, D. (2011). Dead horses and Internet policy: The CRTC's usage-based billing and vertical integration decisions as lost opportunities. Retrieved from http://dwmw.wordpresscom

Discussion Questions

1. From the authors' perspective, why and how is the study of administrative research/communication important to the practice of professional communications?

2. How has the primary focus on critical research in Canadian communications programs limited the development of professional communications in Canada?

3. Given the 70-year old schism between critical and administrative communication research, is it realistic to think that a new, hybrid critical/professional area of study can emerge in Canada?

4. According to the authors, the new definition of public relations states that the practice should be conducted in the public interest. What are the challenges with this type of approach?

5. What three intellectual events in American communication studies established the distinction between critical and administrative research as a means to understand the field?

6. What are six attributes that are used to distinguish critical from administrative research?

7. What are three problems with the Canadian communication studies claim to being "critical?"

PART 2 Media and Social Issues

ISSUE 1 Childhood obesity: Is banning television advertisements to children the best solution?

ISSUE 2 Toxic gaming: Do violent video games make children aggressive?

ISSUE 3 Buckets for the cure: Do the benefits of cause-related marketing outweigh the costs?

ISSUE 4 Representing race: Are Canadian news media racist?

Some of the most debated topics in communication studies have to do with the relationship between the media and contemporary social issues. While we are surrounded by media in various forms—blogs, podcasts, Twitter feeds, video games, television, newspapers, et cetera—they are not without controversy. Myriad questions arise over the impact of media on society. What is the relationship between food advertising and obesity? Do violent media create violent children? Does cause-related marketing benefit corporations more than society? Do news media perpetuate racist perspectives?

Such questions have to do with a spectrum of media, from advertising to video games, but also speak to a variety of audiences. Indeed, the social issues bound up with media are not focused solely on the "vulnerable" audience of children. They also have to do, more generally, with questions of gender, race, community, and citizenship. Starting with childhood obesity and concluding with representations of race, the issues tackled in this section illustrate the wide span of key controversies pertinent to students of communication.

Childhood obesity is a significant public health problem in Canada, which has prompted governments, policymakers, researchers, and advocacy groups (along with health professionals) to consider how the social environment contributes to being overweight. A core part of this environment,

of course, is the media. The first debate addresses the question of whether banning advertisements to children is the best solution for combating childhood obesity in Canada. Bill Jeffery argues that such a ban is essential to addressing the obesity problem. "Flogging disease-promoting foods to impressionable children" is not only unethical, he argues, but also a violation of our Canadian consumer protection laws. Jeffery contends that children are vulnerable to media messages and are not media savvy—that is, they are unable to understand commercial intent. Given this, televised advertising to children should be illegal throughout Canada.

Charlene Elliott, on the other hand, argues that a singular focus on television advertising to children misses the point. Instead, we must to recognize that children's food marketing is situated within a broader social environment, one that promotes food, all-the-time eating, and large portion sizes to all Canadians. Banning or restricting food advertising aimed specifically at children fails to shield them from the deluge of commercial messaging that constantly implores all of us to eat. Childhood obesity will be stemmed only once we, as a society, set aside our preoccupation with nutritionism, recognize the political economic drivers behind food marketing, and focus on transforming our foodscape as a whole. Simply put, if we are serious about combating the problem of childhood obesity, we must combat the problem of food culture and food marketing more broadly.

Debate two pivots on the connection between violent video games and childhood aggression. Rose Dyson views violent video games as deeply corrosive to society, arguing that senseless media violence "is tantamount to child abuse." The consequences of such video games, she explains, play out on both an individual and social level—and she questions the appropriateness of indiscriminately socializing young people into thinking that killing is fun.

James Ivory and T. Franklin Waddell challenge this stance, asserting that we must be more cautious about presuming that violent video games translates directly into violent children. Even though risks are associated with excessive video game use (e.g., evidence suggests violent video games can amplify aggressive thoughts and behaviours), the authors argue that the effects of violent video games on aggression are no stronger than the effects of other violent media on aggression. Given this, the authors argue that directing our public resources to battling video game violence is wrong-headed, as those same resources would do more good "fighting the causes of societal violence" such as unhealthy peer and family environments, poverty, and mental illness.

The third issue under consideration shifts the focus from children to community and corporate players. It questions the relationship between cause-related marketing (CRM) and social good, querying whether the benefits of cause-related marketing outweigh the costs. Josh Greenberg details a number of corporate-driven social campaigns that illustrate the concept of business "doing well by doing good." He suggests that social responsibility initiatives undertaken by corporations can work to generate publicity about a particular problem, allowing charities or nonprofit organizations to reach far broader audiences with their message than otherwise would be possible. While acknowledging the range of critiques levelled at CRM, Greenberg argues that because these schemes generate discourse about social, economic and political issues, they should be seen as valuable

in themselves and as useful to informing how we think about and act in the world.

Samantha King argues that encouraging citizens to shop for a cause is both superficial and misleading. Cause-related marketing wrongly suggests that social problems should be tackled individually and through the marketplace. Yet consumption does not provide the collective action required to solve social problems, nor does it challenge inequality. In short, CRM is not transformative. King affirms that the main goal of cause-related marketing is simply to "sell products through an appeal to the customer's altruistic self-image" while (presumably) demonstrating corporate responsibility. As such, the benefits of CRM do not begin to match the costs.

The final debate moves from marketing and promotion to news coverage. It explores the ways that race is depicted in Canadian news. Faiza Hirji affirms that the Canadian news media promotes racialization—the process of imposing racial characteristics on individuals and/or groups—by marginalizing, underrepresenting, and/or misrepresenting them. Drawing from a series of provocative news articles, Hirji unpacks how the language used to frame certain news stories works to perpetuate (sometimes implicitly, sometimes explicitly) a distinction between "us" and "them." The reasons for this are complex— they are sometimes rooted in attempts to attract attention with "bold" headlines, they may stem from journalistic tendencies to rely on familiar institutional sources, or they may arise partly from the "limited social and financial resources" that allow for minorities to provide their perspective on events. Hirji acknowledges that racialization is "not necessarily a widespread problem in Canadian news media, but it is a serious one."

Sean Hier and Daniel Lett suggest that the issue of media and racism requires more careful analytical attention. Many of the studies on racism and media "misrepresent the diversity of coverage in the mainstream media available in Canada, underrepresent the diversity of media outlets, and remain silent on important patterns of coverage in mainstream and other media pertaining to equity, social justice, and human rights." Part of the problem arising from these studies, Hier and Lett aver, is that analysts tend to "seek out explicit examples of stereotypical, sensational, and spectacular media coverage" at the expense of coverage that contributes to ethno-racial harmony and acceptance in Canada. Greater empirical data are required before claims can be made regarding the overall representation of race in Canadian news coverage. The authors also draw attention to the need to probe the impact of "newer" digital media (such as Facebook, Twitter, blogs, and social networking sites) and "alternative media" on perceptions of race. They argue that Canada offers a diversity of media coverage that tends to be glossed over by analysts who selectively find racism in every (media) treatment of race. Moreover, significant transformations have taken place in Canada, which demand a much more complex reading of the situation.

ISSUE 1

Childhood obesity: Is banning television advertisements to children the best solution?

✔ YES

Advertising and Childhood Obesity: Convincing Legislators Who Refuse to Believe to Ban Advertising to Children Who Will Always Believe
Bill Jeffery

Bill Jeffery, LLB, is the national coordinator of the Centre for Science in the Public Interest in Canada. CSPI is a nonprofit health advocacy organization specializing in nutrition and food safety with staff in Toronto and offices in Ottawa; Washington, DC; and Dallas. CSPI's Canadian advocacy is funded primarily by more than 100 000 subscribers—on average one subscriber within a one-block radius of every Canadian street corner—to the Canadian edition of its *Nutrition Action Healthletter*, which does not carry advertisements. CSPI does not accept funding from industry or government.

INTRODUCTION

Banning advertising and other forms of marketing to children is an essential component of any effective strategy to combat rising childhood obesity and other nutrition-related diseases. Advertising directly to children contributes to poor diets (and probably sedentary behaviour) that ultimately lead to preventable chronic disease and premature death in adulthood. If advertising to children does not already actually infringe untested Canadian federal and provincial consumer protection statutes (and it might), those laws should be amended to explicitly ban such misleading, manipulative, and exploitative marketing practices.

THE TOLL OF POOR DIET AND PHYSICAL INACTIVITY

Nutrition-related disease wreaks a terrible toll on Canadian society. According to the World Health Organization, preventable nutrition-related diseases in high-income countries are responsible for one-fifth of all deaths, or nearly 48 000 deaths annually in Canada, due mainly to cardiovascular disease, diabetes, and certain cancers caused by excess sodium intake, risky blood cholesterol and glucose levels, inadequate fruit and vegetable intake, and excess abdominal body fat. Add in physical inactivity and the burden rises to 57,000 deaths annually. (Statistics Canada, 2011; WHO, 2009). And, for example, in high-sodium-consumption countries like Canada, there is a 90 percent lifetime risk of developing hypertension—the world's leading risk factor for death, due mainly to heart attacks and strokes (Vasan et al., 2010). Nearly two-thirds of Canadian adults are currently overweight or obese (Shields, Gorber, Janssen, & Tremblay, 2011, Table 4, p. 6). Obesity is variously estimated to cost $5 to $7 billion (Public Health Agency of Canada & Canadian Institute for Health Information, 2010), $6 billion for direct health care costs alone (Annis, Zhang, Bansback, Guh, Amarsi, & Birmingham, 2009), and $30 billion annually (Behan & Cox, 2010). This says nothing of the grim death and economic tolls of inactivity-related diseases (Katzmarzyk, Gledhill, & Shephard, 2000; Katzmarzyk & Janssen, 2004), which are also promoted by a barrage of child-directed advertisements for toys, video games, and entertainment products that promote sedentary play. Some have even predicted that we are witnessing the first generation of children to have shorter life expectancies than their parents (e.g., House of Commons Standing Committee on Health, 2007; Ontario Medical Association, 2005).

DOES MARKETING TO CHILDREN ACTUALLY MATTER?

Enormous resources are poured, worldwide, into advertising aimed at children for foods that are generally calorie-dense and nutrient-poor, presumably on the realistic expectation that such ads achieve the intended result: increased sales and profits (American Psychological Association, 2004; Hastings et al., 2003, pp. 7–8; Schor, 2004, pp. 21, 122). In the United States, total expenditures for marketing directed at children by the top forty-four food and beverage companies alone top $1.6 billion annually (Federal Trade Commission, 2008, p. 7), approximately 17 percent of all food advertisements for those companies. McDonald's restaurants alone spend approximately $500 million annually on advertising worldwide, 40 percent of which is targeted at children (Schor, 2004, p. 122).

In Canada, more than $720 million was spent in traditional advertising media (print, radio/TV, and billboard) to promote restaurants, food, and alcohol to children and adults in 1998 (McElgunn, 1999). But this outdated figure may underestimate total marketing expenditures, which now also include promotional contests, package design, kids' clubs, child-oriented food product development, Internet and viral marketing, product placement (on store shelves and in programs), and so on. While there are no good estimates for Canada, some reckon the average American child sees as many as 350 000 TV commercials before graduating from high school, and spends nearly as much time watching TV as attending classes (e.g., Gentile & Walsh, 2002).

Presumably, confidential company evaluations of the effectiveness of their own food and toy advertisements show that advertising is worth the money they continue to spend on it. In fact, critics say that companies should make such research available to independent researchers because of its obvious implications for public health policy (Hastings et al., 2003; Institute of Medicine [IOM], 2006). But two recent systematic reviews of *published* studies confirmed what any sentient parent already knows to be true: advertising works. Gerald Hastings and colleagues were commissioned by the U.K. government's Food Standards Authority to undertake a systematic review of published research examining the extent and impact of television advertising to children. They found that foods marketed to children in the United States and elsewhere tend to be of very low nutritional value (Hastings et al., 2003, p. 172). This finding is consistent with a 1991 survey of Canadian television programming, which found that, for instance, only 3 percent of television food commercials promoted vegetables or fruit (excluding French fries) and approximately 40 percent promoted low-nutrient beverages, butter, margarine, salty snacks, sweets/candy, and chewing gum (Østbye, Pomerleau, White, Coolich, & McWhinney, 1993). Even fifteen years later, only 1 percent of Canadian television advertising targeting children aged two to seventeen promoted vegetables, fruits, or juices (Adams, Hennessey-Priest, Ingimarsdóttir, Sheeshka, Østbye, & White, 2009), even though *Canada's Food Guide* recommends that vegetables and fruit make up more than one-third of food servings (Health Canada, 2007).

Hastings and colleagues also concluded that there is reasonably strong evidence that food promotion affects children's food brand and category preferences, as well as purchasing and purchase-related behaviour (2003, pp. 19, 138). The same year, in a joint report the World Health Organization (WHO) and Food and Agriculture Organization (FAO) concluded that "there is sufficient indirect evidence to warrant [heavy marketing of fast food outlets and energy-dense micronutrient-poor foods] being placed in the 'probable' category and thus becoming a potential target for interventions" (2003, p. 65).

Likewise, the Henry J. Kaiser Family Foundation in the United States concluded that

> it appears likely that the main mechanism by which media use contributes to childhood obesity may well be through children's exposure to billions of dollars worth of food advertising and cross-promotional marketing year after year, starting at the very youngest ages, with children's favorite media characters often enlisted in the sales pitch. Research indicates that children's food choices—and parents' food purchases—are significantly impacted by the advertising they see (2004, p. 10).

In April 2006 the U.S. Institute of Medicine (IOM) of the National Academy of Sciences—a respected scientific review body upon whose advice the Health Canada often relies—released a report entitled *Food Marketing to Children and Youth: Threat or Opportunity?* funded by the U.S. Centers for Disease Control and Prevention. The report recommends that Congress regulate broadcast and cable TV ads if industry does not voluntarily shift emphasis from high-calorie, low-nutrient foods and beverages to healthful ones within two years. In May 2006 the U.S. Federal Trade Commission and Department of Health and Human Services published their own report, which called for more rigorous and transparent self-regulation and greater government oversight.

Since 1980, Quebec has parted ways with the rest of Canada by prohibiting advertising directed at children under age thirteen, offering an enticing natural experiment for health and child protection researchers. One Canadian study looked at recent differences in fast-food consumption among English and French television viewers, with and without children, in Quebec and Ontario in an effort to tease out the impact of the Quebec advertising ban. Researchers concluded that the ban was associated with 13 percent lower consumption of fast-food meals, though the effect can be attenuated by ads leaking across the border from noncompliant U.S. cable networks (Dhar & Baylis, 2011). Another study of 1014 food ads viewed by Quebec children found that 259 ads "targeted" children or preschoolers, including 57 aimed at the French children and 202 ads aimed at English children (Potvin, Kent, & Dubois, 2010). Importantly, this study did not assess how many of the ads reaching children were

- blatant violations of the Quebec *Consumer Protection Act*, exploiting loopholes in the Quebec ban (e.g., advertising during family programming where enough teenagers and adults tune in to make the ban inapplicable[1]);

- abuses of ambiguities in regulatory exemptions, such as a child-oriented fast-food chain advertising salads or coffee during Saturday morning cartoons;

- ads leaking across interprovincial or international borders via Canadian cable networks, U.S. cable networks, satellite TV, or Internet TV; or

- less problematic use of statutory or regulatory exemptions, such as advertising financial planning services, dishwashing detergent, or university enrollment during Saturday morning cartoons.

WHAT IS EASIER (AND LESS ETHICAL) THAN TAKING CANDY FROM A BABY?

Concern about the adverse health effects of promoting junk food to children has animated calls for legislative or regulatory restrictions on such advertising.[2] But the ban on advertising to children (for all products, including food, toys, etc.) in Quebec came into effect in 1980, long before childhood obesity became a cause célèbre[3] (Hawkes, 2004, p. 20). The primary justification for the ban was to address the unique vulnerability of children to deception. In the 1989 decision in *Attorney General of Québec v. Irwin Toy Ltd.*, the Supreme Court of Canada accepted the following explanation of the objective of the legislation: "The concern is for the protection of a group which is particularly vulnerable to the techniques of seduction and manipulation abundant in advertising" (p. 987).

Schor observed that the formula for advertising children's products from the 1920s through the postwar era was to convince mothers (the "gatekeepers") that the advertised product was beneficial for the child (2004, p. 16). Marketers began to abandon the gatekeeper approach in the 1980s and instead promote the idea of "kid power." Advertisers that once depicted mothers as loving and wise now depict parents as "neglectful, incompetent, abusive, invisible, or embarrassing" (Schor, 2004, pp. 54–55, 180). A Toronto-based children's marketing company characterized the new marketing strategy for targeting the so-called tweens market cohort as "gate-crashing" (Valiquette & Farrell, 2005).

Since the 1980s, gate-crashing became even easier for marketers as commercial cable television channels devoted mainly or exclusively to youth audiences (like MuchMusic, YTV, and Teletoon) were launched and more households purchased second television sets; for example, according to a survey of nearly 6000 Canadian students in grades three through ten, nearly half had their own television (Canadian Teachers Federation, 2003, p. 52). The APA Task Force on Children and Advertising noted that, in the days of limited channel capacity, the amount of television programming targeted to children was limited to time slots unpopular with adults, such as Saturday mornings. Now, children can be exposed to child-oriented advertisements all day (APA, 2004, p. 21). While part of this effort will lead to children making their own purchases at the urging of marketers, it also mobilizes "pester power." For instance, a 2002 U.S. poll indicated that 83 percent of children aged twelve to thirteen reported asking their parents to buy or let them buy something they had seen advertised; of those, 71 percent repeated the request an average of eight times, and 11 percent repeated the request more than fifty times (Schor, 2004, pp. 54–55, 62). By contrast, a randomized, controlled trial of grade three and four students demonstrated that reductions in TV viewing led to a 70 percent reduction in children's requests for toy purchases (Robinson, 2001, pp. 179–182).

IF ADVERTISING TO CHILDREN IS NOT ALREADY ILLEGAL IN CANADA OUTSIDE QUEBEC, IT SHOULD BE

Like most countries, Canadian law prohibits false, misleading, deceptive advertising and unconscionable business practices. For example, the federal *Competition Act* prohibits such advertising.[4] Similarly, most provincial governments have enacted some form of consumer protection legislation prohibiting misleading advertising or unconscionable trade practices.[5]

And Canadian appeal court rulings on "misleading advertising" suggest that examining any advertisements targeting children must consider what is "misleading" from the vantage point of the ad's intended target (i.e., not just by applying an adult's logical literal analysis of claims) as interpreted by persons of "average" abilities appropriate to the circumstances (not by well-informed or sophisticated persons) (*R. v. Cunningham Drug Stores*, 1973; *R. v. Imperial Tobacco*, 1971; *R. v. International Vacations*, 1980, p. 284; and *R. v. Suntours Ltd.*, 1974, p. 181). To respect these appeal court rulings, it seems plain that courts should consider developmental psychology research demonstrating the unique vulnerability of children to commercial advertising. In *Attorney General of Québec v. Irwin Toy, Ltd.* (1989), the Supreme Court of Canada examined the constitutionality of the near-total statutory ban on commercial advertising directed at children in Quebec, and concluded that the ban was a permissible limit on commercial freedom of expression under the *Charter of Rights and Freedoms* (*Irwin Toy*, 1989, p. 1000). The law had been challenged by a toy company. The court relied heavily on the 1981 U.S. Federal Trade Commission's report entitled *Final Staff Report and Recommendation, In the Matter of Children's Advertising*. The report concluded that

> the specific cognitive abilities of young children lead to their inability to fully understand child-oriented television advertising, even if they grasp some aspects of it. They place indiscriminate trust in the selling message. They do not correctly perceive persuasive bias in advertising, and their life experience is insufficient to help them counter-argue.... As a result, children are not able to evaluate adequately child-oriented advertising (*Irwin Toy*, 1989, p. 988).

Even after the Supreme Court ruled, the American Psychological Association's *Report of the Task Force on Advertising and Children* concluded that "the ability to recognize persuasive intent does not develop for most children before 8 years of age.... Even at that age ... such capability tends to emerge in only rudimentary form" (APA, 2004, p. 9).

Similarly, the Hastings report found that at around age eight, children are just "beginning to respond to advertising in a more sophisticated way" and that children's ability to retrieve and process information is still developing between the ages of eight and twelve (Hastings et al., 2004, pp. 35–36). Children, because they are still maturing, have very poor cognitive defences against commercial advertisements (APA, 2004, pp. 6–7).

The Supreme Court of Canada also noted the relevance of the common law by stating, "viz. to protect a group that is most vulnerable to commercial manipulation ... [is] reflected in general contract doctrine.... Children are not as equipped as adults to evaluate the persuasive force of advertising and advertisements directed at children would take advantage of this" (*Attorney General of Québec v. Irwin Toy*, 1989, p. 990).

Ironically, given the contribution of its marketing to the diets of youngsters, McDonald's once even argued (unsuccessfully) that lack of legal capacity to enter contracts (just like contracts for the sale of food) should disallow some of its teenage employees from joining labour unions (Wilson, 1994 loose-leaf).

Furthermore, even subsection 9(1) of the *Competition Act*, itself, requires citizens to be at least eighteen years old to petition for an investigation of misleading advertising. Section 16 of the *Canada Evidence Act* also creates a presumption that children under the age of fourteen are not reliable witnesses (and see the Supreme Court of Canada ruling in *Kendall v. The Queen*, 1962).

WHAT IS NEXT IN THE COURTS AND LEGISLATURES?

Since 1980, the government of Quebec has been a world leader in protecting children from the unfairness and adverse health consequences of commercial marketing targeting children under thirteen. The Quebec ban, though imperfect and inadequately enforced, provides significant protection to one-quarter of Canadian children against child-directed advertising (the vast majority of which promotes sedentary play and non-nutritious foods). Parti Québecois and Liberal governments in Quebec successfully defended the popular law for nearly a decade, culminating in a landmark 1989 freedom of expression ruling in which the Supreme Court said that advertising to children is "*per se* manipulative. Such advertising aims to promote products by convincing those who will always believe" (*Irwin Toy*, 1989, pp. 988–989). The same year, Canada adopted the *United Nations Convention on the Rights of the Child*, committing to ensure that policy and legislation prioritize the best interests of children over other interests. Sweden and Norway later enacted similar laws and, two years ago, the U.K. government instituted a ban on many television advertisements for unhealthy foods and beverages targeted at children under age sixteen, which helped reduce the proportion of high fat, sugar, or salt food ads targeting children from four-fifths to three-fifths (Office of Communications, 2010) of all kid food ads. Unfortunately, however, only token safeguards protect Canadian children living outside of Quebec.

Since the Quebec ban and the Supreme Court ruling, mounting evidence has pointed to the harm and unfairness of advertising to children and the value of legal limits on such advertising. Such marketing information obstructs rather than supports informed economic choices and sends misleading market signals to sellers, to say nothing of the adverse health effects of flogging disease-promoting foods to impressionable children. Certainly, Parliament and provincial legislatures could not have intended that misleading advertising provisions of the *Competition Act*, the *Food and Drugs Act*, and other consumer protection statutes be interpreted in a manner that protects adults, but not children. In interpreting the scope of restrictions on advertising in those statutes, one must be mindful of the unique vulnerability of children in order to ensure that they receive more, not less, protection than experienced, intellectually mature adults, though, plainly, even sophisticated adults are not impervious to the effects of advertising.[6] If those laws are deficient, it is incumbent on legislators to fix them to protect children from economic exploitation and to safeguard their health.

Any federal and provincial legislators who are concerned about the ill effects and moral blameworthiness of targeting children with commercial advertising can probably count on plenty of public support for following the path set by Quebec. A 2011 national public opinion poll of 1222 Canadians commissioned by the Public Health Agency of Canada found that the great majority of Canadians support banning ads for nutrient-poor foods targeted to children (77 percent), and nearly two-thirds of respondents thought the federal government is not doing enough to address childhood obesity (Ipsos Reid, 2011). And surveys in Quebec illustrate that the long-standing ban is highly popular among Quebec residents; for instance, 60 percent of Quebecers indicated in a 2007 survey that they would like those limits to be stricter (Dhar & Baylis, 2011).The Organisation for Economic Co-operation and Development stressed the need to curb nutrition-related disease and affirmed the value of regulatory solutions (Sassi, 2010). In March 2007 the House of Commons Standing Committee on Health recommended that the government "explore" limits on advertising directed at children. And Kelly Leitch, who is now a Conservative Member of Parliament, prepared a report called *Reaching for the Top: A Report of the Advisor on Healthy Children and Youth,* recommending that "there be a ban on the advertising of junk food on children's programming targeted to children under 12" (Leitch, 2007).

In the past two years alone, approximately forty health groups and experts added their support to the recommendations of Sodium Working Group,[7] which urged that

> federal, provincial and territorial governments continue to explore options to reduce the exposure of children to marketing for foods that are high in sodium … since 1980 Québec's *Consumer Protection Act* has prohibited all advertising directed at children under the age of 13 years, including ads for all foods as well as for many toys and media products that generally promote more screen time and physical inactivity. (Sodium Working Group, 2010).

The Quebec *Consumer Protection Act* is and should be a source of pride for Canada internationally because it demonstrates a clear commitment to protecting children from economic exploitation. The Quebec law should be supported by the federal and other provincial governments to further reduce the moderate, but significant, inter-provincial cross-border marketing and, of course, to extend similar or tougher protection to the other three-quarters of Canadian children,[8] as the World Health Organization warned is necessary.[9]

Notes

[1] The Quebec law assumes that ads are targeted to children if they appear on programs for which the percentage of the audience aged two to eleven—a standard Nielsen and broadcast media–monitoring demographic category—exceeds 15 percent.

[2] For example, Centre for Science in the Public Interest's "Proposal for an Effective Pan-Canadian Healthy Living Strategy" (at http://cspinet.org/canada/pdf/PanCdn_EffectiveStrat.pdf), which, by the summer of 2006, was supported by about two dozen Canadian health and citizens groups. The unanimous report of the twenty-five–member Sodium Working Group in July 2010 was also supported by seventeen experts in a letter sent to Prime Minister Stephen Harper in January 2012.

[3] It is difficult to assess whether the restrictions on advertising actually improved Quebec children's diets partly because Canadian governments have never conducted regular dietary intake surveys; thirty years passed between national surveys completed in 1974 and 2004. But it is worth noting that overall obesity rates have generally been lower in Quebec than nearly every other province, and per capita soft drink consumption has been lower in Quebec than the rest of Canada since the ban came into effect (Carr, 2004, p. 40). Likewise, Quebec fruit and vegetable consumption rates are among the highest in Canada (Statistics Canada, 2003). Norway and Sweden have also established broad restrictions on advertising to children within the scope of their legislative competence, and other European countries have issued narrower restrictions (WHO, 2004).

[4] See also section 74.01 of the Act.

[5] For example, *Ontario Consumer Protection Act,* R.S.O. 2002, c. 30, ss. 14(1), 14(2)(14–15) and 15(1–2); *Trade Practices Act,* R.S.N.L. 1990, c. T 7, ss. 5(w), 6(f), 7; *Business Practices Act,* R.S.P.E.I. 1988, c. B 7, ss. 2(a) (xiii), 2(b)(i), 3(1); *Business Practices Act,* S.M. 1990-1, c. 6, s. 3; *Trade Practices Inquiry Act,* C.C.S.M. 2006, c. T110, ss. 2(a)(v), 2(a)(viii); *Consumer Protection Act,* S.S. 1996, c. C 30.1, ss. 5, 6(o), 7; *Fair Trading Act,* R.S.A. 2000, c. F 2, ss. 6(2)(b), 4(a), 4(b), 7; *Business Practices and Consumer Protection Act,* S.B.C. 2004, c. 2, ss. 4(1), 4(3)(b)(vi), 8(3)(b), 9 (2004). See also the federal *Food and Drugs Act,* R.S.C. 1985, c. F-27, s. 5.

[6] Adults are not immune to manipulation. A recent note in the *Harvard Law Review* argued that advertising contributes to the development of unhealthful diets (in adults) by distorting consumers' ability to evaluate products, especially about credence attributes, like nutritional features, that cannot be evaluated without expert assistance. See "The Elephant in the Room," 2003.

[7] Sodium Working Group members include the University of Toronto, Canadian Institutes of Health Research, Canadian Stroke Network, Canadian Nutrition Society, Dieticians of Canada, Council of Chief Medical Officers of Health, Hypertension Canada, Heart and Stroke Foundation of Canada, Canadian Council of Food and Nutrition, Centre for Science in the Public Interest, Extenso—Reference Centre for Human Nutrition, Baking Association of Canada, Canadian Meat Council, Dairy Processors of Canada, Food and Consumer Products of Canada, Food Processors of Canada, Canadian Council of Grocery Distributors, Canadian Restaurant and Foodservices Association, Office of Nutrition Policy and Promotion, Health Canada, Public Health Agency of Canada, Food Directorate (Health Canada), Federal Provincial Territorial Group on Nutrition, Agriculture and Agri-Food Canada, and Canadian Food Inspection Agency. More groups indicated support for the strategy in a January 2012 letter to the Prime Minister, including the Canadian Association of Cardiac Rehabilitation, Canadian Nurses Association, College of Family Physicians of Canada, Canadian Cardiovascular Society, Canadian Pharmacists Association, Canadian Council of Cardiovascular Nurses, Canadian Society of Nephrology, Canadian Heart Failure Network, Canadian Society of Internal Medicine, Canadian Hypertension Education Program (CHEP), Canadian National Specialty Society for Community Medicine, and Canadian Medical Association.

[8] According to Statistics Canada, children aged two to eleven spend 89 percent of their TV viewing time watching Canadian stations; however, much of that time is spent watching American programs rebroadcast by Canadian channels, such as Global and CTV (Statistics Canada, 2006, Table 6).

[9] World Health Assembly Resolution on marketing food to children (May 2010). Available at http://apps.who.int/gb/ebwha/pdf_files/WHA63/A63_R14-en.pdf. Nineteen nongovernmental organizations signed a letter (including CSPI) to the federal minister of health prior to the World Health Assembly meeting (May 12, 2010). Available at http://cspinet.org/canada/pdf/protectchildrenfrommarketing.pdf. And see an additional letter from the Chronic Disease Prevention Alliance of Canada (May 16, 2010). Available at http://cspinet.org/canada/pdf/cdpac.letter_to_minister_aglukkaq_may16-10__5_.pdf.

References

Adams, J., Hennessey-Priest, K., Ingimarsdóttir, S., Sheeshka, J., Østbye, T., & White , M. (2009). Food advertising during children's television in Canada and the UK. *Archives of Disease in Childhood, 94,* 658–662 at 680.

American Psychological Association, Task Force on Advertising and Children. (2004). *Report of the APA Task Force on Advertising and Children* (B. Wilcox, Task Force Chair). Washington, DC: Author. Retrieved from http://www.apa.org/pi/cyf/advertisingandchildren.pdf

Anis, A. H., Zhang, W., Bansback, N., Guh, D. P., Amarsi, Z., & Birmingham, C. L. (2010). Obesity and overweight in Canada: An updated cost-of-illness study. *Obesity Reviews, 11*(1), 31–40.

Behan, D. F., Cox, S. H., et al. (2010, December). *Obesity and its relation to mortality and morbidity cost.* Society of Actuaries.

Canadian Teachers' Federation. (2003). *Kids' take on media.* Retrieved from http://www.ctf-fce.ca/bilingual/pubs/ctfreport/kidsenglish.pdf

Carr, S. (2004). *Overweight in Canadian children: Mapping the geographic variation* (Unpublished master's thesis). London School of Hygiene and Tropical Medicine.

Dhar, T., & Baylis, K. (2011, October). Ban on fast-food advertising targeting children *Journal of Marketing Research, 48*, 799–813.

The elephant in the room: Evolution, behavioralism, and counteradvertising in the coming war against obesity. (2003). *Harvard Law Review, 116*(4), 1168–1184.

Federal Trade Commission. (2008). *Marketing food to children and adolescents: A report to Congress.* Retrieved from http://www.ftc.gov/os/2008/07/P064504foodmktingreport.pdf

Gentile, D. A., & Walsh, D. A. (2002). A normative study of family media habits. *Journal of Applied Developmental Psychology, 23,*157–178.

Hastings, G., Stead, M., McDermott, L., Forsyth, A., MacKintosh, A. M., Rayner, M., … Angus, K. (2003). *Review of research on the effects of food promotion to children.* Report prepared for the UK Food Standards Authority. London: UK FSA; Glasgow, Scotland: Centre for Social Marketing, University of Strathclyde. Retrieved from http://www.food.gov.uk/multimedia/pdfs/foodpromotiontochildren1.pdf

Hawkes, C. (Ed.). (2004). *Marketing food to children: The global regulatory environment.* Geneva: World Health Organization. Retrieved from http://whqlibdoc.who.int/publications/2004/9241591579.pdf2004b

Health Canada. (2007). *Eating well with Canada's Food Guide.* Ottawa: Author. Retrieved from http://www.hc-sc.gc.ca/fn-an/alt_formats/hpfb-dgpsa/pdf/food-guide-aliment/view_eatwell_vue_bienmang-eng.pdf

The Henry J. Kaiser Family Foundation. (2004). *Issue brief: The role of media in childhood obesity.* Washington, DC: Author. Retrieved from http://www.kff.org/entmedia/upload/The-Role-Of-Media-in-Childhood-Obesity.pdf

House of Commons Standing Committee on Health. (2007, March). *Healthy weights, healthy kids* (R. Merrifield, Chair). Retrieved from http://www2.parl.gc.ca/content/hoc/Committee/391/HESA/Reports/RP2795145/hesarp07/hesarp07-e.pdf

Institute of Medicine. (2006). Food marketing to children and youth: Threat or opportunity? (J. M. McGinnis, Chair of Committee on Food Marketing and the Diets of Children and Youth). Executive summary available at http://www.nap.edu/execsumm_pdf/11514.pdf and full report on the National Academies Press website at http://www.nap.edu/catalog/11514.html

Ipsos Reid. (2011, November). *Canadian perceptions of, and support for, potential measures to prevent and reduce childhood obesity.* Report prepared for the Public Health Agency of Canada. Retrieved from http://www.sportmatters.ca/files/Reports/Ipsos%20Obesity%202011.pdf

Katzmarzyk, P. T., Gledhill, N., & Shephard, R. J. (2000). The economic burden of physical inactivity in Canada. *Canadian Medical Association Journal, 163*(11), 1435–1440. Retrieved from http://www.cmaj.ca/search.dtl

Katzmarzyk, P. T., & Janssen, I. (2004). The economic costs of physical inactivity and obesity in Canada: An update. *Canadian Journal of Applied Physiology, 29*(1), 90–115.

Leitch, K. (2007). *Reaching for the top: A Report by the Advisor on Healthy Children and Youth.* Ottawa: Minister of Health. Retrieved from http://www.hc-sc.gc.ca/hl-vs/alt_formats/hpb-dgps/pdf/child-enfant/2007-advisor-conseillere/advisor-conseillere-eng.pdf

McElgunn J. (1999, September 27). Canada's top 25 advertising categories. *Marketing Magazine, 44.*

Office of Communications (OfCom). (2010, July). *High fat sugar salt advertising restrictions: Final review.* Retrieved from http://stakeholders.ofcom.org.uk/binaries/research/tv-research/hfss-review-final.pdf

Ontario Medical Association. (2005) *An ounce of prevention or a ton of trouble: Is there an epidemic of obesity in children?* Toronto: Author.

Østbye, T., Pomerleau, J., White, M., Coolich, M., & McWhinney, J. (1993). Food and nutrition in Canadian "prime time" television commercials. *Canadian Journal of Public Health, 84*(6), 370–374.

Potvin, K. M., Dubois, L., & Wanless, A. (2010). Food marketing on children's television in two different policy environments. *International Journal of Pediatric Obesity.* Advance online publication, 1–9.

Public Health Agency of Canada & Canadian Institute for Health Information. (2010). *Obesity in Canada*. Ottawa: Author. Retrieved from http://www.phac-aspc.gc.ca/hp-ps/hl-mvs/oic-oac/assets/pdf/oic-oac-eng.pdf

Robinson, T. N. (2001). Effects of reducing television viewing on children's requests for toys: A randomized controlled trial. *Journal of Developmental & Behavioral Pediatrics, 22*, 179–184.

Sassi, F. (2010). *Obesity and the economics of prevention*. Paris: Organisation for Economic Co-operation and Development. Retrieved from www.sourceoecd.org/socialissues9789264063679

Schor, J. (2004). *Born to buy*. New York: Scribner.

Shields, M., Gorber, S. C., Janssen, I., & Tremblay, M. (2011, August). *Bias in self-reported estimates of obesity in Canadian health surveys: An update on correction equations for adults. Health Reports, 22*(3). Statistics Canada, Catalogue no. 82-003-XPE. Retrieved from http://www.statcan.gc.ca/pub/82-003-x/2011003/article/11533-eng.pdf

Sodium Working Group. (2010). *Sodium reduction strategy for Canada*. Ottawa: Health Canada. Retrieved from http://www.hc-sc.gc.ca/fn-an/alt_formats/pdf/nutrition/sodium/strateg/index-eng.pdf

Statistics Canada. (2003). Dietary practices, by sex, household population aged 12 and over, Canada, provinces, territories, health regions and peer groups, 2003. Retrieved from http://www.statcan.ca/english/freepub/82-221-XIE/00604/tables/html/2188_03.htm using data compiled from Statistics Canada, Canadian Community Health Survey, cycle 2.1 (2003), available at http://www.statcan.ca/bsolc/english/bsolc?catno=82C0025

Statistics Canada. (2006). *Television viewing: Data tables*. Catalogue no. 87F0006XIE. Retrieved from http://www5.statcan.gc.ca/bsolc/olc-cel/olc-cel?catno=87F0006XIE&lang=eng

Statistics Canada. (2011). *Mortality, summary list of causes, 2008*. Catalogue no. 84F0209X. Ottawa: Minister of Industry. Retrieved from http://www.statcan.gc.ca/pub/84f0209x/84f0209x2008000-eng.pdf

United Nations Convention on the Rights of the Child. (1989, November 20). Adopted and opened for signature, ratification, and accession by General Assembly resolution 44/25. Retrieved from http://www.canadiancrc.com/UN_CRC/UN_Convention_on_the_Rights_of_the_Child.aspx

United States Federal Trade Commission. (1981). *Final staff report and recommendation, in the matter of children's advertising*. Washington, DC: U.S. Government Printing Office.

United States Federal Trade Commission & Department of Health and Human Services. (2006). *Perspectives on marketing, self-regulation and childhood obesity*. Washington, DC: Author. Retrieved from http://ftc.gov/opa/2006/05/childhoodobesity.htm

Valiquette, M., & Farrell, M. (2005, December 7). Marketing to young Canadians in 2006 (PowerPoint slides 35–36). "Youth access" *Marketing Magazine* seminar, Montreal.

Wilson, J. (Current loose-leaf service). *Wilson on children and the law* (3rd ed.). Markham, ON: Butterworths.

Vasan, R. S., Beiser, A., Seshadri, S., Larson, M. G., Kannel, W. B., D'Agostino, R. B., & Levy, D. (2002). Residual lifetime risk for developing hypertension in middle-aged women and men: The Framingham Heart Study. *Journal of the American Medical Association, 287*(8), 1003–1010.

World Health Organization. (2009). *Global health risks: Mortality and burden of disease attributable to selected major risks*. Geneva: Author. Retrieved from http://www.who.int/healthinfo/global_burden_disease/GlobalHealthRisks_report_full.pdf

World Health Organization & Food and Agriculture Organization. (2003). *The report of the joint WHO/FAO expert consultation on diet, nutrition and the prevention of chronic diseases*. Technical report series 916. Geneva: Author. Retrieved from http://www.who.int/hpr/NPH/docs/who_fao_expert_report.pdf

Cases

Attorney General of Québec v. Irwin Toy, Ltd., [1989] 1 S.C.R. 927.

Kendall v. The Queen, [1962] S.C.R. 469.

R. v. Cunningham Drug Stores, [1973] 13 C.P.R.2d 244, 248 (B.C. C.A.).

R. v. Imperial Tobacco Prods. Ltd., [1971] 3 C.P.R.2d 178, 195 (Alta. C.A.).

R. v. Int'l Vacations Ltd., [1980] 56 C.P.R.2d 255–56 (Ont. C.A.).

R. v. Suntours Ltd., [1974] 20 C.P.R.2d 179, 181 (Ont. Provincial Ct.).

Statutes

(Generally available at http://www.canlii.org/index_en.html)

Competition Act, R.S.C. 1985, c. C-34.

Canada Evidence Act, R.S.C. 1985, c. E-10 as amended by *An Act to Amend the Criminal Code (Protection of Children and Other Vulnerable Persons)* and the *Canada Evidence Act*, 2005 S.C., ch. 32, § 16.1(1) (assented to July 20, 2005), available at http://www.parl.gc.ca/PDF/38/1/parlbus/chambus/house/bills/government/C-2_4.PDF in force January 2, 2006, per P.C. 2005-1817, C. Gaz. 2005.II.2550, SI/2005-104 (available at page 2550 at http://gazetteducanada.gc.ca/partII/2005/20051116/pdf/g2-13923.pdf).

Food and Drugs Act, R.S.C. 1985, c. F-27.

ISSUE 1

Childhood obesity:
Is banning television advertisements to children the best solution?

✘ NO

The Complexity of Choice: Food Promotion and Our Modern Foodscape
Charlene Elliott

Charlene Elliott is the Canada Research Chair in Food Marketing, Policy and Health, and an associate professor of communication at the University of Calgary. She is jointly appointed with the Faculty of Arts and Faculty of Kinesiology. She has published numerous articles pertaining to issues of communication and the body (ranging from sensorial communication and taste communication to obesity and public health), as well as food promotion and policy. Her current research focuses on food marketing to children within broader questions of taste, popular culture, health, and policy.

What a difference a decade or so makes! When in 1994, Joel Best published *Troubling Children*—an edited volume on children and social problems—it made nary a mention of obesity. Now the World Health Organization has deemed obesity a pandemic, and childhood obesity a major social crisis in the developed nations of the world.

Childhood obesity is not only a social problem, it is a problem linked to communication studies as well.[1] Researchers have traced the relationship between television *exposure* and childhood obesity (Lumeng, Rahnama, Appugliese, Kaciroti, & Bradley, 2006)[2] and the ways in which food-related media messages encourage the consumption of high fat, high sugar foods (Brownell & Horgen, 2004; Chamberlain, Want, & Robinson, 2006; Institute of Medicine, 2006; Horgen, Choate, & Brownell, 2001; Schwartz & Puhl, 2003; Wadden, Brownell, & Foster, 2002). Typically, these studies focus on television advertising targeted at children and the dire consequences of such messages (Adams et al., 2009; Byrd-Brenner & Grasso, 2000; Halford, Boyland, Hughes, Oliveira, & Dovey, 2007; Hastings et al., 2003; Hill & Radimer, 1997; Kotz & Story, 1993; Story & Faulkner, 1990). Indeed, the belief in the effectiveness of food marketing is so firm that governments and public health organizations (at both the national and international level) have suggested regulating the promotion of high sugar, fat, and/or salt foods to children (Public Health Agency of Canada, 2010; World Health Organization, 2010).

In Canada, the focus on advertising directed at children is equally strong. Recent policy recommendations by the federally formed Sodium Working Group encourage Canada's federal, provincial, and territorial governments to strive to "protect children from the marketing of foods and beverages high in fat, sugar and/or salt" (Sodium Working Group, 2010, p. 31). Some technical briefs go even further, advocating for a legal ban on advertising aimed at children under the age of thirteen (Basrur, 2004, p. 49; Jeffery, 2012, p. 9): Quebec has had such a ban in place since 1980. But if childhood obesity is the problem, is banning advertising directed at children—or even restricting the marketing of high sugar, fat, and/or salt foods to children—the *best* solution?

In a word, no. Although I staunchly disagree with targeting young children with commercial messages for ethical reasons, banning "unhealthy" food advertising to children to curb obesity is akin to shining a penlight on a problem requiring broad illumination. The view is hazy and big issues get missed. Make no mistake: advertising has a powerful influence on cultural norms and the way we live our lives. Advertising to very young children—who are cognitively unable to recognize advertising intent—is inherently misleading and manipulative (American Psychological Association, 2004; *Attorney General of Québec v. Irwin Toy Ltd.*, 1989; Graff, Kunkel, & Mermin, 2012). However, food advertising aimed specifically at children represents a tiny piece in a much larger cultural puzzle. Arguments supporting it often fail to capture how the broader environment (including cultural trends and attitudes) works to create substantial limitations on what bans can achieve.

THE NARROW VIEW OF CHILDREN'S FOOD MARKETING

Obesity researchers routinely point out that obesity is a complex, multifaceted problem (Finegood, Karanfil, & Matteson, 2008), but singling out the place of children's advertising in the wider system of food promotion and consumption is problematic at best. Prohibiting the commercial advertising of unhealthy foods to children does very little to transform the broader social environment—an environment sometimes labelled "toxic" or "obesogenic" because of the ways that it promotes constant eating typically of processed, "junk," and/or fast food (Brownell & Horgen, 2004; Swinburn, Egger, & Raza, 1999). Today, cars, strollers, and supermarket carts come with built-in cup holders, the snack and fast-food market is a multi-billion-dollar industry, and it is increasingly rare to encounter a space in which eating is not permitted (or even encouraged).[3] Consumers, it seems, should not be expected to even drive to the grocery store without a beverage to fortify their journey! Given this **obesogenic environment**, placing a restriction on advertising Pop-Tarts and Pepsi-Cola to children is simply a token gesture. It fails to address the wider cultural norms around food, including the promotion of all-the-time eating and the normalization of large portion sizes, which affects all consumers (not just children). Restricting only *child*-targeted advertising would also fail to protect children from the ubiquitous promotion of colas, chips, pizza, fast food, junk food, and other processed edibles ostensibly targeted to an "older" audience base. Food promotion is everywhere. Banning or restricting food advertising aimed specifically at children might be a start, but it certainly does not shield them from the deluge of commercial messaging that constantly implores us to eat.

DEFINITION DILEMMA: THE PROBLEM WITH POLICIES SEEKING TO RESTRICT HIGH FAT, SUGAR, AND/OR SALT (HFSS) FOODS ADVERTISED TO CHILDREN

Restricting "unhealthy" food advertising to children also stumbles when it comes to defining healthy food. As mentioned, many initiatives and policy recommendations seek to limit the promotion of HFSS foods to children. Public opinion also supports this move: a recent survey of 1222 Canadians found that 60 percent "strongly support" restricting "the marketing of unhealthy foods and beverages to children" (Ipsos Reid, 2011, p. 59). Certainly this sounds like a good idea. But what, exactly, constitutes an unhealthy food? In today's food environment, this determination is more complex than one might expect. Part of the reason for this has to do with our current means of evaluating food, which is primarily based on its nutrient composition. Scrinis observes how the "nutrition industry" (i.e., nutrition scientists, dieticians, and public health officials) has cultivated the idea of understanding food in terms of its component parts so that the paradigm of *nutritionism* now sits at the "center of the public's understanding of food and health" (2008, p. 39). Nutritionism, focused on the nutrient level, presumes that "a calorie is a calorie, a vitamin a vitamin, and a protein a protein, regardless of the particular food it comes packaged in" (2008, p. 41). The upshot is that a "nutritionally balanced" diet can be composed of virtually anything, provided that positive nutrients are present. What does this mean in practice? As Mozaffarian and Ludwig observe in their commentary on the current Dietary Guidelines for Americans, "Based primarily on consideration of a few nutrients, a national obesity prevention program categorizes whole-milk yogurt and cheese with donuts and french fries as foods to eat occasionally … and [categorizes] fresh fruits and vegetables with … fat-free mayonnaise as foods to eat almost anytime" (2010, p. 682). Although the nutrition industry has fostered this reductionist approach to food and bodily health, the food industry has boldly capitalized on it, using nutritionism as "a powerful means of marketing their products" (Scrinis, 2008, p. 39).

Thanks to nutritionism, all sorts of foods now qualify as healthy choices, while unhealthy foods become harder to spot. A perfect illustration of this can be found in General Mills' recent move to market its fifty "Big G" cereals (including Cheerios, Cocoa Puffs, Trix, Reese Puffs, and Lucky Charms) in the United States as having "More Whole Grain Than Any Other Ingredient" (General Mills, 2012). Whole grain is a good thing, but as the Public Health Advocacy Institute fairly chided, the "Big G" cereal campaign "is designed to make its entire portfolio of products look healthy by distracting attention from sugar content" (Wilking, 2011). Cereals with nine grams of sugar per serving are binned with those containing one gram. Nutritionism, then, can equally function as a marketing ploy; it allows sweetened cereals to become reframed as health promoting, thanks to the presence of whole grains. A similar example, and one specifically related to the issue of food marketing to children, resides in the Children's Food and Beverage Advertising Initiative (CAI)—a voluntary program whereby nineteen of Canada's leading food and beverage companies have committed to "promote products that represent healthy dietary choices, or not direct advertising primarily to children under 12" (CAI, 2010, p. 2). Launched in Canada in 2007, CAI's stated vision is to market "products to Canadian children in a responsible way to help prepare them to make wise decisions about nutrition and health" (CAI, 2010, p. 1). Participating members draw from "established scientific and/or government standards" in order to create "company developed standards" for products that represent "healthier dietary choices" (2010, p. 2). Essentially, companies (and governing bodies) use nutritionism to determine what constitutes a healthy choice suitable for marketing to children. Yet some of the products that meet these "scientific standards" (and therefore can be marketed to children as healthy dietary choices) defy logic. "Better-for-you" products include Kool-Aid, Fruit Gushers, Dunkaroos Chocolatey Chip cookies, Lucky Charms, Froot Loops, and Reese Puffs cereal. The question arises: How does promoting cookies and chocolate bar–inspired cereals (i.e., Reese) as healthy choices help prepare children "to make wise decisions about nutrition," as per the CAI's vision statement? True, the product formulation or (small) serving sizes might make it possible for these products to fall under the CAI company-determined nutrient threshold for sugar, fat, sodium, and so on, but does this make Reese Puffs or Dunkaroos a "healthy dietary choice" in the same way that eating kale is a healthy dietary choice? Absolutely not. Advertising these highly processed products as healthy dietary choices is clearly an instance of **nutri-washing**—using health-themed marketing to sell ultra-processed foods (Simon, 2006). And such nutritionism and nutri-washing is precisely why some commentators argue that a major shift is needed in which *food*—not its component parts—becomes the "principal dietary targets" (Mozaffarian & Ludwig, 2010, p. 682; also see Nestle, 2000; Pollan, 2009; Scrinis, 2008). Combating the obesity epidemic requires an entire *cultural* shift in terms of how we evaluate food—not merely toying with serving sizes and product formulations so that certain child-targeted cookies are lower in sugar or fat and consequently made acceptable as everyday fare.

THE PROBLEM OF CLASSIFICATION

Sugary breakfast cereal laden with marshmallows or cookies packaged with icing for "dunking" can be classified as healthy choices and therefore advertised to children under the CAI guidelines. Both are key exemplars of why attempts to reduce childhood obesity by reducing the marketing of HFSS foods to children are destined to fail. If certain cookies are promoted as healthy choices, why shouldn't children classify all cookies as healthy? Are children really supposed to classify Dunkaroos Chocolatey Chip cookies as a healthy choice but view Chips Ahoy! and Oreos as treats? All are cookies. Beyond this, Dunkaroos (classified as "better-for-you" and marketed under CAI guidelines) are not nutritionally superior to Oreos or Chips Ahoy! Banning the advertising of HFSS foods to kids will make no difference to the obesity epidemic if companies can still market (presumably low sugar/fat/salt) cookies to children—because what this communicates is that cookies, overall, are not merely a treat but are actually "better-for-you." Such communication normalizes cookies as regular, everyday fare. Key, here, is that this normalization can occur even as companies commit to advertise only those processed foods that meet particular nutritional criteria that qualify for health (e.g., Dunkaroos, Kool-Aid, and Lucky Charms). Simply put, banning the promotion of some cookies as HFSS will make negligible difference to childhood obesity if Dunkaroos can be advertised as healthier fare. Such a move sends ridiculously mixed messages to children regarding how they are supposed to evaluate foods in terms of health.

COUNTER-MARKETING AND THE COMMUNICATION OF HEALTH

Combating childhood obesity requires some careful dialogue about what the real problem is, and we should carefully consider where we draw the lines in the sand. Although calls to ban food advertising to children are well intentioned, they fail to address more important aspects of the broader food environment. *Restricting* Oreo cookie advertising to children will mean little if Dunkaroos are still heavily promoted; *banning* the promotion or Pepsi or Pringles specifically to children under the age of twelve will be a mere ripple in the tsunami of childhood obesity if children can still turn on the television to watch commercials for the exact same products aimed at viewers aged thirteen and above. Indeed, the issue isn't simply about a discrete product being advertised specifically to children; instead, it's a political economic one (see Nestle, 2000; Patel, 2007). And so, while a recent commentary for the journal *Childhood Obesity* affirms that "food marketing directed at youth is pervasive, powerful, and pernicious," this focus is too narrow (Schwartz & Ustjanauskas, 2012, p. 75). Food marketing writ large is pervasive, powerful, and pernicious. As Patel observes, "The food industry is an oligopoly that has transformed not only what we eat but how we eat it, and what we think of food" (2012). Evidence of this transformation can be seen in young children, who can readily define what "kids'" food is versus "adult" food (Elliott, 2011); who often locate foods along a spectrum, with healthier foods as less desirable (Roos, 2002); and who find junk food appealing, not merely because of its taste but because of its transgressiveness or its opposition to "regular" or "adult" fare (Elliott, 2008, 2011; James, 1988; Pires & Agante, 2011). What we consider to be "food" now includes highly processed foodlike substances, evaluated via nutritionism (Pollan, 2008). The food industry, and its marketing practices, has played a powerful role in this. Yet banning advertising directed at children does absolutely nothing to address the fact that there are broad cultural misperceptions about how to evaluate the health qualities of food, misperceptions promoted by commercial advertising to adults even, and ones that children pick up on. In focus groups, for instance, children confidently affirm that the claim "fat free" on a box means that the food is "healthy" or that you can eat "as much as you want and not get fat" (Elliott, 2009). Or they identify calories as the singular determinant of a food's health qualities— just like PepsiCo does with its current "Better-for-You" portfolio of products, which categorizes Diet Pepsi as "better-for-you" because it has zero calories.[4] None of these misperceptions stem from child-targeted advertising.[5] Equally significant is the fact that the core of PepsiCo's food and beverage business (which garners $60 billion in revenue) is its "Fun-for-You" portfolio. This includes products like Pepsi, Doritos, Cheetos, and Fritos—products not necessarily targeted at youngsters under the age of twelve. To truly combat the childhood obesity epidemic, then, perhaps we should start with more significant questions. These would include asking, quite pointedly, how we have managed to accept a foodscape where junk food is framed as "Fun-for-You" (by extension, is healthy fare is "Dull-for-You"?), where cookies are a "healthy" dietary choice, and where we are seeking to curtail particular messages to certain audiences instead of transforming the environment as a whole.

Notes

[1] The point I'm trying to convey here is that the "solution" to childhood obesity isn't simply to place these children on a treadmill. One might intuitively respond, "What does communication have to do with the problem of obesity? Do words make people fat?" Words do not make children fat, but communication— including marketing, advertising, promotion, television/television viewing, and video game playing, along with "food communication" more generally—has much to do with the problem of childhood obesity.

[2] Strangely, this study focused on the number of hours the television was on in a preschooler's room, regardless of whether it was being watched or not.

[3] Even our university library allows food in the building.

[4] True, Diet Pepsi won't make us fat, but it certainly is not something we should consume more of to improve our health.

[5] Current advertising campaigns targeted at women feature a "snack fairy" who informs us that we can "snack happy" because the cookies, chocolate-dipped pretzels and crackers being promoted are in 100-calorie packs; the same holds true for the 100-calorie portions of Cheezies, chocolate bars, cola, and potato chips available. The message is that the content doesn't matter, only the calories do. Again, this reinforces that cookies, Cheezies, chips, and colas are perfectly "good" foods.

References

Adams, J., Hennessey-Priest, K., Ingemarsdóttir, S., Sheeshka, J., Østbye, T., & White, M. (2009). Food advertising during children's television in Canada and the UK. *Archives of Disease in Childhood, 94*, 658–662.

American Psychological Association, Task Force on Advertising and Children. (2004). *Report of the APA Task Force on Advertising and Children* (B. Wilcox, Task Force Chair). Washington, DC: Author. Retrieved from http://www.apa.org/pi/cyf/advertisingandchildren.pdf

Attorney General of Québec v. Irwin Toy, Ltd., [1989] 1 S.C.R. 927.

Basrur, S. (2004). *Report of the Chief Medical Officer of Health: Healthy weights, healthy lives.* Toronto: CMOH. Retrieved from http://www.health.gov.on.ca/english/public/pub/ministry_reports/cmoh04_report/healthy_weights_112404.pdf

Best, J. (1994). *Troubling children: Studies of children and social problems.* New York: Aldine de Gruyter.

Brownell, K., & Horgen, K. B. (2004). *Food fight: The inside story of the food industry, America's obesity crisis and what we can do about it.* New York: Contemporary Books.

Byrd-Brenner, C., & Grasso, D. (2000). Health, medicine, and food messages in television commercials during 1992 and 1998. *Journal of School Health, 70*(2), 61–65.

Children's Advertising Initiative. (2010). Canadian children's food and beverage advertising initiative. Retrieved from http://www.adstandards.com/en/childrensinitiative/default.htm

Chamberlain, L., Wang, Y., & Robinson, T. (2006). Does children's screen time predict requests for advertised products? Cross-sectional and prospective analyses. *Archives of Pediatric and Adolescent Medicine, 160*(4), 363–368.

Elliott, C. (2008). Marketing fun foods: A profile and analysis of supermarket food messages targeted at children. *Canadian Public Policy, 34*(2), 259–273.

Elliott, C. (2009). "Healthy food looks serious": How children interpret packaged food products. *Canadian Journal of Communication, 34*(3), 359–380.

Elliott, C. (2011). "It's junk food and chicken nuggets": Children's perspectives on "kids' food" and the question of food classification. *Journal of Consumer Behaviour, 10*(3), 133–140.

Finegood, D., Karanfil, O., & Matteson, C. (2008). Getting from analysis to action: Framing obesity research, policy and practice with a solution-oriented complex systems lens. *Healthcare Papers, 9*(1), 36–41.

General Mills. (2012). Game helps find whole grain, now the no. 1 ingredient in Big G cereals. Retrieved from http://www.generalmills.com/en/Media/Inside _General_Mills/Library/2012/whole_grain_1_10.aspx

Graff, S., Kunkel, D., & Mermin, S. E. (2012). Government can regulate food advertising to children because cognitive research shows that it is inherently misleading. *Health Affairs, 31*(2), 392–398. doi:10.1377/hlthaff.2011.0609

Halford, J. C. G., Boyland, E. J., Hughes, G., Oliveira, L. P., & Dovey, T. M. (2007). Beyond-brand effect of television (TV) food advertisements/commercials on calorie intake and food choice of 5–7 year-old children. *Appetite, 49*(1), 263–267.

Hastings, G., Stead, M., McDermott, L., et al. (2003). *Review of research on the effects of food promotion to children.* Report prepared for the UK Food Standards Authority. London: UK FSA; Glasgow, Scotland: Centre for Social Marketing, University of Strathclyde.

Hill, J. M., & Radimer, K. L. (1997). A content analysis of food advertisements in television for Australian children. *Australian Journal of Nutrition & Dietetics, 54*(4), 174–192.

Horgen, K. B., Choate, M., & Brownell, K. D. (2001). Television food advertising: Targeting children in a toxic environment. In D. G. Singer & J. L. Singer (Eds.), *Handbook of children and the media* (pp. 447–461). California: Sage.

Institute of Medicine. (2006). *Food marketing to children: Threat or opportunity?* Washington, DC: National Academies Press.

Ipsos Reid. (2011, November). *Canadian perceptions of, and support for, potential measures to prevent and reduce childhood obesity.* Final report prepared for the Public Health Agency of Canada. Retrieved from http://www.sportmatters.ca /files/Reports/Ipsos%20Obesity%202011.pdf

James, A. (1998). Confections, concoctions, and conceptions. In H. Jenkins (Ed.), *The children's culture reader* (pp. 394–405). New York: New York University Press.

Jeffery, B. (2012). *Technical brief of Bill Jeffery, LLB National Coordinator Centre for Science in the Public Interest before the House of Common Standing Committee on Health.* Ottawa: Hearing on Healthy Living. Retrieved from http://cspinet.org/canada/pdf/cspi-technicalbrief.chronicdiseaspreven tionhearings.pdf

Kotz, K., & Story, M. (1993). Food advertisements during children's Saturday morning television programming. *Journal of the American Dietetic Association, 94*(11), 1296–1300.

Lumeng, J., Rahnama, S., Appugliese, D., Kaciroti, N., & Bradley, R. (2006). Television exposure and overweight risk in preschoolers. *Archives of Pediatric and Adolescent Medicine, 160*(4), 417–422.

Mozaffarian, D., & Ludwig, D. S. (2010). Dietary guidelines in the 21st century—A time for food. *JAMA, 304*(6), 681–682.

Nestle, M. (2000). *Food politics: How the food industry influences nutrition and health.* Berkeley: University of California Press.

Patel, R. (2007). *Stuffed and starved: Markets, power and the hidden battle for the world's food system.* London: Portobello Books.

Patel, R. (2012, February 6). Abolish the food industry. *The Atlantic.* Retrieved from http://www.theatlantic.com/health/archive/2012/02/abolish-the-food-industry/252502/

Pires, C., & Agante, L. (2011). Encouraging children to eat more healthily: The influence of packaging. *Journal of Consumer Behaviour, 10,* 161–168.

Pollan, M. (2008). *In defense of food.* New York: Penguin.

Public Health Agency of Canada. (2010). *Curbing childhood obesity: A federal, provincial and territorial framework for action to promote healthy weights.* Retrieved from http://www.phac-aspc.gc.ca/hp-ps/hl-mvs/framework-cadre/pdf/ccofw-eng.pdf

Roos, G. (2002). Our bodies are made of pizza: Food and embodiment among children in Kentucky. *Ecology of Food and Nutrition, 41,* 1–19.

Schwartz, M. B., & Puhl, R. (2003). Childhood obesity: A societal problem to solve. *Obesity Reviews, 4,* 57–71.

Schwartz, M. B., & Ustjanauskas, A. (2012). Food marketing to youth: Current threats and opportunities. *Childhood Obesity, 8*(2), 85–87.

Scrinis, G. (2008). On the ideology of nutritionism. *Gastronomica, 8*(1), 39–48.

Simon, M. (2006). *Appetite for profit.* New York: Nation Books.

Sodium Working Group. (2010). *Sodium reduction strategy for Canada.* Ottawa: Health Canada. Retrieved from http://cspinet.org/canada/pdf/emb_26-232-sodiumredstrat-e.pdf

Story, M., & Faulkner, P. (1990). The prime time diet: A content analysis of eating behaviour and food messages in television programmes and commercials. *American Journal of Public Health, 80*(6), 738–740.

Swinburn, B. A., Egger, G., & Raza, F. (1999). Dissecting the obesogenic environments: The development and application of a framework for identifying and prioritizing environmental interventions for obesity. *Preventative Medicine, 29,* 563–570.

Wadden, T. A., Brownell, K. D., & Foster, G. D. (2002). Obesity: Responding to the global epidemic. *Journal of Consulting and Clinical Psychology, 70*(3), 510–525.

Wilking, C. (2011). General Mills uses whole grain claims to distract from sugar content. The Public Health Advocacy Institute. Retrieved from http://www.phaionline.org/ 2011/12/14/general-mills-uses-whole-grain-claims-to-distract-from-sugar-content/

World Health Organization. (2010). *Set of recommendations on the marketing of foods and non-alcoholic beverages to children*. Geneva: Author. Retrieved from http://www.who.int/dietphysicalactivity/publications/recsmarketing/en/index.html

Discussion Questions

1. Some have called for limits on commercial advertising to children based on nutrient levels of food. Can you think of ways that, for example, fast food restaurants or soft drink companies could skirt such restrictions and undermine the main purpose of the measure?

2. Considering one must be an adult to file an official complaint about advertising or even enter into a legally binding contract (except for the necessities of life) how can marketing aimed at children be justified? Are most/all 12-year-olds or even 16-year-olds as mature and savvy as a typical adult or typical university student?

3. Would food-based limits on ads to children give a free pass to companies that promote—directly to children—video games, movies, and other products that promote sedentary play? Appoint five students to monitor an hour or two of ads on TV on five different channels. What proportion promote sedentary play? Non-starchy fruits and vegetables (ignore potatoes and juices)?

4. What are the implications (positive and negative) of banning advertisements to children as a strategy to combat obesity?

5. Researchers focusing on childhood obesity frequently point to our "toxic" food environment, which prompts unhealthy eating behaviours and contributes to obesity/overweight. Beyond televised advertisements, what other questions should communication scholars consider to properly address the problem of childhood obesity?

6. What do we need to do in order to positively benefit from nutritionism while mitigating the potential for nutriwashing by the food industry?

7. Opponents of legal restrictions on marketing to children often cite the importance of protecting freedom of expression (of advertisers) and instead emphasize parental responsibilities to resist the effects of such marketing. Do food companies have any responsibilities for the consequences of their marketing practices?

ISSUE 2

Toxic gaming: Do violent video games make children aggressive?

✔ YES

Teaching Children that Killing Is Fun
Rose A. Dyson

Rose A. Dyson, Ed.D., is a consultant in media education and president of Canadians Concerned About Violence in Entertainment (C-CAVE.com). She is also a psychiatric nurse, has an undergraduate degree in general arts, holds an M.Ed. in applied psychology and counselling, and was a co-founder of the Cultural Environment Movement at Webster University, St. Louis, Missouri, in 1996. She is an external research associate at the LaMarsh Centre for Research on Violence and Conflict Resolution at York University, Toronto; vice-president of the Canadian Peace Research Association; and a consultant to the International Holistic Tourism Education Centre (ihtec.org). She is author of *Mind Abuse: Media Violence in an Information Age* (2000); co-author of numerous other books, peer-reviewed articles, and book reviews; and editor of *The Learning Edge* (casae-aceea.ca). She has given numerous lectures and speeches, both nationally and internationally.

Research on media effects has historically pointed to the troubling consequences of violent imagery on human beliefs and behaviour, particularly among youth. Many have demonstrated that popular media, from film and television to music and video games, can negatively affect society. Social, medical, and behaviour scientists agree that the voluminous data on harmful effects from television and earlier forms of screen violence are applicable to violent video games (Dyson, 1995). In this chapter she argue that the debate over video games and their social impact is but the tip of the iceberg of deeper cultural and social problems.

INTRODUCTION

In December 2011 *The Economist* reported that the video game Call of Duty: Black Ops had, in one month, taken in more than $1 billion in sales ("All the World's a Game," 2011). On the day of its release a year earlier, fans in countries around the world had queued for blocks to purchase a coveted early copy. In 2010 the global consulting firm PricewaterhouseCoopers estimated that the global video game market was worth around $56 billion, and that sales will continue to grow rapidly, eclipsing an estimated $82 billion by 2015. There is no question that violent video games such as Call of Duty are wildly popular. However, it's important to think critically about the implications for society and culture, and for youth in particular, of glorifying any medium that promotes and normalizes graphic violence, racism, misogyny, and other gruesome images.

Converging technologies, as well as content, fuel the billion-dollar video game industry, whose annual revenues have overtaken music, film, and television production. In the United States alone, sales of computer and video game software in 2010 totalled approximately $25 billion (Bascaramurty,

2011). Graphic violence has been used for decades as a cheap commercial ingredient because it sells well on a global market and translates easily into any language. It can also be relied upon to quickly grab and hold our attention (LaMarsh, 1977). Chris Hedges argues in his book *The Empire of Illusion* that we are now immersed in a culture that has "passively given up the linguistic and intellectual tools to cope with complexity, to separate illusion from reality" (2009, p. 44). Violent media imagery, on television, film, and, increasingly, video games, intensifies the negative impact that media have on society, and overwhelms our capacity for critical thinking. If "the most valued skill [today] is the ability to entertain" (p. 51), as Hedges argues, our culture is in trouble.

POPULAR MEDIA AND COMMUNITY ANXIETY

Ways in which violent video games affect our health, schools, community safety, and ecological sustainability are of growing concern to educators, parents, health professionals, and law enforcement officers. In 2010 California attorneys arguing in defence of a ban on the sale of violent video games to minors cited, among other examples, the game Postal 2, which "includes torturing images of young girls, setting them on fire, and bashing their brains out with a shovel, for no reason other than to accumulate more points in the game" (Biskupic, 2010, p. 1A). State officials agreed that the interactive nature of video games makes these games with extremely violent themes more dangerous than a movie or book that depicts equally brutal violence.

Operant conditioning, a technique widely used in military training to teach soldiers to kill with impunity, is initiated by the reward aspect of points received for brutal action in video games. U.S. Lieutenant Colonel and professor of military science David Grossman argues, "When talking about conditioned reflexes, we must also talk about violent video games, because to understand how we can make killing a conditioned reflex—stimulus-response, stimulus-response, stimulus-response—it is important to understand how the average opponent has been trained" (2004, p. 77). In the military, these techniques are reluctantly employed as a tradeoff for national security, but to indiscriminately reward children for repeatedly blowing off the heads of their virtual playmates is to encourage dangerous and dysfunctional play. In the past, children who beat up their friends or classmates were punished. Today, not only are we teaching them that such violence can be entertaining, we are rewarding them with points for being good at it.

Tapping into teen emotions like love and fear, Addictinggames.com has become one of the Internet's premier casual gaming sites. Every month, over ten million players log on to play games such as Whack Your Soulmate, involving excessive amounts of blood and gore. According to gaming expert and psychologist Douglas Gentile, the video game industry considers addictiveness as a game's "main indicator of success." The industry doesn't think in terms of addiction as a problem for health or well-being. According to Gentile, as in the case of World of Warcraft, whose ten million members pay $15 per month, addiction encourages "repeat play" (quoted in Bakan, 2011, p. 22). Clearly, warnings from the American Pediatrics Association that media violence can contribute to aggressive behaviour, desensitization to violence, nightmares, and fear of being harmed are being ignored (Stein, 2012; Ybarra, Diener-West, Markow, Leaf, Hamburger, & Boxer, 2008).

In 2010 California Senator Leland Yee proposed a ban on violent video games that was backed by the California chapter of the American Academy of Pediatrics, among other health organizations, and supported by eleven other states. Nevertheless, the U.S. Supreme Court ultimately ruled in favour of the software industry, stating that the California law banning the sale or rental of violent video games to minors is unconstitutional because it violates the right to free speech guaranteed in the First Amendment. As Justice Antonin Scalia explained, "California's argument would fare better if there were a long-standing tradition in this country of specially restricting children's access to depictions of violence, but there is none" (Bascaramurty, 2011, p. A13). Although the call for such restrictions is hardly new, it continues to gather momentum within the medical community and among public health organizations. The American Psychological Association, American Psychiatric Association, Canadian Pediatric Society, the U.S. Centers for Disease Control and Prevention, and the Canadian Centre for Science in the Public Interest have all called for restrictions on violent video games in the interest of protecting children's health. As psychologist Craig Anderson points out, "After 40 years of research, one might think that debate about media violence effects would be over" (2003). Many criticisms in the new debate are recycled myths from earlier objections to restrictions on media violence that have repeatedly been debunked on theoretical and empirical grounds. Valid weaknesses have also been identified and often corrected by media violence researchers themselves (Anderson, 2003).

Many of the greatest public health challenges we face today are lifestyle related, from obesity and smoking to media addiction and youth violence. A strong and culturally influential media system profoundly shapes each problem. Yet corporate profits still seem to take precedence over public health concerns. Indeed, efforts by governments or interest groups to restrict the avalanche of advertising targeting children or the violent, blood-drenched thrillers marketed as fun and games to teens and young adults tend to be countered with cries of censorship, moral intolerance, and religious fundamentalism. The popular assumption is that media literacy taught in schools will help students decode and deconstruct messages, enabling them to more critically assess media content and navigate their way toward responsible citizenship and self-sufficiency—together, that is, with input from vigilant parents, who are expected to provide round-the-clock protection if necessary, supervising the media diets of their children.

But the amount of time young people spend on entertainment media has risen dramatically, especially among minority groups. Today, eight- to eighteen-year-olds devote an average of 7.5 hours a day to entertainment media, often using more than one medium at a time, thus intensifying their immersion into a hyper-real, mass-mediated world (www.kff.org). The opportunities to play video games now go far beyond the material games parents used to be able to withhold from their children. These games are now widely available online and can be accessed through a multitude of digital media ranging from desktop and laptop computers to tablets and mobile phones. The ubiquitous presence of violent video games now means that they are increasingly becoming incorporated into the daily rhythms of media use.

VIOLENT VIDEO GAMES AND THE SCIENTIFIC EVIDENCE OF HARMFUL EFFECTS

The Kaiser Family Foundation funded research that involved a meta-analysis of ninety-five published studies and included over 4000 participants, about half under the age of eighteen, which was released in 2010. It found that playing violent video games significantly increases physiological arousal and feelings of anger or hostility, while significantly decreasing prosocial helping behaviour (www.kff.org). In other words, the games make children feel more anxious and aggressive, and numb their capacity for empathy toward others. There is also growing evidence of long-lasting physiological responses from exposure to media violence, in addition to the host of better-known harmful psychological effects, such as desensitization, aggression, fear, anxiety, and attention deficit disorder (Dyson, 1995, 2000; Linn, 2004; LaMarsh, 1977; C-CAVE. com, cmch.tv). Magnetic resonance imaging (MRI) techniques, which are commonly employed for medical diagnostic purposes, have yielded evidence showing that when video game players participate in simulated violence, their heart rate and blood pressure rise, and brain cells that normally counsel empathy are shut down. Furthermore, these images are burned into long-term memory, like post-traumatic stress disorders from real-life events (Atkinson, 2004; Illner, 2003; Linn, 2004). Psychologists regard this kind of powerful operant conditioning as the only technique that will reliably influence the primitive, midbrain processing of a frightened human being, just as fire drills condition terrified school children to respond properly during a fire, and repetitious "stimulus-response" conditioning in flight simulators enables frightened pilots to respond calmly to emergency situations (Grossman, 2004). Now, the operant conditioning that takes place when young people play these games, in which they are frequently rewarded with points for making heads roll and blood splatter, is leading to what Grossman calls "acquired violence immune deficiency syndrome" (p. 205).

CAN'T VIDEO GAMES BE "GOOD" FOR YOU TOO?

Occasionally, reports surface that even violent video games can offer opportunities to learn new skills and facilitate social networking. But at what cost? And for what purpose? These techniques may be extremely effective and useful for military training and recruitment purposes, but that is far different from socializing young people into thinking that killing is fun or promoting play in which rewards are given for killing police and other law enforcement officers. The hidden curriculum in video games and complementary forms of social media constantly reinforces the notion that boys and men should be brutally violent, girls and women are sexual objects, buying and accumulating material things leads to happiness, parents and other authority figures are uncool, and obsessive compulsive behaviour is normal. Representations in these games may not be the sole or even main determinants of what young people think or do. But they are the most pervasive and inescapable. Pioneering media theorist George Gerbner argued, "We distinguish the long-term cultivation of assumptions about life and values from short-term 'effects' that are usually assessed by measuring change as a consequence of exposure to certain messages" (quoted in Morgan, 2002, p. 296). In other words, the accumulation of exposure to negative media imagery over time can have deeply corrosive effects on how we think and the values we espouse, even if those effects appear to be experienced only in the short term.

Indeed, evidence that aggressive marketing of American popular culture is creating a global problem continues to build (Dyson, 2003). The lethal consequences of a seamless blend of combat video games with social media surfaced in the summer of 2011. Norwegian mass murderer Anders Behring Breivik's rampage, which killed seventy-seven people, spawned a lengthy examination of what constitutes empathy, a key personality trait to ward off horrific acts. In one experiment, replicating what has already been known for at least two decades, violent teens who watched a film in which pain was being inflicted showed signs of enjoying the depictions of suffering (Renzetti, 2011). While a definitive link cannot be made between Breivik's murderous actions and his gaming habits, the Norwegian newspaper *Aftenposten* reported that Breivik was a computer game abuser. In just three months he played the computer game World of Warcraft for a total of 500 hours. Police records also showed that Breivik spent more than 8700 hours in front of a computer from July 2006 until the end of 2010 ("Breivik Addicted," 2012).

In August 2011 riots across the United Kingdom dominated international news headlines. Retired British prison doctor and psychiatrist Theodore Dalrymple described how deeply embedded into everyday life criminality has become (2011; see also Dyson, 2003). This normalization of antisocial, criminal behaviour is symptomatic of what Gerbner called "the mean world syndrome" (Morgan, 2002). The model he developed to survey and analyze people's conceptions of social reality demonstrates that long-term, regular exposure to screen violence tends to contribute to the feeling of living in a world that is more cruel and threatening than it really is, and that the anxiety associated with living in a "mean world" leads people (especially youth and children) to feel more dependent on authority and more susceptible to deceptively simple, strong, hard-line postures (Morgan, 2002, p. 297). People who succumb to this "mean world syndrome" tend to accept repressive measures such as more prisons, capital punishment, and harsher sentences for crimes, even though these measures have never proven successful in preventing crime.

The problem is compounded by research showing that children have few restrictions on what they are allowed to watch on television and which video games they can play. Harvard Medical School pediatrician and former television producer Michael Rich argues that children exposed to a torrent of violent media imagery are facing a psychiatric emergency. In "Finding Huck Finn: Reclaiming Childhood from a River of Electronic Media" (ACME, 2011; cmch.tv) Dr. Rich refers to cases where excessive use of Internet and video games creates not only addiction disorders but depression, anxiety, hostility, and paranoia. Excessive screen time also erodes "mind wandering" essential to developing the template for "self," affecting decision-making skills and the ability to relate to other people. The American Academy of Pediatrics recommends no more than two hours of screen time per day, none in the bedroom, and no violent video games at all in homes with young children.

CONCLUSION

Criticisms of media violence production and distribution are always countered by industry-backed studies demonstrating that evidence of harmful effects is inconclusive. The outcome of the aforementioned U.S. Supreme Court decision regarding the California law to ban violent video games to minors is one example. This pattern has been repeated and analyzed in countless studies over the last half century (Dyson 1995, 2000; LaMarsh, 1977). The problem is further exacerbated by media reporting tendencies committed to "balance" that frame any scientific debate, be it on the effects of media violence or climate change, in ways that reinforce the notion of conflicting evidence (Zurawski, 2011). The overwhelming weight of findings pointing to harmful effects becomes distorted and coddles the myth of reasonable doubt, allowing for business as usual. In the process, the news media are, themselves, manipulated by competing interests, particularly when huge corporate profits are at stake.

The perils and rewards of modern life have been heightened both because of and in spite of new communication technologies. Freedom of expression cannot be an absolute guarantee. Although it must be protected and promoted, there is a pressing need for tradeoffs when it impinges upon public health and safety. Some regulation is required to restrict its negative influence on crime. Similarly, as a society, we should not allow the governments we elect to subsidize corporate media through tax shelters, privileges, and credits for the purpose of producing audio-visual material known to be harmful to the public interest. As Calvin H. Johnson, a law professor at the University of Texas in Austin, points out, video game production, most of which is violent, is now one of the most highly subsidized industries in North America (Kocieniewski, 2011). One of the first lessons in media education ought to be that distinctions must be made between individual freedom of expression and corporate freedom of enterprise. Corporations are not the same as individuals. Diversity of opinion, a cornerstone of any healthy democracy, involves conflict in the form of competing ideas. Legislation originally meant to protect political speech is now exploited to protect media violence as entertainment. Along with many media educators, scholars, and public health practitioners, I believe that gratuitous media violence—on television, in film, in popular music, and more than ever in the video game industry—is tantamount to child abuse and should be tightly regulated and controlled.

References

All the world's a game [Special report]. (2011, December 10). *The Economist.* Retrieved from http://www.economist.com/node/21541164

Anderson, C. (2003, October). Violent video games: Myths, facts and unanswered questions. *Psychological Science Agenda: Science Briefs, 16*(5), 1–3.

Atkinson, W. I. (2004, March 13). Video mind games. *The Globe and Mail,* p. F8.

Bakan, J. (2011). *Childhood under seige: How big business targets children.* Toronto: Allen Lane Canada.

Bascaramurty, D. (2011, June 28). U.S. high court rejects video game ban. *The Globe and Mail,* p. A13.

Biskupic, J. (2010, October 28). Can states keep kids from violent video games? *USA Today,* p. 1A.

Breivik addicted to video games. (2012, February 9) *Aftenposten.* http://www.aftenposten.com

Dalrymple, T. (2011, August 11). Lenient justice begets jobs-and London burns. *The Globe and Mail,* p. A18.

Dyson, R. A. (1995). *The treatment of media violence in Canada since publication of the LaMarsh Commission Report in 1977* (Doctoral dissertation). OISE/UT, Toronto; National Library, Ottawa.

Dyson, R. A. (2000). *Mind abuse: Media violence in an information age.* Montreal: Black Rose Books.

Dyson, R. A. (2003). Missing discourse on global media and terrorism. In D. Demers (Ed.), *Terrorism, globalization and mass communication.* Spokane, WA: Marquette Books.

Dyson, R. A. (2011). Media use and misuse: At odds with a sustainable future. In L. Westra et al. (Eds.), *Globalization and ecological integrity in science and international law.* Newcastle Upon Tyne, UK: Cambridge Scholars Publishing.

Grossman, D. (2004). *On combat: The psychology and physiology of deadly conflict in war and peace.* PPCT Research Publications.

Hedges, C. (2009). *Empire of illusion: The end of literacy and the triumph of spectacle.* Toronto: Alfred A. Knopf Canada.

Illner, A. (2003, May/June) Functioning brain imaging: Evaluation of the effects of violent media exposure. *Paediatric Child Health, 8*(5).

Kocieniewski, D. (2011, September 11). Rich tax breaks bolster makers of video games. *The New York Times*, p. A1.

LaMarsh, J. (1977). *Report of the Royal Commission on Violence in the Communications Industry. Volumes 1, 2, 3, 4, 5, 6, 7.* Toronto: Queen's Printer for Ontario.

Linn, S. (2004). *Consuming kids: The hostile takeover of childhood.* New York: The New Press.

Morgan, M. (2002). *Against the mainstream.* New York: Peter Lang.

Renzetti, E. (2011, July 30). The anatomy of evil: Research. *The Globe and Mail*, p. F1.

Stein, M. (2012, January). 2011 year in review: Effects of media use in children. *Pediatrics and Adolescent Medicine, 11*(1).

Ybarra, M., Diener-West, M., Markow, D., Leaf, P., Hamburger, M., & Boxer, P. (2008, November). Linkages between Internet and other media violence with seriously violent behavior in youth. *Pediatrics, 122*(5), 929–937.

Zurawski, R. (2011). *Media mediocrity: Waging war against science.* Halifax and Winnipeg: Fernwood.

ISSUE 2

Toxic gaming:
Do violent video games make children aggressive?

✖ NO

Among a Sea of Influences That Can Increase Aggression, Video Game Violence Doesn't Rise to the Surface
James D. Ivory and T. Franklin Waddell

James D. Ivory is an associate professor in the Department of Communication at Virginia Tech. He is currently the vice chair of the International Communication Association's Game Studies Interest Group and has also served as head of the Association for Education in Journalism and Mass Communication's Communication Technology Division.

T. Franklin Waddell is a doctoral student in the College of Communications at Pennsylvania State Universit. His primary research interests deal with social and psychological responses to video games and interactions between avatars in virtual worlds.

Even taking for granted … conclusions that violent video games produce some effect on children's feelings of aggression, those effects are both small and indistinguishable from effects produced by other media.
—*Justice Antonin Scalia of the Supreme Court of the United States, delivering the opinion of the Court regarding a case involving proposed censorship of violent video games (Brown v. Entertainment Merchants Association,* 2011, p. 13)

A lot of people play video games. Game industry–sponsored research indicates that in the United States, 72 percent of households include video game players and 18 percent of those players are under the age of eighteen (Entertainment Software Association, 2011). Such research has also found that 59 percent of Canadians are video game players, including about 80 percent of Canadians thirteen to seventeen years of age and about 90 percent of those six to twelve years of age (Entertainment Software Association of Canada, 2011).

Further, many of these players spend a lot of time with these games. For example, several studies have indicated that players of the popular massively multiplayer online role-playing game (MMORPG) genre tend to spend more than twenty hours per week with their online games of choice (Griffiths, Davies, & Chappell, 2004; Hussain & Griffiths, 2009; Williams, Yee, & Caplan, 2008; Yee, 2006). A survey of youth eight to eighteen years of age in the United States found that they spent an average of more than thirteen hours per week playing video games (Gentile, 2009), and a survey of children in third, fourth, seventh, and eighth grades in Singapore found that the students spent an average of more than twenty hours per week playing video games (Gentile et al., 2011).

Finally, most of the games that these players are spending so much time with are violent. Analyses of video game content have consistently found that the majority of video games contain **aggression** and violence, including games rated as appropriate for play by young children (Dietz, 1998; Dill, Gentile, Richter, & Dill, 2005; Haninger & Thompson, 2004; Thompson & Haninger, 2001; Thompson, Tepichin, & Haninger, 2006).

It's natural, then, prudent even, to ask how so many video game players might be affected by all the time they spend shooting, stabbing, and bludgeoning their digital foes in video games. Thus, we come to this chapter's question: Do violent video games produce violent children?

Based on our understanding of a large body of existing scientific research on the topic, we don't believe that there is enough evidence to conclude that video game violence is a substantial cause of serious violence.

Before we discuss why we don't consider video game violence a significant factor in serious violence by youth or adults, we should acknowledge that many prominent and respected researchers have come to a different conclusion. A resolution from the American Psychological Association (2005) named violent video games as a cause of aggression, and a policy statement from the American Academy of Pediatrics (2009) goes further to call violent video games "a significant risk to the health of children and adolescents" (p. 1495). Based on these conclusions, both organizations' statements argue for major changes in the content produced by video game makers and for the development of programs to limit video games' negative effects. Let us explain why representatives for these organizations have come to the conclusion that violence in video games represents a significant societal threat based on scientific research findings, and why we disagree with that conclusion based on the same research.

VIOLENT VIDEO GAMES AND AGGRESSION IN USERS

One basis for concerns that violent video games represent a substantial and unique contributor to societal aggression and violence is the argument that violent video games increase aggression in their users. Do we disagree with the conclusion that exposure to violent video games can affect responses related to aggression? No. There have been scores of scientific laboratory studies investigating the effects of violent content in video games on their users' aggressive responses. On the aggregate, published studies in this area have tended to find that in controlled laboratory settings, playing a violent video game can in fact increase some types of aggressive thoughts, feelings, and behaviours in users (see Anderson & Bushman, 2001; Anderson et al., 2010; Sherry, 2001). These studies have used experimental designs, which have typically involved the researchers randomly assigning participants to either a treatment condition where they play a violent video game or a control condition where they play a nonviolent game. This type of research design is effective at isolating causal relationships between violent video games and the outcomes measured in the studies, and the existing experiments have observed many such relationships.

For example, studies have found that people who were assigned to play a violent video game (compared to other people playing a nonviolent game) were more likely to recognize words related to aggression (such as "murder") faster than nonaggressive words (Anderson & Dill, 2000), were more likely to complete an unfinished story by describing characters in the story as being aggressive (Bushman & Anderson, 2002), and were more likely to give a longer blast of loud noise to a competitor in a subsequent competitive activity where they could "punish" their opponent with such a noise blast (Anderson & Dill, 2000). All of these studies have shown that these outcomes, which are all measures of some form of aggression, were influenced by short-term access to video game violence. Not all such studies find effects of violent games (see Ferguson & Kilburn, 2009), and it is difficult to know exactly how much the studies using these types of measures tell us about video games' effects on serious aggression outside of a laboratory setting (see Ritter & Eslea, 2005; Tedeschi & Quigley, 1996), but the findings of some studies do suggest that playing violent video games for even a short period of time affects people's aggression to some extent.

In this regard, though, video games have a lot of company. The list of factors that influence aggression in laboratory studies is a long one. In addition to violent video games, the various stimuli that have been found to increase similar measures of aggressive thoughts, feelings, and behaviours in laboratory studies have included pictures and names of weapons (Anderson, Anderson, & Deuser, 1996; Anderson, Benjamin, & Bartholow, 1998), black uniforms worn in competitive activities (Frank & Gilovich, 1988), words and symbols related to America (Ferguson & Hassin, 2007), violent passages from the Bible (Bushman, Ridge, Das, Key, & Busath, 2007), and hot temperatures (Anderson, Deuser, & DeNeve, 1995). Also, games with severe depictions of violence are not the only video games that can influence laboratory measures of aggression, as similar effects have been found with video games rated as suitable for children (Anderson, Gentile, & Buckley, 2007). Other forms of media, including music with violent lyrics (Anderson, Carnagey, & Eubanks, 2003), violent film clips (Bushman, 1998), and television cartoons featuring violence (Kirsh, 2006), have also been found to influence such measures of aggression.

The problem with viewing violent video games as a unique and substantial cause of aggression based on laboratory studies, then, is not that violent video games don't influence measures of aggression; the issue is that a great many other things influence such measures of aggression as well. Whenever we are exposed to messages, images, and events, these cues can make related ideas, feelings, and behaviours become automatically more accessible in our minds (Berkowitz & Rogers, 1986). Video game violence can make aggression more salient to us, but as the broad range of studies mentioned above shows, so can a host of other cues related to aggression. Therefore, it is difficult to conclude that the effects of video game violence on aggression that have been observed in laboratory experiments are particularly unique compared to the many other stimuli that influence aggression.

Aside from laboratory experiments, **surveys** have also been used to investigate the effects of violent video games on aggression. While surveys cannot isolate causal effects of video games, they can identify correlations between surveyed people's violent video game use and their reports of aggressive behaviour in real life. Typically, these surveys ask their respondents how much they have used violent video games, either recently or over their lives, and then ask them how much they have been involved in a number of different aggressive behaviours (such as fighting) or how aggressive they are in general (such as whether they have a short temper). Some of these surveys are longitudinal, collecting this information over time so that measures of violent video game play can be collected at one point and measures of aggression can be taken later (usually a period of months later, though a period of years would be better).

Some of these surveys have tended to find that people who have played more violent video games have been more likely to be more aggressive (e.g., Anderson & Dill, 2000; Anderson et al., 2008), while others have found no such detrimental effects of violent video game use (e.g., Durkin & Barber, 2002). As with the many experiments dealing with the effects of video game violence on aggression, these surveys have generally tended to find relationships between the use of violent video games and scores on measures of aggression (see Anderson et al., 2010), though a preference for violent video games has also been found to be predicted by children's pre-existing aggressive tendencies (von Salisch, Vogelgesang, Kristen, & Oppl, 2011). Another issue clouding interpretation of survey research on the effects of violent video games is that people who often play violent video games are different from people who do not in many ways, some of which may be measured and some of which may not. Although statistical methods can be used to "control" for the many other factors that might predict aggression, it is difficult to conclude with finality from surveys that violent video game play is responsible for aggression when it is possible that a third factor—measured or unmeasured—influences both of these behaviours (Ferguson, 2011).

It is also important to note that the overall strength of the relationship that these studies have tended to observe is actually weaker than the overall strength of the relationship found in similar studies dealing with the effects of violence in film and television on aggression (Sherry, 2001). In other words, despite speculation that the immersive and interactive nature of violent video games might lead to stronger effects on aggression than other violent media, there is little evidence that any effects of violent video games on aggression are stronger than the effects of other violent media on aggression. Whatever the real effects of video game violence on aggression may be, then, they are not likely to be more powerful than the effects of violence in other media.

VIOLENT VIDEO GAMES, SERIOUS VIOLENCE, AND PUBLIC POLICY

Although a great many studies have been conducted examining the effects of violent video games on aggression, similar studies examining the effects of violent video games on serious violent behaviour, such as violent crime, are limited. One reason this type of research is scarce is that effects on serious violence are difficult to examine with some research methods; it is ethically problematic, for example, to conduct a laboratory experiment that may cause a participant to commit a violent crime. Additionally, relationships between violent video game use and serious violent crime can be difficult to assess because serious violent crime is a relatively rare occurrence (compared to violent video game use and the less serious aggression measures used in many studies), so it can be difficult to measure enough such occurrences with surveys and other methods to produce meaningful analyses.

Despite a shortage of research findings examining whether video games cause serious violent crime rather than less severe measures of aggression, the few studies that have examined effects of violent video game use on serious violent crime have tended to find no important relationship between violent video game use and serious violence (Ferguson, 2011; Ferguson, San Miguel, & Hartley, 2009). For example, one survey study from Christopher J. Ferguson, Claudia San Miguel, and Richard D. Hartley led them to conclude that "depressed mood and delinquent peer associations were the most consistent and strongest predictors" (Ferguson et al., 2009, p. 907) of youth violence, and a longitudinal survey study from Ferguson produced "no evidence to support a long term relationship between video game violence use and subsequent aggression" (Ferguson, 2011, p. 389). Although a number of factors related to personality, peer influences, family environment, socio-economic status, substance use, and other circumstances have been identified as predictors of youth violence (Hawkins et al., 2000), there is limited evidence that violent video game use should be added to the long list of factors known to influence serious violent crime.

Even though there is little support for the conclusion that violent video games have a meaningful unique influence on violent crime, the research has found that at least some effects of violent video game use on other measures of aggression might suggest that it would be prudent to limit access to violent video games as a matter of public policy just in case they increase societal violence. The problem with this line of reasoning, though, is that there are a limited number of public resources (e.g., funds, law enforcement personnel) available to combat societal violence. If some of these resources are dedicated to combat possible effects of video game violence, such as with strict laws censoring violent games, then fewer resources are available to combat the causes of societal violence that are already verified, such as with programs to protect the welfare of children, limit substance abuse, and provide mental health care. Therefore, we should be careful not to make too much of the implications of research on violent video games and aggression until we are able to identify violent video games as a cause of stronger and more societally meaningful effects on serious violence. Also, we must remember not to target the effects of video game violence for scrutiny to the exclusion of violence in other media when there is little evidence that violent games' effects are more pronounced than the effects of violence in other media.

CONCLUSION

Although studies examining the effects of violent video games on aggressive responses in their users have produced mixed findings, there is evidence suggesting that violence in video games can increase aggressive thoughts, feelings, and behaviours—just like other violent media, including violent cartoons, and any number of other stimuli that are reminiscent of aggression, such as pictures of guns or violent scriptures. However important or unimportant these effects of violent video games on scientific measures related to aggression may be, there is a lack of evidence conclusively linking violent video games to more serious violence committed by their users. Given the amount of research devoted to the topic and the increasing sophistication of that research, violent video games may someday be implicated as a meaningful cause of serious violence, but that day has not yet come. Until then, we would do well to stop pointing to violent video games as a cause of violence in our society and focus our efforts on fighting the causes of societal violence that have been unambiguously identified, such as unhealthy peer and family environments, poverty, and mental illness.

This is not to say that playing violent video games may not be harmful. In general, video games appear to entice many of their young users to spend significant amounts of time with them, so much so that excessive video game use may be detrimental to some users' school performance, social activity, and physical health (Gentile, 2009; Gentile et al., 2011; Vandewater, Shim, & Caplovitz, 2004). Concern is also growing about video game content other than violence, such as the way men and women and their bodies are portrayed in games and how that may influence video game users' perceptions of themselves and others (e.g., Behm-Morawitz & Mastro, 2009). Although these concerns are not specific to violent video games, violent video games are just one type of video game that may cause such concerns.

What we want to emphasize, though, is that in the absence of firm evidence that violent video games substantially increase users' violent behaviour, violent video games don't merit the specific attention they have been given as a cause of societal ills. Many factors cause violence in our society, and there are many possible effects that we need to worry about when we consider our children's use of video games. Until there is stronger evidence that violent video games really do have a unique influence on violence committed by their users, perhaps we should spend more of our time on other causes of societal violence, as well as other issues of concern related to video games. When considering both of those topics, plenty of other things are worth worrying about.

References

American Academy of Pediatrics. (2009). Policy statement—Media violence. *Pediatrics, 124,* 1495–1503.

American Psychological Association. (2005). Resolution on violence in video games and interactive media. Retrieved from http://www.apa.org/about/governance/council/policy/interactive-media.pdf

Anderson, C. A., Anderson, K. B., & Deuser, W. E. (1996). Examining an affective aggression framework: Weapon and temperature effects on aggressive thoughts, affect, and attitudes. *Personality and Social Psychology Bulletin, 22,* 366–376.

Anderson, C. A., Benjamin, A. J., & Bartholow, B. D. (1998). Does the gun pull the trigger? Automatic priming effects of weapon pictures and weapon names. *Psychological Science, 9,* 308–314.

Anderson, C. A., & Bushman, B. J. (2001). Effects of violent video games on aggressive behavior, aggressive cognition, aggressive affect, physiological arousal, and prosocial behavior: A meta-analytic review of the scientific literature. *Psychological Science, 12,* 353–359.

Anderson, C. A., Carnagey, N. L., & Eubanks, J. (2003). Exposure to violent media: The effects of songs with violent lyrics on aggressive thoughts and feelings. *Journal of Personality and Social Psychology, 84,* 960–971.

Anderson, C. A., Deuser, W. E., & DeNeve, K. (1995). Hot temperatures, hostile affect, hostile cognition, and arousal: Tests of a general model of affective aggression. *Personality and Social Psychology Bulletin, 21,* 434–448.

Anderson, C. A., & Dill, K. E. (2000). Video games and aggressive thoughts, feelings, and behavior in the laboratory and in life. *Journal of Personality and Social Psychology, 78,* 772–790.

Anderson, C. A., Gentile, D. A., & Buckley, K. E. (2007). *Violent video game effects on children and adolescents: Theory, research, and public policy.* New York: Oxford University Press.

Anderson, C. A., Sakamoto, A., Gentile, D. A., Ihori, M. A., Shibuya, M. A., Yukawa, S., … Kobayashi, K. (2008). Longitudinal effects of violent video games on aggression in Japan and the United States. *Pediatrics, 122,* e1067–e1072.

Anderson, C. A., Shibuya, A., Ihori, N., Swing, E. L., Bushman, B. J., Sakamoto, A., … Saleem, M. (2010). Violent video game effects on aggression, empathy, and prosocial behavior in Eastern and Western countries: A meta-analytic review. *Psychological Bulletin, 136,* 151–173.

Behm-Morawitz, E., & Mastro, D. (2009). The effects of the sexualization of female video game characters on gender stereotyping and female self-concept. *Sex Roles, 61,* 808–823.

Berkowitz, L., & Rogers, K. H. (1986). A priming effect analysis of media influence. In J. Bryant & D. Zillmann (Eds.), *Perspectives on media effects* (pp. 57–81). Hillsdale, NJ: Lawrence Erlbaum Associates.

Brown v. Entertainment Merchants Association, 564 U. S. (2011). Supreme Court of the United States. Retrieved from http://www.supremecourt.gov/opinions/10pdf/08-1448.pdf

Bushman, B. J. (1998). Priming effects of violent media on the accessibility of aggressive constructs in memory. *Personality and Social Psychology Bulletin, 24,* 537–545.

Bushman, B. J., & Anderson, C. A. (2002). Violent video games and hostile expectations: A test of the general aggression model. *Personality and Social Psychology Bulletin, 28,* 1679–1686.

Bushman, B. J., Ridge, R. D., Das, E., Key, C. W., & Busath, G. L. (2007). When God sanctions killing: Effect of scriptural violence on aggression. *Psychological Science, 18*, 204–207.

Dietz, T. L. (1998). An examination of violence and gender role portrayals in video games: Implications for gender socialization and aggressive behavior. *Sex Roles, 38*, 425–442.

Dill, K. E., Gentile, D. A., Richter, W. A., & Dill, J. C. (2005). Violence, sex, race, and age in popular video games: A content analysis. In E. Cole & D. J. Henderson (Eds.), *Featuring females: Feminist analyses of the media* (pp. 115–130). Washington, DC: American Psychological Association.

Durkin, K., & Barber, B. (2002). Not so doomed: Computer game play and positive adolescent development. *Applied Developmental Psychology, 23*, 373–392.

Entertainment Software Association. (2011). Essential facts about the computer and video game industry. Retrieved from http://www.theesa.com/facts/pdfs/ESA_EF_2011.pdf

Entertainment Software Association of Canada. (2011). Essential facts about the Canadian computer and video game industry. Retrieved from http://www.theesa.ca/wp-content/uploads/2011/10/Essential-Facts-2011.pdf

Ferguson, C. J. (2011). Video games and youth violence: A prospective analysis. *Journal of Youth and Adolescence, 40*, 377–391.

Ferguson, C. J., & Kilburn, J. (2009). The public health risks of media violence: A meta-analytic review. *Journal of Pediatrics, 154*, 759–763.

Ferguson, M. J., & Hassin, R. R. (2007). On the automatic association between America and aggression for news watchers. *Personality and Psychological Bulletin, 33*, 1632–1647.

Ferguson, C. J., San Miguel, C., & Hartley, R. D. (2009). A multivariate analysis of youth violence and aggression: The influence of family, peers, depression and media violence. *Journal of Pediatrics, 155*, 904–908.

Frank, M. G., & Gilovich, T. (1988). The dark side of self and social perception: Black uniforms and aggression in professional sports. *Journal of Personality and Social Psychology, 54*, 74–85.

Gentile, D. (2009.) Pathological video-game use among youth ages 8 to 18. *Psychological Science, 20*, 594–602.

Gentile, D. A., Choo, H., Liau, A., Sim, T., Li, D., Fung, D., & Khoo, A. (2011). Pathological video game use among youths: A two-year longitudinal study. *Pediatrics, 127*, e319–e329.

Griffiths, M. D., Davies, M. N. O., & Chappell, D. (2004). Demographic factors and playing variables in online computer gaming. *CyberPsychology and Behavior, 7*, 479–487.

Haninger, K., & Thompson, K. M. (2004). Content and ratings of teen-rated video games. *Journal of the American Medical Association, 291*, 856–865.

Hawkins, J. D., Herrenkohl, T., Farrington, D., Brewer, D., Catalano, R., Harachi, T., & Cothern, L. (2000). *Predictors of youth violence* (OJJDP Juvenile Justice Bulletin). Washington, DC: U.S. Department of Justice, Office of Justice Programs, Office of Juvenile Justice and Delinquency Prevention.

Hussain, Z., & Griffiths, M. D. (2009). Excessive use of massively multiplayer online role-playing games: A pilot study. *International Journal of Mental Health and Addiction, 7*, 563–571.

Kirsch, S. J. (2006). Cartoon violence and aggression in youth. *Aggression and Violent Behavior, 11*, 547–557.

Ritter, D., & Eslea, M. (2005). Hot sauce, toy guns, and graffiti: A critical account of current laboratory aggression paradigms. *Aggressive Behavior, 31*, 407–419.

Sherry, J. L. (2001). The effects of violent video games on aggression: A meta-analysis. *Human Communication Research, 27*, 409–431.

Tedeschi, J. T., & Quigley, B. M. (1996). Limitations of laboratory paradigms for studying aggression. *Aggression and Violent Behavior, 1*, 163–177.

Thompson, K. M., & Haninger, K. (2001). Violence in E-rated video games. *Journal of the American Medical Association, 286*, 591–598.

Thompson, K. M., Tepichin, K., & Haninger, K. (2006). Content and ratings of mature-rated video games. *Archives of Pediatrics and Adolescent Medicine, 160*, 402–410.

Vandewater, E. A., Shim, M., & Caplovitz, A. G. (2004). Linking obesity and activity level with children's television and video game use. *Journal of Adolescence, 27*, 71–85.

Von Salisch, M., Vogelgesang, J., Kristen, A., & Oppl, C. (2011). Preference for violent electronic games and aggressive behavior among children: The beginning of the downward spiral? *Media Psychology, 14*, 233–258.

Williams, D., Yee, N., & Caplan, S. (2008.) Who plays, how much, and why? Debunking the stereotypical gamer profile. *Journal of Computer-Mediated Communication, 13*, 993–1018.

Yee, N. (2006). The demographics, motivations, and derived experiences of users of massively multi-user online graphical environments. *Presence: Teleoperators and Virtual Environments, 15*, 309–329.

Discussion Questions

1. What are the main arguments involving the harmful effects of violent video games?

2. Why is there so much opposition to any restrictions on the production and distribution of violent video games?

3. How does the "hidden curriculum" in violent video games impact on ethical issues, public health and community safety?

4. Despite the evidence that the effect of violent video games on aggression is often similar to the effects of other media on aggression, the relationship between video games and aggression often receives more public attention than similar effects of other media. Does a focus on violent video games at the expense of other media potentially limit awareness of potentially harmful effects of other media? What advice would you give the parents of young children who are deciding what media they should allow their children to view?

5. Aggression in experiments is often measured either by the accessibility of game players' aggressive thoughts and feelings or by their subsequent behaviour in a laboratory task. Some scholars suggest that measuring the short-term accessibility of aggressive thoughts and feelings following video game use is not a valid predictor of actual aggression. What challenges would a media effects researcher encounter when examining the effect of violent video games on aggression? What types of problematic behaviour that might be influenced by violent video game play cannot be studied in the laboratory? Alternatively, what types of problematic behaviour might be less likely to be reported by game players in a questionnaire?

6. Aside from the potential effects of violent video games on aggression, are there any other reasons that some people should not be exposed to violent video games? In other words, are there reasons that you believe access to violent video games should be restricted regardless of whether they increase users' aggression? If so, what do you think it the fairest and most responsible way to restrict access to violent video games? Should similar restrictions be put in place for other violent media?

ISSUE 3

Buckets for the cure:
Do the benefits of cause-related marketing
outweigh the costs?

✔ YES

Cause-Oriented Marketing and the Benefits
to Democratic Discourse
Josh Greenberg

Josh Greenberg is an associate professor in the School of Journalism and Communication at Carleton University. His research interests and areas of teaching and publication include public relations and promotional culture, emergency-risk communication, social movements and the media, and media representations of social problems.

INTRODUCTION: DOING WELL BY DOING GOOD

In March 2012 Cenovus Energy, a Calgary-based oil company, announced a donation of $1 million (Cdn.) to assist in the creation of the Calgary Child Advocacy Centre (CAC), a treatment facility for children who are survivors of violence and abuse. The CAC offers a range of services for victims, their families, and the community, including treatment programs to stop the cycle of abuse, programs that seek to change victims' lives, crime prevention, and support for the prosecution of perpetrators of abuse. Although rates of violent crime in Canada have been declining for decades, family violence remains a pervasive problem. In 2009 almost 55 000 children aged seventeen or younger had been victims of physical assault or sexual violence, of which 84 percent had been victimized by a family member, friend, or acquaintance (Statistics Canada, 2011).

While it might seem unusual for an energy company to invest in a community social service, it isn't a surprise that a corporation like Cenovus would become involved in such an initiative. According to a recent survey from Abacus Data, Canadians have high expectations of the private sector when it comes to its community contributions (Abacus Data, 2011). More than 60 percent of respondents to the Abacus study indicated that a company's contribution to a social cause or charity was an important factor in their decision to purchase a product or service from that company. And it reported that Canadians care most about corporate programs that assist in reducing poverty, protecting the environment, promoting health research, and providing health services for children. Yet, while Canadians believe it is important for the private sector to help address social problems, Canadian industries tend to underperform in relation to these expectations. Thus, for Cenovus not only is it seen as morally virtuous to contribute to the battle against a societal problem like violence and abuse, but it also makes good business sense to give back to the community by investing in projects its employees care about.

Let's consider another example. At the 2010 South by Southwest Interactive Festival (SXSWi), an annual event in Austin, Texas, the geo-location service Foursquare partnered with Microsoft and PayPal in a "Check-In for Charity" event to increase Foursquare's visibility and help raise money for Save the Children's Haiti Relief Fund. Save the Children is an international aid and human rights NGO that focuses on improving the lives of children. Every time an SXSWi attendee checked into an Austin location on Foursquare during the festival, PayPal and Microsoft would donate twenty-five cents to Save the Children up to a maximum of $15 000. By the end of the festival, more than 135 000 check-ins had been registered on Foursquare, the $15 000 maximum donation had been reached in less than forty-eight hours, and the project partners all benefited from a considerable volume of social media buzz and earned media attention, including a story in *The Wall Street Journal* (Valentino-DeVries, 2010). For Save the Children, the publicity and funding (although small by comparison to the enormous demand) were instrumental in raising awareness about the challenges facing the Haitian people in the aftermath of the 2010 earthquake's devastating consequences.

The Cenovus and Foursquare initiatives illustrate the familiar adage that business can "do well by doing good." It's an expression referring to the idea that companies which demonstrate care for those in need or less fortunate will be rewarded by greater loyalty and support from their customers. This chapter looks at business philanthropy and cause-oriented marketing as examples of corporate communication that do not take profit-making as their only motive (though this may inform a company's interests) but focus also on delivering a range of benefits to a community or to society. These benefits might include awareness about an issue or problem of community importance, money for research, or institutional support to inform other activities. Through the presentation of different cases, I outline these benefits but also point to several important critiques. The practices themselves are important for the ethical issues they raise about the relationship between business, the state, and society. However, for students in communication, it's the discourse these practices generate—the questions they raise, the language they use, and the debates they produce—that should be of primary interest. Ultimately, because cause-oriented marketing schemes generate discourse about social, economic and political issues, they should be seen as valuable in themselves and as useful to informing how we think about and act in the world.

PERFORMING SOCIAL RESPONSIBILITY: PHILANTHROPY AND CAUSE-ORIENTED MARKETING

Corporations demonstrate their commitment to social causes in a number of ways. First, as the Cenovus example illustrates, they can make direct donations to a social cause through conventional philanthropic activity. **Corporate philanthropy** involves the donation of money or resources to a charity or cause with no obvious tie to the donor's core business. Although business philanthropy began during the sixteenth century, corporate giving emerged in a significant way in the period surrounding World War I, when nonprofit organizations like the YMCA developed "systematic solicitation and carefully organized 'whirlwind campaigns'" that targeted wealthy corporations (Soskis, 2010, p. 13). Soskis shows that the first nonprofit organization to be a recipient of major corporate philanthropic support was the American Red Cross, established by President Wilson to be the official relief agency of the U.S. armed forces during World War I. In 1917 alone, the Red

Cross received gifts of $1 million from General Electric, $1.5 million from Anaconda Copper, and 5000 Model T Fords from Henry Ford, while the YMCA received $500 000 from subsidiaries of U.S. Steel and $250 000 from Standard Oil. It's important to ask critical questions about the political and economic self-interest of corporations that give large sums of money to charity. At the turn of the century, large corporations such as GE, Ford, and Standard Oil were arguably motivated to support social causes not primarily for altruistic reasons, but to amass wealth and power, and to legitimize the role of big business in the lives of Americans (Marchand, 2001). Nevertheless, and ulterior motives aside, business leaders are among the largest donors to social causes, and the major donations of money and other support they provide do enable charities to carry out a range of important activities.

Second, as illustrated by the Foursquare campaign, through **cause marketing** a business or corporation will partner with a charity to generate publicity about a particular problem (e.g., child abuse, environmental degradation, illiteracy) and solicit donations to help respond to it. In cause marketing, societal value and business value are no longer seen to be mutually exclusive. Rather, social investments come to be seen as important to the values and business interests of the company, its shareholders, and employees (Beaudoin, 2010). A good example is Subaru America's "Share the Love" campaign, launched in 2008. The campaign offered customers who bought or leased a new Subaru a donation incentive, in which the company would contribute $250 (up to $5 million) to a variety of organizations and causes: the American SPCA (animal welfare), Big Brothers and Big Sisters of America (mentoring for at-risk youth), Habitat for Humanity (homelessness and social housing), Meals on Wheels (outreach to seniors), and the Ocean Conservancy (environmental stewardship). Subaru gave vehicle owners the opportunity to select which charity would receive its donation, or to split the donation across all five, and it provided additional information about other ways of contributing to each of the charity causes. In 2008 the campaign generated $4.6 million, and by the end of 2010 the company had raised almost $10 million. While the charities benefited from the infusion of money and the increased visibility through one of the largest car companies in the United States, Subaru sales and market share continued to rise at a time when industry sales overall had been declining. The campaign was arguably a win for each of the charities and a win for their corporate partner.

Another approach to cause-oriented marketing is **social marketing**. Whereas traditional cause marketing involves partnerships between corporations and nonprofit organizations, in social marketing a nonprofit or charity brings the tools and strategies of business marketing to bear on a social issue or problem. Social marketing is said to have emerged in response to G.D. Wiebe's (1951) famous question, "Why can't you sell brotherhood like you sell soap?" (implying that while corporations are effective at influencing consumer thought and behaviour, social change organizations do a lousy job by comparison). Although there is debate about how best to define social marketing (Lee & Kotler, 2011), most researchers and practitioners agree that it involves using principles and strategies of product branding to effectively promote social causes like sustainability, community well-being, and social welfare. For example, social marketing has been used widely in public health campaigns to reduce smoking, promote safe sex and responsible diet, and encourage parents to vaccinate their children against communicable disease and seasonal flu (e.g., Cheng, Kotler, & Lee, 2011). Yet critics argue that poverty is not the same as perfume, and that the commitment citizens make to solving the former is fundamentally different in both substance and scale from the commitment that consumers would make to buy the latter.

Ultimately, corporate philanthropy and cause-oriented marketing campaigns appeal to consumers because they generate positive feelings about purchasing decisions and help them to manage the ambiguity that might arise with the knowledge that corporate profits often come at the expense of others, whether those others are workers in overseas factories, the environment, or wildlife habitat. These campaigns also resonate because they represent what many consider to be a "pragmatic" solution to the distorting effects of modern capitalism: for many consumers and nonprofit organizations that cannot envision (or that may not wish to pursue) a revolutionary transformation of the market economy, cause partnerships at least ensure the economy's longevity and sustainability. When McDonald's Europe gave in to consumer demands for more ethical sourcing of fisheries products for its Filet-O-Fish sandwich, it not only demonstrated a willingness to act on customer and critic demands, but it also ensured that its supply chain could operate more effectively over the longer term (Hill, 2012).

CRITIQUING CORPORATE PHILANTHROPY AND CAUSE MARKETING

Despite their appeal, business philanthropy, cause-marketing, and social marketing initiatives have been criticized on a number of grounds, and the problems that critics have pointed to are important.

Let's revisit Foursquare's "Check-In for Charity" campaign for Save the Children. How meaningful is "check-in giving" for addressing or helping to solve the deep structural problems (which persist today) that contributed to Haiti's devastation following the 2010 earthquake? For consumers who use social or mobile media as a gateway to participating in charity campaigns, episodic donations allow them to feel good by giving a little of what they have without significantly altering their everyday lives. But is this an effective way of combating social problems, or is it merely an elixir to mask the emotional discomfort that comes with low levels of problem awareness? In a provocative and much-debated essay published in *The New Yorker*, Malcolm Gladwell (2010) argued that the rise of digital giving and activism (or "slacktivism"—see the chapters by Saunders and McCurdy in Part III) could have the adverse effect of promoting only casual support rather than the deep commitment necessary for achieving justice. If we really want to address problems like environmental degradation, racism, illiteracy, human rights abuses, or violence against children, Gladwell suggests that we need to spend less time making it easy for people and more time encouraging them to become long-term advocates and supporters. The criticism of click-based campaigns is that they not only promote one-time giving but also turn crises and problems into episodes that are often quickly forgotten. Haiti remains in crisis today, more than two years after the devastating earthquake. However, except for the most committed advocates and organizations that have always been there, public and media attention has shifted elsewhere.

A second criticism pertains to the ways in which cause marketing commodifies the social problems it purports to combat or resolve. Commodification is a concept originating in Karl Marx's critique of capitalism, and has come to refer to a process in which something that does not have inherent economic value is transformed into a commodity for sale or exchange. Samantha King articulates a compelling thesis about cause marketing and the commodification of breast cancer (King, 2006). She argues that despite the fact that breast cancer campaigns are designed to raise needed money for research and public education, they do so by turning an ugly disease into an attractive and appealing "product": promoted with branded merchandise, high-profile celebrity endorsements, and "tyrannically cheerful" events. Rather than exploring the devastating toll that breast cancer has had on women, men, and their families, or challenging corporate sponsors (such as those in the cosmetics or automotive industries) for making products that are known to produce dangerous carcinogens, breast cancer pink ribbon campaigns are designed essentially to make participants feel good about *themselves* by raising money (King, 2006). For critics, including many breast cancer survivors, the notion that pink ribbon events should be about anything other than the disease and its victims is shocking.

A third criticism pertains to the negative economic impacts that charitable giving in the West can have in the developing world. The key to lifting communities out of poverty is to help build *local capacity* so that the people in those communities can sustain their *own* economies and livelihoods. However well intentioned donations from outside sources may be, they can unwittingly undercut local markets, thereby hurting the very people they are trying to assist (Wadhams, 2010). If a corporation like Toms Shoes sends millions of used shoes from North America to Rwanda, it may very well make donors feel good about repurposing an item they no longer need, and which they believe will make a difference in the life of a poor child overseas. But this can also come at the expense of actually providing effective aid that can help that child and the community escape long-term poverty. As one study estimates, between 1981 and 2000, donations of second-hand clothing were responsible for 40 percent of the decline in production and 50 percent of the decline in employment within the African apparel industry (Frazer, 2008).

CORPORATE GIVING: BEYOND GOOD OR BAD

So are corporate philanthropy and cause-oriented marketing good or bad? The examples presented in this chapter illustrate that one can answer this question in both ways. However, they also show how the debate is too often framed in either-or terms: corporate giving is *either* a new and potentially destructive form of market imperialism, *or* it's a force for good. Appealing as this line of thinking may be, it doesn't get us very far. Rather than thinking about corporate giving as an either-or proposition (good or bad, right or wrong), I would argue that we need to think of corporate philanthropy and cause-oriented marketing through the concept of simultaneity (Beck, 1997). In other words, it's not a question of either-or (good *or* bad) but rather of both and more (good *and* bad): more awareness but also more unhelpful ideas; more donations but also more aid dependency; more "brand" visibility for charities but at the expense of rendering their beneficiaries less visible. When we think analytically about the simultaneous and nonlinear effects of cause-oriented marketing, we open ourselves to the production of a plurality of perspectives. In other words, the *discourse* that these debates generate is itself a "public good" because it becomes the ingredients from which citizens can make their own determinations about whether a company is genuinely interested in contributing to the social good or in using social causes to advance their own self-interest. This requires citizens to move beyond thinking about corporate causes and cause campaigns in only either-or terms, and to explore the range of effects these initiatives produce, as well as the ideas that come with them. And this body of discourse—in other words, of practices and their accompanying ideas about corporate responsibility and cause marketing—is precisely the kind of good that should be important to students in communication.

References

Abacus Data. (2011). *Industry CCSR performance and cause alignment: Part 6 of the Corporate and Community Social Responsibility Research Series.* Retrieved from http://abacusdata.ca/wp-content/uploads/2011/11/CCSR-Conference-Part-6-Industry-Performance-and-Cause-Marketing.pdf

Beaudoin, S. (2010, May 10). The end of corporate philanthropy? *PR Week Online.* Retrieved from http://www.prweekus.com/the-end-of-corporate-philanthropy/article/169834/

Beck, U. (1997). *The reinvention of politics.* London: Sage.

Cheng, H., Kotler, P., & Lee, N. R. (2011). *Social marketing for public health: Global trends and success stories.* Sudbury, MA: Jones and Bartlett.

Frazer, G. (2008). Used-clothing donations and apparel production in Africa. *The Economic Journal, 118*(532), 1764–1784.

Gladwell, M. (2010, October 4). Why the revolution will not be tweeted. *The New Yorker.* Retrieved from http://www.newyorker.com/reporting/2010/10/04/101004fa_fact_gladwell

Hill, A. (2012, April 13). By being selfish, leaders can boost the greater social good. *The Globe and Mail.* Retrieved from http://www.theglobeandmail.com/report-on-business/careers/careers-leadership/leadership-advice/by-being-selfish-leaders-can-boost-the-greater-social-good/article2400219/

King, S. (2006). *Pink Ribbons, Inc.: Breast cancer and the politics of philanthropy.* Minneapolis: University of Minnesota Press.

Lee, N. R., & Kotler, P. (2011). *Social marketing: Influencing behaviors for good* (4th ed.). Thousand Oaks, CA: Sage.

Marchand, R. (2001). *Creating the corporate soul: The rise of public relations and corporate imagery in American big business.* Berkeley: University of California Press.

Soskis, B. J. (2010). The pre- and early history of American corporate philanthropy. History of Corporate Responsibility Project, Working Paper no. 3. Center for Ethical Business Cultures at the Opus College of Business, University of St. Thomas, Minnesota.

Statistics Canada. (2011). *Family violence in Canada: A statistical profile.* Catalogue no. 85-224-X. Ottawa: Minister of Industry.

Valentino-DeVries, J. (2010, March 12). Big at the SXSW Interactive Fest: Location, location, location. *The Wall Street Journal.* Retrieved from http://blogs.wsj.com/digits/2010/03/12/big-at-the-sxsw-conference-location-location-location/

Wadhams, N. (2010, May 12). Bad charity? (All I got was this lousy T-shirt!). *Time.* Retrieved from http://www.time.com/time/world/article/0,8599,1987628,00.html

Wiebe, G. D. (1951). Merchandising commodities and citizenship on television. *Public Opinion Quarterly, 15,* 679–691.

ISSUE 3

Buckets for the cure:
Do the benefits of cause-related marketing outweigh the costs?

✗ NO

Shopping ≠ Social Change: The Case of Breast Cancer Marketing
Samantha King

Samantha King is associate professor and associate director in the School of Kinesiology and Health Studies at Queen's University, where she is also a member of the Cultural Studies Program and the Department of Gender Studies. Her research and teaching focus on the politics of health, sport, and the body. At present, she is working on a project that explores the place of prescription painkillers in contemporary culture. Her book *Pink Ribbons, Inc: Breast Cancer and the Politics of Philanthropy* (2006) is the subject of a National Film Board documentary by the same name.

In April 2010, when KFC and the Susan G. Komen for the Cure foundation announced the launch of a new breast cancer marketing campaign, a Facebook group quickly sprung up in opposition. What would be next, asked the administrators of "Pink Buckets of Kentucky Fried Chicken for the Cure? Really?"—cigarettes for the cure? ("Pink Buckets," n.d.).

Frankly, I would not be surprised. After all, earlier that year a breast cancer gun, complete with interchangeable bubble gum pink grip, was released in the United States. The following October, Ultramar gas stations in Canada were once again emblazoned with giant pink ribbons as part of a partnership with the Quebec Breast Cancer Foundation. Handguns? Gasoline? Hormone-inflated chickens? Known threats to public health are clearly not a primary concern for some breast cancer charities. Indeed, it appears that organizations such as Komen may have lost sight of their core vision—"to achieve a world without breast cancer"—as they scramble to attract commercial sponsors (Susan G. Komen Breast Cancer Foundation, 2010).

When critics such as myself challenge cause-related marketing (CRM) campaigns, we are usually told that the money and awareness raised by the sale of specially branded products supersedes concerns about their negative effects. "It's a win, win situation," we hear. Charities receive much-needed income and an opportunity to educate the public; corporations improve their bottom line, enhance their image, and differentiate their brands from those of their competitors. But how much money is actually accrued through such promotions? How is that money spent? And of what, exactly, is the public taught to be aware? More fundamentally, what vision of society and approach to those in need does CRM promote? And what social, economic, and environmental problems does it perpetuate?

A deeper consideration of these questions suggests that the benefits of CRM do not, in fact, outweigh the costs. The financial gains of CRM campaigns for their ostensible beneficiaries are ambiguous and incredibly hard to track. The educational components of these efforts are generally superficial, if not misleading. Most crucially, CRM promotes the idea that social problems are best dealt with individually and through the marketplace, rather than collectively and in ways that question the role of capitalism in creating inequalities in the first instance. In encouraging citizens to shop for a cause, CRM conceals the pernicious effects of overconsumption on the environment and on social and economic well-being more generally.

WHAT IS CAUSE-RELATED MARKETING?

Traditional corporate philanthropy, whereby businesses donate a portion of their profits or products to nonprofit organizations, is usually based on the personal preferences of high-ranking corporate executives and conducted without much concern for the bottom line (King, 2006). While many corporations continue to give in this manner, over the past three decades, CRM has emerged as an alternative model of charity in which particular products are sold with the promise that a proceed of the sales will be made to a particular cause. In this model, synergy between the meaning of the brand and the resonance of the cause is sought and promoted. The primary purpose is to sell products through an appeal to the customer's altruistic self-image and an apparent desire to support corporate responsibility (King, 2006).

CRM has been used to raise money for a wide range of charitable concerns, not just breast cancer. The 1983 American Express effort to collect money for the renovation of the Statue of Liberty is widely recognized as the first such campaign in North America, if not the world. Since then, domestic violence, homelessness, HIV, education, and a host of other causes have become targets of this new promotional tool. Here I illustrate my argument with reference to breast cancer marketing for two primary reasons: first, it is the subject of my ongoing research, and second, it is arguably the most prominent of all commercialized charitable concerns in Canada at this time and therefore a phenomenon that I hope will resonate with readers as they contemplate their respective positions on CRM.

HOW MUCH MONEY DOES CRM RAISE AND HOW IS THAT MONEY SPENT?

There is no denying that, taken collectively, CRM campaigns have raised considerable money over the past three decades. In 2011 the Susan G. Komen for the Cure foundation predicted it would raise approximately $50 million annually from CRM (Singer, 2011). Its "Save Lids to Save Lives" partnership with Yoplait, the yoghurt manufacturer alone has raised $22 million since its inauguration in 1999 (Singer, 2011). The Canadian Breast Cancer Foundation (CBFC), by far the most successful procurer of CRM agreements in Canada, raised 6 percent of its funds, or $1.16 million, through such partnerships in 2011 (CBFC, 2011a). These figures are boosted by companies such as Ford, the automobile manufacturer, which has given CBCF a minimum of $50 000 per year since 1997 (CBFC, 2011b).

The overall financial impact of CRM remains extremely nebulous, however. Regardless of the revenue they may generate, CRM campaigns also cost corporations and their nonprofit partners money. According to nonprofit researcher Angela Eikenberry (2009), IEG Inc., a company that tracks CRM in the United States, estimated that corporations spent approximately $1.3 billion on CRM in 2006. Perhaps more surprising is the claim (oft-repeated in mass media, but not substantiated as far as I can discern in academic literature) that nonprofit organizations spend roughly $7.6 billion per year on marketing and public relations (Chong, 2010). If $9 billion is spent annually on persuading consumers to buy cause-related products, it seems reasonable to expect a strong and unambiguous return on this investment.

Supporters of CRM point to the numerous community service programs, biomedical research projects, and educational opportunities that have received funds through this approach as evidence of its positive impact. There is no doubt that some of the money from CRM campaigns flows out of corporations, through the large and wealthy foundations they tend to partner with, and into the lives of those for whom the funds are intended. But companies are rarely explicit about the fact that a customer's purchase will make no difference to the cause if the maximum promised amount has already been reached, in which case the money from their well-intentioned purchase stays firmly within the company's coffers. While some companies include a clear statement of what they have promised to give in the small print accompanying their product, in other cases such small print is absent and inquiries to head offices are met with the response that the contract with their foundation partner is governed by a confidentiality clause. Even when maximum donations are plainly stated (in Canada, $50 000 is a typical amount for a single breast cancer campaign), I have found that companies are usually reluctant to reveal how much they spend on marketing these products or the amount of the exclusive licence fees they pay to foundations to use their names in the promotion.

It is also worth noting here that funding through CRM tends to make up a small percentage of most foundations' total returns, even for leaders in this sector such as the Canadian Breast Cancer Foundation (CBCF, 2011a). In both Canada and the United States, schools, hospitals, museums, art galleries, recreational facilities, and public foundations receive substantial (if shrinking) amounts of their income from local, regional, and national governments. Although religious organizations and private foundations rely primarily on private donations, the majority of funds tend to come from individuals, from wealthy families, or from more traditional corporate philanthropy. In other words, revenues through CRM represent a drop in the ocean of charitable giving.

Given the partnerships between large breast cancer foundations and oil and gas companies, car manufacturers, and cosmetics merchants, it should come as no surprise that the research agenda has been skewed away from projects focused on primary prevention and the environmental causes of the disease and toward projects focused on more optimistic-sounding avenues like "genetic breakthroughs" and "miracle drugs." Sadly, those avenues have not lived up to expectations thus far, and, in the meantime, corporations and their foundation partners continue to encourage consumers to help end breast cancer by purchasing products (for example, cosmetics containing parabens or cars that produce polycyclic aromatic hydrocarbons) that may in fact be linked to the disease. This might help explain why, in spite of all the money that has been raised and all the attention that has been generated around the disease, incidence and mortality rates for breast cancer remain stubbornly high.

AWARENESS OF WHAT?

When confronted with concerns about the financial viability of CRM, supporters often argue that regardless of how much money is raised or where that money goes, campaigns help build awareness of their respective causes. But what does awareness actually mean? That we must learn that breast cancer, HIV, or homelessness exist? Or that we are all at risk for such misfortunes? There is not much more that can be said in the five to ten words that usually compose contemporary marketing slogans and messages.

When breast cancer campaigns do venture into specifics, awareness usually means preaching the benefits of early detection through mammograms or breast self-exams. Although this approach might prompt people to discover if they already have the disease, this selective brand of awareness asks people to take personal responsibility for fending it off, while ignoring more difficult questions related to what might be done to stop it at its source. Hyperawareness has other worrisome effects too: research suggests that women now overestimate their risk of breast cancer while underestimating their risk of other conditions—heart disease, lung cancer, or stroke— that are more likely to kill them (Fagerlin, Zikmund-Fisher, & Ubel, 2005; Lloyd-Jones, Larson, Beiser, & Levy, 1999). As a result, growing numbers of women are taking up drastic interventions such as prophylactic double mastectomies in an effort to prevent an occurrence of the disease (McLaughlin, Lillqujist, & Edge, 2009).

Beyond the potentially harmful physical effects of awareness, there are also negative political effects. Although the educational messages conveyed through breast cancer marketing—"Get squished!" "Get felt up!" "Feel your boobies!"—may appear benign at first glance, they also tend to trade in objectifying, sexualized language, a harmful irony given the logic of "women's empowerment" that simultaneously characterizes breast cancer campaigns. If contemporary breast cancer awareness means encouraging women to worry disproportionately about their risk of diagnosis through retrograde anti-feminist language and a logic of individual responsibility, it does not seem worth defending.

WHAT VALUES DOES CRM PROMOTE?

The emergence of CRM is part of a broader societal shift in which participation in voluntary giving—of time or money—is touted as a preferable way to fund public services and to instill civic and self-responsibility among citizens. In this new vision of an ideal society, citizenship services (for example, nationalized health care or income assistance) and practices (for example, political protest or the paying of taxes) are viewed as divisive and apathy inducing. In contrast, donning a brightly coloured silk ribbon or participating in a leisurely 5 K fundraising run on a Sunday afternoon are thought to help rekindle "traditional" cultures of personal generosity, and constitute a more harmonious, benevolent, active, and personally responsible citizenry (King, 2006).

As governments in Canada and the United States have sought to cut expenditures on public goods such as education and health care, a dramatic "upward redistribution of a range of resources" (Duggan, 2003, p. xi) has occurred; this shift has been accompanied by widespread tolerance of increasing inequality in the context of a gradual elimination of the concept of collective well-being. Under this regime, the consumer marketplace and individual and corporate giving are promoted as morally and economically viable means through which to respond to societal needs, in place of the state's role in alleviating the negative effects of capitalism.

CRM is a perfect tool for realizing a vision of a society unfettered by social programs. CRM does not encourage citizens to think about "the public good" or to contemplate the role of consumer capitalism or other economic, political, or social structures in creating the need for charity in the first place. Indeed, a variety of research projects have shown that if individuals purchase a CRM product, they are less likely to think collectively or to make direct donations to nonprofits; they may also become desensitized to other social needs, particularly those that are less marketable than breast cancer (for example, heart disease or poverty) (Flaherty & Diamond, 1999; Krishna, 2011; Lichenstein, Drumwright, & Braig, 2004). Rather than alleviating social problems, then, CRM might best be understood to mask or even perpetuate them if the example of marketing toxic products through breast cancer awareness gives any indication.

BEYOND CRM?

Perhaps because of a broader and frequently moralizing societal panic around obesity, as well as increasing recognition that food quality is an important component of good health, the Komen Foundation's "Buckets for the Cure" promotion elicited a quicker and more vexed response than other dubious endeavours brought to the North American public by the pink ribbon industry (King, 2010). If high-fat diets are linked to breast cancer—an unsubstantiated but nonetheless widely held belief—what is the self-described "global leader of the breast cancer movement" doing promoting a fat- and sodium-laden product, commentators asked. In reply, Komen claimed that KFC offers a range of healthy menu options and placed responsibility squarely with the individual: "Consumers ultimately have a choice about what they will eat," spokesperson Andrea Radar told NPR ("Are Charities Doing Enough," 2010). More pointedly, Komen's partnership with a corporation embroiled in a lawsuit with the state of California over the use of a known carcinogen—PhIP—in the preparation of its chicken brings into question Komen's legitimacy as an organization supposedly dedicated to saving lives.

But KFC is likely laughing all the way to the bank. With the promise to donate fifty cents for every bucket sold (although the small print notes that "customer purchases will not directly increase the total contribution"), their fundraising target was $8.5 million. This means KFC would have had to sell 17 million pink buckets of chicken over the five-week campaign to reach their goal. It was just as well they were only committed to a minimum of $1 million. As San Francisco–based Breast Cancer Action (2010) asked in their response to the promotion, "How much does KFC stand to gain from this campaign?" Surely KFC—owned by the world's largest restaurant company—could afford to donate this amount without making it conditional on a sales drive?

If there is a glimmer of hope to be found in this story, it is that it has piqued the interest of a broad range of activists who might not otherwise have paid attention to the problems with breast cancer marketing, and it has highlighted how the struggle against the disease is connected to other social issues. Some critics have pointed to the underserved communities that Komen claimed to be reaching through their campaign and have asked why the foundation doesn't instead partner with community clinics and other organizations concerned about the health of marginalized populations. KFC has a reputation for installing themselves in neighbourhoods without grocery stores, where food insecurity is endemic—wouldn't Komen's efforts be better channelled toward changing these conditions? Meanwhile, animal welfare advocates have drawn attention to the ghastly treatment of birds at KFC processing plants. Other commentators have questioned the working conditions of those who process and serve these chemically saturated avians.

Does public outrage over "Buckets for the Cure" suggest that the sheen is slowly fading on the pink ribbon machine? I certainly hope so. But what about CRM more generally? The last few years have seen increasing amounts of critical mass media coverage of this phenomenon (Krishna, 2011; Singer, 2011), but as long as CRM continues to move products off shelves, corporations will continue to use it as a strategy. Critics could simply persuade consumers to change their purchasing habits, or push corporations to improve the payouts from their CRM campaigns, but these changes would leave bigger questions related to consumer capitalism untouched. Instead, it may be time to more directly, and explicitly, question the role of foundations and charities in the problematic practices of CRM. If nonprofits are to contribute to real social change, they are going to have to question how they relate to big business. A move away from corporate partnerships might allow them to fund more transformative projects while also relieving consumers of the myth that the benefits of CRM outweigh the costs.

References

Are charities doing enough to fight breast cancer? (2010, October 25). *NPR*. Retrieved from http://www.npr.org/templates/story/story.php?storyId=130810038

Breast Cancer Action. (2010). What the cluck?! Think Before You Pink. Retrieved from http://thinkbeforeyoupink.org/?page_id=1011

Canadian Breast Cancer Foundation. (2011a). Financials. Retrieved from http://www.cbcf.org/ontario/AboutUsMain/Financials/Pages/default.aspx

Canadian Breast Cancer Foundation. (2011b). Our corporate partners in action. Retrieved from http://www.cbcf.org/bc/PartnersSponsors/NationalPartnersSponsors/Pages/Corporate-Partners-in-Action.aspx

Chong, R. (2010, January 4). Cause-related marketing: Just plain ol' marketing. *Huffington Post*. Retrieved from http://www.huffingtonpost.com/rachael-chong/cause-related-marketing-j_b_409633.html

Duggan, L. (2003). *The twilight of equality? Neoliberalism, cultural politics, and the attack on democracy*. New York: Beacon Press.

Eikenberry, A. (2009, Summer). The hidden costs of cause marketing. *Stanford Social Innovation Review, 17*. Retrieved from http://www.ssireview.org/articles/entry/the_hidden_costs_of_cause_marketing

Fagerlin, A., Zikmund-Fisher, B. J., & Ubel, P. A. (2005, June). How making a risk estimate can change the feel of that risk: Shifting attitudes toward breast cancer risk in a general public survey. *Patient Education and Counseling, 57*(3), 294–299.

Flaherty, K., & Diamond, W. (1999). The impact of consumers' mental budgeting on the effectiveness of cause-related marketing. *American Marketing Association Conference Proceedings, 10*, 151–152.

King, S. (2006). *Pink Ribbons, Inc: Breast cancer and the politics of philanthropy*. Minneapolis: University of Minnesota Press.

King, S. (2010, Fall). Pink cigarettes for the cure? *Breast Cancer Action Montreal Bulletin, 18*(3). Retrieved from http://www.bcam.qc.ca/content/"pink-cigarettes-cure"

Krishna, A. (2011, October 15). Philanthropy and marketing. *Toronto Star*. Retrieved from http://www.thestar.com/opinion/editorialopinion/article/1070419--philanthropy-and-marketing

Lichenstein, D. R., Drumwright, M. E., & Braig, B. M. (2004). The effect of corporate social responsibility on customer donations to corporate-supported nonprofits. *Journal of Marketing, 68*(4), 16–32.

Lloyd-Jones, D. M., Larson, M. G., Beiser, A., & Levy, D. (1999). Lifetime risk of developing coronary heart disease. *The Lancet, 353*, 89–92.

McLaughlin, C. C., Lillqujist, P. P., & Edge, S. B. (2009). Surveillance of prophylactic mastectomy: Trends in use from 1995 through 2005. *Cancer, 115*(23), 5404–5412.

Pink buckets of Kentucky Fried Chicken for the cure? Really? (n.d.). Retrieved from http://www.facebook.com/group.php?gid=113440285356592

Singer, N. (2011, October 15). In the breast cancer fight, the pinking of America. *The New York Times.* Retrieved from http://www.nytimes.com/a2011/10/16/business/in-the-breast-cancer-fight-the-pinking-of-america.html?pagewanted=all

The Susan G. Komen Breast Cancer Foundation, Inc. (2010). Consolidated statements of activities. Retrieved from http://ww5.komen.org/uploadedFiles/Content/AboutUs/Financial/AUDIT_FINAL_FY2010.pdf

Discussion Questions

1. Is it important to you that a company contributes to helping solve a community problem, either through direct financial support (corporate donation) or through a cause-marketing partnership? Why or why not?

2. Now think about every purchasing decision you have made in the past week. In how many of those decisions did you think about the company's impact on the environment or its workforce? In how many of those decisions did you consider whether the company has exercised "community responsibility"? Is there a gap between your expressed support for cause-marketing and your actions? If so, how do you explain that gap?

3. What are some cause-marketing campaigns that you find particularly compelling in terms of influencing how you act and think as a citizen and consumer? What about these campaigns attracts your interest? Identify the alleged benefits and limitations of these campaigns— does thinking more critically about the competing perspectives change your support?

4. Why do you think that cause-related marketing has become so popular among businesses and consumers over the past two decades?

5. Why do you think breast cancer, in particular, is such a popular focus of cause-related marketing campaigns?

6. Do the benefits of cause related marketing outweigh the costs?

7. What are some alternatives to cause related marketing that citizens can use in their efforts to raise awareness of social causes and bring about social change?

Representing race:
Are Canadian news media racist?

✔ YES

Overachievers, Homegrown Terrorists, and Exceptional Cats: Constructing Race in the Media
Faiza Hirji

Faiza Hirji is an assistant professor in the Department of Communication Studies and Multimedia at McMaster University. She specializes in research exploring media representation of race, religion, ethnicity, and gender; the use of media in the construction of identity; popular culture and youth; and the importance of media within diasporic/transnational communities. She is currently working on two research projects, one investigating overlapping musical cultures and their associated politics within South Asian and black diasporas, and the other looking at media representations of Muslim women. Her recent book, *Dreaming in Canadian: South Asian Youth, Bollywood and Belonging* (2010), details her work on audience readings of nationalism and religion in Bollywood cinema. She has published articles on the formation of online communities by Muslim Canadians, the depiction of Islam in Indian cinema, e-health, and feminism in television, film, and music. Her work has appeared in *Global Media Journal*, *Journal of Communication Inquiry*, *Information, Communication and Society*, *Canadian Journal of Communication*, and *TOPIA*.

ALL ABOUT RACE? DISCRIMINATION IN CANADIAN NEWS MEDIA

Are the Canadian news media racist? Yes. Is this always the case? No. Is this racism intentional? Probably not. Then why does it occur? These are important questions and provide the focus for this chapter.

The question of racism in the media is a difficult one to examine for a number of reasons. In the first place, there are different ways of understanding racism and the related process of **racialization**. Henry and Tator explain that racism

> refers to the assumptions, attitudes, beliefs, and behaviours of individuals and to the institutional policies, processes, and practices that flow from these misunderstandings. Racism as racialized language or discourse manifests itself in euphemisms, metaphors, and omissions that support given ideologies and policies. It is reflected in the collective belief systems of the dominant culture. (2002, p. 11)

Related to this, racialization affects groups that are not necessarily tied together by race, yet "they are groups by virtue of being racialised (socially defined as a 'race'), not vice versa. They are defined as a 'race' by others, acquire a group identity and become oppressed, and then use the idiom of 'race' in relation to themselves, their identities and their grievances" (Miles & Brown, 2003, p. 6). The distinction between racism and racialization may be less straightforward than the difference between black and white. Miles and Brown suggest that our history highlights the importance of understanding a concept as complex as racialization. The physical difference between, for instance, Bosnian Muslims and Bosnian Serbs may seem almost irrelevant to us, and yet "imagined distinctions between these groups produced discourses of racism" and a horrific case of genocide (Miles & Brown, 2003, p. 6). In times of economic or political stress, racialization may easily give way to racism, in the media and in society at large. Thus, this chapter is concerned both with racism and with the more predominant problem of racialization, which can affect individuals on the basis of race, culture, or religion. Discrimination against Muslims, for instance, is due only partly to differences of race. A white Canadian may practise Islam and be subject to harassment or misunderstanding.

To combat such misunderstanding, Henry and Tator argue, it is necessary to investigate the role that media play in promoting it: "The media are one of the most powerful institutions in a democratic society because they help transmit its central cultural images, ideas, and symbols, as well as a nation's narratives and myths" (2002, p. 4). Owing to its complexity, racialization in media is difficult to detect and to prevent. It can occur in a number of forms: through marginalization, underrepresentation, or misrepresentation. For instance, some groups may be depicted very infrequently, or they may appear in the media in ways that do not provide an accurate picture of their activities or beliefs. Misrepresentation need not be intentionally malicious or even negative. While the use of **stereotypes** to describe a people can be damaging, it is entirely possible that those citing the stereotypes may see them as positive.

TOO ASIAN? *MACLEAN'S* AND THE ENROLLMENT CONTROVERSY

A recent case in the Canadian media illustrates the concept of racialization. In what would be a controversial article, the national news magazine *Maclean's* reported that high-achieving Asian students were negatively affecting "Canadian" (i.e., white) students, who were experiencing difficulty obtaining admission to the universities of their choice as a result of the increasingly high levels of competition (Findlay & Köhler, 2010). The conclusion of the report was not that the average Canadian student needed to work harder, or that governments needed to open up more spots in universities—rather, there was a distinct implication that Canadian students could not possibly compete. After all, according to the stereotype, Asian students are such abnormally high achievers that their very presence in Canadian postsecondary institutions constitutes a threat:

> Many white students simply believe that competing with Asians—both Asian Canadians and international students—requires a sacrifice of time and freedom they're not willing to make. They complain that they can't compete for spots in the best schools and can't party as much as they'd like (too bad for them, most will say). Asian kids, meanwhile, say they are resented for taking the spots of white kids. (Findlay & Köhler, 2010, para. 5)

Maclean's went on to issue a response to the controversy, changing the title of the article from "Too Asian?" to "The Enrollment Controversy," and insisting that it supported the merit-based admissions standards found in Canada. However, the article itself seems to suggest that administrators need to rethink merit-based policies that favour high achievers rather than considering the resulting racial balance on campuses. This is certainly an interesting twist on educational concerns in countries such as the United States, where affirmative action quotas were once seen as pushing bright young (white) American students to the sidelines while mediocre minorities stormed the citadels of higher education.

In the Canadian case, where no such quotas exist, *Maclean's* nevertheless managed to conjure up a story that is sympathetic to the thinly veiled anti-immigrant sentiments of some parents and students. Indeed, the article attempts to validate open racism, as when a young woman quoted in the report rejected the possibility of attending the University of Toronto on the basis of its "reputation of being Asian" (Findlay & Köhler, 2010, para. 3). The *Maclean's* story actually manages to be doubly racist, misrepresenting Asian and white students alike. Asian students, whether Asian Canadian or Asian international students, are described as scholars who are so obsessed with academics that they contribute very little socially to campus life, while white Canadian students are depicted as lazy and uninterested in academic achievement.

"HOT FOR JIHAD": REPRESENTING ISLAM IN THE MEDIA

A tendency to emphasize difference is not new to *Maclean's*. In 2008 the magazine defended its decision to continue publishing the work of Mark Steyn, who has written columns suggesting, among other things, that Muslims are terrorists (2006a, 2006b), that they are associated with bestiality (2006a), and that Islam is fundamentally violent (2006a, 2006b). In one *Maclean's* column, Steyn ruminated on the dangers of Muslim reproduction to European civilization:

> On the Continent and elsewhere in the West, native populations are aging and fading and being supplanted remorselessly by a young Muslim demographic. Time for the obligatory "of courses": of course, not all Muslims are terrorists—though enough are hot for jihad to provide an impressive support network of mosques from Vienna to Stockholm to Toronto to Seattle. Of course, not all Muslims support terrorists— though enough of them share their basic objectives (the wish to live under Islamic law in Europe and North America) to function wittingly or otherwise as the "good cop" end of an Islamic good cop/bad cop routine. But, at the very minimum, this fast-moving demographic transformation provides a huge comfort zone for the jihad to move around in. (2006b, para. 40)

Maclean's defended Steyn's writing by citing his right to free speech. This sounds compelling—and yet Canadian laws on hate speech were established in recognition of the fact that there can be very real consequences to comments that demonstrate bias against adherents of a specific faith or culture.

These consequences have been evident with the history of **anti-Semitism** and can now be seen with **Islamophobia**, particularly after the World Trade Center attacks of September 11, 2001, and the subsequent wars in Afghanistan and Iraq. The case of the so-called Toronto 18, the young men who were allegedly engaged in a terrorist plot against a number of Canadian institutions (including Parliament), prompted journalists to refer excitedly to "homegrown terrorism," further stoking the fears of those who believe that minorities living in Canada are necessarily suspect (for one example, see Teotonio, 2009). Karim H. Karim describes the cases of other individuals who have been accused by the media of terrorist activity when little evidence existed to support these claims. He argues that the "increasing humiliation of innocent Muslim men and women by Northern states can probably be attributed to the continually negative media references to Islam" (2000, p. ix; also see Walton & Kennedy, 2002).

TERRORISTS OR VICTIMS? DEPICTING REFUGEE CLAIMANTS

A similar example can be seen in the case of nearly 500 Tamil migrants who attempted to come to Canada on a boat that docked in British Columbia in 2010. Before the migrants had arrived, there was a strong implication from politicians and from the media that these migrants might actually be criminals. A *Globe and Mail* story referred to the migrants as "illegals" and mentioned a human smuggling operation as well as the possibility of terrorism, based on intelligence sources relied upon by the government. This use of anonymous sources by the government to hint at terrorist links is not unusual, according to Karim, who argues that while "the mass media may often contradict government statements, there is a high degree of alignment of views on issues such as terrorism" (2000, p. 93). The use of the term "terrorist" to describe Tamil migrants is also familiar, as Henry and Tator demonstrate. Examining *National Post* articles from the year 2000 regarding Tamil migration, they found that the word "terrorist" was most often used to describe Tamils living in Toronto, and the newspaper drew consistent links between Tamil Canadians and the Tamil Tigers, an alleged terrorist organization, ensuring that "an entire group has been tainted by the actions of a few" (Henry & Tator, 2002, p. 123).

Like the Chinese "boat people," 600 Chinese migrants who attempted to migrate to Canada in 1999, the Tamil migrants were desperate, coming in terrible conditions. The way they immigrated was certainly not ideal, and as with the Chinese migrants, human smugglers may have taken advantage of them. Some might argue that they deserved our compassion, and yet the coverage implied that these migrants posed a threat to Canadian society. In the case of the migrants from China, Hier and Greenberg argue, the media constructed their arrival as a crisis that threatened the nation's security, resonating with "Canadians' collective anxieties stemming from social change, racial integration, and contested Euro-Canadian hegemony" (2002, p. 138).

There is nothing new in this, of course—on the one hand, Canadians often applaud the immigrant success story embodied by our society, but on the other, any sign that immigrants may present risk to our way of life is quickly seized upon and emphasized. Indeed, much of the reporting that exists on immigration, race, ethnicity, and religion makes some reference, explicit or not, to "us" and "them." There are those who have a fundamental right to belong to Canadian society, and those who exist on the outside. They may be granted right of entry, but their belonging is conditional. Is this, however, a construction of the media, or is it merely the media's reflection of existing social inequality? The truth may lie somewhere in between. As Hier and Greenberg (2002) discuss, it is unlikely that the news media can independently create public panic. At the same time, media are able to call attention to some cases more than others, and to frame them in particular ways if they employ dehumanizing or threatening language such as "illegal," "aliens," "detainees," and "human cargo" (Hier & Greenberg, 2002).

RACISM AND RESPONSIBILITY IN THE MEDIA: EXPLANATIONS AND THE WAY FORWARD

Many media outlets, and many journalists, do practise responsible journalism, making an effort to consider the implications of the terminology they employ and the allegations they report. However, in too many cases, reporters and editors employ headlines and inflammatory language intended to attract attention. Slim profit margins and shrinking newsroom budgets can lead to an increasing tendency to rely on popular columns rather than factual news reports, to reproduce reports from news agencies rather than conducting independent research, and to rush to complete stories rather than taking the time to investigate all the facts (Karim 2000, p. 14; Shoemaker & Reese, 1996, p. 118).

Teun van Dijk (1996), who has written extensively on racism in the press, adds that bias may be due partly to limited social and financial resources for minorities to provide their perspective on events, as well as to a persistent perception by journalists that minorities are not credible sources when compared to white institutional sources. For reasons such as these, Jiwani (2009) argues, the plight of missing Aboriginal women in Canada was largely downplayed by the national press from 2000 to 2007, with an emphasis on the women as drug addicted or sex workers, rather than victims of a violent crime that needed to be investigated urgently. In such cases, reporters may have found it more difficult to approach the victims' families or acquaintances than to rely on familiar institutional sources such as police officers. Beyond this, stereotypes about minorities may come to mind more frequently in newsrooms that are staffed by members of the Canadian majority: in other words, white and middle class (Cottle, 2000).

Newsrooms that are not representative of the Canadian population are ones where journalists are less likely to be familiar with or understand all the cultural, religious, and racial nuances of certain stories. Moreover, in the digital age, when deadlines are more pressing than ever and competition is more fierce, media outlets need to provide stories that attract the reader, which can happen through portraying subjects in simplistic terms such as good vs. evil, lawful vs. threatening.

One common rebuttal to these points is to suggest that media simply report the news. If the media make a link between Islam and terrorism, or report on illegal immigration, or cover crime committed by minorities, perhaps they have a reason: could it be that Muslims/Tamils/Chinese are fundamentally dangerous?

Here, as I view it, is the problem. In cases like these, the media focus on the problems, not on the larger picture. The Ismaili Muslim spiritual leader and media owner, the Aga Khan, refers to this as the case of the exceptional cat:

> These failures are compounded by our pernicious dependence on what I call crisis reporting—the inclination to define news primarily as that which is abnormal and disruptive. As one journalist puts it: "It is the exceptional cat, the one who climbs up in a tree and can't get down, that dominates our headlines, and not the millions of cats who are sleeping happily at home."
>
> Most of the public, however, has no context in which to place the story of the exceptional cat that climbs a tree. And without that context, the casual reader or viewer, never hearing about the cats that stay home, comes to think of all cats as tree-climbing pests who are forever imposing on the fire departments of the world to bring out their ladders. (1996, para. 54–55)

Yes, there may be some extremists out there who cite religion to justify their actions. There are just as certainly many immigrants who have difficulty adapting to Canadian society, or minorities who commit crime. And yet, adopting the parlance of the Aga Khan's speech, are these ordinary cats?

The problem with these portrayals is that they take a negative depiction and apply it to entire groups of people. This is how stereotypes are born, and how misunderstanding is fostered. Arguably, this is not the role of journalism. Journalists are meant to speak truth to power, and spreading stereotypes and promoting misunderstanding furthers marginalizes those who are most disempowered.

To their credit, many media outlets do recognize this, and have worked hard to moderate their language and check their facts, an increasingly challenging endeavour as they rush stories to print, broadcast, and the web. Racialization is not necessarily a widespread problem in Canadian news media, but it is a serious one. The consequences can be severe. Canadians who watch, read, or listen to the news rely upon the media to provide them with information about the society in which they live. At times, their only exposure to some minority groups may be through these media. If the media present these groups as criminal, dishonest, or otherwise threatening, they leave an impression that may be hard to erase. In conclusion, then, are the Canadian news media racist? Yes. All the time? No. Too often? Absolutely.

References

The Aga Khan. (1996, October 17). Speech at the Commonwealth Press Union Conference in Cape Town, South Africa. Retrieved from http://www.akdn.org/Content/979/Commonwealth-Press-Union-Conference-in-Cape-Town-South-Africa

Cottle, S. (Ed.). (2000). *Ethnic minorities and the media: Changing cultural boundaries.* Buckingham, UK: Open University Press.

Findlay, S., & Köhler, N. (2010, November 10). The enrollment controversy. *Maclean's.* Retrieved from http://www2.macleans.ca/2010/11/10/too-asian/

Henry, F., & Tator, C. (Eds.). (2002). *Discourses of domination: Racial bias in the Canadian English-language press.* Toronto: University of Toronto Press.

Hier, S., & Greenberg, J. (2002). News discourse and the problematization of Chinese migration to Canada. In F. Henry & C. Tator (Eds.), *Discourses of domination: Racial bias in the Canadian English-language press* (pp. 138–162). Toronto: University of Toronto Press.

Jiwani, Y. (2009). Symbolic and discursive violence in media representations of Aboriginal missing and murdered women. In D. Weir & M. Guggisberg (Eds.), *Violence in hostile contexts e-book.* Oxford: Inter-Disciplinary Press. Retrieved from http://www.inter-disciplinary.net/ptb/hhv/vcce/vch7/Jiwani%20paper.pdf

Karim, K. H. (2000). *The Islamic peril: Media and global violence.* Montreal: Black Rose Books.

LongmanSteyn, M. (2006, April 28). Celebrate tolerance, or you're dead—Oriana Fallaci appeals to Europe to save itself. Good luck. *Maclean's.* Retrieved from http://www.macleans.ca/culture/books/article.jsp?content=20060501_125827_125827

Miles, R., & Brown, M. (2003). *Racism* (2nd ed.). London and New York: Routledge.

Shoemaker, P., & Reese, S. (1996). *Mediating the message: Theories of influence on mass media content* (2nd ed.). White Plains, NY.

Steyn, M. (2006, October 20). The future belongs to Islam. *Maclean's.* Retrievedfrom http://www.macleans.ca/culture/entertainment/article.jsp?content=20061023_134898_134898

Teotonio, I. (2009, September 4). The making of a homegrown terrorist. *Toronto Star,* p. A1.

Van Dijk, T. A. (1996). Discourse, power and access. In C. R. Caldas-Coulthard & M. Coulthard (Eds.), *Texts and practices: Readings in critical discourse analysis* (pp. 84–104). London and New York: Routledge.

Walton, D., & Kennedy, P. (2002, September 7). Muslims feel forced to explain their faith. *The Globe and Mail,* p. A11.

ISSUE 4

Representing race:
Are Canadian news media racist?

✗ NO

Racism, Media, and Analytical Balance
Sean P. Hier and Daniel Lett

Sean P. Hier is associate professor and chair of sociology at the University of Victoria. His areas of research interest and expertise are race and ethnicity, surveillance, moralization, and media studies. His recent books include *Moral Panic and the Politics of Anxiety* (2011) and *Panoptic Dreams: Streetscape Video Surveillance in Canada* (2010).

Daniel Lett is a Ph.D. candidate in sociology at the University of Victoria. His areas of research interest and expertise are surveillance, cultural studies, racism, and criminology. He is co-editor of *Racism and Justice: Dialogue on the Politics of Identity, Inequality and Change* (2009).

In their critique of racial bias in the Canadian English-language press, Frances Henry and Carol Tator (2002) provide six case studies to explain how journalists (re)produce "discursive spaces" (p. 6) that contribute to the denigration and marginalization of people of colour, First Nations communities, and other minorities. They argue that white Canadian journalists and editors unconsciously reproduce and transmit "discourses of domination" that pass as everyday, commonsense truths about the social world. They also argue that white journalists and editors reaffirm and propagate racist ideologies that legitimize and reinforce patterns of social inequality in the country (Henry & Tator, 2006). For Henry and Tator, it is not necessarily that individual journalists and editors are racists, but rather that news production and journalistic activity take place in a cultural-ideological system that normalizes and naturalizes Euro-Canadian beliefs, values, and ways of life.

Henry and Tator's argument about racism, ideology, and the cultural production of meaning is representative of studies concerned with racism and media generally (see, for example, Mahtani, 2001, pp. 99–109; Mahtani, 2009). The general point that Henry and Tator make is an important one, namely, that the production of media discourse takes place in a wider cultural-ideological system of meaning (see also Henry, Tator, & Mattis, 1997). Their case studies effectively debunk the notion of journalism as a neutral or objective practice that is free of cultural biases and stereotypical imagery. Their argument about the cultural production of media discourse is also important because it reminds us of the dangers of relying on actual media content (what appears on the evening television news, for example) or on specific media outlets (such as mainstream newspapers) to understand the complexity of relations involved in systems of cultural representation.

Henry and Tator offer important case study findings that contribute to our understanding of media and racism. However, as we argue below, the relationship between media and racism requires more analytical attention than their analyses permit. Researchers who examine racism and media in Canada commonly argue that analyzing and understanding what appears in media coverage is insufficient for gaining a complete understanding of media representations of diversity. What is additionally required to fully understand the relationship between racism and media is analysis of what does *not* appear in media coverage. In identifying this problem, studies tend to foreground one of three mutually reinforcing arguments: first, slanted or stereotypical representations in media coverage narrowly represent the complexity of ethno-racial minority achievements, thereby presenting a distorted view (misrepresentation); second, an insufficient amount of coverage highlighting the positive achievements of ethno-racial minorities inhibits complete appreciation of difference in the country (underrepresentation); and third, significant ethno-racial minority achievements are not addressed in media coverage at all (silence). These three foregrounded arguments are commonly situated in the context of a fourth "foundational" argument about Euro-Canadian cultural hegemony. What this means is that foregrounded arguments about misrepresentation, underrepresentation, and silence are supported by the taken-for-granted argument that Canadian society is fundamentally racist. The latter argument is used to provide rhetorical credibility for the foregrounded arguments—that is, claims about Canadian culture and institutional life that are asserted rather than demonstrated (Alford, 1999).

Addressing interrelated patterns of misrepresentation, underrepresentation, and silence is crucial for gaining a complete understanding of the cultural production of knowledge generally, and the relationship between racism and media particularly. The same kinds of arguments, however, can also be applied to scholars who study racism and media. Regardless of the good intentions motivating research, racism and media studies misrepresent the diversity of coverage in the mainstream media available in Canada, underrepresent the diversity of media outlets, and remain silent on important patterns of coverage in mainstream and other media pertaining to equity, social justice, and human rights.[1] They also fail to address (or simply ignore) important changes taking place in Canadian culture over the past three decades. By reproducing patterns of misrepresentation, underrepresentation, and silence, and by ignoring changes to Canadian cultural life, analysts fail to assess the potential influence that media have on patterns of ethno-racial harmony, acceptance, and incorporation in the country.

In examining the first foregrounded pattern of misrepresentation in the mainstream media, analysts commonly use case studies to generalize about the nature of racism in the media specifically, and about racism in the country generally. Case studies take one of two forms: they either involve investigations of particular events (e.g., news coverage of editorial diversity during times of war), or they focus on certain groups (e.g., representations of black men in the mainstream press or the scripting of visible minority characters on television). Studying media representations in this manner, analysts select media coverage over certain periods of time or select coverage pertaining to certain events, thereby ignoring other periods of time and other events.

Given that almost all analysts have a self-avowed commitment to exposing racism in all its forms and manifestations, they tend to seek out explicit examples of stereotypical, sensational, and spectacular media coverage (after all, they often get their information from mainstream media). Studies of this nature are important because they help us to understand how ethno-racial signifiers can be invoked to produce negative or stereotypical portrayals of groups of human beings (e.g., post-9/11 representations of Arabs), but they cannot be presented independently of positive coverage on anti-racism, anti-oppression, and social justice. Why, for example, is there almost no research on Canadian news coverage of anti-racism or reparation/redress politics? Has there been no mainstream media coverage that contributes to ethno-racial harmony and acceptance in Canada? What about the increasing presence of visible minority characters occupying influential social positions on prime-time television shows (e.g., as lawyers, doctors, and news anchors)? Or changes in ethno-racial diversity in women's magazines? Is it empirically and analytically sound to draw from a limited number of studies in the 1980s and 1990s to generalize about misrepresentation in mainstream magazines in 2012? And consider the growing number of popular films that deal with cultural and generational complexity (e.g., *Bollywood/Hollywood, Bend It Like Beckham*) and explicit racism (e.g., *Higher Learning, American History X, Crash*), or those that portray same-sex interracial couples in a positive light (e.g., *The Family Stone*). Do the positive social messages transmitted in these films fail to resonate with "white" Canadian viewers? Do we have sufficient data to even know? We are not suggesting that analysts' misrepresentation of racialized discourses in the mainstream media is insidious, underhanded, or even lazy. The point, rather, is that we require a greater amount of empirical data before we can definitively conclude that Canadian media misrepresent minorities and reinforce white Euro-Canadian hegemony.

Related to patterns of mainstream media misrepresentation is the underrepresentation of the diversity of Canadian and, necessarily, international media outlets. It is understandable that analysts take a special interest in media discourse appearing in mainstream media outlets, but it is difficult to find current investigations that include media other than mainstream newspapers and television (the latter is less common than the former). Considering the proliferation of new digital media over the last ten years, this is indeed a curious oversight. Newer media, such as Facebook, Twitter, and other social networking sites, have a profound influence on the ways that people make sense of, communicate, and live in the world, and any comprehensive understanding of racism and anti-racism must attend to the significance of these technologies.

While a few studies investigate organized racism on the Internet (see Hier, 2000, for an examination of Canadian racist groups), there has been no systematic attempt to understand the diversity of representations about race that are transmitted through other digital media (e.g., blogs, chat rooms, tweets, message boards, online communities). Additionally, analyses of ethnic press or non-English-, non-French-language newspapers are rare (see, however, Bright et al., 1999); studies of the significance of racism in music have focused primarily on hate rock (see Futrell, Simi, & Gottschalk, 2006), showing little interest in anti-racist messages in popular music and their effects on values and beliefs; and analyses of the significance of changing representations in comics, local street papers (e.g., Vancouver's *Georgia Straight*), billboards, street advertisements, flyers, micro media (e.g., buttons and stickers), email distribution lists, independent/alternative media, and popular books are almost nonexistent. Again, our point is not to qualify the significance of studies that demonstrate underrepresentation of ethno-racial diversity in mainstream Canadian and international media. Our point, rather, is that studies of racism and media underrepresent the diversity of media outlets, and thereby misrepresent media coverage on diversity.

The third pattern that is reproduced in racism and media studies is silence. Silence can take many forms, including failure to analyze the significance of minority media profiles or experiences and the impact of anti-racist education in the niche or micro media. Given that analysts usually set out to examine racism in mainstream media coverage, it is not surprising that they remain silent on anti-racism and social justice discourses in **alternative media**. To illustrate the diversity of media discourse that has been hitherto ignored by analysts, we will offer three examples drawn from the mainstream press, educational documentaries, and the Internet. While we do not argue that these three examples buttress claims that Canadian and international media transmit racist images and information, they do complicate generalizing claims about the Canadian and international media as unequivocally racist.

The first example concerns two stories drawn from *The Globe and Mail*. In the wake of the devastation left in New Orleans after Hurricane Katrina hit the United States in August 2005, claims of Katrina's unequal "racial toll" proliferated in the international press. Despite evidence revealed later that year that age rather than race was the biggest factor in the deaths associated with the catastrophe (Sharkey, 2007)—of the 623 bodies identified by December, 293 were black, 262 were white, and two-thirds were over age sixty—the front-page headline of *The Globe and Mail*'s Saturday, September 3, 2005, edition read: "Katrina's Unequal Toll: Disaster Bares Divisions of Race and Class Across the Gulf States." In the ensuing story (surrounding a half-page photograph of a crowd of African Americans appearing frustrated and tired), *Globe* columnist Christie Blatchford (2005) argues that race and class intersected in New Orleans to produce a racially stratified society that was reflected in the unequal toll of natural disaster. It is not our purpose to dispute Blatchford's claims, but rather to reflect on the significance of one of Canada's major newspapers running a front-page story of this nature. Is it fair to assume that this is an example of Euro-Canadian racism? Can we simply infer that it is a "discourse of domination" (Henry & Tator, 2002)? Is covert "othering" at work? And is it fair to assume that the majority of (white) Canadian readers of this Saturday edition believed that black Americans deserve to suffer in this way? Or is this instead an example of a mainstream Canadian newspaper openly addressing an important social issue in our world? Is it possible that news coverage of this kind could motivate Canadians of all backgrounds to consider the relationship between race and class? And is it beyond the pale of imagination that thousands of white Canadians endorsed Blatchford's discourse? We do not wish to minimize the significance of race and representation in the press, but this story is not an isolated example of explicit engagement with debates about social inequality and race in the Canadian press.

The second example of silence on anti-racism discourse concerns the ways in which analysts ignore the diverse editorial stances adopted *among* mainstream media. Consider the response of several Canadian newspapers to *Canada's Colour Coded Labour Market* (Block & Galabuzi, 2011), a study released by the Canadian Centre for Policy Alternatives (CCPA) and the Wellesley Institute in 2011. The principal findings of this study—comprising a secondary analysis of Statistics Canada 2006 census data—are that "racialized Canadians continue to face differential labour market experiences, which include higher levels of unemployment and lower employment earnings … racialized groups face a labour market in which racially defined outcomes persist" (Block & Galabuzi, 2011, p. 17). Yet far from ignoring (i.e., remaining silent on) the report, many mainstream Canadian newspapers approached the study with concern and alarm. Headlines declared, "Skin Colour Matters in Access to Good Jobs" (Keung, 2011b, *Toronto Star*); "Discrimination to Blame for Prosperity Gap: Study" (Abma, 2011, *The Montreal Gazette*); "Colour Code Keeps Canadian Workforce Inequitable" (QMI Agency, 2011, *The Toronto Sun*); "Oh, Canada: Diverse but Not Inclusive" (Myrie, 2011, *The Hamilton Spectator*). Readers of Keung's *Toronto Star* article responded with 132 online comments, including those by self-identified minorities and whites who recounted personal experiences of discrimination, expressions of dismay at the findings, and also fierce rebuttals. What these headlines and exchanges suggest is that Canadian print media might be far more engaged with racism and equity debates than analysts are (or have been) willing to acknowledge.

Not only are mainstream Canadian news media attentive to exclusionary practices, but they also consistently highlight the negative aspects of stories that might otherwise have been made to fit with a discourse of denial about the persistence of racism in Canada. One example is the coverage afforded to the British Council and Migration Policy Group's 2011 report on the state of thirty-one countries' immigrant integration policies (Huddleston, Niessen, Chaoimh, & White, 2011). The *Migrant Integration Policy Index* (MIPEX) report claims that Canada's integration policies compare favourably with those of the United States and the European countries that make up the sample, ranking third best overall. While the Canadian mainstream media duly reported the positive news, editorials broadly focused on Canada's remaining shortcomings. *The Globe and Mail* (Friesen, 2011) devoted over half of an article covering the report to critical assessment of Canada's record on political integration, visa restrictions, and inadequate integration advisory boards. Similar critiques appear in the *Toronto Star* (Keung, 2011a) and *The Montreal Gazette* (Chai, 2011), and the CBC phrased the headline of their mixed report in the form of a question: "Immigration: Does Canada Do a Good Job of Integrating Newcomers?" (Community Team, 2011). These examples of diverse coverage do not foreclose on the possibility that mainstream coverage is informed by conscious or unconscious racism. However, neither do they support the thesis that a racist ideology shapes mainstream media reporting.

The third example of silence on anti-racism discourse in Canadian media pertains to educational documentary films produced and funded by the National Film Board (NFB). Over the past twenty-five years, the NFB has produced a number of films dealing with Aboriginal inequality, racism, immigration, and the enduring legacy of hardship. In films including, but not limited to, *Sisters in the Struggle, Speak It! From the Heart of Black Nova Scotia, The Road Taken, Moving the Mountain, In the Shadow of Gold Mountain*, and *The War Between Us*, the NFB critiques racism in Canada's past and present. Despite the significant impact these films could have on students and their knowledge of Canada's history with racism, there is not a single study of the influence of these or related films on public attitudes and beliefs. Indeed, these titles are used in university courses on racism and anti-racism in Canada. The films never fail to lead students to evoke strong emotional reactions and interest in anti-racism and social justice—among white students and students of colour alike. If nothing else, these experiences suggest that the ideological effects of the films are profoundly anti-racist and inspirational.

In addition to the three examples showing how analysts remain silent on the diversity of media coverage in Canada, there is also evidence of the growing political power wielded by those who produce and engage with online alternative media. Consider the role of online media in drawing attention to an ongoing humanitarian crisis at the Attawapiskat reserve in Northern Ontario—a community whose housing and sanitation infrastructure has degraded to hazardous standards over recent years. NDP MP Charlie Angus vociferously articulated what he perceived as government indifference to the suffering of First Nations people of the Attawapiskat reserve through Twitter, Facebook, and a widely shared and cited *Huffington Post* article (Angus, 2011). Angus credits the subsequent "digital storm"—his blog post was shared over 60 000 times via Facebook in just three days—with prompting an immediate humanitarian intervention by Red Cross Canada, pressuring the Aboriginal Affairs department to visit and assess the community, and sparking an "international outcry" backed with donations of thousands of dollars from Europe and the United States (Nurwisah, 2011). While one might expect such a mobilization of support to follow the declaration of emergency by a Canadian community, it is noteworthy that the chief of the Attawapiskat reserve, Theresa Spence, had also declared a state of emergency in 2009 and 2010, with little effect (Lindell, 2011). A key difference in 2011 appears to be the critical attention that originated in and disseminated through the use of digital media.

The three main patterns of misrepresentation, underrepresentation, and silence highlighted above find support in a fourth, mutually reinforcing background argument that the extent of racism in Canada is not as pervasive as many analysts suggest. We are not arguing here that racism does not exist in Canadian society; however, it behooves a serious analyst to note that there have been important changes in Canada, particularly in the past three decades, which partially explain the growing complexity of media coverage today. While Canadian history is fraught with explicit forms of institutional racism, demographic changes since 1970 have profoundly influenced Canadian culture, as well as Canadian political and social institutions. Although racism persists in Canadian institutions and in everyday life, there have been significant changes to levels of institutional participation among and within Canada's diverse ethnic, racial, cultural, and religious populations. These progressive, albeit uneven, changes can be observed in institutional domains, including immigration practices, educational attainment rates, labour market participation, and patterns of civic-democratic participation. Advances in educational attainment rates, labour market returns, and occupational distribution for Canadian-born members of visible minority groups, in particular, have been comparable if not in excess of those of Canadians of Western European ancestry. It is important to realize, too, that the changes taking place in Canada are not simply outcomes of interrelated social-structural transformations underway since the 1960s; they are, importantly, also catalysts for interrelated changes that continue to transform the country (see Hier & Bolaria, 2006; Hier, Lett, & Bolaria, 2009; Hier & Walby, 2006). In fact, scholarly interest has recently come to focus on the emergence of "Canadian" as an ethno-racial identity among English-speaking, non-Aboriginal Canadians (Howard-Hassmann, 1999). While many researchers offer important studies laying claim to institutional or systemic forms of racism in Canada, a significant body of evidence also contests the extent to which the social categories of race and ethnicity function as *categorical determinants* for the inequitable distribution of services and resources in the country (Hier, 2007).The four mutually reinforcing patterns in studies of racism and media that have been highlighted above are not presented with the intention of dismissing arguments that media misrepresent, underrepresent, and remain silent on issues of significance to ethno-racial minority groups in Canada and elsewhere. They are presented, rather, with the intention to open debate about the diversity of media representation in Canada, and to contest claims that the media (as an institution comprising many different organizations) in Canada are racist. That analysts persist in misrepresenting the diversity of coverage in the mainstream media, underrepresenting the diversity of media outlets, and remaining silent on the diversity of anti-racism and social justice media discourses probably says more about the structure of the production of academic knowledge about race and racism than it does about the empirical world (see Mahtani's [2009] assessment and Hier's [2010] response). Of course, this argument may provoke those who believe that the media are unequivocally racist. Our purpose here is not to undermine or debunk the research of these analysts, but to encourage them to strive for greater analytical balance and more proportional representation of media coverage in Canada.

To conclude, students interested in seeking greater analytical balance in their research on media and racism will want to ensure that they adhere to principles of sound research design where matters of sampling and generalization are concerned. To put this differently, it is incumbent on researchers to formulate hypotheses, design empirically rigorous research strategies, and minimize bias or preconceived assumptions about how things "really are." As we argue above, one way to do so is to begin to balance media reporting on racism and anti-racism, analyze a variety of media outlets, and avoid the pervasive tendency to remain silent on progressive media activity in the area of racism and social change. Concomitantly, analytical balance also involves taking seriously progressive social changes in Canadian society and avoiding polemical argumentation that frames the question of racism and the media in either-or terms: racism is either there or it is not. By striving for analytical balance, it is conceivable and entirely possible that we will conclude that media coverage of racism and anti-racism is much more complicated than the existing literature suggests.

Note

[1] We define mainstream media as newspapers, radio, television, and Internet sites, predominantly owned by corporations or governments, which produce content and widely disseminate it for a general audience.

References

Abma, D. (2011, March 21). Discrimination to blame for prosperity gap: study. *The Montreal Gazette.* Retrieved from http://www.montrealgazette.com/business/Discrimination+blame+prosperity+study/4476030/story.html

Alford, R. (1999). *The craft of inquiry.* Oxford, UK: Oxford University Press.

Angus, C. (2011, November 21). What if they declared an emergency and no one came? *The Huffington Post Canada.* Retrieved from http://www.huffingtonpost.ca/charlie-angus/attawapiskat-emergency_b_1104370.html#undefined

Blatchford, C. (2005, September 3). Katrina's unequal toll: Disaster bares divisions of race and class across the Gulf States. *The Globe and Mail,* p. A1.

Block, S., & Galabuzi, G.-E. (2011). *Canada's colour coded labour market: The gap for racialized workers.* Retrieved from http://www.policyalternatives.ca/publications/reports/canadas-colour-coded-labour-market.

Bright, R., Coburn, E., Faye, J., Gafijczuk, D., Hollander, K., Jung, J., & Srymbos, H. (1999). Mainstream and marginal newspaper coverage of the 1995 Quebec referendum: An inquiry into the functioning of the Canadian public sphere. *Canadian Review of Sociology and Anthropology, 36*(3), 313–330.

Chai, C. (2011, March 1). Canada welcoming to newcomers, but wait list a "major weakness". *The Montreal Gazette,* p. A13.

Community Team. (2011, February 28). Immigration: Does Canada do a good job of welcoming newcomers? *CBC News.* Retrieved from http://www.cbc.ca/news/yourcommunity/2011/02/immigration-does-canada-do-a-good-job-of-integrating-newcomers.html

Friesen, J. (2011, February 28). Canada near top in integrating immigrants, survey says. *The Globe and Mail.* Retrieved from http://www.theglobeandmail.com/news/national/canada-near-top-in-integrating-immigrants-survey-says/article1923091/

Futrell, R., Simi, P., & Gottschalk, S. (2006). Understanding music in movements: The white power music scene. *Sociological Quarterly, 47*(2), 275–304.

Henry, F., & Tator, C. (2002). *Discourses of domination: Racial bias in the Canadian English language press.* Toronto: University of Toronto Press.

Henry, F., & Tator, C. (2006). *The colour of democracy.* Toronto: Harcourt Brace.

Henry, F., Tator, C., & Mattis, W. (1997). *Challenging racism in the arts.* Toronto: University of Toronto Press.

Hier, S. (2007). Researching race and racism in 21st century Canada. In S. Hier & S. Bolaria (Eds.), *Race and racism in 21st century Canada: Continuity, complexity, and change* (pp. 19–33). Peterborough, ON: Broadview Press.

Hier, S., & Bolaria, S. (2006). *Identity and belonging: Rethinking race and ethnicity in Canadian society.* Toronto: Canadian Scholars' Press.

Hier, S., Lett, D., & Bolaria, S. (Eds.). (2009). *Racism and justice: Critical dialogue on the politics of identity, inequality and change.* Halifax, NS: Fernwood Press.

Hier, S., & Walby, K. (2006). Competing analytical paradigms in the sociological study of racism in Canada. *Canadian Ethnic Studies, 26*(1), 83–104.

Hier, S. P. (2000). The contemporary structure of Canadian racial supremacism: Networks, strategies, and new technologies. *Canadian Journal of Sociology, 25*(4), 471–493.

Hier, S. P. (2010). Beyond vernacular commentary: A response to Minelle Mahtani. *Canadian Journal of Communication, 35*, 173–178.

Howard-Hassman, R. (1999). "Canadian" as an ethnic category. *Canadian Public Policy, 25*(4), 523–537.

Huddleston, T., Niessen, J., Chaoimh, E. N., & White, E. (2011). *Migrant Integration Policy Index III.* British Council/Migration Policy Group. Retrieved from http://www.mipex.eu/sites/default/files/downloads/migrant_integration_policy_index_mipexiii_2011.pdf

Keung, N. (2011a, February 28). Canada ranked third in integrating newcomers. *Toronto Star.* Retrieved from http://www.thestar.com/news/canada/article/945735--canada-ranked-3rd-in-integrating-newcomers?bn=1.

Keung, N. (2011b, March 21). Skin colour matters in access to good jobs. *Toronto Star.* Retrieved from http://www.thestar.com/news/investigations/immigration/article/957009--skin-colour-matters-in-access-to-good-jobs-study

Lindell, R. (2011, November 29). Putting Attawapiskat on the map. *Global News.* Retrieved from www.globalnews.ca/timeline/6442531868/story.html

Mahtani, M. (2001). Representing minorities: Canadian media and minority identities. *Canadian Ethnic Studies, 33*(3), 99–133.

Mahtani, M. (2009). Report: Critiquing the critiques about media and minority research in Canada. *Canadian Journal of Communication, 24*, 715–719.

Myrie, E. (2011, March 23). Oh, Canada: Diverse but not inclusive. *The Hamilton Spectator.* Retrieved from http://www.thespec.com/opinion/editorial/article/505924--oh-canada-diverse-but-not-inclusive

Nurwisah, R. (2011, November 24). Pressure grows on governments to help Attawapiskat reserve. *The Huffington Post Canada.* Retrieved from http://www.huffingtonpost.ca/2011/11/24/attawapiskat-reserve-housing-funding_n_1112145.html#undefined

QMI Agency. (2011, March 21). "Colour code" keeps Canadian workforce inequitable. *The Toronto Sun.* Retrieved from http://www.torontosun.com/news/canada/2011/03/21/17699986.html

Sharkey, P. (2007). Survival and death in New Orleans: An empirical look at the human impact of Katrina. *Journal of Black Studies, 37*, 482.

Discussion Questions

1. On the basis of the arguments and evidence presented in these chapters, can we reach a definitive conclusion that Canadian media are racist? Explain how you have been persuaded to take your position.

2. How can the existing literature on racism and Canadian media be understood as a place to *begin* social analyses and not as a place to *end* them?

3. What does Hier mean when he calls for analytical balance to the study of racism and the media? How would an analytically balanced approach change how we understand the role of the media in sustaining or challenging racism in Canadian society?

4. Why is it important to examine the discursive dimensions of ideology in the media?

5. Apply critical discourse analysis (CDA) by examining another newspaper column. What explicit and implicit coded messages did you find in this column? What challenges and opportunities arose from employing this method to analyze the text?

PART 3 Technology and Everyday Life

ISSUE 1 The promise and problems of mobility: Power, agency, and cell phones

ISSUE 2 Activism or slacktivism: Can social media drive political change?

ISSUE 3 Sexting: Should teens have the right to sext?

ISSUE 4 We are Big Brother: Is social media surveillance a threat to our sense of community?

Henry Ford II, grandson to the eminent American industrialist, famously stated that "the technological triumphs of the past few years have not solved as many problems as we thought they would, and, in fact, have brought us new problems we did not foresee." Ford, writing in the post–World War II era during his tenure at the helm of his family's automotive empire, was speaking about the negative environmental effects of industrialization. Ford's remarks suggest that technology can be a double-edged sword: while offering what are seemingly unlimited conveniences that promise to make our lives easier, technology also produces negative and sometimes unanticipated consequences that may create problems in social relations and actually make our lives more difficult.

This section offers competing arguments about some of the key communication technology issues and events of our time. The first debate pertains to the liberating and potentially dangerous implications of mobile phones. Unlike every other topic in this book, in which competing perspectives are written by different authors, this debate features competing arguments presented by the same author. Richard Smith explores some of the key questions that define the study of mobile phones from the perspective of communication studies:

Is their increased use beneficial or detrimental to society? Are they positively or negatively affecting social relations? Are we becoming more liberated or losing our freedom in personal matters? Smith does not advocate in favour of one view over another, but instead provides readers with a framework for exploring how the ever-presence of mobile phones can both increase domination and control of everyday social life by technology while providing new opportunities for human agency and creativity. Ultimately, for Smith, the impacts of communication technology aren't simple and "should never be reduced to one thing." For students in communication, the objective ought to be to understand how technology is both enabling and constraining and to look for ways of minimizing the control technology exercises over our lives while maximizing its creative potential.

The popular uprisings that took hold in North Africa and across parts of the Middle East in what has become known as the Arab Spring touched off a heated debate in the media, among politicians, and within academia about the influence of social media on politics and its impact on social change. For some, the latest digital technologies associated with social media are "game changing" because they are seen to significantly reduce the opportunity and mobilization costs of activism and social organization. For others, social and political change comes only from deep moral and ethical commitments by activists to improve the world around them. For these writers, Facebook, Twitter, email, and text messaging may assist in political organizing, but these technologies do not drive change on their own. Moreover, to the extent that social media may enable more democratic politics, they can also assist oppressive regimes by enhancing their capacity to monitor and police dissent.

The second debate features two essays that engage these issues. Patrick McCurdy argues that digital media provide activists with valuable resources to assist in the planning, coordination, and enactment of social change. Yet, he also argues that to determine whether these technologies can actually "drive" social change we need to be sensitive to a variety of contextual (economic, political, and cultural) factors. His essay provides a conceptual framework to help students define social media, and he challenges the argument made popular by writers such as Malcolm Gladwell that one of the damaging effects of new technology is that it has given rise to a generation of lazy activists, or "slacktivists," who only exercise political agency with the click of a mouse. According to McCurdy, while we shouldn't blindly celebrate the emancipatory potential of social media, "dismissing [their] potential … to act as a catalyst for social change would be a terrible mistake."

Eileen Saunders presents a complementary if contrasting argument. In agreement with McCurdy, she doesn't discount the potential of social media to inspire and facilitate social and political activism. However, she argues that it is important for communication scholars to "temper our enthusiasm" by focusing on the empirical record and recognizing the significant limitations these technologies present. For example, proponents of digital activism herald the ease with which new media can assist in the quick mobilization and organization of social movements. Yet this comes with an important downside. Citing the long-time civil rights activist Angela Davis, Saunders cautions that with ease of mobilization comes a difficulty in getting people to "think about protracted struggles,

protracted movements that require very careful organizing." Ultimately, Saunders strikes a skeptical tone, arguing that despite our hope and faith in the emancipatory potential of technology, there simply is too little research or empirical evidence to support the argument that social media can be a driver of social change.

In April 2012, *The Telegraph* in Britain published a story describing a new public health epidemic for youth. The paper was reporting the case of a teen girl who committed suicide after nude photos she had sent to a boy were posted on Facebook, triggering a wave of online bullying by schoolmates. "Sexting" involves the sending of sexually provocative images, messages, or video clips with a mobile phone or via an Internet site. For many adults, it's seen as yet another example of how lackadaisical youth are with their sexuality and sense of privacy, and it has even given rise to calls for harsh punishment, including charging people who sext with possession and distribution of child pornography, or for remedial education, such as requiring youth who sext to enter abstinence programs to correct bad behaviour. But for many teens, sexting is nothing more than harmless fun, a way of playing with and expressing sexuality identity. Whichever way you look at it, sexting has emerged as a controversial moral and cultural issue. And given the centrality of digital technology in the debate about sexting, it's an issue of importance to communication studies.

The third debate focuses on the issue of sexting and presents competing arguments about how dangerous it may be to youth and whether teens should have the right to sext. Amy Hasinoff argues that teens should have the right to sext provided they are able to give consent and that appropriate laws are in place to protect and punish those who violate the privacy of others. Her chapter provides a valuable primer on the legal status of sexting, examining why consent is crucial to understanding the discourse about the alleged dangers of sexting, and offers practical and progressive ways of dealing with sexting when it becomes associated with abusive behaviour. "While further legal reforms are needed to protect online privacy," Hasinoff argues, "allowing teens the right to sext is the first step in clarifying that people who receive these images have no right to distribute them further without permission."

Nora Draper offers a slightly different perspective. Her chapter helps to historicize sexting by locating it in a deeper context which explains that access to digital media has not changed the way teens actually explore their sexuality, or how they seek to document and share their sexual experiences with friends. Yet, at the same time, Draper argues that digital media changes how much control individuals have over the images they create (sexually explicit or otherwise) and that these changes are significant to the debate about sexting. One of the dangers posed by new technologies is that they "increase the risk of loss of control over personal and sensitive content" by providing a "false sense of security." For teens, as for individuals of any age group, sexting increases the risk of compromising one's personal reputation and makes youth more vulnerable to abusive behaviour from others.

The final debate in this section explores social media from the perspective of online surveillance and community building. Christopher Parsons argues that while we regularly receive warnings about how our social media activity might be tracked and monitored by employers or police, a more sinister form of online surveillance exists in the monitoring that occurs between citizens. Social media sites, he argues, are not only unregulated spaces where surveillance, harassment, and denigration of individual rights are encouraged, but they are also designed in a way to limit the legal liability of their architects. Beyond the issues of law and liability, Parsons explores how social media sites can give rise to a mob mentality that poses a threat to civility and social order. Citing the case of the 2011 Vancouver riots, he describes how in the search for perpetrators of violence and disorder online vigilantes turned to Facebook, Flickr, and other social media sites to name and shame alleged rioters, and in some cases individuals faced threats of violent retribution and abuse. Parsons reminds us that our justice system is not built on the principle of mob rule but rather on due legal process that demands guilt be demonstrated in a court of law, and not in the court of social media opinion.

Kate Milberry takes a different approach in her case study of the Toronto G20 protest. Milberry describes the myriad of ways that community organizers used social media and other new media platforms during the lead up to the Group of 20 (G20) summit in Toronto in 2010. From using email and text messaging to social networking sites like Facebook and Twitter, activists engaged in what she calls "open source organizing," not only to share critical information and to organize meetings and events that would increase participation and involvement of people concerned about the economic agenda of the G20, but also to give rise to a sense of shared purpose and collective identity. Milberry shows how activists used a range of digital technologies to report police brutality and how in the aftermath of the summit, activists continued to use social media to develop community cohesion by supporting those who were arrested and facing prosecution. She argues that while the Toronto G20 was a massive experiment in reshaping the global political economy (for the worse), it was also "an experiment in community [building], fuelled by social media." And like other contributions in this section, she shows that although technology does not define social movements, it does provide activists with an important tool to support their ongoing goals of building community and sparking progressive social change.

ISSUE 1

The promise and problems of mobility: Power, agency, and cell phones

✔ Yes and ✘ No

The "Danger" of Cellphones: Power and Agency
Richard Smith

Richard Smith is a professor in the School of Communication at Simon Fraser University and director of the Centre for Digital Media in Vancouver. His research focus is social inclusion (and exclusion) brought on by the introduction of new media. He has an ongoing interest in technology for education, privacy, and surveillance in public spaces, online communities, and the wireless information society. He is the publisher of the *Canadian Journal of Communication* and is co-author of *Mobile and Wireless Communications* (2006, with Gordon Gow) and *New Media: An Introduction* (2011, with Terry Flew).

Canadians were pioneers in the development of mobile phones. An Alberta company, NovAtel, launched a private cellular service for the oil industry in 1982, a year before Motorola and Ameritech launched the first commercial cellular service, in Chicago, with the famous "brick" phone, the DynaTAC.[1] Another Canadian company, Northern Telecom (later Nortel), did some of the early work on digital mobile phones, and when the company was dissolved recently, Apple and others bid $4.5 billion for those patents (Foresman, 2011).

Despite this history of innovation, Canadians were not initially heavy users of mobile phones. Service was spotty and expensive, and innovations such as the iPhone and the 3G network were late coming to this country (Pedersen, 2008). Now, however, Canada is catching up to other countries in its mobile phone use, and a similar pattern, in which smart phones (those with access to the Internet, apps, and rich media capabilities) displace regular mobile and home phones, is under way (Canadian Wireless Telecommunications Association, n.d.).

Now that mobile phone use is no longer a novelty, some folks are wary of their impact. With the growing use of mobile phones have come complaints that the devices are being misused or are detrimental to society. But are they? Is this new media form hurting our social relations? Are we losing our freedom, our grace in personal matters?

PART ONE: POWER

In an introductory essay to a book about two centuries' worth of "new media," authors Lisa Gitelman and Goeffrey Pingree (2003) argue persuasively that when we consider a new media technology, the question we should ask is not what the technology is capable of but how people use it to communicate. The two centuries they cover, by the way, end in 1915.

Wariness of new communication technologies is not new. And, as I'll argue below, concerns about "the impact" of mobile phones are not unfounded. Without making light of those concerns, however, I will suggest that the impact of cellphones might reasonably fall into the category of what Adam Gopnik (2011) has termed the "Ever-Was" effect of information technology:

> All three kinds [of argument about technology] appear among the new books about the Internet: call them the Never-Betters, the Better-Nevers, and the Ever-Wasers. The Never-Betters believe that we're on the brink of a new utopia, where information will be free and democratic, news will be made from the bottom up, love will reign, and cookies will bake themselves. The Better-Nevers think that we would have been better off if the whole thing had never happened, that the world that is coming to an end is superior to the one that is taking its place, and that, at a minimum, books and magazines create private space for minds in ways that twenty-second bursts of information don't. The Ever-Wasers insist that at any moment in modernity something like this is going on, and that a new way of organizing data and connecting users is always thrilling to some and chilling to others—that something like this is going on is exactly what makes it a modern moment. (Gopnik, 2011, p. 4)

More than two decades ago in his book *Under Technology's Thumb* (1990), William Leiss tackled a similar question, but one more broadly focused on information itself. In a recent summary of that work, Leiss argues that

> more information (or a society and economy that is more information-intensive) is not an unambiguous good because the concept of information itself carries some crucial ambiguities. What one ideally seeks out in either "gaining information" or "gaining better access to information," either individually or collectively, is: enlightenment, understanding of complex situations, insight, pertinence, etc.—and, above all, truth. But like anything else that has value, both intrinsic and market value, information is a contested domain in a society that is intensely competitive and also highly unequal (in terms of access to income and resources), and therefore, with respect to distributional equity, grossly unfair. This type of society reacts to better and more accessible information by, in effect, contaminating the source, through ubiquitous "spin," social-interest-based interpretive bias, and simple distortions and lies.[2]

How mobile phones are deployed in our society, the information they convey, the databases they have access to, and even the very networks they run on are all subject to this bias and based in the power relations of our society.

We know that technological change almost always results in winners and losers (Leiss, 1990). Leiss's other early work pointed to the ways humans use technology to dominate nature and each other (Leiss, 1994). As we shall see, the mobile phone can also be used in this way.

So what *are* the social, political, and interpersonal "dangers" of cellphones? Should we be concerned? In many ways the answer to this question can be found in the answer to another, more basic question: What is our appetite for change? Or, more precisely, is change a good thing? If we take Leiss's perspective, we might see in information technology the potential for further domination of our lives.

We can see numerous examples of this domination in the spread of mobile technology in our society. For example, Sam Ladner (2008) has documented the way in which interactive agency workers are "tied" to their jobs after hours by the BlackBerry cord. Work life might have ended at 5 p.m. in the old days, but nowadays a quick call to the mobile by the bedside table can retrieve you to the office or, more likely, impel you to read a text message or answer an email. This extra work, often unpaid, is a concern to many people who talk about the mobile phone as a "tether."

Taking the "Ever-Was" approach, we might argue that these intrusions are not unique to mobile phones, but rather cellphones are the latest in a long line of communication technologies—starting with the telegraph—that have been used to remotely control workers' lives. In fact, the information revolution, of which mobile phones are just the latest iteration, has been called a control revolution (Beniger, 1986) for the way in which it has allowed remote monitoring and direction of work and workers. Importantly, Beniger shows how the control revolution was not initiated by digital devices but in fact traces its roots to the earliest days of industrialization and the need to better manage fast-moving steam-powered production and distribution processes.

Some of the earliest work on computers and networks pointed to their role in providing feedback in what Norbert Wiener (1948) termed a "**cybernetic**" system. The mobile phone, and especially the smart phone with its GPS, compass, accelerometer, and gyroscope, is an extension of this control system into the pockets of workers, wherever they may be. In a very real way the modern worker is wearing a leash or a tether when carrying a mobile phone.

This leash has its family equivalent in the mobile phones that so-called helicopter parents press on their children. So-named because of their tendency to hover, ever-present, in the lives of their children (and their children's teachers), helicopter parents are a phenomenon not unfamiliar to many of today's undergraduate students. Mobile phones—sometimes without the child's permission or awareness—are used to track the location and speed of children borrowing the family car, their presence (and absence) at school, and more.

The modern smart phone is a powerful network-attached computer with a complex sensor array that surpasses almost anything that has come before it. Depending on the circumstances, it can give rise to all three of Gopnik's scenarios (Never-Better, Better-Never, and Ever-Was). To illustrate this, let us imagine a hypothetical smart phone–carrying teenager with a part-time job, a girlfriend in the countryside, access to the family minivan, and cautious (and tech-savvy) parents. We will call him "Steve."

Now let us imagine that Steve's part-time job is in a warehouse filled with valuable goods. A few years ago, in response to numerous employees losing or forgetting their keys, the company opted to install an "access pass" on the back of employees' mobile phones. Let us also imagine that Steve's parents decided to have tracking software installed on his mobile phone when they bought it for him, unbeknownst to Steve.

Now let us further imagine a scenario given this configuration. Steve's job in the warehouse is after school and he uses the family minivan to make the trip. He is under instructions to return directly home after work, as it is "a school night." At work, Steve is distracted. He has had a fight with his girlfriend and finds a quiet place at the back of the warehouse to make a long phone call, trying to get things back on track. Just as things seem to be going well, he is paged to the office. The supervisor has noticed that Steve hasn't moved in over an hour. While installing Steve's access pass the company had recorded the Bluetooth ID of his phone, and their array of sensors throughout the warehouse has reported his lack of movement—and lack of productivity—as an anomaly. Steve is given a warning and sent home early.

Frustrated, Steve decides to head to his girlfriend's house in the country. Still in a daze from the day's events, he takes a wrong turn and slides off the road as it abruptly narrows. A quick query to the artificial intelligent agent on his phone not only reveals his precise location but offers up the name of a local tow truck company. The agent even makes the call for him. A truck is dispatched, and while he is waiting, Steve calls his girlfriend and completes patching things up via a video call from the front seat of the van.

Once the van is out of the ditch, Steve gets back on the road. He realizes that he'll have to push it a bit to get home before his curfew. Things are going well and with a bit of tricky driving he pulls into the driveway just before 11 p.m. Steve slams his hand on the dash. Yes! He's back with the girlfriend, the job incident only resulted in a warning, and his parents will never know about the fast driving and detour. As he walks up the steps, however, the look on his father's face suggests that something is amiss. Steve's father has been tracking his whereabouts since receiving a text message earlier in the evening about a variation in his routine, when he left his job two hours early. Watching on the live web feed for his son, he saw not only the diversion to the countryside and the strange amount of time in what looked like a farmer's field (from Google Maps) but also the erratic and high-speed driving on the way home. Car privileges are about to be suspended.

In this story[3] we see all three of Adam Gopnik's (somewhat sarcastic) characterizations of the world of modern information technology.

Steve's father's spying is a classic case of "Better-Never," in that without such a (spyware-enabled) mobile phone, Steve would never have been caught by his father and had his car privileges suspended.

Steve's quick access to roadside aid and video call relationship mending are both examples of technology that is "Never-Better." Lost and stuck in the mud, he would have likely faced a long walk. Instead, he is out of the ditch and headed home on time.

Steve's workplace monitoring is a great example of "Ever-Was." Employees and employers have had different motivations since the days of the very first job, and the term "surveillance" derives from the activity of watching over employees to make sure they are not shirking their duties. Aside from the Bluetooth sensors making the job a little easier, the boss overseeing Steve is a perfectly standard workplace activity, and the role of technology—reinforcing power relations and implementing a control relationship—is a textbook example of managerial control.

What this story highlights, for me, is that "the impact" of communication technology on society is never simple and should never be reduced to one thing. Even the simplest of technologies have differences in how they are used, who uses them, for what, and in what circumstances. As a programmable, networked device, the smart phone is amenable to all of that variability plus the additional variance that comes from being mutable, depending on the software that is loaded in, the features that are activated, and the capabilities the network has. It is always important, when considering the impact of technology, to see who benefits, and who is harmed and in what circumstances. And, as Leiss tells us, there is systematic bias in our current society such that these configurations often favour the strong over the weak, the current owners in favour of the emerging ones.

While one might decry the waste of time, distraction, and misadventures resulting from teenagers' preoccupation with mobiles, these same young people have used mobile technologies to engage with and try to change their world. The Arab Spring and Occupy Wall Street movements, despite their differences, made extensive use of mobile phones to both coordinate and document the activities of protest and reactions to that protest.[4] Our knowledge of the protest activities in Egypt, Libya, and elsewhere in the region was greatly enhanced by the ability of people on the scene to share their experience instantly via mobile phone networks. The very fact that those networks were from time to time shut down completely by government forces speaks to their importance for political purposes. Similarly, it is highly unlikely that the UC Davis "pepper-spraying cop" Internet meme would have had the salience, broad reach, and resonance that it did without the many on-the-scene videos captured on cellphone cameras. Whether these sorts of interventions have a major impact remains to be seen, but we should think carefully before we dismiss mobile communication devices as mere distractions.

PART TWO: AGENCY

There is another reason not to let the easy critique of mobile devices (e.g., "They are leading to iPod zombies, cellphone boors, and crackberry dropouts!") stand unchallenged. To do so is to deny the active decision making and creativity of the people who buy and use these gadgets. In other words, it denies their **agency**.

In the context of mobile phones, individuals with agency are the ones who imagine uses for the devices beyond anything dreamed up by the designers and sometimes with entirely unanticipated results. User-driven creativity often results in situations and outcomes that the companies that build these gizmos did not predict.

A hue and cry has gone out that mobile phones are not just annoying but are harming our society by pushing the private and the public worlds together in ways that are damaging to public discussion and debate (in other words, they are contributing to the degradation of the public sphere).

These gadgets are supposed to do damage in several ways. One way is that they allow us to retreat into our private sphere when we are in public. This can take the form of zoning out with wireless email on the bus, surfing on a laptop in a café, or just listening to (or watching) your iPod on the street. You are actively partaking of media and messages of your own choosing and, in so doing, neglecting those around you in the immediate physical world.

Another impact of using gadgets to turn inward is the potential narrowing of perspective. By selecting your own news sources, perhaps attending only to a particular set of blogs and podcasts, you can develop a very idiosyncratic view of the world and be unwilling to accept the compromises or accommodations that make democratic politics possible in a diverse and rapidly changing country such as Canada. Some political commentators have pointed to the rise of specialty news sources as a factor in the increase in special interest politics.

The other way gadgets can harm civil society, and the aspect that is more familiar to people these days, is the extent to which they push the private sphere out into the public sphere. This is what we might associate with the annoying person who speaks loudly on the phone or who has his iPod turned up so loud that you can hear the music, too.

And yet, something else is possible with this technology. There are alternative outcomes for mobile technology in public space. The Arab Spring and Occupy Wall Street initiatives are a subset of a wider phenomenon first described in the groundbreaking 2002 book *Smart Mobs*. In that book, technology pundit and commentator Howard Rheingold brought to wider public attention a social and technological phenomenon that was spreading across the globe, namely activism enabled by the mobile phone. In countries ranging from the Philippines to Egypt, we've seen significant political changes brought about or hastened by mass political participation through widespread access to mobile phones and, in particular, text messages.

Rheingold provides several examples in his book, ranging from the anarchic and largely whimsical "flash mobs" to the concerted and impassioned campaigns waged through phone messages to unseat corrupt and despotic governments. The power of these messages is sufficiently potent that the government of Syria recently took the extreme step of shutting down the nation's phone system rather than endure endless activism facilitated through the phone networks.

What these phenomena have in common, however, is the way in which a personal portable communication device—the mobile phone—becomes a catalyst for local, regional, and even national political activism. Text messages typically come from your friends—it is much less common to receive the kind of "spam" that email does—and so they may be more likely to spur the recipient to action. Mobile phones also provide a connection to the global system of communication via the Internet, as when text messages are sent to Twitter, Facebook, and similar services. And, with the ubiquitous cellphone camera that comes with the smart phone, we have not just the words but the images to back up what people are saying. Whatever the reason, the cellphone is now a potent tool in the hands of the activist and a key feature of political campaigns worldwide.

Although the technology is more than twenty years old, the mobile phone is relatively new as a mass phenomenon in Canadian society. As such it is not surprising that there is no shortage of annoying and undesirable actions related to mobile phones. And it isn't surprising that people like to project other larger issues in society onto the new phenomenon in their midst. Rudeness, political apathy, even narrow-mindedness have all be ascribed to mobile phone use.

But that isn't the whole story. Rather, as the examples above illustrate, mobile phones can also be used toward pro-social ends. More importantly, these examples show that in order to chart a different course for mobile technology—or any technology, for that matter—it is necessary to think consciously and proactively. It is also necessary to create the type of use pattern and habits that you think are desirable and not merely accept the default path of least resistance, which is too often the path of commercialization.

Finally, I hope these examples illustrate something very important about the public sphere and civil society. Civility is not a thing that exists in the world apart from people. Rather, it is the ongoing creation of people who care about the world around them. Civility doesn't exist apart from the actions of everyday people in their everyday lives. It is, instead, the creation of activists, citizens, and just common people with uncommon aspirations and actions. That is what agency means in this context, and it is up to us to use our communication technology in a way that enhances our world and doesn't detract from it.

Notes

[1] For more on the history of mobile in Canada, see Langford, Wood, & Ross, n.d.; "Mobile Phone," n.d.; Telus Communications, 2011; and Treviño, Doutriaux, & Mian, 2006.

[2] Personal communication with the author, 2011.

[3] Although the story is fictional, none of the technologies or applications described are made up. They are all available in the market today.

[4] The role of mobile and social technologies in activism was vigorously debated in 2010/2011 following an

essay in *The New Yorker* by Malcolm Gladwell, "Small Change: Why the Revolution Will Not Be Tweeted" (October 4, 2010, available at http://www.newyorker.com/reporting/2010/10/04/101004fa_fact_gladwell). Clay Shirky, a long-time proponent of the power of online and social media, replied to Gladwell's post in the journal *Foreign Affairs*, with an article titled "The Political Power of Social Media" (January/February 2011, available at http://www.foreignaffairs.com/articles/67038/clay-shirky/the-political-power-of-social-media). A later issue of *Foreign Affairs* (March/April 2011, available at http://www.foreignaffairs.com/articles/67325/malcolm-gladwell-and-clay-shirky/from-innovation-to-revolution) brought both authors together for a debate. Students of mobile media and social media should read all three of these articles.

References

Beniger, J. (1986). *The control revolution: Technological and economic origins of the information society.* Cambridge, MA: Harvard University Press, 1986.

Canadian Wireless Telecommunications Association. (n.d.). Wireless communications make Canada stronger. Retrieved from http://www.cwta.ca/CWTASite/english/index.html

Foresman, C. (2011). Big bidding: Apple, Microsoft, RIM nab Nortel patents for $4.5 billion. *Ars Technica.* Retrieved from http://arstechnica.com/apple/news/2011/07/apple-ms-rim-nab-nortel-mobile-patents-for-45-billion.ars

Gitelman, L., & Pingree, G. (2003). Introduction. In L. Gitleman & G. Pingree (Eds.), *New Media, 1740–1913.* Cambridge, MA: MIT Press. Retrieved from http://web.mit.edu/transition/subs/newmediaintro.html

Gopnik, A. (2011, February 14). The information: How the Internet gets inside us. *The New Yorker.* Retrieved from http://www.newyorker.com/arts/critics/atlarge/2011/02/14/110214crat_atlarge_gopnik#ixzz1fUvo0nJE

Ladner, S. (2008). Laptops in the living room: Mobile technologies and the divide between work and private time among interactive agency workers. *Canadian Journal of Communication, 33*(3), 465–490. Retrieved from http://www.cjc-online.ca/index.php/journal/article/view/1981

Langford, C. H., Wood, J. R., & Ross, T. (n.d.). *The origins and development of the Calgary Wireless Cluster* [PDF]. Retrieved from http://www.thecis.ca/cms3/userfiles/File/Origins%20Dev%20wireless%2016%2009%2007.pdf

Leiss, W. (1990). *Under technology's thumb.* Montreal and Kingston: McGill-Queen's University Press.

Leiss, W. (1994). *The domination of nature* (2nd ed.). Montreal and Kingston: McGill-Queen's University Press.

Mobile phone. (n.d.). Wikipedia. Retrieved from http://en.wikipedia.org/w/index.php?title=Mobile_phone&oldid=464971489

Pedersen, I. (2008). "No Apple iPhone? You must be Canadian": Mobile technologies, participatory culture, and rhetorical transformation. *Canadian Journal of Communication, 33*(3), 491–510.

Rheingold, H. (2002). *Smart mobs: The next social revolution.* Cambridge, MA: Perseus.

Telus Communications. (n.d.). Telus history, 2011. Retrieved from http://about.telus.com/community/english/news_centre/company_overview/company_history

Treviño, L. C., Doutriaux, J., & Mian, S. A. (2006). *Building knowledge regions in North America: Emerging technology innovation poles.* Northhampton, MA: Edwin Elgar.

Wiener, N. (1948). *Cybernetics: Or control and communication in the animal and the machine.* Paris: Hermann & Cie; Cambridge, MA: MIT Press.

Discussion Questions

1. Using examples from your own experience with mobile technology, discuss the ways that users demonstrate agency in their use of mobile devices such as smart phones, tablet computers, or iPods.

2. Do you agree that surveillance is on the increase because of mobile phones? How do you respond when you observe or are affected by surveillance involving mobile technology? Have you become desensitized or immune to such phenomena?

3. Have you ever taken part in civil discourse at the behest of a message viewed or received on a mobile? How was it organized?

ISSUE 2

Activism or slacktivism: Can social media drive political change?

✔ YES

Societal Game Changer: The Political Potential—and Power—of Social Media
Patrick McCurdy

Patrick McCurdy is an assistant professor in the Department of Communication at the University of Ottawa. His research interests include the media strategies and counter-strategies of social movements and other political actors in an age of media saturation. Patrick received his Ph.D. from the Department of Media and Communications at the London School of Economics and Political Science (LSE) in May 2009 for his dissertation, entitled *"I Predict a Riot"—Mediation and Political Contention: Dissent!'s Media Practices at the 2005 Gleneagles G8 Summit.* His work has been published in academic journals including the *International Journal of Communication, Critical Discourse Studies, Media, War & Conflict,* and *Communications—European Journal of Communication Research.* He has just finished the co-edited book *Mediation and Protest Movements* and is currently working on the co-authored book *Protest Camps: Imagining Alternative Worlds.*

Just as the invention and spread of the printing press in the middle of the fifteenth century was a catalyst for fundamental political upheaval, the rise and diffusion of social media is a societal game changer. However, the printing press on its own did not "cause" revolutions, and the same can be said about social media such as Facebook or Twitter. Technology does not cause revolutions, people do. That said, it would be a terrible mistake to overlook how the rise of social media and the Internet more generally has provided activists with a repertoire of valuable resources that can assist in planning, coordinating, and enacting social change.

This chapter is based on the premise that understanding the political potential and power of social media requires moving beyond both cynical and utopian technological determinist perspectives. Instead, social media must be understood as an important yet context-dependent feature of our contemporary media environment. To this end, I begin this chapter by establishing a working definition of social media and unpack what it means to "drive" change. Next, I examine the idea of "slacktivism" and argue that this label is too broad and is often wrongly used to hastily dismiss the potential of social media. In this section I address two common critiques of slacktivism and social media more generally to show how social media can help activists in the quest for political change.

DEFINING SOCIAL MEDIA

Arguing that social media can drive political change first requires clarifying what is meant by the term **social media**. The concept of social media can be traced to the rise of social networking sites such as MySpace and Facebook and even to its predecessors of the 1990s, such as Sixdegrees (Ellison & boyd, 2007; Kaplan & Haenlien, 2010; Kietzmann, Hermkens, McCarthy, & Silvestre, 2011). Yet social media go well beyond sites such as Facebook and include "email, discussion forums, blogs, microblogs, texting, chat, social networking sites, wikis, photo and video sharing sites, review sites and multiplayer gaming communities" (Hansen, Shneiderman, & Smith, 2010, p. 12). Thus, social media may be understood as web-based and mobile applications and technologies that allow individuals and groups of people to create, collaborate, comment, discuss, share, and remix user-generated content (Kietzmann et al., 2011, p. 242). It is the *social* aspect of social media that must be emphasized, because it allows often physically disperse individuals to form connections and communities, and to share and create content, and has proven itself to be a valuable resource for activists both online and offline.

A flaw in much of the popular discourse on the relationship between social media and political change is that social media have often been presented as a deterministic force that directly causes popular protest. For example, the BBC aired a two-part documentary entitled *How Facebook Changed the World: The Arab Spring,* which explored "the story of how the Arab world erupted in revolution, as a new generation used the internet and social media to try to overthrow their hated leaders" (Pollack, 2011). Headlines such as this instill an anthropomorphic quality upon social media, as if it is Facebook itself that is in control. Such prominent media narratives tell us less about the *actual* role of social media in political change and more about the popular "myths" (Barthes, 1957) of our time, such as the liberating and transformative potential of Western technology in nondemocratic states or the dystopian fear of technological advances. Unfortunately, such deterministic headlines are often drawn upon by critics and skeptics as a means to dismiss outright the importance of social media in actualizing change. Yet instead of a blanket dismissal of social media, we need to reposition what is meant by "driving" social change. While both the determinist and skeptical views see social media as driving or "in control" of change, "drive" can also mean to propel or to advance. By using this definition of "drive" we can break the binaries of "All change" or "Small change" (Gladwell, 2010) that have plagued this debate and move toward exploring *how* social media can and do advance political change. This is particularly true for addressing the critiques lobbed at social media as a form of slacktivism.

SOCIAL MEDIA AND DEBATING SLACKTIVISM

The term "slacktivism" has recently gained traction as a derogatory word used to describe "feel-good online activism that has zero political or social impact … [but creates] an illusion of having a meaningful impact on the world without demanding anything more than joining a Facebook group" (Morozov, 2009a). Examples of what counts as slacktivism include the signing and forwarding of online petitions, the "liking" on Facebook or other social media sites of campaigns or political statements, and the sharing, status updating, tweeting, and/or retweeting of campaign goals or political statements (Clements, 2009; Kingsley, 2011; Morozov 2009a, 2009b). Micah White, a senior editor at the Canadian activist magazine *Adbusters*, has branded this type of activism "clicktivism" and argues polemically that "clicktivism is ruining left activism" (2010; see also White, 2012). In short, the concerns that White, Morozov, and others hold about the rise of slacktivism are first, that it encourages activists to be lazy and therefore deters individuals from engaging in "real" activism, and second, that it is generally ineffective. Yet, as argued below, both of these concerns can be addressed and rebuked.

SOCIAL MEDIA AS PART OF ACTIVISM AND NOT SEPARATE FROM IT

Critics charge that individuals who engage in social media–driven slacktivism are "lazy" (Morozov, 2009a) and less likely to undertake "real" activism. Such claims are premised on the misplaced belief that activism facilitated by social media displaces real-world activism. Just as someone who signs a paper petition may never engage further with said issue, for some, signing or tweeting about an electronic petition may also mark the virtual endgame. However, this is certainly not the case for all activists, and therefore it is unfair to make such sweeping claims about the negative impact of social media–facilitated slacktivism—especially when they are not based on any empirical evidence. Moreover, the bigger problem with this argument is that it perpetuates a false dichotomy between online and offline activism, viewing each as separate realms that never meet. In doing so, such claims fail to acknowledge how activists may use the resources afforded by social media such as Facebook groups or other networking tools to develop, coordinate, or push forward a campaign on the ground. This can be illustrated with the following example of the "Save BBC 6Music" campaign. I have intentionally selected this campaign in an effort to broaden how we think about politics. Too often our understanding of what is political is limited to "big P" politics—the activities of formal political parties and professional politicians. Yet campaigns undertaken by everyday citizens to alter the decisions, policies, or production practices of government and corporations are also political. And, as outlined below, social media can play an important role in such campaigns.

In the United Kingdom, on January 24, 2010, Mark Thompson, director general of the British Broadcasting Corporation (BBC), announced his intention to close the digital radio station BBC 6 Music as part of a collection of strategic budget cuts (Plunkett, 2010a). The proposed closure of 6 Music sparked large debate about the station's future both in the British mainstream media and in social media such as blogs, chat forums, Twitter, and, of course, Facebook. It also marked the beginning of a listener-driven campaign to challenge the decision taken by the head of the public service broadcaster.

On the heels of Thompson's announcement, a Facebook group called "Save BBC 6Music" was formed and, by March 3, 2010, had amassed 88 000 members (Taylor, 2010).[1] The Facebook group was public and anyone could join with the click of a button; thus, it became a common virtual space for concerned individuals to converge, connect, discuss, and coordinate action, such as the collection of protests held outside the BBC's Broadcasting House office building in London (Plunkett, 2010c). In mid-March 2010 the BBC Trust—the governing body of the BBC—decided to open a public consultation into 6 Music's planned closure (Plunkett, 2010a). By the end of March 2010, membership in the Save BBC 6Music Facebook group had grown to over 160 000 members (Glanfield, 2010; Plunket, 2010b).

The Save 6 Music campaign also saw the deployment of e-petitions by groups such as 38Degrees, which amassed 40 000 signatures against cuts to the BBC in general (Matt.L, 2010), and Love6music.com, which collected 62 874 online signatories against cutting 6 Music specifically (Lewis, 2010). While critics have panned online petitions as hollow acts of slacktivism, I would argue, in line with Clay Shirky (2011), that such tactics should be seen as part of a wider campaign strategy. Thus, the Facebook groups and e-petitions were not separate from a "real" campaign to challenge BBC cuts and rescue 6 Music, *they were an integral part of it.* Moreover, they played an important role in boosting the visibility of the campaign and its impact.

Social media also made it easier for 6 Music supporters to spread information about how to submit their views to the public consultation run by the BBC Trust, and, because the consultation was online, submitting feedback to the Trust was easy. By the time the BBC Trust closed its public consultation, it had received almost 50 000 responses and over 25 000 emails about the planned closure of 6 Music (Robinson, 2010). On July 5, 2010, the BBC Trust released the findings of its consultation and announced that as there had been "significant public support" for 6 Music, the station will continue operating (Robinson, 2010). Of course, social media alone did not keep 6 Music open. Mark Thompson's proposed closure sparked a public backlash among radio station listeners and supporters, who, in turn, used social media platforms as part of a wider campaign to challenge and eventually successfully overturn this decision. However, the use of social media by campaigners increased visibility, facilitated individuals getting information about and becoming involved in the campaign, and simplified the process of providing feedback to the BBC. In the case of 6 Music, what some critics have hastily dismissed as slacktivist tactics, such as signing e-petitions and joining Facebook groups, played an integral role in a campaign that successfully combined online and offline elements (Plunkett, 2010c; Taylor, 2010).

Obviously, Save 6Music is just one example of a campaign that used social media. The global Occupy or Occupy Wall Street (OWS) movement began on September 17, 2011, with the occupation of Zuccotti Park in New York City. Focusing on the broad issue of social inequality and economic injustice, members of the OWS movement drew upon a diverse repertoire of Twitter accounts, Facebook groups, YouTube accounts, blogs, and live streams to recruit, coordinate, create, and spread information about the movement. Many local manifestations of the Occupy movement (including those in Calgary, Toronto, Ottawa, Montreal, and Halifax) created Twitter accounts and used Facebook groups as a means to connect individuals in their communities and share information about relevant meetings and actions. Social media platforms also allowed physically disparate Occupy groups to build and maintain global connections and thus share experiences, tips, reports, pictures, and video both locally and globally.

The value and impact of such coordination can be seen in the global response to a call made by the International Commission of Sol, in Madrid, Spain, for a Global Day of Action on October 15, 2011 (October 15th United for #Globalchange, 2011; OccupyWallSt, 2011). The call to protest was spread by both word of mouth and social media platforms, including email listservs, Facebook groups, blog posts, and Twitter. In total, protests were held offline in at least 950 cities across 82 countries from London, Ontario, to London, England (October 15th United for #Globalchange, 2011; Taylor, 2011). The protest realized by the Occupy movement on October 15, 2011, was on a global scale rarely, if ever, seen before. Perhaps the closest event was the February 15, 2003, protests against the impeding war on Iraq, which also used online communication to coordinate and report back on demonstrations held on the streets of over 600 cities worldwide (Gillan, Pickerill, & Webster, 2008). In both cases, it was the *issue* and not the technology that caused the protest. Nonetheless, social media played a crucial role in mobilizing people for change, facilitating and creating spaces for conversation, self-representation, and expression.

SLACKTIVISM, SOCIAL MEDIA, AND CHANGE

All forms of activism are driven by the goal of bringing about some kind of change. Naturally, debates about the effectiveness of slacktivist tactics or social media more generally focus on how social media can have an impact on a campaign. Debates concerning the effectiveness of social media have not been helped by the overzealous claims of, for example, the role of Twitter in Iran's Green Revolution (which Evgeny Morozov [2009b] has debunked; see also Morozov, 2011). Yet, as argued earlier, social media are not a cure-all and, as Clay Shirky (2011) rightly states, their use does not have a single or guaranteed outcome.

The example of Save 6 Music discussed earlier illustrates how social media can certainly be part of a successful campaign. Measuring success in the case of 6 Music is relatively easy based on outcome: the station was saved. Admittedly, pinpointing the exact contribution of social media in this instance is more difficult. However, my broader point is the need to view social media—and the battery of tools they offer—as part of larger campaign repertoire, and the campaign should be assessed against the goals and change it set out to achieve.

Micah White, social media critic and inventor of the word "clicktivism," has written with contempt of the growing obsession by campaigns with web metrics, hits, likes, e-signatures, follows, retweets, and twibbons (White, 2010, 2012). White is correct to express concern that campaigners and activists may become obsessed with *output* (e.g., the number of followers) over *outcome* (the result of the campaign), but this is not the fault of the technology per se but the user. Indeed, statistics such as the number of web hits and Twitter followers provide fodder for year-end reports; however, they become meaningless if one's focus switches from outcome (the objective) to output. Thus, White's concern is not that social media are being used, but *how* social media are being used. The fact that some activists and campaigners may decide to use social media in a certain way for their campaign, to the disdain of some, should not detract from the fact that they have proved an effective tool in mobilizing, coordinating, and undertaking protest.

Malcolm Gladwell, in a *New Yorker* polemic against the futility of Twitter and other social media resources in bringing about social change, does acknowledge that social media can be effective in small campaigns. However, Gladwell argues that beyond these "small changes," of which he would surely classify the 6 Music victory as one, large-scale or "revolutionary" social change cannot be brought about by social media. For Gladwell this is because social media encourage only "weak ties" between individuals and do not foster the kind of "strong ties" needed for "high-risk" activism such as direct action. Gladwell's argument about the futility of social media in effecting change is premised on a false dichotomy between online and offline activism. Of course, Facebook groups cannot and should not be used as a substitute for on-the-ground organizing; however, the resources afforded by social media, such as texting and secure chat, can certainly facilitate undertaking direct action. Put differently, those with "weak ties" and "strong tries" can both use social media, but they may do so differently.

Perhaps the largest debate about the effectiveness of social media has been around what has become known as the Arab Spring, which saw protests and revolutions in many countries in the Middle East and North Africa (MENA) region, beginning with Tunisia. On December 17, 2010, after being humiliated by police and having his goods confiscated, twenty-six-year-old Tunisian street vendor Mohamed Bouazizi set himself on fire in an act of protest and desperation at the repressive and poverty-stricken conditions faced by many Tunisians (Ryan, 2011b). Mr. Bouazizi's protest struck a chord with the people of his hometown in Sidi Bouzid, Tunisia, where protests were held that same day. On the evening of December 17, 2010, the Al Jazeera channel Mubasher aired video footage of the protests in Sidi Bouzid that it obtained from Facebook (Ryan, 2011c).

Protests continued in Sidi Bouzid, began to spread elsewhere in the country, and were quickly met with punishing force by then-president Ben Ali's government. Video from the protests in Tunisia was uploaded to file-sharing sites such as YouTube, which allowed those within and outside of Tunisia's borders to witness the protests and the repressive response from the Ali regime. Moreover, Facebook was one of the only social networking sites that the Tunisian government had not censored and thus was used by some, if only a minority, of Tunisians to share experiences, images, and videos of the protests (Ryan, 2011a). Through the use of common hashtags on Twitter such as #sidibouzid and #tunisia, users of the micro-blogging site could learn about, follow, comment on, and react to ongoing events in Tunisia and other countries, bolstering awareness and solidarity.

Given the tight control that the Tunisian government (and similar governments) held over state radio and television, social media provided a vital source of information for those following the protests within and beyond the borders of affected countries. A recent and rigorous study on the role of social media in Tunisia and Egypt conducted by the Project on Information Technology and Political Islam at the University of Washington supports this, arguing that "social media played a central role in shaping political debates in the Arab Spring … [and] helped spread democratic ideas across international borders" (Project on Information Technology and Political Islam, 2011, pp. 2–3). To be clear, social media did not cause the protests in Tunisia or elsewhere; they were spurred by local social, political, and economic conditions. However, social media did provide a platform to amplify the plight and struggles of Tunisians, Egyptians, and citizens of other MENA countries seeking to overthrow their autocratic rulers, which, in turn, encouraged other people to join in the struggle. Social media also allowed for the rapid dissemination of accounts from citizen journalists within these countries and, at least in the case of Egypt, served as a key resource in the planning and undertaking of protests (Khamis & Vaughn, 2011).

CONCLUSION

In late December 2011, *Time* magazine named the protestor as its "person of the year." Indeed, 2011 was a year that appeared to be ripe for protests, from those of the Arab Spring in Tunisia, Egypt, Libya, and Bahrain, to demonstrations against austerity measures in Greece and Spain, and riots and social unrest in the United Kingdom. We also must not overlook the rise of the Occupy Wall Street movement, which quickly evolved from a small encampment in New York`s Zuccotti Park to a movement that spread around the world, and Quebec's student movement, which has garnered world attention.

Social media played a role in each of these protests, from providing a virtual space for activists to coordinate material protests, to offering a digital arena where supporters separated by physical distance could witness and support the movement in solidarity. Of course, the ability to benefit from the resources afforded by social media depends on the social, political, and economic context of the movement, not to mention the desired outcome. Nonetheless, social media stand as a powerful tool that can be used by activists to speed up communication as well as reduce barriers to participation in campaigns seeking to bring about social change.

However, social media are only a tool and cannot or must not replace on-the-ground organizing and activism. Moreover, social media are not a panacea for activism and certainly have their shortcomings. That said, it is time we move beyond the simplistic dichotomies that draw hard lines between online and offline activism and patronizing claims of slacktivism. Instead, we must acknowledge the fact that social media have become a significant feature of our contemporary media environment and have proven to be a key tool in the repertoire of social movements. Dismissing the potential of social media to act as a catalyst for social change would be a terrible mistake. Instead, we must accept the idea that social media can indeed drive political change and examine how, and under what circumstances, they can do so.

Note

[1] The Facebook archive of the Save BBC 6Music group, whose name was changed to Saved BBC 6Music, may be accessed at http://fb.com/saved6music.

References

Barthes, R. (1957). *Mythologies*. Paris: Seuil.

Clements, W. (2009, May 16). A slacktivist and his crackberry are seldom parted. *The Globe and Mail*. Retrieved from Canadian Newsstand Major Dailies. (Document ID: 1712694571).

Ellison, N. B., & boyd, d. (2007). Social network sites: Definition, history and scholarship. *Journal of Computer-Mediated Communication, 13*(1), 210–230.

Gillan, K., Pickerill, J., &Webster, F. (2008). *Anti-war activism: New media and protest in the information age*. Basingstoke, UK: Palgrave McMillan.

Gladwell, M. (2010, October 4). Small change: Why the revolution will not be tweeted. *The New Yorker*. Retrieved from http://www.newyorker.com/reporting/2010/10/04/101004fa_fact_gladwell

Glanfield, T. (2010, March 14). 6 Music: "The consultation is the key" say the accidental Internet campaigners. *Beehivecity*. Retrieved from http://www.beehivecity.com/radio/6-music-%E2%80%9Cthe-consultation-is-the-key%E2%80%9D-say-the-accidental-internet-campaigners/

Hansen, D., Shneiderman, B., & Smith, M. A. (2010). *Analyzing social media networks with NodeXL: Insights from a connected world*. Burlington, MA: Morgan Kaufmann.

Kaplan, A. M., & Haenlein, M. (2010). Users of the world, unite! The challenges and opportunities of social media. *Business Horizons, 53*(1), 59–68.

Khamis, S., &Vaughn, K. (2011). Cyberactivism in the Egyptian revolution: How civic engagement and citizen journalism tilted the balance. *Arab Media and Society, 13*. Retrieved from http://www.arabmediasociety.com/?article=769

Kietzmann, J. H., Hermkens, K., McCarthy, I. P., & Silvestre, B. S. (2011). Social media? Get serious! Understanding the functional building blocks of social media. *Business Horizons, 54*(3), 241-251.

Kingsley, P. (2011, July 20). Avaaz; activism or "slacktivism"? *The Guardian*. Retrieved from http://www.guardian.co.uk/world/2011/jul/20/avaaz-activism-slactivism-clicktivism

Lewis, P. (2010). 6 Music Petition. Retrieved from http://web.me.com/ideasci/Love_6Music/THE_PETITION.html

Matt.L. (2010, July 6). BBC announcement: They listened to us! [Blog post]. Retrieved from http://blog.38degrees.org.uk/2010/07/06/bbc-announcement-they-listened-to-us/

Morozov, E. (2009a, May 19). The brave new world of slacktivism. *Foreign Policy*. Retrieved from http://neteffect.foreignpolicy.com/posts/2009/05/19/the_brave_new_world_of_slacktivism

Morozov, E. (2009b). Iran: Downside to the "Twitter Revolution." *Foreign Affairs, 56*(4), 10–14.

Morozov, E. (2011). *The net delusion*. Toronto: Penguin Books.

OccupyWallSt. (2011, October 12). October 15th Global Day Of Action. Retrieved from http://occupywallst.org/article/october-15th-global-protest-info/

October 15th United for #Globalchange. (2011). Retrieved from http://15october.net/

Plunkett, J. (2010a, March 2). BBC confirms plans to axe 6 Music and Asian Network. *The Guardian.* Retrieved from http://www.guardian.co.uk/media/2010/mar/02/bbc-6-music-asian-network

Plunkett, J. (2010b, March 12). BBC logs "just under 8,000" complaints about plan to close 6 Music. *The Guardian.* Retrieved from http://www.guardian.co.uk/media/2010/mar/12/bbc-complaints-close-6music

Plunkett, J. (2010c, March 29). 6 Music: Adam Buxton and Liz Kershaw join protest at BBC. *The Guardian.* Retrieved from http://www.guardian.co.uk/media/2010/mar/29/bbc-6-music-protest

Pollack, R. (Producer). (2011, September 5). *How Facebook changed the world: The Arab Spring* [Television series]. London: BBC Two.

Project on Information Technology and Political Islam. (2011). *Opening closed regimes: What was the role of social media during the Arab Spring?* Working Paper. Retrieved from http://pitpi.org/index.php/2011/09/11/opening-closed-regimes-what-was-the-role-of-social-media-during-the-arab-spring/

Robinson, J. (2010, July 5). 6 Music saved from closure. *The Guardian.* Retrieved from http://www.guardian.co.uk/media/2010/jul/05/bbc-6-music-saved

Ryan, Y. (2011a, January 6). Tunisia's bitter cyberwar. *Al Jazeera.* Retrieved from http://www.aljazeera.com/indepth/features/2011/01/20111614145839362.html

Ryan, Y. (2011b, January 20). The tragic life of a street vendor. *Al Jazeera.* Retrieved from http://www.aljazeera.com/indepth/features/2011/01/201111684242518839.html

Ryan, Y. (2011c, January 26). How Tunisia's revolution began. *Al Jazeera.* Retrieved from http://www.aljazeera.com/indepth/features/2011/01/2011126121815985483.html

Shirky, C. (2011, January/February). The political power of social media. *Foreign Affairs, 90*(10), 28–41.

Taylor, M. (2010, March 3). BBC 6 Music: fans and stars join growing protest. *The Guardian.* Retrieved from http://www.guardian.co.uk/media/2010/mar/03/bbc-6-music-protest

Taylor, A. (2011, October 17). Occupy Wall Street spreads worldwide. *The Atlantic.* Retrieved from http://www.theatlantic.com/infocus/2011/10/occupy-wall-street-spreads-worldwide/100171/

White, M. (2010, August 12). Clicktivism is ruining leftist activism. *The Guardian.* Retrieved from http://www.guardian.co.uk/commentisfree/2010/aug/12/clicktivism-ruining-leftist-activism

White, M. (2012). Clicktivism.org. Retrieved from http://www.clicktivism.org

ISSUE 2

Activism or slacktivism:
Can social media drive political change?

✘ NO

Social Media and Political Change: Beyond the Hype
Eileen Saunders

Eileen Saunders is the associate director of the School of Journalism and Communication at Carleton University. Previously she served as the director of the Arthur Kroeger College of Public Affairs and associate dean of the Faculty of Public Affairs. Her research interests are in the field of youth, media, and political engagement; social inequality and gender; and children and the media. She is the author of numerous publications concerning such topics as youth and civic engagement, representation of youth in mainstream media, public opinion about social inequality, and access of visible minority groups to news media. Her current research focuses on the potential of social networking sites for civic engagement.

The year 2011 was a heady time for social media; they were credited with bringing democracy to countries formerly ruled by dictators and heralded as the fuel that lit the fire under the various "Occupy" protests that challenged inequity and capitalism. Indeed, 2011 was dubbed "The Year of Social Media" by *The Globe and Mail*, which devoted a weeklong series in December 2011 to the myriad ways that social media are reshaping the world. In particular, the media were captivated by the role of social media in the political protests that swept across the Arab world in 2011: "Arguably, without social media the Arab Spring wouldn't have happened as quickly and as decisively as it did" (Verma, 2011, p. A8).

In a similar vein, Mark Pfeifle, former deputy national security advisor to George W. Bush, suggested in June of 2009 that Twitter should be nominated for a Nobel Peace Prize for the role it was assumed to have played in pro-democracy protests in Iran. Media pundits, Internet gurus, and political advisors alike appear to agree that social media play a powerful role as a driver of political change. In this view, activism as we know it has been transformed, making it easier for the dispossessed and the disenchanted to organize for change. A narrative of triumphalism pervades the various accounts of the role played by Twitter, Facebook, YouTube, and other social media platforms in a range of activist engagements.

So what are the claims regarding political change made by the apostles of social media? They range from the obvious—that the viral capacities of applications such as Facebook and Twitter allow us to spread information faster and further than we ever could have imagined—to the hyperbolic (witness the title of Clay Shirky's presentation posted on TED in June of 2009: "How Social Media Can Make History"). The problem is compounded when attempts to sort out the place of social media in the contemporary political landscape dissolve into competing claims based on scant empirical evidence. My objective is to address the assumptions underlying some of the arguments made on behalf of social media. While not discounting the contributions that social media can make to activist movements, I want to suggest that we need to temper our enthusiasm with a clear understanding of where the limitations and pitfalls lie.

WHITHER ACTIVISM?

"We seem to have forgotten what activism is," lamented Malcolm Gladwell in *The New Yorker* in 2010, in an essay in which his skepticism outraged social media advocates. Gladwell was responding to a euphoria he detected in public and political discourse about the potential of social media to drive political change. He makes a distinction between "**Facebook activism**," those gestures of political engagement, whether in the form of online petitions or Facebook fundraising for worthy causes, and what he identifies as "high-risk activism," exemplified in the U.S. civil rights movement of the 1960s.

His problem is that social media activism demands so little of us, while promising so much: "It makes it easier for activists to express themselves, and harder for that expression to have any impact" (Gladwell, 2010). Moreover, he sees it as diverting and displacing real activism. If individuals feel they have "done their bit" for their cause by joining a Facebook group or pledging funds online to a worthy campaign, they are less likely to engage in the kinds of action needed to forge real change. Other critics go further and label this kind of protest politics as "slacktivism," defined as "feel-good online activism that has zero political or social impact.... Slacktivism is the ideal type of activism for a lazy generation" (Morozov, 2009). As Micah White (2010) argues, we are moving toward a digital model of activism that privileges numbers over action and "uncritically embraces the ideology of marketing," equating every click on a link with political engagement. "Most tragically of all, to inflate participation rates, these organizations ask less and less of their members" (White, 2010). The most cynical might suggest that slacktivism is about collecting political causes the way earlier generations might have filled autograph books.

WHAT ARE SOCIAL MEDIA AND WHAT ARE THEIR AFFORDANCES FOR ACTIVISM?

Social media include a wide range of Web 2.0–based applications, many of which have little to contribute to political change. The defining characteristics generally cited as separating the first-generation applications and those that define Web 2.0 are user-generated content and interactivity. Consumers are also producers and have the potential to seek out and interact with like-minded individuals. Kaplan and Haenlein (2010), in an attempt to add some classificatory rigour to the use of the term "social media," identify six categories:

- *social networking sites* (of which Facebook would be the most popular),

- *content communities* (e.g., YouTube or Flickr),

- *blogs* (we would add micro-blogs such as Twitter),

- *collaborative projects* (Wikipedia being the best-known application),

- *virtual game worlds* (e.g., World of Warcraft), and

- *virtual social worlds* (such as Second Life).

It is primarily the first three categories where attention is focused on their value for activism and political change.

It is important to distinguish between the *technical capacities* of social media and the *social practices* related to their use. Earl and Kimport refer to the former as the affordances of digitally enabled technologies: "the type of action or a characteristic of actions that a technology enables through its design (2011, p. 10). In particular, they identify two key affordances for activism: lowered costs and a reduced need to be physically present in order to coordinate and act. Social media allow "collective action at a lower cost, on a larger scale, and more quickly" (Earl & Kimport, 2011, p. 5). In the case of the first, social media can make information dissemination, communication, and organization much cheaper and easier than earlier channels such as printing posters, mailing supporters, or knocking on doors. It is cheaper to post an online petition and ask followers to click on the link than to print and distribute those petitions, to say nothing of the labour power saved and the wider geographical reach. In reference to the second affordance, or technical capacity, of social media, Earl and Kimport point to the advantages of being able to bring activists together around common goals without the restrictions of time and space: "Signers of a petition need not stumble by the same signature gatherer in order to sign" (Earl & Kimport, 2011, p. 11).

But one needs to ask whether these technical capacities of social media can transform activism or whether other factors are involved in driving political change. One also needs to address the social practices and the social context of the use of social media tools in order to fully understand what they have to offer.

KEY STAGES IN ACTIVISM

What is required to organize people around a political goal? And what factors play a role in whether that collective action is successful? Garrett suggests we need to understand how social movements come together, evolve, and succeed, by way of understanding three different yet interrelated stages: mobilizing structures, opportunity structures, and framing processes (2006).

A key assumption behind much of the optimistic rhetoric surrounding social media is that increasing the ease, speed, and interactive capacity of online communication has enhanced mobilization efforts and increased levels of participation. Lievrouw defines **mobilization** as "the process in which people convert their collective *concerns* into collective *action* to bring about change" (2011, p. 154; emphasis in original). How are people mobilized to act collectively? Garrett suggests this first depends on the presence of adequate mobilizing structures, identified as those social structures—both formal and informal organizations or networks—and those "tactical repertoires" that enable individuals to organize around a common issue (2006, pp. 203–204). More specifically, activist mobilization depends on three factors: "reduction of participation costs, promotion of collective identity and creation of community" (Garrett, 2006, p. 204).

While it would be hard to dispute the fact that organizing off-line can be costlier and more time-consuming than organizing through online tactics, the role of social structures in activist movements bears further investigation. One of the claims trumpeted by social media advocates like Clay Shirky—whose book *Here Comes Everybody* is subtitled *The Power of Organizing Without Organizations*—is that organizing with social media is more decentralized and more democratized. Lievrouw, for example, suggests the loosely formed networks that are replacing more traditional established activist organizations represent a "move toward increasingly flexible, adaptable and 'flat' social movement organizing" (2011, p. 175).

While this may be true, one needs to ask whether it is desirable. The new methods of organizing may be advantageous for some types of collective action—crowdsourcing of knowledge comes to mind—but effective political activism requires planning, deliberation, coordinated action, and strategic decision making. Do non-hierarchical networks provide the best means of accomplishing this? Citing the example of Iran's failed Twitter revolution in 2009, which he claims "may have drowned in its own tweets," Morozov quotes an Iranian blogger: "A protest movement without a proper relationship with its own leaders is a not a movement. It is no more than a blind rebellion in the streets which will vanish sooner than you can imagine" (2011, p. 197). This speaks to the need for strategic coordination and setting of political goals, things not easily carried out in decentralized networks. One could also point to the various incarnations of the Occupy movement, which blossomed with the aid of social media in September 2011 with a call to protestors to occupy Wall Street in opposition to growing income inequality. Protestors filled tent cities that quickly spread, first throughout North America and western Europe and then to Asia, Africa, and Australia. Leaderless and seemingly lacking in clearly defined goals for the movement—other than the unifying slogan of "We are the 99 percent," in reference to the concentration of wealth in the hands of the 1 percent—Occupiers have included groups who seem to have little in common. (I was struck by this when walking by Harvard Yard in late November of 2011. The renowned square at this Ivy League institution was blocked off to only registered students and faculty of Harvard due to the fact that it was being "occupied." If the students and faculty of Harvard don't represent the 1 percent—either now or in the future—then who does?) This may explain why, by late December 2011, many of the encampments had been dismantled and the movement was largely dormant aside from sporadic outbursts.

The question is whether movements that lack hierarchy and formal organization have long-term staying power, to say nothing of impact. Long-time civil rights activist Angela Davis argues that the ease with which we can mobilize large crowds of people over the Internet makes it "difficult to encourage people to think about protracted struggles, protracted movements that require very careful organizing interventions that don't always depend on our capacity to mobilize demonstrations" (Davis, 2005, cited in Morozov, 2011, p. 196).

The jury is also still out on the benefits of social media for creating a shared identity and a sense of belonging to a community. We need to ask, for example, what kinds of ties and networks social media foster. Gladwell points out that the type of connections social media create are at best "weak ties" and "weak ties seldom lead to high-risk activism" (2010). As Morozov adds, "Social psychologists have long understood that while it doesn't take much to make a group of people feel they have a common identity, it is considerably harder to make them act in the interests of that community or make individual sacrifices in its name" (2011, pp. 187–188).

Clay Shirky cites the 2001 downfall of Philippine president Joseph Estrada as an important example of the value of social media in mobilizing activists as a community, claiming it represents the "first time that social media had helped force out a national leader" (2011). It did so, according to Shirky, because of the speed with which political activists were able to mobilize over one million protesters in Manila calling for Estrada's ouster; this was made possible by the use of text messaging. But is this a case of media mobilizing previously unengaged or passive individuals, or did they rather provide another outlet for already mobilized individuals who had a shared political identity and common goal? Bimber's research on political engagement and the Internet suggests the latter; new media seem to provide another channel for citizens who are already politically engaged (Bimber, 2001.) Text messaging may have amplified the speed with which protesters were encouraged into the streets of Manila and even the size of the crowd, but it is unlikely that the medium created opposition where it did not already exist. Morozov sees this as a problem of seeing protests "through the lens of the technology through which they were organized—rather than, say, through the demands and motivations of the protesters" (2011, p. 293).

What seems to be missing in much of the cyber-rhetoric about the inherent capacities of social media is an appreciation for context. If social media drive political change, how does one explain success in Egypt but not in Iran? Tunisia but not Syria? One way of looking at context is to examine activism in terms of what Garrett calls "opportunity structures," defined as "the attributes of a social system that facilitate or constrain movement activity" (2006, p. 212). In order to avoid technology-centric explanations of political change, we need to see that the historical and political space in which activists operate is critical. In Syria, for example, we have seen that the pro-democracy Arab Spring supposedly ushered in by social media has met with fierce resistance and a crackdown by the state. It is not that activists there are not using social media; rather, the particular configuration of the state, military, and other elite allies has violently suppressed them. A similar fate befell the 2009 Iranian protests against election rigging; despite the hype at the time of the role played by Twitter, government forces crushed the protests.

Finally, we are told that activism is enhanced by social media's capacity to bypass normal information channels and traditional media such as television or newspapers in order to distribute information on their own terms and to challenge mainstream or dominant views. Garrett refers to the framing processes involved in social movements, and describes their "strategic attempts to craft, disseminate and contest the language and narratives used to describe a movement" (2006, p. 204). In order to do this effectively, they need to develop alternative accounts that get their message out, challenge the mainstream press or government propaganda, and avoid the gatekeeping filters of traditional media institutions. This is where social media tools are presumed to be crucial. Information moves freely, globally, and often anonymously. Content-sharing sites such as YouTube or Flickr allow videos and photos to be uploaded and shared from any location. Videos and photos that expose corruption or political violence and might never be seen in the mainstream press—particularly in authoritarian regimes—are thus made available to new publics. DIY journalism is made easy through camera-equipped cellphones or micro-blogging platforms like Twitter. And not only does this facilitate sharing of information among activists, but the global reach of social media can create communities of support and new allies.

Again, we need to scrutinize these claims. First, one needs to be cautious about dismissing the role of traditional media in the coverage of activism. Former Canadian diplomat David Malone rejects the argument that social media were central in the overthrow of authoritarian regimes during the Arab Spring, arguing instead that television footage from the Arab network Al Jazeera played a key role in mobilizing protestors in a region that was already ripe for change (cited in Blanchfield, 2012). Gaffney, in an interesting attempt to quantify the role of online activism in Iran during the 2009 protests, suggests that online activism via Twitter was not a key means of engaging until *after* access to traditional media sources was cut: "The spike in account creation began the day reporters started being arrested" (2010).

Second, the lack of editorial control or gatekeepers to information enabled by social media creates its own set of problems. How can one distinguish fact from fiction; whose version of events can one trust? Rumour, conspiracy myths, and propaganda all circulate freely in the world of social media. An illustration of this is the now-classic case of a Danish psychologist who in 2009 created a Facebook group which indicated that a well-known landmark in Copenhagen (the Stork Fountain) was about to be dismantled by the city. The Facebook protest against the fictitious city proposal quickly went viral (cited in Morozov, 2011, p. 179).

A third problem connected to the apparent ability to bypass traditional media controls with the ease of user-generated content is that of information overload. This is a concern that has routinely been raised in the past regarding the Internet in general. Commenting on the contemporary demands for more and more information, Scott notes, "But there is a point at which one has enough information to act; the acquisition of more information beyond this point can be confusing and paralyzing—and can effectively block the taking of effective action" (quoted in Wright, 2004, p. 85). Connected to the problem of overload is the problem of diluting key messaging for the movement. With so many activist channels and voices available via social media, the spectre of "frame clouding" or loss of thematic focus is very real (Garrett, 2006, p. 214).

CONCLUSION

How effective are social media tools in driving political change? Here, faith trumps evidence. In fact, there is very little research or empirical evidence on the actual impact of social media in social movements. Even social media high priest Clay Shirky conceded, when reflecting on the contribution of these tools to democratic change, "[they] probably do not hurt in the short run and might help in the long run" (2011).

While Shirky dismisses the potential for harm, others are less sanguine. Morozov details the myriad ways in which activists have had these technologies of liberation turned against them. Privacy and security have always been an issue on the Internet, and social media amplify that concern. Whether through identifying protesters using videos of demonstrations on YouTube, learning of planned events through Facebook postings, or following the tweets of suspected activists, surveillance has never been easier. Morozov cites Iran's chief of police, who boasted in January of 2010, "The new technologies allow us to identify conspirators and those who are violating the law, without having to control all people individually" (Morozov, 2011, p. 146).

The question of harm is a separate matter from the effectiveness of social media, but perhaps it is one we should pay more attention to. After all, with the major social media platforms owned by private corporations, should activists put their faith in tools that at the end of the day must turn a profit? When Twitter announces, as it did on January 26, 2012, that it is now able to selectively censor and remove content when requested to do so by offended nations, maybe we should question our assumptions about how open and accessible these tools really are.

A little humility and a little perspective, please; it is perhaps premature to start drafting that Nobel acceptance speech.

References

Bimber, B. (2001). Information and political engagement in America: The search for effects of information technology at the individual level. *Political Research Quarterly, 54*(1), 53–67.

Blanchfield, M. (2012, January 9). Twitter, YouTube and social media not major players in Arab Spring: Ex-diplomat. *Winnipeg Free Press*. Retrieved from http://www.winnipegfreepress.com/canada/breaking-news/twitter-facebook-had-little-role-to-play-in-arab-spring-ex-diplomat-136968003.html

Earl, J., & Kimport, K. (2011). *Digitally enabled social change: Activism in the Internet age*. Cambridge, MA: MIT Press.

Gaffney, D. (2010, April 26–27). #iranElection: Quantifying online activism. *Proceedings of the WebSci 10: Extending the Frontiers of Society On-line*, Raleigh, NC. Retrieved from http://journal.webscience.org/295/

Garrett, R. K. (2006). Protest in an information society: A review of literature on social movements and new ICTs. *Information, Communication and Society, 9*(2), 202–224. doi:10.1080/13691180600630773

Gladwell, M. (2010, October 4). Small change: Why the revolution will not be tweeted. *The New Yorker*. Retrieved from http://www.newyorker.com/reporting/2010/10/04/101004fa_fact_gladwell

Kaplan, A. M., & Haenlein, M. (2010). Users of the world, unite! The challenges and opportunities of social media. *Business Horizons, 53*, 59–68. doi:10.1016/j.bushor.2009.09.003

Lievrouw, L. (2011). *Alternative and activist new media*. Cambridge, UK: Polity Press.

Morozov, E. (2009, May 19). The brave new world of slacktivism. *Net Effect, Foreign Policy*. Retrieved from http://neteffect.foreignpolicy.com/posts/2009/05/19/the_brave_new_world_of_slacktivism

Morozov, E. (2011). *The net delusion: The dark side of Internet freedom*. New York: PublicAffairs.

Shirky, C. (2011, January/February). The political power of social media: Technology, the public sphere and political change. *Foreign Affairs, 90*(1). Retrieved from http://www.foreignaffairs.com/articles/67038/clay-shirky/the-political-power-of-social-media/

Verma, S. (2011, December 19). After a Tunisian youth died protesting corruption, a global torrent of messages saw dictators topple. *The Globe and Mail*, pp. A8–A9.

White, M. (2010, August 12). Clicktivism is ruining leftist activism. *The Guardian*. Retrieved from http://www.guardian.co.uk/commentisfree/2010/aug/12/clicktivism-ruining-leftist-activism

Wright, S. (2004). Informing, communicating and ICTs in contemporary anti-capitalist movements. In W. van de Donk, B. Loader, P. Nixon, & D. Rucht (Eds.), *Cyberprotest: New media, citizens and social movements* (pp. 77–93). London: Routledge.

Discussion Questions

1. What do supporters of the term "slacktivism" think is wrong with online activism?

2. What is the difficulty with the "slacktivism" perspective?

3. How can we move beyond a "slacktivism" viewpoint to better understand the role of social media in change?

4. Are there types of activism that social media might foster better than traditional media? Provide examples.

5. Changes in media technology are often accompanied by promises of promoting and expanding democracy. Are social media any different than the telephone, radio, television or the fax machine? Is there something unique about social media that make them more likely than older technologies to drive social change?

6. In what ways might the openness of social media be seen as a threat to social movements just as much as it may be an opportunity for collective action?

ISSUE 3

Sexting:
Should teens have the right to sext?

✔ YES

Privacy, Consent, and Social Media
Amy Adele Hasinoff

Amy Adele Hasinoff is a postdoctoral fellow in the Art History and Communication Studies department at McGill University. Her work appears in *Critical Studies in Media Communication* and *Feminist Media Studies*. Her book about the media and legal responses to sexting is forthcoming.

In early 2009, parents of nearly twenty students at a high school in Pennsylvania received a letter from the district attorney that opened with this statement: "[Your child] has been identified in a police investigation involving the possession and/or dissemination of child pornography" (Searcey, 2009). He explained that school officials had found sexually explicit photos of classmates on some of the students' mobile phones, and those appearing in or possessing the photos could face child pornography charges unless they agreed to complete an education program and serve six months of probation, including random drug testing (Walczak, Burch, & Kreimer, 2009). Most of the students agreed to a version of this deal, while three girls and their parents took legal action to obtain a restraining order preventing the district attorney from filing child pornography charges.

"**Sexting**," which is often defined as the practice of sending sexually explicit images or text through mobile phones or via Internet applications, has been widely discussed in U.S. mass media since December 2008, when a national survey reported that 20 percent of teenagers had sexted (National Campaign to Prevent Teen and Unplanned Pregnancy, 2008).[1] Educators typically advise abstinence from sexting, while law enforcement officials sometimes respond to sexting with child pornography charges for the adolescents involved (Hasinoff, forthcoming). Neither adequately separates the abusive forms of sexting, such as maliciously distributing a private image, from the relatively harmless practice of **consensual sexting**.

A consensus has emerged in the United States that a criminal justice response is necessary to address sexting. While few legal analysts argue that felony charges are necessary, most recommend reducing the penalty for consensual sexting between teenagers to a misdemeanour or applying other lesser consequences, such as in the Pennsylvania case. To date, most legal reforms that U.S. state legislatures are considering involve this type of reduction in the severity of the crime for sexting teenagers who meet a narrow set of conditions (Greenberg, 2010; Sacco, Argudin, Maguire, & Tallon, 2010). By maintaining that sexting should be at the very least a misdemeanour offence, U.S. laws reflect the dominant idea that teenagers should not have the right to sext.

My central argument is that teens should have the right to consensually sext. Sexting is risky and yet teens (and adults) continue to engage in it. Giving teens the right to sext is crucial—it would reduce the potential for unfair prosecutions and help everyone avoid blaming the victims of abusive sexting.

SEXTING AND THE LAW

Advances in digital photography and distribution technologies have made it easy for many people to produce and distribute images of their sex acts. When teenagers do this, the photos and videos they create and share can be legally classified as child pornography since the law makes no exception for minors (people under age eighteen) who create sexually explicit images of themselves. For example, in a U.S. state such as Pennsylvania, two seventeen-year-olds can legally have sex, but if they create a digital image of their sex acts, even for their own use, this depiction can meet the legal definition of child pornography. The fact that child pornography laws are vague enough and broad enough to use against sexting teenagers amplifies the panic about sexting: the label "child pornography" makes sexting seem more dangerous and deviant, while the law allows prosecutors to pursue these cases, adding to the public discussion of the issue.

While the *Canadian Charter of Rights and Freedoms* and the U.S. First Amendment both provide some protections for freedom of expression for people of all ages,[2] child pornography laws in both countries take priority. Child pornography laws were designed to address child sexual abuse and exploitation, but when applied to minors they criminalize teens who distribute images without permission as well as self-expression and consensual behaviours between teenagers. These laws were also intended to combat the sexual exploitation of all minors more broadly by seeking to reduce the distribution and availability of sexual images of minors.

To date, no minor in Canada has been charged with child pornography offences for private, consensual sexting. This is in part because a 2001 Canadian Supreme Court decision (*R. v. Sharpe*) established that privately held images depicting lawful sexual activity do not qualify as child pornography. In Canada, then, two minors who engage in legal sex acts are allowed to photograph these acts but not share these images with any third parties. There is no such exception for private use in the United States, and indeed parents and school officials have discovered private images on adolescents' mobile phones and then initiated child pornography charges against teens and/or their young adult partners.

If an image is explicit enough to qualify as child pornography, a prosecutor who is alerted by a parent or school about it can choose to charge the minors involved with producing, distributing, and possessing child pornography. When a common behaviour like sexting is subject to harsh punishment, authorities decide whom to investigate and whom to prosecute—and these decisions are not always fair.

Laws that prohibit all forms of sexting are particularly troubling because girls are disproportionately punished for sexting, even if it is consensual. Though some surveys indicate that adolescent boys and girls sext at similar rates, much of the attention and punishment for sexting is directed at teenage girls who take photos of themselves. Few people seem concerned about teenage boys involved in sexting (unless they become registered sex offenders) because boys are not usually required to maintain the ideals of sexual purity and chastity imposed on teenage girls. The double standard that teenage boys who are sexually active are often praised or tolerated while girls are criticized and shamed for engaging in the same activities has a significant impact on the responses to sexting. This means that girls who sext may be punished—supposedly to protect them from harming themselves—while boys who sext are often ignored, since many people think "boys will be boys." This leads to cases like one in Seattle in which two girls were suspended for sexting while the boys who distributed their private images without permission were not punished at all (Blanchard, 2008).

The illegality of sexting does not just affect girls excessively; it also affects queer[3] youth, racialized youth, and low-income youth, whose sexual activities are often scrutinized more thoroughly and punished more severely. For example, in a 2010 Oregon case, the mother of a sixteen-year-old girl disliked that her daughter was dating a young woman (who was nineteen years old), so she took her daughter's mobile phone and turned it over to local police. Since the girls had exchanged some explicit text messages and suggestive photos, the older girl was charged with producing child pornography, which could have netted her six years in prison and mandatory sex offender registration (Slovic, 2010). Race may have also played a role in this case, as both girls are African American and the U.S. justice system has a long history of enforcing laws more harshly on people of colour (Alexander, 2010). In another case in Ohio, a prosecutor singled out a girl in the foster care system for sexting. In a TV news segment, a state public defender commenting on this case criticized the prosecutor for misusing child pornography law by "[choosing] an economically disadvantaged person to make an example of" ("Teen Faces," 2008). Ensuring that adolescents have the right to sext is the most effective way to protect them from these kinds of unfair prosecutions.

Some legal analysts and prosecutors contend that punishment for sexting is necessary because sexually explicit images of minors, regardless of the conditions of their production, could facilitate adults' sexual abuse of other minors. This argument contends that adult abusers may have been aided or encouraged by viewing a teen's self-created image without her permission. On U.S. television news-commentary program *The O'Reilly Factor*, a former prosecutor argues for criminal consequences for a fifteen-year-old girl who posted images of herself online. She argues, "This isn't a crime just against this one child. This is against all children. Because those pictures, while they may not have injured her, led perpetrators to seek more images, more pictures of kids, which puts more kids at risk as victims" (O'Reilly, 2004). This kind of attempt to protect minors from objectification and exploitation is well-intentioned, but it paradoxically blames teenage girls for contributing to the broad social problem of child sexual abuse. More importantly, the vague possibility that a sext may contribute to an abuser's fantasies is not a good enough reason to prohibit the practice, especially given all the other problems this prohibition creates.

In addition to worries that sexts will enter the child pornography market, some commentators also refer to the dangers of online predators to argue that sexting must be criminalized and prevented. A former prosecutor speaking on a CNN program argues that criminal charges for sexting are necessary because, she says, "Adults in the real child pornography business will hunt you down and take advantage if they find these pictures, and they will" ("Teen Faces Porn Charges," 2009). This comment implies that taking a nude picture of oneself virtually guarantees that a predator "will hunt you down." Prosecutors and media commentators tend to refer to victimization by online predators as the ultimate and potentially deadly consequence of sexting. However, the concern about online predators targeting minors whose photos they have found online is greatly exaggerated, since the vast majority of physical and sexual assaults against adolescents are still committed by family members, intimate partners, and acquaintances, as they were before digital media were invented (Finkelhor, Mitchell, & Ybarra, 2008).

SEXTING AND CONSENT: MAKING CRUCIAL DISTINCTIONS

While the risks of online predators are inflated in discussions of online safety, the more common problem that private images can be distributed without permission is a serious issue. Just as it is now easy to send a sexual partner a nude photo, it is also very easy for someone to send that photo to many other people—though both of these acts are often called "sexting," they are very different behaviours with different motivations, intents, and outcomes. Some of the commentary about sexting views all forms of sexting (consensual or abusive) as equally damaging and harmful (Hasinoff, forthcoming). Part of the problem is that child pornography laws do not account for the fact that teens sometimes produce and share such images; if the image is explicit enough, the law considers all parties involved (the victims, perpetrators, and consensual participants alike) as child pornography producers, distributors, and possessors.

People may enjoy sharing images consensually, but girls report being traumatized and humiliated if someone distributes their private images without permission (Powell, 2010). It is vital to carefully distinguish between types of sexting and to fully consider questions of consent and intent in any sexting incident. If a consensually produced image is shared between partners or friends, this type of sexting can be a sex act and a form of interpersonal communication and media production. On the other hand, if one or more people distribute this private image without permission, this type of sexting is a form of abuse and sexual harassment. While the aim of consensual sexting is pleasure and communication, the goal of **abusive sexting** is often to harm and humiliate someone. These are each very different behaviours that demand different responses. In short, consensual sexting should be okay, abusive sexting should not.

The fact that adolescents currently have no right to sext means that it's possible to presume that a teen who consensually sexted her partner is just as guilty of crime and wrongdoing as someone who maliciously distributes her photos with the intent to harm and humiliate her. Currently, a teenager who suffers from abusive sexting has few options for recourse against the person who purposefully harmed her, since reporting the incident to authorities makes her vulnerable not only to harsh judgment and punishment but potentially to child pornography charges, especially in the United States. The problem with viewing sexting as deviant and criminal for everyone involved is that it makes the malicious distribution of private images seems like a normal and inevitable part of sexting (Slane, 2010). In fact, most private sext images remain private.[4] If the typical sexting scenario is instead viewed as the consensual exchange of images, it is obvious that sexting is not inherently harmful, but that the malicious distribution of private images certainly is. I argue that in order to accurately recognize harmful, malicious behaviours, it is necessary to first recognize and acknowledge teenagers' right to engage in consensual sexting.

A BETTER RESPONSE TO SEXTING

Minors already have some limited rights to sext in Canada, and thus the need for legal reform is currently less urgent than in the United States. However, in both Canada and the United States, many online safety programs exclusively counsel sexting abstinence. Since a significant number of teens are sexting, it seems unlikely that any school program or public service announcement could convince them to avoid the practice. Educational messages could instead give youth (and adults) practical advice about the precautions they might take when using the Internet and mobile phones as a part of their sexual relationships.

In order to reduce the incidence of abusive sexting, online safety messages could focus on discouraging unauthorized forwarding. For example, one component of MTV's online safety campaign advises against forwarding images. The website explains, "When you get a sext, you might not know if the person would be cool with you sending it around, so better to hit delete rather than forward" ("Sexting," 2012). The site also warns that forwarding may "help humiliate the person in the pic—contributing to their emotional distress" (Gatti, 2009). While this kind of advice might seem obvious, it is actually very different from most educational messages about online safety, which often target girls and advise them to simply abstain from sexting in order to protect themselves (Hasinoff, forthcoming; Shade, 2007).

Abusive sexting occurs within the larger context of gender- and sexuality-based victimization in schools. Girls, queer youth, and other marginalized youth are most likely to be harassed and bullied if someone distributes their private sexual images. Many education researchers stress that bullying and harassment reflect broad social norms and school cultures, and can be addressed effectively only through collective action by administrators, teachers, and students (see, for example, Meyer, 2009; Perrotti & Westheimer, 2001). Neither legally prohibiting sexting nor advising abstinence is likely to reduce the incidence of abusive sexting or sexting-related harassment. The problem is much larger than mobile phone cameras and requires broadly addressing gender and sexual harassment by making significant changes in the attitudes and policies that underlie these recurring issues. If teens had the right to sext, it would be clear that addressing abusive sexting and sexual harassment is the way forward.

CONCLUSION

While many legal and educational commentators believe they are protecting youth from victimization by making sure sexting is illegal, I argue that they are actually exacerbating the problem. This is because when sexting is illegal for everyone, it lets abusive sexters off the hook. One of the ways that abusive sexters avoid blame is through the idea that no teenager should be creating sexting images in the first place. This leads to the problematic consensus in mass media and law that everyone involved in sexting—regardless of whether their behaviour was consensual or abusive—is equally guilty of wrongdoing.

Teens should have the right to sext: this means they would have the same rights as adults to produce sexual images of themselves without fear of prosecution for creating child pornography. The right to sext is also about the right to demand that these images are kept private. While further legal reforms are needed to protect online privacy (for youth and adults), allowing teens the right to sext is the first step in clarifying that people who receive these images have no right to distribute them further without permission. The panic about sexting teens highlights the need for broader conversations about social media that can fully account for the complicated issues of privacy and consent in new digital media environments.

Notes

[1] A different study reports that only 4 percent of teenagers have sexted, though it defines sexting more narrowly (Lenhart, 2009).

[2] Each country has a different history and approach to protecting citizens' freedom of expression rights.

[3] Here I use "queer" as an umbrella term to refer to lesbians, gay men, transgender people, bisexual people, and anyone who does not fit into dominant norms of gender and sexuality.

[4] In a survey conducted for Cox Communications, only 2 percent of teens (thirteen to eighteen years old) who sent a sext report that their image was forwarded to someone they did not want to see it (Cox Communications, 2009, p. 38). In a survey commissioned by MTV, 14 percent of teens who sexted report that the person they sent the image to shared it with other people without their permission (Gatti, 2009, p. 15). Both the Cox and the MTV studies were produced in partnership with the National Center for Missing and Exploited Children, but Cox may be biased nonetheless toward reporting lower rates of victimization because they are invested in demonstrating that mobile phones are safe.

References

Alexander, M. (2010). *The new Jim Crow: Mass incarceration in the age of colorblindness.* New York: The New Press.

Blanchard, J. (2008, November 21). Cheerleaders' parents sue in nude photos incident: Two were the only ones suspended. *Seattle Post-Intelligencer.* Retrieved from http://www.seattlepi.com/local/article/Cheerleaders-parents-sue-in-nude-photos-incident-1292294.php

Cox Communications. (2009, May). *Teen online and wireless safety survey: Cyberbullying, sexting, and parental controls.* Atlanta, GA: Cox Communications, National Center for Missing & Exploited Children, and John Walsh.

Gatti, J. (2009). *The MTV-Associated digital abuse study: A Thin Line* [Report]. Retrieved from http://www.athinline.org/MTV-AP_Digital_Abuse_Study_Full.pdf

Greenberg, P. (2010, March 15). 2010 legislation related to "sexting." *National Conference of State Legislatures: Issues & Research.* Retrieved from http://www.ncsl.org/default.aspx?TabId=19696

Hasinoff, A. A. (forthcoming). *Sexting: The politics of sexuality and social media.* Champaign, IL: University of Illinois Press.

Lenhart, A. (2009, December 15). *Teens and sexting: How and why minor teens are sending sexually suggestive nude or nearly nude images via text messaging.* Pew Internet & American Life Project. Retrieved from http://pewresearch.org/assets/pdf/teens-and-sexting.pdf

Meyer, E. J. (2009). *Gender, bullying, and harassment: Strategies to end sexism and homophobia in schools.* New York: Teachers College Press.

The National Campaign to Prevent Teen and Unplanned Pregnancy. (2008). *Sex and tech: Results from a survey of teens and young adults.* Washington, DC: Author.

O'Reilly, B. (2004, April 4). Impact. *The O'Reilly Factor* [Transcript]. Retrieved from NewsBank database.

Perrotti, J., & Westheimer, K. (2001). *When the drama club is not enough: Lessons from the Safe Schools Program for Gay and Lesbian Students.* Boston, MA: Beacon Press.

Powell, A. (2010). *Sex, power, and consent: Youth culture and the unwritten rules.* New York: Cambridge University Press.

R. v. Sharpe, [2001]1 S.C.R. 45, 2001 SCC 2.

Sacco, D. T., Argudin, R., Maguire, J., & Tallon, K. (2010, June 22). *Sexting: Youth practices and legal implications.* Prepared for the Youth and Media Policy Working Group Initiative, Berkman Center for Internet & Society. Retrieved from http://cyber.law.harvard.edu/sites/cyber.law.harvard.edu/files/Sacco_Argudin_Maguire_Tallon_Sexting_Jun2010.pdf

Searcey, D. (2009, April 21). A lawyer, some teens and a fight over "sexting": Revealing images sent via mobile phones prompt district attorney to offer seminars but threaten felony charges. *Wall Street Journal.* Retrieved from http://online.wsj.com/article/SB124026115528336397.html

Sexting: What is it? (2012). *A Thin Line.* Retrieved from http://www.athinline.org/facts/sexting

Shade, L. R. (2007). Contested spaces: Protecting or Inhibiting girls online? In S. Weber & S. Dixon (Eds.), *Growing up online: Young people and digital technologies* (pp. 227–244). New York: Palgrave Macmillan.

Slane, A. (2010). From scanning to sexting: The scope of protection of dignity-based privacy in Canadian child pornography law. *Osgoode Hall Law Journal, 48*, 543–593.

Slovic, B. (2010, December 10). Sext crimes: Oregon has a name for teens who take dirty photos with their mobile phones: Child pornographer. *Willamette Week.* Retrieved from http://www.wweek.com/portland/article-16544-sext_crimes.html

Teen faces charges for her own nude photos: An Ohio public defender is disputing the child pornography charges [Video]. (2008, October 14). *ABC News.* Retrieved from http://abcnews.go.com/video/playerIndex?id=6034996

Teens face porn charges [Video]. (2009, January 15). *CNN Prime News.* Retrieved from http://www.cnn.com/video/#/video/bestoftv/2009/01/15/pn.sexting.teens.cnn

Walczak, W. J., Burch, V. A., & Kreimer, S. F. (2009, March 25). United States District Court for the middle district of Pennsylvania: Verified complaint. *Miller, et al. v. Skumanick:* Legal Documents. Retrieved from http://www.aclupa.org/downloads/MillerComplaintfinal.pdf

Wolak, J., Finkelhor, D., Mitchell, K., & Ybarra, M. (2008). Online "predators" and their victims: Myths, Realities, and implications for prevention treatment. *American Psychologist, 63*(2), 111–128.

ISSUE 3

Sexting:
Should teens have the right to sext?

✖ NO

Familiar Issues, New Implications: Why Teens (and Adults) Should Not Sext
Nora A. Draper

Nora Draper is a Ph.D. student in the University of Pennsylvania's Annenberg School for Communication. She is interested in the evolution of privacy norms and policies in the digital era with a specific focus on digitally mediated consumer surveillance. Her current research focuses on the development of an industry supporting the management of online reputations for "ordinary" individuals. Her work has been published in the *Journal of Children and Media* and *Surveillance and Society*.

The potential consequences of teen sexting are not trivial. Consider a November 2011 *Globe and Mail* story on a website run by twenty-five-year-old Hunter Moore called IsAnyoneUp.com. According to the article, "the site encourages visitors to submit nude photos of their exes, hookups, friends or anyone else who's ever 'sexted' them, and then cross references the racy photos with screen grabs of the unconsenting subjects' actual Facebook, Twitter or Tumbler accounts—whatever's floating out there" (Bielski, 2011). The North American public was first introduced to sexting in 2009 thanks to a flurry of media coverage about the growth of this practice among teenagers. Commonly defined as the production and exchange of nude or semi-nude images or videos via mobile phone, sexting quickly caught the public's attention.

Due to the lack of nuanced coverage of this topic, commentators have largely failed to acknowledge the complexities surrounding the issue. One important oversight—sexting is not strictly a teen issue. Mr. Moore's website, with thousands of submissions, has a strict policy against child pornography, suggesting that adults are also sexting. The panic around a single type of content—sexual images—also obscures the central issue embedded in questions around sexting: How can digital technologies be used without the risk of losing control over one's personal content? While there is much to criticize about the media, legal, and public response to sexting, it would be a mistake to adopt the "kids will be kids" approach taken by some commentators. The "right" to sext is bound up with some problematic and unintended consequences that will be explored in this chapter.

PUTTING SEXTING IN (HISTORICAL) PERSPECTIVE

It is essential to acknowledge that sexting does not represent a unique phenomenon motivated by newly realized impulses. By representing this practice in the absence of its historical referent, commentators are able to create distance between themselves and the behaviour, making it easier to ignite fears about its consequences. Media coverage of sexting has tended to ignore the occurrence of sexual experimentation in previous generations, choosing instead to compare sexting with "wholesome" teen behaviours like spin the bottle and drinking milkshakes in malt shops (Draper, 2012). Despite this fantasy of an innocent past, there are historical analogues to sexting. The advent and proliferation of home photography and video recording technology allowed people to record images at their leisure and likely supported the growth of a do-it-yourself pornography culture (Coopersmith, 2000). The introduction of instant camera technology, which allowed people to produce and develop images without the intruding eye of a commercial developer, may have altered the range of images amateur photographers felt comfortable producing (Buse, 2010). In fact, in a 1982 article, Charles Edgley and Kenneth Kiser introduce the notion of "Polaroid sex," which they define as "the use of instant photography devices to create homemade pornography" (1982, p. 59). These authors argue that the Polaroid instant camera changed the production capabilities of the individual, making the creation of amateur porn easier.

Peter Buse outlines a number of defining characteristics of the instant chemical images produced by Polaroid cameras: the speed of development, the elimination of the external darkroom, and the lack of a usable negative (2010, pp. 220–221). Buse notes that the first two characteristics are shared with digitally produced images, but the third is not:

> Amateur Polaroid and digital image making could not be further apart in their technologies of production and dissemination, but the speed with which the image appears and the way in which it "develops" inside the camera mean that the former nevertheless anticipates the latter as a practice and a cultural form. (2010, p. 221)

It is precisely this ease of replication and dissemination implicit in digital photography that means instant chemical cameras, and even the practice of Polaroid sex, could not anticipate the inherent risk in the production and distribution of sexually explicit digital images. Without control over the reproduction and transmission of the image, the emancipatory potential often associated with new production-oriented technologies is threatened. There may be room for individual agency in the creation and even sharing of sexual images, and this potential should be explored and perhaps celebrated; however, the loss of control over such an image and the accompanying vulnerability necessitates thinking about the potential risks associated with sexting.

WHAT'S NEW ABOUT SEXTING?

Given the opportunities created by digital photography for private production spaces that support experimentation with intimate subject matter, it is essential to consider the inherent risks associated with this new medium. Social media researcher danah boyd (2008) notes four properties of networked, digital content that separate it from its unnetworked, analogue counterpart. While boyd is talking primarily about the speech acts that take place on social networking sites, the characteristics are similarly applicable to digital content, including images. The first property is the *persistence* of digital content. While unmediated speech acts vanish almost immediately after they are rendered, digital content does not disappear automatically once it is sent or received. Rather, digital content is inscribed, lending it a type of permanence. The second characteristic is the *searchability* of information in a networked community. While images may be more difficult to search than text, once a piece of personally identifiable information is tied to an image—for example, a name or email address—it becomes easily searchable. Moreover, with the increasing sophistication of facial recognition software and its use by companies like Google and Facebook, text may soon be unnecessary when searching for images.

The third characteristic boyd describes is *replicability*. She notes that information in a networked public "can be copied from one place to another verbatim such that there is no way to distinguish the 'original' from the 'copy'" (2008, p. 126). Combined with the persistence of digital content, the ease of replication makes complete deletion of networked digital content very difficult. Finally, boyd notes the existence of an *invisible audience* for those embedded in networked publics. Unlike communication that takes place in "unmediated spaces," it is very difficult to know who is receiving the information being sent. According to boyd, this invisibility is further complicated by the asynchronous nature of this type of communication, which means information may be read out of context. Given the desire among teens to facilitate belonging through the sharing of digital images (Scifo, 2005, p. 368), it is likely that a single digital image could find multiple audiences very quickly. Unlike a Polaroid photo—a truly singular image with no usable negative (Buse, 2010)—which can be passed physically but not easily reproduced—each time a digital image is shared, an identical copy is created. This contributes to the difficulty of maintaining control over an image once it has been sent.

The circulation of information about others is not a new phenomenon. The accumulated mass of information about an individual that coalesces into a personal reputation has traditionally been used as a tool for social control by creating an incentive to conform to social norms (Solove, 2007). However, the difficulty of controlling digital information, whether it is text or image based, is an important feature of the contemporary era. In the digital era, the increasing ability to preserve, replicate, and search information has brought notions of personal reputation to the fore. Daniel Solove notes that these features of digital media "transform [gossip and rumours] from forgettable whispers within small local groups to a widespread and permanent chronicle of people's lives" (2007, p. 11). While the media have tended to focus on the consequences of sexual content that goes viral, the loss of control over any personal information can have potentially negative consequences. These changes are not insignificant and represent a dramatic shift in how we think about reputation management in the digital era. This is not to say that positive outcomes from sexting do not or cannot exist, but this potential loss of control of personal information and the associated reputational damage must be considered.

NEW MEDIUM, NEW MESSAGE?

Lapsing into **technologically deterministic** rhetoric, media coverage of sexting suggests that new digital technologies seduce young people into dangerous and risky sexual behaviours (Draper, 2012). By situating the power to incite action within the technology itself, this discourse ignores the agency of the individual in determining *how* to use the medium and disregards the cultural forces that shape the ways societies create, understand, and use new technologies. Offering a variation on technological deterministic rhetoric, Nancy Baym outlines the media choice model in which "technological features are seen as having direct consequences, but people are seen as making strategic, and usually rational, choices about which media they use for differing purposes" (2010, p. 27). The media choice model acknowledges that while new technologies are not powerful enough to *create* new behaviours, by making certain activities easier, these technologies may shift cultural practices in important ways. Moreover, the media choice model allows for a discussion about the ways in which new technologies can alter the circumstances around existing behaviours with dramatic consequences. For example, this theory suggests that while the desire for revenge on an ex through public humiliation is not caused by new technologies, websites like IsAnyoneUp. com, which make it easier to aggregate discrete content from a number of sites around the web, facilitate the creation of a single profile for the purposes of public embarrassment.

Following the media choice model, it is important to acknowledge that digital photography has not *created* new impulses among teens. Penny Tinkler (2008) notes the persistent role cameras have played in helping young people to explore their identities, create a sense of belonging, and collect memories. Digital technologies, however, have opened up new opportunities for self-expression. While young people have traditionally used photography in the "production of identity statements," Tinkler argues that using the camera for identity *experimentation* was less common owing in part to the high cost of film (2008, p. 259). Digital cameras and camera phones, which do not rely on film and create easily disposable images, allow for playful photography that focuses on subject areas—the intimate and mundane—traditionally left out of the photographic frame (Tinkler, 2008). Digital cameras do not, therefore, incite people toward sexually risky behaviour. By changing the nature of production, however, they may alter the types of photographs that are taken, thereby changing the content.

Similarly, mobile devices do not *create* new behaviours. They do, however, offer alternative strategies for communication that may facilitate different patterns of interaction. Importantly, digital media have created a communication model where individuals are always accessible. By tying communication devices to an individual rather than a location, mobile devices create a state of "perpetual contact" (Katz & Aakhus, 2002). A number of scholars have also noted that the asynchronous and mediated communication made possible by mobile phones—particularly through texting—helps alleviate some of the inhibitions people feel when communicating about sensitive issues, which may lead to the adoption of a braver persona when communicating via text message (Ellwood-Clayton, 2003; Kasseniemi & Rautiainen, 2002). Moreover, mobile technology has created new norms around the exchange and storage of communication content. The sharing of photos, particularly via mobile phone, constitutes an important form of gift-giving for teens that helps establish social belonging within a peer group (Ling & Haddon, 2008; Scifo, 2005; Vincent, 2003). The ease with which these digital images can be stored and accessed, particularly in smart phones, allows for the creation of a "portable photo archive" (Scifo, 2005, p. 265), providing adolescents with an easily accessible tool to illustrate their identity to others and create an archive of memories. While it is important not to overstate the seductive potential of the mobile phone, it is necessary to think about how the intimacy fostered through the **asynchronous communication** of text messaging, combined with the availability of a camera in one's phone—and the new types of content afforded by digital technology—creates an environment where sexting is possible.

SEXTING: A TEEN THING?

The new opportunities and norms for information exchange facilitated by digital technologies introduce important risks around the control and management of personal information. However, by catering to public anxieties around youth, sexuality, and digital technology, the media have misrepresented the likely cause and most important implication of this emergent phenomenon. Kirsten Drotner (1992) notes that **media panics**—defined as concerns about the uses of new media technologies and their cultural implications—are often disproportionately targeted at young people. Like the media coverage around the use of social networking sites by sexual predators that was pervasive in the early 2000s (Cassell & Cramer, 2009), discourse around sexting tends to drastically overstate its incidence (Draper, 2012). Research into the prevalence of sexting among teens has used inconsistent definitions that help to obscure its pervasiveness. In the early coverage of sexting, the news media widely reported results from a survey conducted by the National Campaign to Prevent Teen and Unplanned Pregnancy (2009) to suggest that one in five teens had sexted. The National Campaign study included eighteen- to twenty-six-year-olds in their sample rather than restricting participation to minors. Although the report split findings for respondents aged thirteen to nineteen and those twenty to twenty-six, these figures tended to be combined in media reports. While later surveys that focused specifically on teens found much lower rates of sexting (Lenhart, 2009; Mitchell, Finkelhor, Jones, & Wolak, 2011), these studies were released after the media flurry allowing the exaggerated figures to define the discourse.

The early framing of sexting as a "teen issue" has meant a lack of empirical research on the prevalence of the practice among adults. The absence of such research has helped to entrench sexting as primarily a youth behaviour and has circumvented the need for research that attempts to understand the practice as a broader social phenomenon. Recent high-profile scandals involving the exchange of sexually explicit text messages and images by mobile phone—including Brett Favre, Tiger Woods, and U.S. Representative Anthony Weiner[1]—suggest that the construction of sexting strictly as a teen behaviour is problematic. There is an important distinction between the exchange of sexually explicit texts among consenting and nonconsenting partners. By ignoring the occurrence of sexting among adults, this distinction tends to be overlooked. Instead, the focus on teens allows sexting to be framed as a necessarily exploitative extension of child pornography.

The legal implications of teen sexting are immense. A number of U.S. states have used child pornography laws, originally designed to protect children, to prosecute young "offenders" who create and distribute "obscene" images. For example, a Wisconsin court charged a seventeen-year-old boy with possession of child pornography for posting naked pictures of his sixteen-year-old girlfriend on the Internet (Corbett, 2009). Demonstrating the flexibility of the courts in assigning blame in such instances, a Pennsylvania court charged a group of girls between fourteen and fifteen with child pornography for sending semi-nude images of themselves via cellphone to two teenage boys who were then charged for receiving them (Corbett, 2009). On top of concerns about the loss of control of personal information, these laws mean that some teens have to worry about the legal ramifications of sexting.

The use of child pornography laws, originally intended to protect children from violence and abuse, to punish teens is the wrong approach to dealing with sexting. Moreover, the use of child pornography laws to prosecute these cases limits our ability to understand the implications of these behaviours when they occur among adults. Recognizing the problems with draconian legal approaches to teen sexting, some states are amending sexting laws in favour of "educational reform programs" that avoid the need to prosecute youth as child pornographers (Gershman, 2011). These legal reforms promote education around the unintended consequences and potential risks of sharing digital information and may provide a more appropriate forum for discussion.

If, however, these programs rehash the discourse found in the media coverage of sexting, which focuses on the dangers of teen sexuality and the seductive nature of new technologies (Draper, 2012), they will continue to misdiagnose the true risks inherent in sexting. These programs must focus on the characteristics of digital content that increase the risk of loss of control over personal and sensitive content—sexually explicit or otherwise.

CONCLUSION

Sexting does not denote a fundamental shift in the dispositions of young people. Suggestions that exposure to digital media creates impulses and hypersexualized behaviours that did not exist in the past invest technologies with far too much power over the user and dehistoricize the practice of sexting in unhelpful ways. There is nothing new about the exploration of sexuality among teens. Nor is there anything new about a desire to document and share these experiences with friends. Much of the literature that celebrates the production of erotic images by amateurs focuses on individual agency and the ability undermine and subvert traditional hegemonic norms found in commercial pornography (see, for example, Coopersmith, 2000; Kibby & Costello, 2001). Technologies that conflate the roles of producer, subject, and consumer help to create intimate spaces of production where experimentation is both possible and enjoyable. However, it is when this heightened feeling of privacy allows for a false sense of security around individuals' control over the content they are producing and sharing that problems arise.

With the development of digital technologies come new opportunities and risks around the ability to control personal information. This is true for sexual content, but not just for sexual content. Discussions that focus on the taboo topics of nudity, sex, and pornography ignore the myriad of other types of personal information about an individual that help create a reputation. These new technologies also create risks for teens, but not just for teens. The presence of websites like IsAnybodyUp.com forces us to reconsider the consequences of sexting across age groups. The potential for personal information to go viral may raise specific concerns for teens, for example, around issues of bullying and, in some cases, criminal charges. While we must not allow anxieties about teen sexuality to dominate the discourse, it is essential that we continue to educate teens about the inherent risks of sexting related to the control of personal information in the digital era.

Note

[1] National Football League star Brett Favre was implicated in a 2010 scandal for sending "lewd messages and photos" to a female employee of the New York Jets franchise (Thomas & Viera, 2011). Tiger Woods saw his marriage fall apart after a woman who claimed to have had an affair with him released flirty text messages, which were later published by some media outlets (Holson, 2009). In 2011, U.S. Representative Anthony Weiner resigned his congressional seat after sending "lewd messages and photos" to women he had met online (Hernandez, 2011).

References

Baym, N. (2010). *Personal connections in the digital age.* Malden, MA: Polity Press.

Bielski, Z. (2011, November 11). "Making money off your mistakes": Meet the creator of "stalker porn." *The Hot Button Blog: The Globe and Mail.* Retrieved from http://www.theglobeandmail.com/life/the-hot-button/making-money-off-your-mistakes-meet-the-creator-of-stalker-porn/article2233399/

boyd, d. (2008). Why youth [heart] social networking sites: The role of networked publics in teenage social life. In D. Buckingham (Ed.), *Youth, identity and digital media* (pp. 119–142). Cambridge, MA: MIT Press.

Buse, P. (2010). Polaroid into digital: Technology, cultural form, and the social practices of snapshot photography. *Continuum, 24*(2), 215–230. doi:10.1080/10304310903363864

Cassell, J., & Cramer, M. (2009). High tech or high risk: Moral panics and girls online. In T. McPherson (Ed.), *Digital youth, innovation, and the unexpected* (pp. 53–75). Cambridge, MA: MIT Press.

Coopersmith, J. (2000). Pornography, videotape, and the Internet. *IEEE Technology and Society Magazine, 19*(1), 27–34. doi:10.1109/44.828561

Corbett, D. (2009). Let's talk about sext: The challenge of finding the right legal response to the teenage practice of "sexting." *Journal of Internet Law, 13*(6), 3–8. Retrieved from http://proxy.library.upenn.edu:2441/pqdlink?did=1916479051&sid=1&Fmt=3&clientId=3748&RQT=309&VName=PQD

Draper, N. R. A. (2012). Is your teen at risk? Discourses of adolescent sexting in United States television news. *Journal of Children and Media, 6*(2), 221–236. doi:10.1080/17482798.2011.587147

Drotner, K. (1992). Modernity and media panics. In M. Skovmand & K. C. Schroder (Eds.), *Media cultures: Reappraising transnational media* (pp. 42–62). New York: Routledge.

Edgely, C., & Kiser, K. (1982). Polaroid sex: Deviant possibilities in a technological age. *Journal of American Culture, 5*(1), 59–64.

Ellwood-Clayton, B. (2003) Virtual strangers: Young love and texting in the Filipino archipelago of cyberspace. In K. Nyíri (Ed.), *Mobile democracy: Essays on society, self and politics* (pp. 225–235). Vienna: Passagen Verlag Ges.m.b.H.

Gershman, J. (2011, June 6). Lawmakers propose teen "sexting" law. *The Wall Street Journal.* Retrieved from http://online.wsj.com/article/SB10001424052702304474804576367960734408624.html

Hernandez, R. (2011, June 12). Despite plan to enter rehab, Weiner still faces calls to resign. *The New York Times.* Retrieved from http://www.nytimes.com/2011/06/13/nyregion/despite-rehab-plan-more-calls-for-weiner-to-quit.html

Holson, L. M. (2009, December 8). Text messages: Digital lipstick on the collar. *The New York Times.* Retrieved from http://www.nytimes.com/2009/12/09/us/09text.html

Kasseniemi, E., & Rautiainen, P. (2002). Mobile culture of children and teenagers in Finland. In J. Katz & M. A. Aakhus (Eds.), *Perpetual contact: mobile communication, private talk, public performance* (pp. 170–192). Cambridge, UK: Cambridge University Press.

Katz, J. E., & Aakhus, M. (Eds.). (2002). *Perpetual contact: Mobile communication, private talk, public performance.* New York: Cambridge University Press.

Kibby, M., & Costello, B. (2001). Between the image and the act: Interactive sex entertainment on the Internet. *Sexualities, 4*(3), 353–369. doi:10.1177/136346001004003005

Lenhart, A. (2009, December 15). *Teens and sexting: How and why minor teens are sending sexually suggestive nude or nearly nude images via text messaging.* Retrieved from www.pewresearch.org/millennials

Ling, R., & Haddon, L. (2008). Children, youth and the mobile phone. In K. Drotner & S. Livingstone (Eds.), *International handbook of children, media and culture* (pp. 137–151). London: Sage.

Mitchell, K. J., Finkelhor, D., Jones, L. M., & Wolak, J. (2011). Prevalence and characteristics of youth sexting: A national study. *Pediatrics.* doi:10.1542/peds.2011-1730

National Campaign to Prevent Teen and Unplanned Pregnancy. (2009). *Sex and tech survey.* Retrieved from http://www.thenationalcampaign.org/sextech

Scifo, B. (2005). The domestication of camera-phone and MMS communication: The early experiences of young Italians. In K. Nyíri (Ed.), *A sense of place: The global and the local in mobile communication* (pp. 363–373). Vienna: Passagen Verlag.

Solove, D. J. (2007). *The future of reputation: Gossip, rumor, and privacy on the Internet.* New Haven, CT: Yale University Press.

Thomas, K., & Viera, M. (2011, January 4). N.F.L. declined to view Favre texts, lawyer says. *The New York Times*. Retrieved from http://www.nytimes.com/2011/01/05/sports/football/05nfl.html

Tinkler, P. (2008). A fragmented picture: Reflections on the photographic practices of young people. *Visual Studies, 23*(3), 255–266. doi:10.1080/14725860802489916

Vincent, J. (2003). Emotion and mobile phones. In K. Nyíri (Ed.), *Mobile democracy: Essays on society, self and politics* (pp. 215–224). Vienna: Passagen Verlag Ges.m.b.H.

Discussion Questions

1. Do you think teenagers should be legally allowed to sext? Why or why not?

2. How do you think schools should address sexting?

3. Which concerns about the risks of sexting are legitimate and which are exaggerated?

4. Does the ability to aggregate discrete content found on the web present new threats to an individual's reputation? How?

5. Think about the various digital media that allow for asynchronous communication. How do these media change the *context* of communication in ways that might encourage intimate disclosure, including sexting?

6. Which social institution do you think is best situated to deal with teen sexting: the legal system, the education system, families or peer groups, or some combination of these? If you were a policy maker tasked with creating new legislation to deal with teen sexting, what approach would you suggest?

ISSUE 4

We are Big Brother:
Is social media surveillance a threat to
our sense of community?

✔ YES

Sex, Lies, and Digital Memory: How Social Surveillance Threatens Communities
Christopher Parsons

Christopher Parsons is a Ph.D. candidate in the Department of Political Science at the University of Victoria. His research interests focus on how privacy is affected by digitally mediated surveillance, and the normative implications that such surveillance has in (and on) contemporary Western political systems. Specifically, he thinks through how digital surveillance technologies influence citizens' decisions, and capacities, to openly express themselves and associate with others. Christopher has spoken across Canada about social media, surveillance, and security; Internet service provider network surveillance practices; and the relationships between copyright and free speech. He has also given presentations addressing the short- and long-term risks associated with various government and corporate surveillance programs. Christopher has published in *CTheory*, *Canadian Privacy Law Review*, with the Canadian Centre for Policy Alternatives, and contributed to Open Media's *Casting an Open Net* report. He also has forthcoming publications on the topics of e-passports and privacy literatures.

Employers commonly check up on prospective, current, and past employees' social media activities. The press regularly warns that we shouldn't say anything on social media that we wouldn't want revealed on the front page of a major daily newspaper. In essence, we are warned that everything we do using social media will be tracked and monitored by organizations, large and small, for business and security purposes alike.

Less often, however, do we hear about how citizens monitor each other, using Facebook, Twitter, and other social networking sites. Moreover, we do not tend to interrogate whether our surveillance of one another is harmful. Instead, we casually say that the technology is here and that the genie out of the bottle. Such utterances let us avoid critical reflection concerning the harm that can arise from (re)producing a surveillance culture using social networks. This chapter investigates how surveillance in combination with social media can harm our sense of community. It focuses on two separate scenarios. The first looks at social media communities that are intentionally designed to reduce members' accountability for their surveillance and speech. The second turns to social media networks that are designed for positive purposes—such as connecting with friends and colleagues—and how they can be transformed into sites of collective surveillance and damaging speech. Both scenarios can undermine social bonds in offline communities; when online communities report on the result of real or alleged offline monitoring, and link those reports with people's addresses, phone numbers, and other personal information, the targeted are often emotionally and financially wounded. Moreover, combining such surveillance with calls for mob justice threatens our capacity to generate safe, respectful, and integrated offline communities.

After investigating these case areas, the chapter concludes with some suggestions for mediating the worst impacts of ill-considered speech acts on social media sites. The question that will remain, however, is how to encourage technologists, legislators, and citizens to advocate for basic transformation in the web's technical infrastructure.

DEVELOPING (UN)REGULATED SPACES

Lurking throughout the web are social networking spaces designed to encourage surveillance, harassment, and denigration of individuals. Many of these sites are crafted so their web designers and those who communicate on them assume limited (or no) liability for their actions. Because most major social media websites are developed and operated out of the United States, American law is often key in encouraging and protecting such sites. Specifically, section 230 of the *Communications Decency Act* makes such sites possible. This section reads, "No provider or user of an interactive computer service shall be treated as the publisher or speaker of any information provided by another information content provider." Section 230 indemnifies Internet service providers (ISPs) and other communications carriers from liability for copyright infringement and harmful speech coursing across their networks. These protections were granted because legislators presume that communications carriers are not encouraging infringement or hate speech; their business is transmitting communications, not encouraging or advocating particular kinds of communication. Unfortunately, the same section that ensures that ISPs are not prosecuted for their subscribers' words and deeds lets malicious sites thrive.

When developers create social networking sites meant for malicious or harmful purposes, they can retreat behind section 230 to avoid personal liability for actions taken on those sites; so long as they are not making comments, they are minimally liable for what is said on their networks. Further, developers can code the sites to minimize the personal data collected on each user. Consequently, while users *are* liable for their speech acts, authorities cannot identify users using the sites' own records. Such sites often encourage "low-value" speech, which is not protected as political in nature and instead includes bullying, harassing, or hateful communications. Such low-value speech is often predicated on monitoring of people offline. After monitoring a person's actions or behaviours, they are (mis)reported in intentionally harmful ways via social media.

Juicy Campus, a website based in the United States, has been used to shame and harm those targeted by its members. A twenty-one-year-old at Baylor found that "her name surfaced on the site in a discussion of the 'biggest slut' on campus" and police temporarily detained another student after false allegations that the young man planned to start a shooting rampage (Morgan, 2008). This website was intentionally designed to minimize the amount of personally identifiable information collected from users, and site designers encouraged users to spread gossip about individuals who were on their college campuses. The designers retreated behind section 230 to avoid liability for humiliating and repugnant speech, and openly stated that administrators were unlikely to remove harmful or hateful content (Solove, 2010). Another website, AutoAdmit, is described by Professor Brian Leiter as constituting a "cyber-cesspool." Members of AutoAdmit regularly demean female law students in discussion threads that describe these students' alleged sexual exploits and alleged condemnable academic behaviours. Leiter argues that affording low-speech websites full section 230 protection increases "speech that causes dignatory harms" and that law should not encourage or protect individuals from creating sites encouraging harmful speech (2010, p. 156).

Such speech acts on social networking sites do more than simply perpetuate and reproduce violent behaviour among community members because what happens online tends to stay online forever. When analyzing men's comments toward women on AutoAdmit, Nussbaum writes, "In effect, he hijacks her agency more or less completely, by colonizing her mind, her social relationships, her access to employment" (2010, p. 80). When employers, colleagues, and friends discover these online hate statements, the targets may be perceived as tainted because of their (forced) associations with pornographic, racist, and slanderous statements. Women who attempted to bring charges against the AutoAdmit administrators suffered financially as a result of the community's slander, insofar as they received no job offers after successfully completing their law degrees. Moreover, the targets admit feeling uncomfortable in classrooms because they know some of their colleagues have sexualized, objectified, and defamed them. Corporeal peer surveillance, combined with the online reporting and slanderous remarks, weakens community bonds within physical classrooms and college campuses by undermining the safe and trusted nature of the classroom. Such surveillance transforms college from a site of exploration and creativity to one of self-censorship and restraint in the face of hidden and malicious voyeurs.

It is important to recognize that both of these social networking sites emerged because developers deliberately created communities to encourage hateful content that exploited American legislation. Further, those same designers protected site members by failing to collect information that could identify them. Turning from this online scenario, let us now address how users can transform otherwise positive social networks into hostile spaces. Specifically, we turn to Facebook and WordPress to discuss how some members used them to encourage mob-like monitoring and punishment in response to the riots following the 2011 Stanley Cup finals.

SOCIAL MEDIA, SHAME, AND MOB RULE

In 2011 a riot erupted in downtown Vancouver in the aftermath of game seven between the Vancouver Canucks and Boston Bruins. During and following the riot, the Vancouver Police Department asked citizens to provide photos and videos of riotous behaviour so that authorities could conduct investigations and bring charges. Authorities requested that citizens send their media directly to them. Unfortunately, this appeal was drowned out in the earliest days after the riot. Prominent local bloggers encouraged their readers/visitors to upload recordings of the riot to social media sites so that the community could identity those caught on camera (Bollwitt, 2011).[1] Moreover, the premier of British Columbia condoned using social media to "share information about events and images of troublemakers captured on mobile phones" (Clark, 2011). These encouragements, combined with claims that social media users were justified in reporting on actions as "citizen-journalists" and the discursively limited natures of online social networks, promoted intense mob-like monitoring, reporting, and shaming of alleged rioters.

The online community identified individuals as soon as the calls went out. As individuals were identified, online vigilantes that mobilized using Facebook called for direct community justice. Photos were sent to employers, which led to alleged rioters being fired. Many photos were intentionally made public with the result that future searches of those individuals would reveal photos of alleged riotous behaviour combined with uncorroborated commentary. In addition to vigilantes trying to digitally "brand" individuals who they believed had destroyed public and private property, the online community urged violent retribution for those assumed guilty before trial. Statements in Facebook groups, such as "They look guilty to me. String em up," were common. Photos often showed individuals posing in front of wreckage without any context of the broader situation, which might clarify whether those photographed were responsible for the destruction. Despite this lack of context, the Facebook mob identified those "responsible" for the riot based on their collected evidence and implied—rather than proved—guilt.

While considerable discussion occurred on Facebook, blogs were also established to "out" individuals. The Public Shaming Eternus WordPress blog was created to publicly shame individuals caught on camera. The (anonymous) site owner wrote,

> There are those who would say that our court system is for the public record to view. When was the last time the average person sat in on a trial and read court transcripts? They are all there for the viewing to see. Public shaming thru the use of social media and blogging shall place them into a world that is engraved into history. It shall be chiseled into the hard stone of the internet and last eternally. (Anonymous, 2011)

Such politics of shame operate as a dangerous response to criminal activity, insofar as shame strikes at the heart of a person's dignity rather than toward the integrity of their actions. Our justice system is not designed to stigmatize individuals with the digital equivalent of scarlet letters, and community efforts to stigmatize individuals threaten to undermine a sense of community by stepping away from integrative and rehabilitative conceptions of justice and politics (Nussbaum, 2004).

Social media users justified a considerable amount of their surveillance, captured on and disseminated across social networks, under the auspice of "citizen journalism." Such journalists recognize themselves as members of the Vancouver community and claim that they report on the world as they see it. The alacrity with which citizen-journalists press "post," "like," or "tweet this" when the implications are potentially far-reaching diverges from the alacrity of well-trained journalists. The latter are trained in what is appropriate and inappropriate to publish, whereas the former rarely possesses similar training. Further, formal journalists (as opposed to their columnist colleagues) who are at newsworthy events describe facts as they arise instead of advocating for harm toward individuals or shaming them pre- (or post-) trial.

Beyond the notion that journalistic ethics and reserve are often lacking when citizens turn to social media, most citizens are simply not trained as investigators. As such, their investigations often depend on crowd-sourced, mob-based fact finding. While online expression in social networks is often heralded as a way for citizens to correct facts and improve the quality of discourse, such positions are often challenged (Hindman, 2009; Sunstein, 2006, pp. 75–102). People engaged in online discussions frequently amplify factually inaccurate information, fail to effectively elicit members' information, go along with the crowd to maintain the good opinion of others, and tend toward extreme positions that accord with positions held prior to deliberating with others. Failure to elicit information and willingness to go along with the group are closely related; in both cases, group members who could clarify or contribute facts either avoid doing so or are prevented from doing so. As a consequence, the deliberative process is stunted, which often leads to increasingly polarized discussions (Sunstein, 2006). As a result, especially in online mobs, the vitriol and surveillance of offline behaviour are amplified by integrating discrete online community members and groups into a much larger online body.

Being hunted down by an amorphous mob is a terrifying experience. Those who believe they are being wrongly persecuted cannot confront the mob because doing so runs "the risk of sustaining the life of the attacks rather than slowing them down" (Keats Citron, 2010, p. 38). Those who are targeted often experience emotional and physical suffering, a loss of personal security, fears that digitally stated sexual threats may be physically realized, anxiety as their online and offline anonymity is eviscerated, and serious fears that online threats may lead to real-world stalking. While celebrities and other newsworthy individuals have oft been targeted, the Internet has democratized surveillance. Whereas **panoptic surveillance** entails the few watching the many, we are now in an age of **synoptic surveillance**, where the many watch the few. Both forms of surveillance discipline discourse and mediate our relations with others (Lyon, 2007). The power accompanying synoptic surveillance is considerable, as manifest following the Vancouver riots. Specifically, after being monitored and identified online, some alleged rioters were afraid to remain in their homes and members of the online community visited alleged rioters' places of employment.

Synoptic surveillance facilitated and empowered the mob's justice, and this "justice" threatens our racially, socially, and culturally mixed communities. Our communities depend on redressing criminal behaviour through impartial evaluation of facts and rehabilitation processes to integrate individuals back into the community; this remedies criminality while also limiting prospective mob-driven harms to minority groups. Mob-like justice limits individuals' capacities to open up, hinders their sense of autonomy, infringes upon their dignity, and reduces the likelihood of feeling that they are full members in a wider, inclusive community. Such capacities are limited because mob-governed horizontal surveillance, of us watching us, carries with it a norm that if people are not "good" all the time then they should expect mob-issued punishment (Turkle, 2011 pp. 241–264). For minority and at-risk groups, who already experience discrimination and condemnation for their entirely legal practices and activities, the slide toward mob-justice can have significant chilling effects. As such, we cannot dismiss threatening online speech as harmless or simply as a way for individuals to safely express anger and rage. While such expressions might feel safe for those making the speech act, the targets of hatred and vitriol, and other community groups most threatened by such targeting, can feel considerably less safe and pushed outside of their offline communities.

MOVING FORWARD

So what does all this mean for social networking? First, the Internet has enabled entrepreneurs to create sites devoted to low speech and to protect themselves (and their users) via regulations that were intended to promote high-value political and legitimate commercial speech. Platforms of speech can themselves possess a dispositional agency, insofar as they can be intentionally designed to reduce the barriers to hostile speech by limiting the capacity to monitor, identify, or out members who engage in tortious or criminal online activities.[2] Second, even platforms that are ostensibly "speech neutral" such as Facebook and WordPress can be used to generate, spread, and reinforce speech that might harm individuals. Both venues of harmful expression can weaken real-world community bonds by undermining otherwise safe communities and imposing a politics and justice of shaming. The surveillance that occurs in both of these platforms operates as a form of **scopophilia**, or love of looking, that manifests "as a sort of voyeurism that reduces the rights of the watched" (Lyon, 2007, p. 40). Consequences of scopophilia can be serious: citizens can be seduced into viewing surveillance—and its accompanying power discrepancies and prejudicial categorizations—as acceptable while blurring conceptions of what is, and should be, public and private. This blurring can have larger societal consequences, as citizens may be less willing to defend the right to privacy because such a defence might make illegal their own voyeuristic pleasures.

In light of these prospective harms from social networking spaces, how might we move forward? Is there an overarching solution that will banish the bad parts of the Internet and leave us with its good, or at least grey, elements? Perhaps.

Authorities might inspect social networking sites that they perceive as having been deliberately designed to promote hateful communications. Such investigations have to tread a fine line because online sites that explicitly ensure secure and anonymous communications for beneficial purposes (e.g., enabling dissidents to communicate with one another) but that are also used for destructive purposes (e.g., hate mongering) should not be closed. Only sites that are explicitly designed to encourage violent speech and limit speakers' and designers' liability should be investigated. Moreover, individuals who actively engage in tortious or criminal behaviour on social networks by inciting violence, encouraging illegal offline surveillance, or violating individuals' reasonable expectations of privacy should be investigated by authorities and punished accordingly.

Unfortunately, shutting down intentionally harmful networks and punishing flagrantly harmful speakers will not cause major search engines to "forget" the utterances that harm individuals or communities (Solove, 2007). This stands in contrast to our past, where actions were once (largely) lost to the mists of time. In the digital era we default to remembering over forgetting, and thus open ourselves to potentially devastating overreactions over past transgressions, regardless of their being real or false (Mayer-Schönberger, 2009). While the initial harm cannot be stopped—we don't want to require state approval to engage in free speech—we could mediate the worst of the long-term damage. The original construction of the web allowed authorized individuals to annotate other people's comments (Berners-Lee, 2000); perhaps (with appropriate court oversight), search engines and web pages could be annotated by authorities to acknowledge that a court has found a statement illegal, false, or otherwise inappropriate. Such annotations might mitigate the worst long-term consequences of speech acts and remind those browsing the web that egregious surveillance and reporting the (alleged) offline actions of other citizens can be ethically and legally suspect.

Annotations might mitigate the long-term consequences of destructive comments in social media, limiting their potential to promote hatred and injustice in perpetuity. Combined with rapid and appropriate judicial rulings against abusive speech online, an ethic of self-reflection and critical evaluation might result. Annotations, rulings, and ethics might tame some of the most harmful uses of social media, ones that threaten to undermine our open, integrative, and democratic communities.

Notes

[1] It should be noted that Ms. Bollwitt subsequently retracted her call for public outings of alleged rioters.

[2] Tortious activities are those that can lead to civil wrongs and charges, and are juxtaposed against wrongs to society, which can lead to criminal charges.

References

Anonymous. (2011, June 16). The case for public shaming of Vancouver rioters. Public Shaming Eternus. Retrieved from http://publicshamingeternus.wordpress.com/2011/06/16/the-case-for-public-shaming-of-vancouver-rioters/

Berners-Lee, T. (2000) *Weaving the Web: The original design and ultimate destiny of the World Wide Web.* New York: HarperBusiness.

Bollwitt, R. (2011, June 15). Vancouver Canucks riot aftermath, how to help. Miss 604. Retrieved from http://www.miss604.com/2011/06/vancouver-canucks-riots-aftermath-how-to-help.html

Clark, C. (2011, June 16). An open letter to British Columbians from Premier Clark. Government of British Columbia statement. Retrieved from http://www2.news.gov.bc.ca/news_releases_2009-2013/2011PREM0070-000730.pdf

Hindman, M. (2009). *The myth of digital democracy.* Princeton, NJ: Princeton University Press.

Keats Citron, D. (2010). Civil rights in our information age. In S. Levmore & M. Nussbaum (Eds.), *The offensive Internet: Speech, privacy, and reputation* (pp. 31–49). Cambridge, MA: Harvard University Press.

Leiter, B. (2010). Cleaning cyber-cesspools: Google and free speech. In S. Levmore & M. Nussbaum (Eds.), *The offensive Internet: Speech, privacy, and reputation* (pp. 155–173). Cambridge, MA: Harvard University Press.

Lyon, D. (2007). 9/11, synopticon, and scopophilia: Watching and being watched. In K. D. Haggerty & R. V. Ericson (Eds.), *The new politics of surveillance and visibility* (pp. 35–54). Toronto: Toronto University Press.

Mayer-Schönberger, V. (2009). *Delete: The virtue of forgetting in the digital age.* Princeton, NJ: Princeton University Press.

Morgan, R. (2008, March 18). Juicy Campus: College gossip leaves the bathroom wall and goes online. *The New York Times.* Retrieved from http://www.nytimes.com/2008/03/18/travel/18iht-gossip.1.11208865.html

Nussbaum, M. (2004). *Hiding from humanity: Disgust, shame, and the law.* Princeton, NJ: Princeton University Press.

Nussbaum, M. (2010). Objectification and Internet misogyny. In S. Levmore & M. Nussbaum (Eds.), *The offensive Internet: Speech, privacy, and reputation* (pp. 68–87). Cambridge, MA: Harvard University Press.

Solove, D. J. (2007). *The future of reputation: Gossip, rumor, and privacy on the Internet.* New Haven, CT: Yale University Press.

Solove, D. J. (2010). Speech, privacy, and reputation on the Internet. In S. Levmore & M. Nussbaum (Eds.), *The offensive Internet: Speech, privacy, and reputation* (pp. 15–30). Cambridge, MA: Harvard University Press.

Sunstein, C. (2006). *Infotopia: How many minds produce knowledge.* Toronto: Oxford University Press.

Turkle, S. (2011). *Alone together.* New York: Basic Books.

ISSUE 4

We are Big Brother: Is social media surveillance a threat to our sense of community?

✗ NO

Social Media for Social Cohesion: The Case of the Toronto G20
Kate Milberry

Kate Milberry is an expert in online privacy and surveillance, specializing in social movements and the Internet. She researches the implications of digital technology for democratic communication, including the right to political dissent. Dr. Milberry is a technology commentator for CBC radio and blogs at http://geeksandglobaljustice.com. She has a Ph.D. in communication from Simon Fraser University.

INTRODUCTION

The evolution of the Internet, Web 2.0, and social media has enhanced the potential for community building online, which has increased dramatically as the interface between the digital and the social has become more user friendly. This, in turn, has developed the potential of online community building for strengthening community offline. While not uniformly tech savvy, activists have begun adopting and adapting a wide range of digital tools for their social justice work. During the lead up to the Group of 20 (G20) Summit in Toronto in 2010, community organizers relied upon email, texting (SMS), social networking (SNS), and the roster of Google products to mobilize opposition to the G20's economic austerity agenda. They engaged in **open source organizing**, eschewing security culture and using corporate digital technologies rather than the more security conscious online services and applications provided by tech activists.

This strategy of openness created solidarity among activists organizing both locally and remotely. But it also facilitated police infiltration of their groups, and led to pre-emptive arrests of "ringleaders" and the ensuing criminal charges, court cases, and jail sentences. From this perspective, social media appear to be a threat to community, and dangerous for political activists and dissidents critical of current governing and economic regimes. However, in the aftermath of the G20 weekend, which saw widespread civil liberties infractions and "virtual martial law" (Marin, 2010), as well as the largest mass arrests and the largest domestic spying operation in Canadian history, activists again turned to digital technology. Drawing upon the same social networks used before and during the G20, activists shifted from mobilizing the resistance to organizing jail solidarity, court support, legal defence fundraising, and other activities intended to rebuild community and create cohesion.

G20 ORGANIZING: USING SOCIAL MEDIA FOR ENGAGEMENT

For several months prior to the Toronto G20 Summit (June 26–27, 2010), community organizers planned the G20 "Days of Action"—a weeklong series of protests and demonstrations. The Toronto Community Mobilization Network (TCMN) worked to engage residents of the city by educating them about the G20, its global economic agenda, and the negative impacts on local communities. The focus was not simply on organizing a protest but on "building community power" (Stimulator, 2010). Organizers did this "by holding community forums, free barbecues, free lunches and dinners … going into immigrant communities, shelters, welfare lines and talking to people" (Stimulator, 2010). Facebook, a privately owned social networking service, was an important outreach tool for TCMN in the engagement process, used to announce the meetings and events and get people involved in the planning sessions associated with this advance organizing.

Preparations for the G20 Alternative Media Centre (AMC) also began in earnest several months before the summit. The Toronto Media Co-op, part of a network of grassroots online news outlets, provided the foundation for the AMC, hosting its web presence as well as the physical media centre. The AMC website, www.2010.mediacoop.ca, was designed as a central hub for incoming social network feeds, gathering all posts from Twitter, Flickr, and YouTube tagged with the hashtag #g20report. This meant that as tweets, photographs, and videos were uploaded to the Internet, they would be aggregated in real time on the AMC site, which became a clearinghouse for breaking news during the G20. About 10 days before the summit, independent journalists from Montreal arrived in Toronto to help launch the media centre's physical site. Throughout its weeklong operation, the AMC served as a convergence space for independent journalists from across North America, as well as a locus of news production. Google Groups, a discussion forum that operates as a listserv, and Google's email service, Gmail, were key communication tools for AMC organizers, facilitating internal communication among dozens of volunteers, as well as external communication with more than 100 journalists seeking AMC accreditation.

TWITTER REPORTING: SOCIAL MEDIA FOR BROADCASTING

As much as digital technology, particularly social media, was useful for activists preparing for the G20, it became more crucial as the summit weekend unfolded. "Twitter reporting" emerged as an important news source for both journalists and protesters. Twitter is a social networking service that allows users to send and read text-based posts, or "tweets," to their followers. Hashtags are a key feature of Twitter, enabling users to mark key words or topics, thus categorizing messages in a way that makes it easy for other users to find and follow them (e.g., #g20, #g20report). During the summit, G20-related posts dominated Canadian Twitter feeds, acting as a conduit for information, misinformation, and likely disinformation. Twitter acted as a "gateway" app to the wider Internet, with embedded links pushing readers to Flickr, YouTube, and the blogosphere, as well as to established media outlets, where more information could be found. Thus Twitter acted as a broadcast medium, albeit one that facilitates audience response, allowing activists to disseminate news and information to potentially vast audiences, including other citizens, mainstream journalists, and politicians.

AMC journalists either tweeted their own reports from the streets or called them in to the media centre, where at least one volunteer was posting official AMC tweets under the Twitter account @2010mediacoop. Other activist organizations also provided regular Twitter coverage, including the Movement Defence Committee (@MDCLegalUdates), a group of lawyers offering free legal advice to activists, and the TCMN (@G20mobilize). "Long after the network crews had packed up, hours after reporters had filed their stories, Twitter was there, providing real-time news plus links to videos from the protest frontlines" (Zerbisias, 2010). Twitter also served a practical function: by monitoring G20-related hashtags, alternative media journalists could find each other in the midst of actions that often turned dangerous. They could also hear about events as they unfolded, allowing them to deploy quickly to any given scene to provide live updates on the action. Twitter helped protesters to mobilize quickly for a particular action or to avoid "hot spots," such as police kettles, mass arrests, or raids.

G20 SOUSVEILLANCE: SOCIAL MEDIA FOR SELF-DEFENCE

The police presence for the G20 was the largest in Toronto's history, comprising 20 000 public and private officers. The protest turned violent after about 100 activists using the Black Bloc tactic engaged in a vandalism spree in the city's shopping district on Saturday, June 26. Police stood down, despite monitoring events live via video surveillance cameras that were part of the $510 million security apparatus (Office of the Auditor General, 2011). They later swept through the downtown core, conducting illegal searches and detentions, including kettles; terrorizing and assaulting peaceful citizens; and arresting more than 1100 people.

Reacting to the police brutality, activists and onlookers alike used social media defensively. They did so by conducting "inverse surveillance," filming instances of apparent unlawful police behaviour and uploading footage to social networking sites like Facebook, Twitter, Flickr, and YouTube (Milberry & Clement, forthcoming 2013). According to Mann (2004), inverse surveillance involves "the recording or monitoring of a high ranking official by a person of lower authority" (p. 627). It is a form of "sousveillance," a method of surveillance inquiry that engages in "watchful vigilance from underneath" (Mann, 2002). Inverse surveillance "intervenes in the process of surveillance and attempts to undermine or reverse the authoritative power associated with the technology" (Institute for Applied Autonomy, n.d.). Thus, it is a political strategy of individuals "who know very well that mediated visibility can be a weapon in the struggles they wage in their day-to-day lives" (Thompson, 2005, p. 31). Videos and photographs posted in real time to the Internet documented shocking police violence as well as blatant disregard for civil liberties and legal protocol during the G20. The infamous "Officer Bubbles" incident showed Toronto Police officer Adam Josephs threatening to arrest a protester and charge her with assault for blowing bubbles (Freeston, 2010). Captured on video and uploaded to YouTube, the piece went viral, receiving almost a million views and fuelling calls for a public inquiry into G20 policing.

Police abuse of power was not indiscriminate; it soon became clear that police were targeting journalists, both mainstream and independent. AMC journalist Amy Miller was arrested and held for thirteen hours in the temporary G20 jail after she filmed police detaining and searching a group of young demonstrators. "My press pass was ripped off me and I was throttled at the neck," she recounts ("G20 Toronto," 2010). Jesse Rosenthal, a freelancer for

The Guardian and AMC affiliate, was punched in the stomach and back by police while covering a kettling incident. A member of the Toronto Police Service (TPS) punched Real News Network and AMC journalist Jesse Freeston twice in the face after he filmed the violent arrest of a deaf man. Police seized his microphone, and when he demanded it back, a Toronto Police supervisor gave the order to "just give him another shot" ("Real News Network," 2010). Familiar with police tactics of harassment and intimidation during protests, AMC journalists created an "emergency response plan" for the media centre in case of a police raid. Part of this plan included filming police with two cameras that stayed on site at all times. On Sunday, June 27, police made two visits to the AMC, and both times, activists filmed the police and streamed the footage live to the web using Qik, a mobile phone application. In one video, the police inform AMC journalists they are there owing to a complaint, to which one journalist responds, "You've been on a riot all over the city. And we've been documenting it. That's why you're here harassing us" ("Police Harassment," 2010). Over the G20 weekend, at least nine AMC journalists were arrested (Dent, 2010).

G20 AFTERMATH: THE FAILURE OF SOCIAL MEDIA

The footage gathered by mainstream and independent media, bloggers, protesters, and onlookers was widely posted on the Internet and circulated via social networking services. Some of it also became evidence in cases investigating police misconduct, including those of Adam Nobody (his real name) and Dorian Barton. Two years later, however, only two officers had been charged with offences relating to the Toronto G20, while multiple calls for an official public inquiry by the provincial government had been rejected (Leslie, 2011). This despite the fact that G20 policing was "at times, disproportionate, arbitrary and excessive" (Canadian Civil Liberties Association, 2011), resulting in what Ontario's ombudsman called the "most massive compromise of civil liberties in Canadian history" (Marin, 2010).

Despite bringing about a "new visibility" in policing (Goldsmith, 2010), the use of social media during the G20 clearly failed to hold police to account, either by shaming or "outing" them, or by otherwise proving misconduct. Worse, in some cases, digital **data doubles**—shadows and trails created by activists using corporate social media tools—proved a boon to police surveillance operations, with some of the intelligence gathered becoming evidence used against them in court. In the high-profile trial of Byron Sonne, a computer security expert and alleged "G20 bomber," police amassed his feeds from Twitter and Flickr, a photo-sharing website, as well as his personal blog postings to build their case against him (Balkissoon, 2011). Sonne was critical of G20 security spending and conducted a "white hat hack"—a benevolent probe—of the G20 security system, which he publicized across his social media networks.

Activists' use of Facebook to plan the G20 resistance made it easy for police to infiltrate and monitor their groups. Many activists used unencrypted email and text communications via insecure corporate service providers such as Gmail, Hotmail, and Yahoo. Their vulnerability was heightened during the G20 weekend, when Twitter emerged as a key communication platform, creating streams of publicly available cached data regarding the activities, opinions, and locations of activists. The "open source organizing" that activists undertook on the premise that they were doing nothing illegal and thus had nothing to hide rejected the security culture that is common in activist circles, and that works to minimize exposure to harm by law enforcement. In hindsight, casual or careless use of social media seemed only to provide fodder for the "open source spying" conducted by the G20 Integrated Security Unit (Thompson, 2006).

BEYOND THE G20: SOCIAL MEDIA FOR COMMUNITY COHESION

Nevertheless, the activist community turned to social media to rebuild their communities in the aftermath of the G20. The Toronto Community Mobilization Network, which had relied heavily on Facebook and Twitter for communication, public outreach, and information dissemination, took on a new role. Though the G20 Days of Action had concluded, there was much work to be done in terms of court support and legal defence fundraising, not to mention in mending the torn fabric of its community. Using the same mailing lists, email account, and web domain, the group re-formed as the Community Solidarity Network (CSN). They renamed their Facebook and Twitter accounts, keeping the same active member base. Shifting gears from mobilizing action to rebuilding community, communication efforts focused on informing members about upcoming court dates, including "bus to court" pickups, fundraising events, and ongoing news stories and press releases about G20-related issues. CSN has been successful in creating community cohesion by rallying around those who faced criminal charges as a result of their G20 organizing, and in keeping the spotlight on the court cases, some of which dragged on for nearly two years.

The Alternative Media Centre's use of social media throughout the G20 convergence was novel, although it drew from a decade-long tradition of media making in the Global Justice Movement(s) (Kidd, 2003). The Independent Media Centre (Indymedia) innovated the open publishing model, which eschews editorial gatekeeping and allows anyone with an Internet connection to upload stories to its newswire. Indymedia also initiated the tactic of launching temporary media centres during protests to accompany the online presence. The AMC adopted other aspects of the Indymedia model, including a consensus-based decision-making process, a general commitment to social justice, and an overall **anarchist philosophy**. Where the AMC differed significantly, however, was in its use of social media to anchor its media-making project. The aggregation of social networking feeds alongside the unedited open publishing wire and featured stories was an important supplement to AMC reporting. Anything posted to YouTube, Twitter, or Flickr tagged #g20report was funnelled through the AMC website in real time. This meant that viewers could receive more information on G20 action faster than they could through traditional news outlets.

In the days following the G20 summit, the AMC disbanded: the website shut down and the media centre reverted to its role as an erstwhile farmers' market. AMCistas—journalists associated with the Alternative Media Centre—returned to their various cities and communities, but the AMC Google group continued to function in much the same way as it did over the course of the G20 resistance. Although traffic is much lower than it was during the height of G20 action, g20altmedia@gmail.com still acts as a listserv for movement journalists covering G20-related issues and other resistance efforts, such as the Occupy phenomenon. Former AMCistas now use the list to stay in touch with one another, share information about upcoming media projects, and promote affinity-based events. Friendships and alliances developed during the G20 have evolved into a national network of independent and activist journalists who regularly collaborate on local, national, and international projects.

FINDINGS/CONCLUSION

There is ample evidence of the potential for community building online (Benkler, 2006; Feenberg & Bakardjieva, 2004; Rheingold, 1994; Shirky, 2010). Despite the Internet's use in both promoting and contesting capitalism, its technical flexibility and continual reconstruction create openings. These openings are virtual spaces of hope in which community building and progressive social change can take root. Social media have contributed to the Internet's metamorphosis from an information-sharing platform to a network that promotes participatory community building.

Social justice activists involved in the G20 resistance appropriated social media in three distinct ways. In advance of the summit, they used social media for engagement through open source organizing. The interactive nature of Facebook, with its "like," "comment," "share," and "join" functions, made it a valuable public outreach tool, helping to engage activists and nonactivists alike. During the G20, activists used social media, especially Twitter, to report on events as they unfolded from within the action, in real time. While this broadcast function is a throwback to traditional or "old" media, it was reinvented for the social web as users re-posted, re-tweeted, and otherwise re-broadcast information about the protests unavailable anywhere else. As a gateway leading to the wider Internet, the blogosphere, and beyond, Twitter provided an alternative historical record to the one offered by the mainstream media. It was also an important communication medium for journalists and protesters alike, allowing them to move safely and strategically across the city. Finally, in addition to engaging communities and broadcasting information, activists and others used social media defensively by documenting police misconduct, tweeting eyewitness accounts, and using their digital cameras (and the implied Internet connection) as their weapon.

Despite social media's usefulness for engagement, broadcasting, and sousveillance, their overall efficacy is questionable. The widespread police abuses during the course of the G20 summit remain inadequately addressed, despite their broad documentation and dissemination on social networking sites. To date, only two police officers have been charged with G20-related offences. Further, the police infiltration and surveillance, along with the pre-arrests, house arrests, and ultimately criminal convictions, brought home to activists the danger of open source organizing. Data trails left by Twitter feeds, Facebook activities, Flickr postings, YouTube uploads, and blogs became evidence in court cases where activists faced serious G20-related charges. The "open source spying" conducted by police was evidently simplistic, consisting mainly of using the Google search engine, yet the information this method uncovered served to bolster government cases against G20 activists.[1]

The negative fallout of organizing online did not prevent activists from turning to social media to rebuild their communities. Once again, they reached out through Facebook (3000+ members) and Twitter (1700+ followers) to rally supporters around those arrested, charged, and jailed. This included important fundraising work that helped pay for lawyers and living expenses for those under house arrest, in pretrial detention, or in jail. It also included court support—getting allies to attend bail hearings and trials—and jail support, such as letters, phone calls, and visits to those incarcerated. AMCistas remain connected through the AMC Google group and have built up a national community of independent media activists. This network is formally embodied in the Media Co-op, a national collective of online grassroots media outlets, and is maintained through informal networking on Facebook and Twitter, and ongoing collaboration on media projects. The Toronto G20 resistance was an experiment in community, fuelled by social media, that withstood the failures of social media. This moment, still unfolding, showed that technology does not define contemporary movements for social justice; rather, activists adopt and adapt technologies for their movement goals in an ongoing process of community building and change making.

Note

[1] Author field notes, Byron Sonne pretrial hearing, February 2011.

References

Balkissoon, D. (2011, November 11). The ruse that violated Byron Sonne's rights. *OpenFile*. Retrieved from http://toronto.openfile.ca/toronto/text/ruse-violated-byron-sonnes-rights

Benkler, Y. (2006). *The wealth of networks: How social production transforms markets and freedom*. New Haven, CT: Yale University Press.

Canadian Civil Liberties Association. (2011). Breach of the peace: A citizens' inquiry into policing and governance at the Toronto G20. Retrieved from http://ccla.org/2011/02/28/take-action-g-20/

Dent, G. G. (2010). Journalists illegally detained and searched en masse. Toronto Media Co-op. Retrieved from http://toronto.mediacoop.ca/story/journalists-illegally-detained-and-searched-en-mass/3931

Feenberg, A., & Bakardjieva, M. (2004). Consumers or citizens? The online community debate. In A. Feenberg & D. Barney (Eds.), *Community in the digital age: Philosophy and practice*. Oxford: Rowman & Littlefield.

Freeston, J. (2010). The whole "Officer Bubbles" story: Toronto neighbourhood responds to G20 policing [Video file]. *The Real News Network*. Retrieved from http://www.youtube.com/watch?v=bVwXOKZh4Os

Goldsmith, A. (2010). Policing's new visibility. *British Journal of Criminology, 50*, 914–934.

G20 Toronto Police rape threats + strip searched—Amy Miller. (2010). Alternative Media Centre press conference. Retrieved from https://www.youtube.com/watch?v=RcXhEd_mDt4

Hiscocks, A. (2012). Last day on the outside. *Bored but Not Broken* [Blog]. Retrieved from http://boredbut-notbroken.tao.ca/lastdayontheoutside

Institute for Applied Autonomy. (n.d.). Inverse surveillance. Retrieved from http://www.appliedautonomy.com/projects.html

Kidd, D. (2003). Indymedia.org: A new communications commons. In M. McCaughey & M. D. Ayers (Eds.), *Cyberactivism: Online activism in theory and practice*. New York and London: Routledge.

Leslie, K. (2011, May 6). McGuinty rejects call for public inquiry into G20 secret law. *The Globe and Mail*. Retrieved from https://www.theglobeandmail.com/news/national/ontario/mcguinty-rejects-call-for-public-inquiry-into-g20-secret-law/article2013400/

Mann, S. (2002). Sousveillance, not just surveillance, in response to terrorism. *Metal and Flesh, 6*(1). Retrieved from http://wearcam.org/metalandflesh.htm.

Mann, S. (2004). Sousveillance: Inverses surveillance in multimedia imaging. *Proceedings of the ACM International Conference on Multimedia (MM '04)*, 620–627.

Marin, A. (2010). Caught in the act: Investigation into the Ministry of Community Safety and Correctional Services' conduct in relation to Ontario Regulation 233/10 under the Public Works Protection Act. Retrieved from http://ombudsman.on.ca/Investigations/SORT-Investigations/Completed/G20-summit—Caught-in-the-Act-br---December-2010.aspx

Milberry, Kate and Clement Andrew. (2013). Policing as spectacle and the politics of surveillance at the Toronto G20. In Margaret E. Beare & Nathalie Des Rosiers (eds.) *The state on trial: Policing protest.* Vancouver, BC: UBC Press.

Office of the Auditor General. (2011). *2011 spring report of the Auditor General of Canada.* Retrieved from http://www.oag-bvg.gc.ca/internet/English/parl_oag_201104_e_35230.html

Police harassment at amc [Qik video]. (2010). Retrieved from http://qik.com/video/8282541

Real News Network journalist attacked at G20 [Video transcript]. (2010). *The Real News Network.* Retrieved from http://therealnews.com/t2/index.php?Itemid=74&id=31&jumival=5326&option=com_content&task=view

Regarding our plea deal. (2011). *Conspire to Resist* [Blog]. Retrieved from http://conspiretoresist.wordpress.com/about-2/

Rheingold, H. (1994). *The virtual community: Homesteading on the electronic frontier.* New York: HarperPerennial. Retrieved from http://www.rheingold.com/vc/book/intro.html

Shirky, C. (2010). *Cognitive surplus: Creativity and generosity in a connected age.* New York: Penguin.

Stimulator. (2010). Escape the freedom fence [YouTube video]. Retrieved from http://www.youtube.com/watch?v=0dkDzJg_jhc

Thompson, C. (2006, December 3). Open source spying. *The New York Times.* Retrieved from https://www.nytimes.com/2006/12/03/magazine/03intelligence.html?_r=1&pagewanted=all

Thompson, J. B. (2005). The new visibility. *Theory, Culture & Society, 22*(6), 31–51.

Zerbisias, A. (2010, July 11). Coverage of the G20 proved Twitter's news edge. *Toronto Star.* Retrieved from http://www.thestar.com/news/insight/article/834367--coverage-of-the-g20-proved-twitter-s-news-edge

Discussion Questions

1. This chapter focuses on negative elements of online speech and suggests means of alleviating long-term harms. Do you think that the suggested means are adequate or should alternate techniques be adopted, such as purging or deleting content from the Internet?

2. While Canada has stricter laws governing speech than the United States, a considerable amount of Canadians' slanderous and libelous speech is physically stored on, and processed by, computer servers in the United States. Given this, should Canadian or American courts decide whether speech is inappropriate? Which nations' courts should oversee the annotation of web pages that violate Canadian speech laws? Should the court's decisions be globally enforced or should they only apply to jurisdiction in which the court has standing?

3. The Internet has afforded individuals the capacity to publish information in ways that only broadcasters enjoyed a few decades ago. Given that broadcasters and journalists must adhere to regulations and ethical codes before publishing comments about individuals, should citizens have to assume similar responsibilities when they publish statements online about other people?

4. What do you see as the main benefits and limitations of "open source organizing" for political activism? Discuss your answer by considering the difference between "surveillance" and "sousveillance" and explaining how these practices were put into use during the G20 summit?

5. In what ways did community activists and citizen journalists use social media sites like Twitter for public engagement and education during the G20 summit? Whom do you think were the intended audiences for activist social media "broadcasts", and how might those audiences have used this content differently?

6. In what ways was social media used by community activists to strengthen offline relations and build community before, during, and after the G20 summit? What does this case tell us about the argument that social media only fosters weak and superficial relationships between individuals and groups?

PART 4 Culture and Regulation

Movies, music, "talk radio" and intellectual property: all of these "products" influence Canadian culture in significant ways, and all are subject to various forms of regulation. But how much regulation should exist—and to what extent should it influence the Canadian marketplace and, by extension, the lives of Canadians?

The section begins with a debate about Canadian cultural identity and to what extent it's represented in film. André Loiselle explores the poignant image of blood on snow, common in the Canadian horror genre, as a way of thinking about the paradox of Canadian identity and culture. For Loiselle, the contrast of red blood on white snow is more than just a visual metaphor for our national flag. "These images stunningly evoke the clash between the peaceful, calm, wintery temperament that putatively distinguishes Canadians and the deep-seated, repressed violence that feeds our collective nightmares." Loiselle's chapter introduces students to a range of "pure" Canadian films and co-productions that were shot in Canada. Students will want to make a weekend of watching the films Loiselle discusses and considering their Canadian distinctiveness.

Peter Urquhart takes the opposite position and argues that "Canadian film does not exist." This isn't to say there is no such thing as a movie made in Canada. Rather, Urquhart's is a methodological argument about how we categorize films for the purposes of programming, critique, or even subsidizing costs of production in the name of cultural goals or industrial strategies. Urquhart provides students with a valuable primer on how the category "Canadian film" is defined in policy and academic discourse: we call films "Canadian" if they are made by Canadians, if they are primarily shot in Canada, if they are made by Canadian companies, or if they are films that reflect something called a "Canadian experience." But these are unhelpful categories, Urquhart argues, because they don't actually tell us anything. He reminds us that the blockbuster movie *Avatar* was made by the Canadian director James Cameron. Is calling this a Canadian film useful in any way? The Hollywood smash hit *Chicago*, which earned Catherine Zeta-Jones an Oscar for best supporting actress and took the big award home for best picture, was actually shot in Toronto. Would it be helpful to call this film a "Canadian production"? Urquhart argues that it would not. And in response to the notion that there is something thematically distinct about some films that should qualify them as Canadian, he argues that Canada's cultural, linguistic, and geographic diversity militate against the possibility that we could ever have an essential category of "Canadian film." He concludes, therefore, that "Canadian film" is a useless analytical category because nobody can agree about what it means.

The second debate moves from film to music and examines the long-standing debate about the necessity of Canadian Content (CanCon) regulations for promoting Canadian musicians and the Canadian music industry. These are regulations that help provide ways for defining what counts as "Canadian music" for purposes of categorization as well as funding and promotion. In an age when Canadian artists like Drake and Justin Bieber can achieve global superstardom thanks to the Internet and social media, does it make sense for Canada to have regulations that, for example, require radio stations to play quotas of Canadian music? David Young argues that global superstars are quite exceptional, and for many Canadian artists CanCon regulations are necessary to their survival. He presents students with a summary of where these regulations came from and how they have been shown to be effective. Young argues, for example, that CanCon not only initially helped put a lot of Canadian talent onto commercial radio, but also led to the development of a domestic recording industry that helped support Canadian studios and producers. Young contends that the increased pressure to deregulate Canadian broadcasting puts these achievements at risk. And citing survey data showing that Canadians still discover new music mostly from radio, he argues that these are achievements worth protecting.

Ira Wagman dismisses the arguments in favour of CanCon regulations as mere myths. He claims that CanCon was not so much about preserving Canadian music or culture as it was about creating a strategy for developing a Canadian industry. Thus, while culture has been the object of CanCon regulations, economics has been its underlying rationale. Wagman observes that the criteria for determining Canadian content might actually work against the efforts of Canadian musicians, allowing some songs to qualify while rejecting others. And he argues that perhaps the greatest problem with this system of regulation is that it "overlooks the numerous venues in which Canadians experience music in the course of their daily lives." Against Young's argument that Canadians privilege traditional radio as a primary source for experiencing and consuming new music,

Wagman argues that local music festivals, Internet radio, websites, iTunes, and various other channels or platforms for music distribution are becoming more prominent in terms of influencing the ways Canadians experience, share, and talk about music.

The third debate explores the issue of free speech, focusing specifically on whether Canada should censor "shock jocks" and other media personalities who seek to entertain or "inform" audiences with what are often offensive jokes and commentary. Ronald Cohen argues that the speech of shock jocks and other media personalities (he includes the prominent Canadian evangelical Christian leader Charles McVety, known for his strong right-wing views about homosexuality and same-sex marriage) should be restricted. Although Canadians have a high tolerance for dissenting speech and benefit from a world of information abundance, this does not mean that Canadian audiences should be subject to any and all forms of speech. Cohen provides a valuable distinction between what Canadians call "freedom of expression" and what is termed "free speech" in the United States, and he notes the irony that while Americans get morally exercised over the brief exposure of a woman's breast during the halftime show of the Super Bowl, they have no problem defending the rights of radio personalities to verbally abuse women with sexist speech. In Canada, by contrast, our broadcast regulations tend to be more tolerant of sexual imagery but more restrictive about abusive commentary targeting minorities.

Josh Paterson, on the other hand, argues that freedom of expression constitutes an essential feature of democratic society. Canada should not censor or otherwise muzzle shock jocks, he insists, because censorship is a "clumsy tool" that can cause much more harm than good. Although Paterson's chapter does not extend to televangelists or other media personalities, the philosophical position he takes does apply. He argues that censorship can actually work to "hide prejudicial views and ensure that nobody is able to challenge them—because nobody is allowed to hear them." To make his case, Paterson examines the Canadian Radio-television and

Telecommunications Commission (CRTC) licensing regulations and outlines how the justifications for regulation are inappropriately suited to Canada's current media environment.

Music industry organizations, including the major record labels, are currently engaged in a long-standing campaign to convince Canadian policymakers, and those in other countries, to legislate against unauthorized copying of copyrighted materials. Through a variety of strategies, including the ability to monitor and surveil Internet websites, to block sites that encourage peer-to-peer (P2P) file sharing, and even to terminate Internet access for people accused of violating copyright laws, they are looking for ways of exerting tremendous control over how Canadians access and enjoy films, books, television shows, and music. The final debate in this section addresses the issue of copyright and the ubiquitous practice of P2P file sharing, asking the question of whether file sharing harms the music industry.

George Barker argues that file sharing through BitTorrent websites and other illegal services poses a significant harm to the music industry, costing it "hundreds of millions of dollars in stolen product." Music piracy provides a valuable example of what economists like Barker call the "free rider" problem: people who steal and distribute music they've not paid for online are riding for nothing off the investment of artists and their distributors in the music industry. The challenge is that people are not inclined to pay for something they know they can get for free, and especially for something that is incredibly easy and quick to obtain. Barker argues that this is harmful because it reduces legitimate

sales that will have a trickle-through effect within the industry, which employs hundreds of thousands of artists, musicians, songwriters, engineers, and other professionals. And to the extent that it harms those in the music industry, Barker argues that music lovers will also be harmed as the quality and quantity of music over time will be less than it would be without unauthorized music file sharing.

John Shiga challenges Barker's assumptions, and argues that industry claims about the harmfulness of file sharing rest on a series of fallacies. His notes that music industry sources frequently undervalue their revenue streams by never including things like concert sales, merchandising, ring tones, and other music-related products in their earnings profiles. However, if they did talk about music industry sales overall, they would have to conclude that revenue is actually growing, not declining, overall. Shiga also challenges the industry argument that illegal downloads are necessarily equivalent to "loss of sales" of legitimate digital music, and he confronts the industry claim that file sharing is its most serious economic challenge by pointing to the effects of broader structural changes in the economy (e.g., recession) and in the music and entertainment industry specifically (e.g., consolidation in music distribution, concentration of ownership and its impact on CD "price fixing"). Finally, Shiga shows that while certain "high-profile artists periodically denounce file sharing in their media appearances," many other artists are more likely to identify traditional contractual relations with recording studios as a greater threat to their rights and livelihood.

ISSUE 1

Red and white on the silver screen: Is there such a thing as "Canadian film"?

✔ YES

Red and White on the Silver Screen: An Iconography of the Canadian Film
André Loiselle

André Loiselle is professor of film studies and associate dean of graduate studies at Carleton University in Ottawa. His main areas of research are Canadian and Québécois cinema, screen adaptations of drama, theatricality in cinema, and the horror film. He has published ten books, including *Stages of Reality: Theatricality in Cinema* (2012, with Jeremy Maron), *Denys Arcand's* Le Déclin de l'empire américain *and* Les Invasions barbares (2008), *Cinema as History: Michel Brault and Modern Quebec* (2007), and *Canada Exposed* (2009, with Pierre Anctil and Christopher Rolfe). He has appeared as an "expert on zombie movies" in the documentary *Zombiemania* (2008, Donna Davies), along with Tom Savini and George A. Romero.

The image of a red-and-white, maple-leaf-adorned flag waving proudly in the front yard of a peaceful suburban bungalow is relatively rare in English-Canadian cinema.[1] Unlike American directors, who generally signal their patriotic penchant through prominent shots of the Stars and Stripes, Canadian filmmakers have traditionally chosen to express their sense of national belonging in other ways. Cineastes in this country seem to agree with Keith Spicer when he says that "we Canadians are reluctant enough to wrap ourselves in our own flag" (1995, p. 14). As I have discussed elsewhere, "irony," "mosaic narratives" (Loiselle, 2002, pp. 257–262), and "quirkiness" (Loiselle, 2011, p. 372) have been the preferred cultural markers of our "distinct" identity on film. Much has been written on the unassumingly flagless distinctiveness of our cinema over the last fifty years, and there is no doubt that this persistent discourse has been at once reflexive and constitutive of something that can definitely be called "Canadian film." Yet, there has been a peculiar use of red and white in Canadian films that has haunted our screens but has rarely been theorized: the poignant image of blood on snow. The bloody connotation of the Canadian flag has not gone unnoticed. Margaret Atwood, among others, has noted the violence imbedded in our most official national symbol. As she once put it, "You thought the national flag was about a leaf, didn't you? Look harder. It's where someone got axed in the snow" (2004, p. 14). Canadian film critics, however, have generally been oblivious to this vivid iconographic analogy. From the shot of an old man crawling in the snow with his face mysteriously torn off by a possessed doll in *Cathy's Curse* (1977) to the close-up of a wounded pigeon on the frozen ground getting crushed with a brick by an evil little girl in *Orphan* (2009), images of gooey red liquid colliding with the whiteness of the frosty surface with which we are all too familiar appear in a number of cinematic tales of terror shot in this country. These images stunningly evoke the clash between the peaceful, calm, wintery temperament that putatively distinguishes Canadians and the deep-seated, repressed violence that feeds our collective nightmares and at times explodes in the form of a downtown shootout on Boxing Day or a savage riot after a hockey game.

Staunch cultural nationalists would probably take issue with the two examples above: Eddy Matalon's *Cathy's Curse* and Jaume Collet-Serra's *Orphan*. "These are not Canadian films!!!" one might say. As co-productions, they are not "pure" Canadian films; they were directed by *non-Canadians* (the former is French, the latter Spanish); and, perhaps most damningly, they are formulaic horror films that seek to appeal to the spectator's baser instincts, rather than trying to edify them through the earnest discourse of compassionate, tolerant, open-minded Canadianness. Yet both films were shot in Canada and foreground the frigid environment that defines much of Canadian identity. The same is true of many other "un-pure" films shot in Canada, which display a vivid red-and-white iconography, from *Ilsa, the Tigress of Siberia* (1977, Jean LaFleur) and *Ghostkeeper* (1981, Jim Makichuk) to *Yeti: Curse of the Snow Demon* (2008, Paul Ziller) and *Red Riding Hood* (2011, Catherine Hardwicke). These might all defy the conventional definitions of our national cinema as advocated by culturally conservative Canadian film critics, but these and other similar tales of bloody terror on ice nevertheless generate stunningly effective visual metaphors for the red-and-white banner.

CONVENTIONAL WISDOM ABOUT CANADIAN FILM

Since the 1960s, the critical discourse around English-Canadian cinema has sought to demonstrate not only that there is such a thing as a true "Canadian film," but that motion pictures worthy of the term "Canadian" are undeniably *distinct* from their Hollywood counterparts. As I have discussed at length elsewhere, cultural nationalists who contributed to landmark anthologies such as *Canadian Film Reader* (1977) and *Self Portrait: Essays on the Canadian and Québec Cinemas* (1980), which defined English-Canadian film studies for years, took it "upon themselves to promote a kind of cinema that was *not* Hollywood [... and] set forth the admittedly uncertain project of defining our national cinema through an exploration of the 'unique characteristics of Canadian cinema'" (Loiselle, 2011, p. 367). The "unique characteristics of Canadian cinema" that were highlighted by cultural nationalists in an attempt to promote the distinctiveness of our national cinema helped to create over time a canon of films that are "small-scale, narratively and stylistically innovative" and that shun "the slick look and contrived, action-packed stories of Hollywood movies" (Loiselle, 2011, p. 366).

Over the past fifty years, the critical discourse around Canadian cinema has changed somewhat. But to this day, Canadian critics continue to praise those films that are distinctively *not* clones of mindless American entertainment. Films that are quirky and ironic yet understated and unassuming, narratively daring yet realist in style, cutting-edge yet inoffensive—those are the true Canadian films (Loiselle, 2011, p. 372). But this definition of Canadian cinema cannot hold. There are many American films that are as quirky and understated as any Canadian film ever was (think of films by directors ranging from Jim Jarmusch to Alexander Payne), and, conversely, there are Canadian films that are as stupidly patriotic as anything Hollywood ever produced (think of Paul Gross's insipidly romantic and moronically pro-militaristic *Passchendaele* [2008]).

Trying to establish a clear-cut distinction between American and Canadian cinema is an exercise in futility. The American film industry has had, and continues to have, too profound an influence on

Canadian film culture for any "distinct" mainstream cinema to exist in this country. However, there can be, undeniably, a recognizable Canadian "spin" in cinema. This spin, to me, is most obvious in films that dare to tackle the peculiar aberrations that emerge from a context where cultural and environmental repressions overlap to engender characters who are compelled by their well-meaning hypocrisy, aggressive tolerance, and callous civility to obstinately stifle the natural urges that people living in less "courteous" nations can express unreservedly. When this exercise in fanatical self-restraint fails—as it necessarily will—red splashes on white in a pattern most evocatively depicted on the poster of Bruce McDonald's darkly droll tale of linguistic zombies, *Pontypool* (2009).

Courtesy of Big Picture Group. Reproduced with permission.

BLOOD ON SNOW: MOMENTS OF BRUTAL RECOGNITION IN CANADIAN CINEMA

The arresting iconography of the *Pontypool* poster finds many moving equivalents in Canadian films that deal with this quintessential moment when our repressed brutality returns with a bloody vengeance to paint the vivid red on white of our flag. In *The Dark Hours* (Paul Fox, 2005), for instance, a fatally wounded dog, wrapped in a blood-stained white sheet, crawls on snow toward the disturbed female psychiatrist who just shot it. This hallucination, one of many, reminds the doctor of her tragic professional failures, her own terminal illness, and the fact that she axed to death her cheating husband and sister minutes earlier. At this moment of horror, the visual analogy with the Canadian flag signals the correlation between the cruel vindictiveness beneath the psychiatrist's pretense of sensible rationalism and the vicious hostility that underlies the agreeable façade of our collective ethos.

Of course, I am not the first film critic to have pointed out the analogy between bloody gore and the Canadian flag. In her analysis of the *Ginger Snaps* trilogy, Sunnie Rothenburger describes a moment early in *Ginger Snaps: Unleashed* (Brett Sullivan, 2004) when, on a cold wintery night, a young man falls victim to a werewolf. As he is torn to pieces in his car, a huge splash of blood covers the windshield upon which a small Canadian flag proudly stands. Rothenburger notes:

> The gore on an official symbol of nation insinuates that, against the common stereotype of peacekeeper, not only is violence possible in Canada, but it may even help constitute the nation. As [Justin] Edwards argues, "the history of colonization in Canada enables us to consider the nation as a threatening, powerful force that has mangled, mutilated, and marginalized those who have stood in its path." (2010, p. 102; see Edwards, 2005, p. 111)

This moment in *Unleashed* undoubtedly bespeaks a Canadian cinematic strategy whereby our holier-than-thou attitude gets a well-deserved slap in the face. But I personally prefer another moment in the *Ginger Snaps* trilogy, which occurs in *Ginger Snaps Back: The Beginning* (Grant Harvey, 2004), the early-nineteenth-century prequel to the other two.

Unlike *Unleashed*, *The Beginning* makes no direct visual reference to the flag—not surprisingly, since the flag did not exist in 1815. But there is still one moment of bloody snow that provides a vivid reflection on Canada's unspeakable potential for brutality. As the colonial ancestors of the twenty-first century, Ginger and Brigette, find refuge from the cold in a fort inhabited by unpleasant soldiers, we are thrown in the middle of Northrop Frye's worst nightmare: a small garrison "confronted with a huge, unthinking, menacing, and formidable physical setting" (Frye, 1971, p. 226) and surrounded by werewolves! The film quickly constructs the soldiers as reprehensible colonialists and the two sisters as defiant victims of patriarchy who use their connections to the ungodly beasts as weapons against men. From a feminist perspective, as

Rothenburger notes, the Ginger-led werewolf attacks against the fort can be read positively: "the audience's potential empathy with these characters [Ginger and Brigette] suggests that these are celebratory moments, where the sisters turn violence back against their oppressors and reshape Canada as subversively brutal" (2010, p. 105). The bond between the two women is so strong that when the Hunter, an indigenous man who had been an ally, urges Brigette to kill Ginger, she proceeds to stab him ruthlessly. Any man who threatens the sister's "feminist solitary"[2] must be disposed of.

But the film becomes more broadly critical, beyond a feminist reading, when it paints all white characters with the same brush in a striking scene where a teenage indigenous boy offers to guide the sisters through the dark, looming forest. He is not a menacing character, threatening neither to the sisterhood nor to the masculinist fort. And yet he is lacerated by the werewolves. For the boy, the werewolves are the wendigo: "a disease that the White men brought with them from Europe" (Rothenburger, 2010, p. 102). His bloody body lying in the snow signals that the werewolves are not so much a tool of female power against patriarchy as an embodiment of the (self-)destructive Canadian settler mentality—male and female. Canadians, in their ravenous thirst for civility, their irrational obsession with being reasonable, their rabid fixation on appearances of equality and fairness, will destroy anything and everything that stands in their path—allies and enemies alike—to satisfy their need for hostile graciousness.

Courtesy of Copperheart Entertainment. Reproduced with permission

In many ways, therefore, Canadians are like the murderous little creatures of David Cronenberg's best horror film, *The Brood* (1979): bland, innocuous little things that look rather ridiculous in their awkward snowsuits. But do not stand in the way of their self-righteous mission to manifest their mother's repressed rage or they will beat you to a pulp with a meat tenderizer. While there is a lot of snow and blood in *The Brood*, I do not believe there is a single shot of blood *on* snow. But the red-and-white iconography is still central to the film's main moment of horror. The infamous scene in which the monstrous mother, Nora, reveals the external womb from which she gives birth to the killer brood projects an image of gruesome patriotism. Dressed in white and covered in blood, Nora stands for Canada's matriarch. A repressed Brit (the accent is unmistakable), she gives birth to preposterous little Canadians who generally behave inoffensively, until fury overtakes them.

Like many other Canadian films, *The Brood* uses the red-and-white iconography as a metaphor for the consequence of oppressive good manners and **repressive politeness**. Another, even more striking example is the selective use of red in Guy Maddin's *Dracula: Pages from a Virgin's Diary* (2002). Shot in black and white, the 1920s-looking film adaptation of the Royal Winnipeg Ballet's performance of Mark Godden's *Dracula* includes only a few moments of colour, and in particular the conspicuous use of red for blood, which clashes with the overexposed pale greys that dominate the screen.

The film revolves around the age-old Canadian conflict between reason and passion. The "immigrant" Dracula embodies all that is sensual, exotic, irrational, and forbidden. For their part, the "normal" men who surround Lucy, the main female character and first victim of the vampire's bite, are rationalists who fear the woman's threatening sexuality as much as they despise Dracula's lascivious potency. While they hide behind the cloak of reason, science, and civilization, the men are depicted by Maddin as vile hypocrites and brutal perverts. In a scene where the men, led by Dr. Van Helsing, give a collective blood transfusion to Lucy, to "save her" from Dracula's venom, Maddin uses extreme camera angles and distorted perspectives to link the transfusion to a gang rape, with Lucy contorting and the men grimacing with painful pleasure as they pump their vital fluid into her. Not surprisingly, red blood appears during the scene in stark contrast with the white flesh of the learned scientists. This is Canada, Maddin seems to suggest: highly cultured and enlightened men who, under the guise of reason and knowledge, rape, pillage, and abuse.

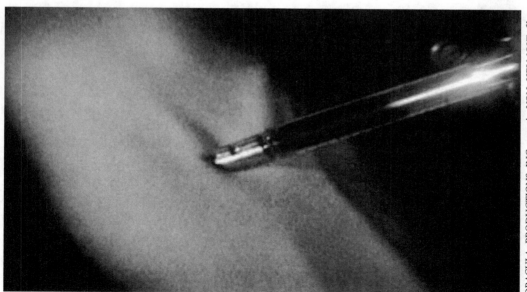

DRACULA PRODUCTIONS INC. vonnie VON HELMOLT film. Reproduced with permission.

Significantly, when Lucy—now a vampire—and Dracula suck each other's blood, there is no shot of red against white. The bichromatic iconography would not be fitting here, for the two characters are now on the same plane of impolite lust, bad-mannered desire, undemocratic horniness—nothing could be less Canadian. It is only when the repressive urges of perversely quirky civility encounter inappropriate concupiscence and offensive courtship that the red-and-white icon materializes as a suitable emblem of appalling Canadian contradictions. And one of the most evocative uses of red blood against a white backdrop occurs when the nauseatingly sensible men decide to eliminate Dracula and the threat he represents against caution, propriety, and triteness.

Armed with their crosses and stakes, Van Helsing and his disciples track down Dracula in his castle and swiftly proceed to poke at the rogue aristocratic figure. Each rational, level-headed stab from the decent men produces a streak of red blood upon white surroundings that visually associates the victory of neurotic sanity and perilous prudence with the colours of our fanatically prosaic nation. At this moment, when the mundane hunts down the extraordinary in a pathetic effort to maintain respectability, health, and social equity, the red-and-white iconography is too salient to ignore. As such, the obliteration of Dracula reverberates cinematically as a typically Canadian gesture.

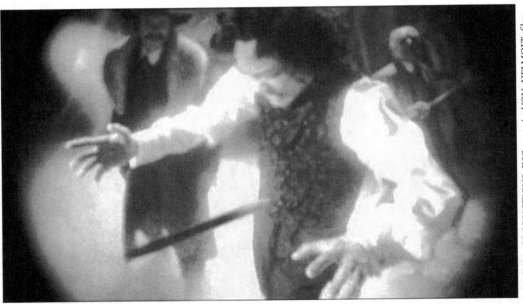

DRACULA PRODUCTIONS INC. vonnie VON HELMOLT film. Reproduced with permission.

CONCLUSION

Whether it is a "pure" Canadian ballet film directed for the mighty CBC by Winnipeg's homegrown cinematic genius, or a bastard child co-production that tries to deny its origins, like *Orphan*, the movies that explore the more unpleasant facets of our all-too-pleasant collective identity often foreground red and white as a conspicuous visual reminder of the gory national wounds we desperately try to veil. Of course, not all Canadian films include shots of blood on snow, or some bichromatic equivalent; nor does red-and-white iconography appear exclusively in Canadian films. But there is an intriguing tendency in cinematic tales of terror shot in this country to flag our contradictions through images of a bloody stain smudged on a pristine frozen surface. Most Canadian spectators are probably oblivious to these moments of patriotic repulsion. But for those of us who have noticed them, their recurrence serves as haunting evidence that Canadian cinema is most gripping when it dares to tap into our disturbingly pleasant nightmares.[3]

Notes

[1] In this essay, I will conveniently ignore French-language Québécois cinema, which is a different creature altogether.

[2] See Bianca Nielsen's (2004) well-known reading of "feminist solidarity" in the original *Ginger Snaps*.

[3] I wish to thank my students Gina Freitag and Frederick Blichert for drawing my attention to some of the elements discussed in this paper.

References

Atwood, M. (2004). *Strange things: The malevolent North in Canadian literature*. London: Virago.

Edwards, J. (2005). *Gothic Canada: Reading the spectre of a national literature*. Edmonton: University of Alberta Press.

Frye, N. (1971). *The bush garden: Essays on the Canadian imagination*. Toronto: House of Anansi Press.

Loiselle, A. (2002). The radically moderate Canadian: Don McKellar's cinematic persona. In W. Beard & J. White (Eds.), *North of everything: English-Canadian cinema since 1980* (pp. 256–269). Edmonton: University of Alberta Press.

Loiselle, A. (2011). A "distinct" national cinema or "plus ça change plus c'est pareil": English Canadian film studies since 1980. In K.-D. Ertler et al. (Eds.), *Canadian studies: The state of the art* (pp. 365–389). Frankfurt am Main: Peter Lang.

Nielsen, B. (2004). "Something's wrong, like more than you being female": Transgressive sexuality and discourses of reproduction in Ginger Snaps. *Thirdspace: A Journal of Feminist Theory & Culture, 3*(2). Retrieved from http://www.thirdspace.ca/journal/article/view/nielsen/176

Rothenburger, S. (2010). "Welcome to civilization": Colonialism, the gothic, and Canada's self-protective irony in the Ginger Snaps werewolf trilogy. *Journal of Canadian Studies/Revue d'études canadiennes, 44*(3), 96–117.

Spicer, K. (1995). Values in search of a vision. In R. L. Earle & J. D. Wirth (Eds.), *Identities in North America: The search for community* (pp. 13–28). Stanford, CA: Stanford University Press.

ISSUE 1

Red and white on the silver screen: Is there such a thing as "Canadian film"?

✘ NO

Canadian Film Does Not Exist
Peter Urquhart

Peter Urquhart is an associate professor in communication studies at Wilfrid Laurier University. He has published widely on Canadian film and television and is currently completing a book on Canada's cultural industries, co-edited with Dr. Ira Wagman of Carleton University.

Some of you are thinking right now, "*Of course* there is such a thing as a Canadian film. How could there not be?" I begin by acknowledging the apparent obviousness of the answer to this question because this reaction—that there is an obvious answer to this question—illustrates one of the many utterly habitual ways we think about film, about how films are categorized, critiqued, programmed at film festivals, advertised, and discussed by film scholars, critics, and historians and in our everyday conversations about movies. Other habitual and commonplace categorical tools—*Raging Bull* is a "Martin Scorsese picture," for example—seem equally obviously accurate at first (Scorsese *did* direct it, after all) but also help to show us that if we really want to understand film as a cultural, textual, industrial, artistic form of expression, then we need to recognize the failings of some of our everyday understandings of the cinema. I say this because describing *Raging Bull* as "a Martin Scorsese picture" actually tells us very little about the way this film was created and the effects it has on audiences. In fact, categorizing *Raging Bull* this way certainly obscures far more than it reveals. Assigning films to **auteur** directors regularly misassigns credit, confuses audiences about the collaborative nature of filmmaking, and is, in most cases, simply wrong.

I have selected the case of *Raging Bull* because excellent recent research has demonstrated the extremely high degree of input the film's star, Robert De Niro, actually had in not only shaping the screenplay—largely writing or rewriting several drafts of it—and providing the crucial performance at the centre of the film, but also initiating its production, convincing an originally totally uninterested Scorsese to direct it, and using his star persona to sell it after its completion (Tate, 2011). If this is any one person's "picture," it's demonstrably Robert De Niro's, but the habitual pull of what we call the auturist tendency helped categorize and define *Raging Bull* in the commonsense way we still do.

The question of national cinema is at least as, if not more, fraught as a categorical tool. Just because we all continue to use it almost nearly every time we think of a film does not make it a useful category. If there is such thing as a "Canadian film," we should be able to define what that might be. If we cannot define "Canadian film," why ever evoke this useless category?

There are several ways of thinking about this question. Here are the most common.

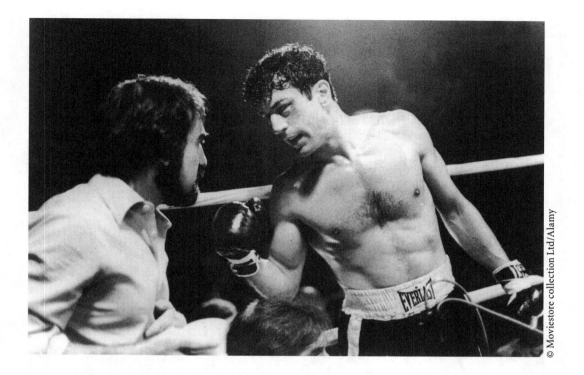

© Moviestore collection Ltd/Alamy

A CANADIAN FILM IS ONE MADE BY CANADIANS

Among the many problems with this notion, the first has to be the one this assertion shares with the failure of the auturist paradigm: that it fails to acknowledge the collaborative nature of all professional filmmaking. Many, many people contribute to a completed film in most cases, and the entire history of cinema shows how frequently collaborators are an international mixture. We think of "classical Hollywood" cinema as an inherently American cultural form, but such a huge percentage of the creative talent that made these films were foreigners, mostly Europeans: Charlie Chaplin, Billy Wilder, Fritz Lang, Douglas Sirk, Alfred Hitchcock, and the list goes on. Other key creative individuals integral to the look, sound, and appeal of classical Hollywood were also foreigners in large part, from celebrated cinematographers to screenwriters, editors, composers, and, of course, stars. How can the birthplace of the people who make films tell us anything at all about the "nationality" of the work they produce?

Another way of looking at this question is to ask, are *Avatar*, *Titanic*, *Ghostbusters*, *In the Heat of the Night*, or Mack Sennett's Keystone Kops slapstick comedies Canadian films simply because they were directed by Canadians? And if they are, how useful is "Canadian film" as a category of analysis or description? If the highest-grossing film in the history of cinema— *Avatar*, at approximately $2.8 billion worldwide—is a Canadian film simply because it was directed by Canadian James Cameron, I think we need to look for another, more useful way to define "Canadian film." The definition of "national cinema" needs a better definition than this one, otherwise *Psycho* and *Modern Times* are British films (by virtue of the nationalities of Alfred Hitchcock and Charlie Chaplin), *All That Heaven Allows* is German (Douglas Sirk), and *Chinatown* is a Polish film (directed as it was by the Polish-born French citizen Roman Polanski).

CANADIAN FILMS ARE THOSE PRIMARILY SHOT IN CANADA

No, they're not. If they were, once again we find the concept "Canadian film" reduced to uselessness because annually billions of dollars worth of so-called runaway productions made by foreign firms, with foreign talent, are shot in Canada due to various incentives that bring these productions to Canada. Vancouver, Toronto, and Montreal are centres of what is called the "service" sector of the Canadian film industry, which explicitly encourages foreigners, chiefly based in Hollywood, to make films in Canada for the sole purpose of generating capital and creating employment. There are far too many Hollywood films that you will have heard of, but that were shot in Canada, for me to list. A great example here is the Jackie Chan vehicle *Rumble in the Bronx*, which was shot in Vancouver. The more observant viewers of this film will notice the majestic North Shore mountains in the background of some shots of this film ostensibly set in a New York City borough. Last I checked, there are no mountains in the Bronx. But my favourite example is the film *Chicago*, a huge Hollywood hit that met with much critical acclaim around the world as well, and that was shot in Toronto. *Chicago*. Toronto. No, these examples show that "made in Canada" cannot define what a Canadian film is.

© AF archive/Alamy

A subset, or related, part of this possible definition of what might count as a Canadian film are those films *set* in Canada. But this definition cannot work either, for a number of reasons. First, think about what this definition would mean for the designations of any other national cinema. Should we think of *An American in Paris*, the luscious MGM musical starring Gene Kelly, as a French film? What could be more ridiculous? And what about those films that purposely, often for thematic or artistic reasons, choose to leave their setting ambiguous, unidentified, or unknowable: Are these films with no national designation at all? Finally, consider the problem this definition poses for a hypothetical Canadian filmmaker who wants to use her Canadian investors' money to collaborate with her all-Canadian creative team and crew to shoot in, say, Winnipeg her futuristic science fiction movie—which is about beavers playing hockey but is *set* near a Tim Hortons outlet on Mars. Canadian films clearly cannot be defined as those set in Canada.

CANADIAN FILMS ARE THOSE MADE BY CANADIAN COMPANIES (AND/OR WITH CANADIAN MONEY)

This initially appealing possible definition has the virtue of working well when held up by comparison against the notion of Hollywood films as "American" or against studio productions in other countries. For example, it gets around the clear problems of defining Canadian cinema by the nationality of the filmmakers and of the problems with shooting location and setting as defining features because a film produced by Universal Pictures or 20th Century Fox *is* a Hollywood (and therefore American) film, in spite of the likelihood of foreigners being in the cast or directing *and* even if it was set in Vietnam or on Mars (or in Toronto). Another of the habitual "commonsense" through-lines of film history is to adopt this criterion, hence the centrality in standard film histories given to entities like Paramount in Hollywood, and the studios Ufa in Germany, Gaumont in France, Ealing studios in Britain, and Toho in Japan.

In fact, if we look at film history through this lens, we can see how dominant this definition is, using the example, again, of Alfred Hitchcock. British born, Hitchcock is generally known as a master Hollywood filmmaker, but film history also acknowledges the British part of his career (actually called by historians "British Hitchcock") where he made films in Britain in the 1920s and '30s for the British companies Gainsborough Pictures and British International Pictures, among others. Thus, although the more celebrated part of his career began with *Rebecca* in 1940—a film set in England, starring British actors Joan Fontaine and Laurence Olivier and based on the British novel by Daphne du Maurier—is the beginning of "Hollywood Hitchcock" chiefly due to the fact that the film was produced by David O. Selznick's Selznick International Pictures? No matter who starred in or wrote the films Englishman Alfred Hitchcock made after 1940, *or* where they were set, the fact that they were produced by American firms makes them Hollywood pictures.

Let me now introduce some ambiguity and doubt about the idea of defining Canadian films as those produced by Canadian companies and/or with Canadian money. To begin, we must deal with the relatively large percentage of so-called Canadian films that are actually international co-productions. Many other nations, of course, participate in international co-production, normally in official treaty arrangements with other nations, but Canada is especially active in international co-production and has treaties with over fifty nations. In the words of Telefilm Canada, the federal agency that oversees treaty co-production, "Coproduction agreements enable Canadian and foreign producers to pool their creative, artistic, technical and financial resources to coproduce projects that enjoy the status of national productions in the countries involved" (2012). Thus, under these treaties, the film *Barney's Version*, based on Montrealer Mordecai Richler's novel and starring Americans Paul Giamatti and Dustin Hoffman, counts as a Canadian film in Canada for purposes of tax credits and opportunities for other Canadian state funding because of the participation of Toronto-based Serendipity Point Films. But it also counts as an Italian film in Italy for these same purposes because of the participation of Rome-based production company Fandango. Consider another recent example: Canadian David Cronenberg directed *Eastern Promises* with an international cast including American Viggo Mortensen, German Armin Mueller-Stahl, Frenchman Vincent Cassel, and Brit Naomi Watts. The film was written by Steve Knight, another Brit; shot by cinematographer Peter Suschitzky (born in Poland); and set in England. Like *Barney's Version*, *Eastern Promises* counts to the Canadian government as a Canadian film because it was co-produced by Serendipity Point Films. But this film is *also* a British film because it is an official treaty co-production with the United Kingdom's Kudos Pictures.

Some of you are probably thinking that international co-production *obviously* complicates things under this possible definition, but what about films produced by a single Canadian firm? Surely *these* are Canadian films. One problem with reducing film to a purely economic/industrial model is that it renders the designation more or less meaningless as a descriptive category. Consider this hypothetical example. A Canadian production firm decides to shoot a "faithful" adaptation of Mark Twain's *The Adventures of Tom Sawyer*. To lend authenticity to their production, which they hope will increase the commercial appeal of the film, they decide to hire exclusively local people for all aspects of the production, from cast and crew to writer and director, to the Missouri town on the Mississippi River where they will shoot. Post-production will take place on a riverboat on the Mississippi as well. What would it mean, what would it *tell us*, to define this film as a Canadian film solely based on the fact that the company that produced it was incorporated in Canada, and that it was made with Canadian money? This proposed definition, upon closer examination, seems, like the others examined so far, to render the category relatively meaningless. Does the company that produced it define the nationality of a film? If it does, how are we to use this information in any meaningful way? Would this definition in any way aid in an interpretation or understanding of this *Tom Sawyer* film?

CANADIAN FILMS ARE THOSE THAT REFLECT SOMETHING OF THE "CANADIAN EXPERIENCE"

We come now to the "thematic" definition of Canadian film. As many readers will know, this definition has had several high-profile supporters over the years, including Canadian literary icon Margaret Atwood. In fact, it would be reasonable to claim that Canadian scholarly and popular criticism has overwhelmingly endorsed the thematic definition of Canadian film for many decades. The proposal here is that by virtue of a shared set of social, historical, geographical, and cultural experiences that are at the centre of what it means to be Canadian, and which may sometimes be described as our "national identity," something of our Canadian nature *reveals itself* in the thematic terrain of Canadian films. Underlying this is the premise that Canadians *are* Canadians because we all share something cultural that makes us different from citizens of other nations (this premise lies beneath understandings of every other nation too, of course).

The thematic approach to defining Canadian film has its roots in the literary criticism of the world-famous Northrop Frye, who identified what he called the "garrison mentality" prevalent in Canadian literature. Frye observed the frequency of characters who feel threatened by hostile environments and seek to establish metaphorical garrisons in defence against this perceived hostility. Frye further theorized that this thematic concern is prevalent because it represents something of the historical conditions of the Canadian experience. Another world-famous Canadian, Margaret Atwood, advanced Frye's theory in her 1972 book *Survival: A Thematic Guide to Canadian Literature*, in which she argues that survival is the central thematic motif of Canadian literature, which tends to be peopled by characters who are victims.

Following these celebrated works, one of the compelling and enduring "thematic" explanations for what defines the essence of Canadian films is provided by Robert Fothergill's 1973 article "Coward, Bully or Clown: The Dream-Life of a Younger Brother." In this still frequently cited article, Fothergill observes a preponderance of "loser" characters in Canadian films, which he contrasts with the "hero" character's dominance in Hollywood narratives. Fothergill theorizes that loser characters people Canadian films in disproportionate numbers because they represent Canadians' national inferiority complex vis-à-vis the cultural domination by our powerful neighbour to the south. Hollywood has heroes because Hollywood and America are powerful and dominant; Canadian films have losers because we are less powerful and culturally dominated.

Appealing though this thematic explanation of Canadian film might be, it has to be scrutinized. There are sound objections to using thematic consistency to define what might be a Canadian film. The first of these is that it commits what we call "essentialism." How could there possibly be some cultural or historical experience or attitude, an *essential essence*, shared by all Canadian filmmakers? When we think of the incredible diversity of the country in every single way—geographically, linguistically, religiously, historically—is it reasonable to speak of an "essence" of Canadian experience that will necessarily (or even frequently) manifest itself in a film made by Canadians? Are we willing to accept the notion that a female, Chinese Canadian, high school dropout filmmaker from Vancouver shares so much culturally with a gay, Cree, doctorate-holding filmmaker from Shamattawa, Manitoba, or with a unilingual Farsi-speaking, aged, Canadian filmmaker who lives in Sherbrooke, Quebec, that somehow the Canadian experience is going to emerge thematically in all their work? Furthermore, what are we to make of the films that do not fit the thematic paradigm? How can we account for all those Hollywood films with protagonists who are not heroes, and all those films from Canadian filmmakers that *do* have heroic characters? In addition to its inherent essentialism, the thematic definition also commits a **tautology** in that Canadian films that do not feature loser characters are not really Canadian, thus circularly maintaining the purity of the definition. No, the thematic definition of Canadian film is not tenable.

CANADIAN FILMS ARE THOSE THAT CANADIANS ACTUALLY SEE

The whole point of defining Canadian film is that this category should tell us something about either the film or the country that produced it. Film festivals categorize films this way because of the understanding that audiences will make some kinds of assumptions before deciding to see a film of a particular national origin. Parts of the premise underlying this assumption are found in some of the above proposals: we may anticipate it to be shot or set in Canada, we may expect it to be made exclusively by Canadian citizens, and we may expect it represent *something* about Canada (and not Sweden or France). In other words, the assumption is that a relationship exists between films' texts and the countries they come from. If we are willing to go along with the assumption

TWENTIETH CENTURY-FOX FILM CORPORATION/THE KOBAL COLLECTION

that the distinctive culture of a nation is reflected through its films, and that films influence the distinctive culture of a nation, does it not make sense to consider the films that a nation's citizens actually see to be the definition of that nation's cinema? The films we see are those that have the possibility of affecting the way we see the world, so we could define Canadian film this way.

But it would be unreasonable to do so. To do so would mean that, since Canadians overwhelming see Hollywood films, these are Canadian films, and that would not tell us anything, would it? Unfortunately, none of the possible definitions of what a Canadian film is manages to tell us anything. There may be such a thing as a "Canadian film," as far as the government is concerned and as it pertains to industry growth objectives. And there may be such a thing as a "Canadian film" as far as film festivals are concerned, and as far as some critics and audiences are concerned. But if a term is useless as an analytical category because nobody knows what it means, there is no reason to have this category. Thus, if "Canadian film" is a category that does not meaningfully describe anything, we can only be left to conclude that Canadian films do not exist.

References

Tate, R. C. (2011, Spring). Robert De Niro's *Raging Bull*: The history of a performance and a performance of history. *Canadian Journal of Film Studies, 20*(1), 20–40.

Telefilm Canada. (2012). Guidelines. Retrieved from http://www.telefilm.ca/en/coproductions/coproductions/guidelines

Discussion Questions

1. Should films that were directed by non-Canadians and set in non-Canadian locations, but shot in Canada and financed in part through Canadian taxpayers money (through governmental funding agencies) be considered "Canadian"?

2. Are Canadians truly characterized by well-meaning hypocrisy, aggressive tolerance, and callous civility?

3. When you see the red & white of the Canadian flag, do you immediately think "Blood on Snow"?

4. Do you agree that in spite of our stereotypical reputation as peace-keepers, Canadians have a history drenched in blood and violence?

5. Why do we habitually assign a "nationality" to films? What is it about films and nations that make this connection seem normal? What is problematic about this practice?

6. As an incredibly international medium for over a century, should we see the cinema as an early instance of what we now call "globalization"?

7. The Canadian government supports the creation of Canadian films through various incentive programs that cost tax-payers millions of dollars every year. What are the reasons for doing so? Do you think they are good reasons?

ISSUE 2

Music matters:
Are CanCon regulations necessary to promote Canadian music?

✔ YES

Why Canadian Content Regulations Are Needed to Support Canadian Music
David Young

David Young is an assistant professor in the Department of Sociology at McMaster University. His areas of research include awards shows, the political economy of Canadian cultural industries, media policy, and media history. He is the author of several journal articles, including three that report research on the Juno Awards for the Canadian music industry.

INTRODUCTION

After decades in which Canadian music was rarely heard on the radio, 1971 marked a turning point. "Signs" by the Five Man Electrical Band, "Sweet City Woman" by the Stampeders, and "Put Your Hand in the Hand" by Ocean are just a few of the many now-classic Canadian songs that dominated the airwaves that year. The success of these songs has a lot to do with Canadian content (CanCon) regulations that came into effect in 1971 (Breithaupt, 1999, p. 5). CanCon regulations have been controversial ever since they were implemented, and they have increasingly come under attack in recent years. It is argued, for instance, that the popularity of Drake and Justin Bieber means that "there has been no need to force these regulations" (Sutherland, 2011). However, in this chapter, I will make three arguments in defence of CanCon. First, CanCon regulations were crucial in light of conditions that largely precluded music by Canadians. Second, the regulations have supported various components of the Canadian music industry. Third, while the doctrine of neoliberalism has generated pressure to eliminate CanCon, the regulations are still needed because prevailing economic interests threaten to undermine the further development of Canadian musical artists.

THE EMERGENCE OF CANCON REGULATIONS

From the 1950s to the end of the 1960s, there was little production and airplay of Canadian music. The few Canadian-owned record companies (such as Quality) primarily made money by pressing foreign master tapes into records and only occasionally produced records by Canadian acts (Straw, 1993, pp. 56–57). Although some Canadian acts received airplay, including Gordon Lightfoot and the Guess Who, American or other foreign music was emphasized on Canadian commercial radio (Haysom, 1996, p. F1). The popularity of this music drew listeners, which in turn generated high advertising rates and therefore profit for private radio stations. Under these circumstances, it is not surprising that only 4 to 7 percent of the music on private radio during 1968 was Canadian (Audley, 1983, p. 8).

The concept of a **promotional state** helps to shed light on developments in Canadian music from the 1970s onward. Reacting to the dominant presence of foreign music, a promotional state attempts to support domestic music through a number of interventionist strategies (Cloonan, 1999, p. 204). Public broadcasting and government funding are key aspects of Canada's promotional state, but another important factor is CanCon regulations (Young, 2004, p. 272). The CRTC, the federal government agency that sets rules for broadcasting, announced in 1970 its proposal to establish Canadian content regulations for music on Canadian radio stations. The CRTC's public hearings on the issue revealed sharp divisions between various groups. Private radio stations opposed the idea of CanCon. However, the CRTC's proposal was strongly supported by Canadian record companies, music publishers, trade unions, and musicians (CRTC, 1971, pp. 19–20).

On the basis of the public hearings, the CRTC proceeded with CanCon regulations. Starting in 1971, a minimum of 30 percent of music in the entire broadcast day had to meet at least one of the following criteria: the music must be written by a Canadian; the performance must be by a Canadian artist; the production must be recorded in Canada; and the lyrics must be written by a Canadian. After one year, a minimum of 30 percent of the music needed to satisfy at least two of these criteria (CRTC, 1971, pp. 16–17, 20). The four criteria of what became known as the MAPL system (music, artist, production, and lyrics) have continued to provide the basis for determining what constitutes Canadian content. The CRTC has stated that the *cultural objective* of CanCon regulations is "to encourage increased exposure of Canadian musical performers, lyricists, and composers to Canadian audiences," while the *industrial objective* is "to strengthen the Canadian music industry, including both the creative and production components" (CRTC, 2009).

THE EFFECTIVENESS OF CANCON REGULATIONS

When considered in relation to these objectives, CanCon regulations have been effective. Wright notes that the emergence of CanCon "opened the recording industry to Canadian talent as nothing had done previously, and a great scramble to build record companies and to sign artists followed" (1987–88, p. 30). By encouraging production in Canada, the regulations helped to support Canadian recording studios and producers (Dafoe, 1991, p. C1). As a result of radio airplay in the first half of the 1970s, the copyright royalties paid to Canadian composers and lyricists more than tripled (Spurgeon, 1992, p. 2). Of course, recording artists also received airplay as a result of CanCon. For instance, Randy Bachman (of Bachman-Turner Overdrive) and Rich Dodson (of the Stampeders) have stated that CanCon regulations helped their bands to get on the radio during the 1970s. Similarly, Sass Jordan noted that the airplay she enjoyed in the 1980s and 1990s can be partially attributed to the regulations (Breithaupt, 1999, p. 5; Leary, 2003).

Although CanCon regulations have been effective, some Canadian recording artists and private radio broadcasters have attacked the regulations or attempted to undermine them. Bryan Adams criticized the CRTC in 1992 after songs from his latest album failed to qualify as CanCon because the music and lyrics were co-written with a foreigner. However, Adams also conceded in a column he wrote for the *Toronto Star* that CanCon has assisted many Canadian artists by giving them exposure (1992, p. J1). Representatives of the private radio industry have made similar admissions (McCabe, 2001, p. R1). Nevertheless, because private stations still wanted to emphasize foreign music, a "**CanCon ghetto**" had emerged at a number of stations by the 1980s. Even though the CRTC required CanCon selections to be played throughout the entire broadcast day, some stations were not playing them during peak listening periods (morning and afternoon). Instead, the stations attempted to meet the requirement by playing Canadian music during low-listening times (Lanthier, 1989, pp. 2–3). According to a study conducted by the Canadian Independent Music Association (CIMA) and the Society of Composers, Authors and Music Publishers of Canada (SOCAN), this ghettoization of Canadian content continued into the 1990s (Jones, 1996, p. 16). The CRTC addressed the problem in the late 1990s by establishing tighter rules regarding the hours for playing CanCon while also increasing the minimum level of CanCon for popular music stations from 30 percent to the current 35 percent (CRTC, 2006).

THE CONTINUING NEED FOR CANCON REGULATIONS

The practices of private radio broadcasters demonstrate that CanCon regulations are needed and must be enforced, but the rise of neoliberalism presents challenges to the regulations. Neoliberalism is a philosophical and economic doctrine that has been influential since the late 1970s. It advocates a minimalist role for the state, the centrality of the individual, and the importance of a free market (Naiman, 2000, p. 337). These elements of neoliberalism provide the basis for three key arguments against CanCon regulations, and all three must be critically interrogated.

The Ongoing Impact of Radio

To begin with, while neoliberalism favours a significantly limited role for the state, private radio broadcasters have not offered compelling reasons for reducing or eliminating CanCon. Believing they should be able to play whatever music their listeners want, these broadcasters have long complained that the regulations are an "assault on broadcast freedom" (Hoy, 1998). However, since the Canadian airwaves are public property that is subject to the *Broadcasting Act* (the legal foundation for CanCon), the public interest overrides the freedom of individual broadcasters (McPhail, 1986, pp. 46–48). A more recent position adopted by private radio broadcasters is also problematic; they have contended that CanCon regulations are a burden due to the competition they face from music sources such as the Internet (Shecter, 2006, p. FP4). It is true that radio is no longer the only way in which Canadians can access music, but "it will be some time before the Internet becomes as ubiquitous as radio and even then there is no guarantee that it will displace it in terms of its importance for music" (Sutherland, 2002, p. 13).

This conclusion is supported by a national survey that Decima Research conducted in 2008 for the Department of Canadian Heritage (2010). The survey results indicate that radio occupied 36 percent of the time Canadians aged fifteen and over spent listening to music each week during 2008. CDs were in a distant second place at 18 percent, followed by portable digital players at 13 percent, computer files at 12 percent, the Internet at 7 percent, and social networks (websites such as Facebook) at 4 percent (p. 17). Furthermore, 65 percent of Canadians stated that they discovered new music through radio (p. 18). Although the Internet and social networks played a larger role for young Canadians aged fifteen to nineteen, radio was still important. People in this age category devoted 12 percent of their weekly music listening to radio, 12 percent to the Internet, and 8 percent to social networks. While 18 percent of young Canadians stated that they discovered new music through the Internet and social networks, 14 percent indicated that they discovered it through radio (p. 18).

All of this demonstrates the ongoing impact of radio, which, in turn, helps to explain purchases of Canadian music. The 2008 survey by Decima Research found that music by Canadian artists accounted for 34 percent of the CDs and 29 percent of the music DVDs that Canadians bought. Among Canadians who used the Internet, Canadian artists accounted for 27 percent of the full albums they downloaded and 25 percent of the individual tracks (Canadian Heritage, 2010, p. 19). Since the Internet and social networks expose people to much more than just Canadian music, these data suggest that radio still has an important role to play in familiarizing Canadians with Canadian music and influencing their music purchases. Even if the Internet eventually displaces the impact of radio, new media do not necessarily mean the end of old media; old media like radio "almost inevitably find new niches, new methods, new audiences and new leases on life" (Taras, 2001, p. 66). There is no reason, then, to loosen the obligations imposed on private radio broadcasters for using the public airwaves.

The Existence of Organizational Barriers

Some arguments against CanCon reflect a view of the individual that is associated with neoliberalism, and they consequently ignore conditions in capitalist society that make the regulations essential. Liberal ideology subscribes to the notion of a meritocracy and engages in blaming the victim (Naiman, 2000, p. 233). If people do not succeed, they must lack ability or a willingness to work hard enough. Such thinking is often applied to people who are unemployed or on welfare (even though capitalism generates the elimination of jobs and other conditions that are the real source of their misfortune), and this becomes a justification for cutting employment insurance or social assistance. The same reasoning is used to call for the elimination of CanCon regulations. In the above-mentioned column he wrote for the *Toronto Star*, Bryan Adams suggested that "real talent will always win out whether or not it is supported by the government. It's time to shut off the government tap as it relates to music" (1992, p. J1). Adams's arguments are problematic since they focus on the individual rather than considering larger organizational barriers. Talent alone is not necessarily going to get Canadian performers on the radio. Many private radio stations ignore Canadian artists who are not signed to (or at least distributed by) one of the multinational conglomerates that dominate the music industry. Even if they qualify as CanCon, performers such as Drake and Justin Bieber are linked to powerful conglomerates and do not need CanCon regulations for support. However, Canadian acts associated with independent record companies face obstacles at commercial radio (Everett-Green, 2001, p. R3; McLean, 1996, p. 1).

These circumstances mean that CanCon regulations or other measures are needed to secure airplay for emerging artists, a number of whom are signed to independent firms. The independent music industry has pushed for quotas through changes to CanCon, but the CRTC has recently opted to require applicants for new radio licences and licence renewals to make specific commitments regarding support for emerging Canadian artists (CRTC, 2006).

The Threat of Globalizing Influences

While neoliberalism advocates free trade and global competition, CanCon regulations are a crucial aspect of the fight to protect Canadian culture from globalizing (and Americanizing) cultural influences. Opponents of the regulations suggest that they are inconsistent with globalization and run counter to Canada's support for international free trade agreements (Stanbury, 1998, pp. 67–68). Although there is a contradiction between free trade and the continuing existence of CanCon, this is arguably positive because it shows that Canada has been willing to put limits on free trade. The United States has long seen music, television programs, films, and so on, as products for trade rather than reflections of culture. Because American entertainment industries have economic interests in accessing foreign markets, the United States has objected to domestic content regulations (quotas) and other protective measures on the ideological grounds that they restrict the free flow of information. However, in the view of less powerful countries, such measures are needed to ensure space for media expressing their own culture (Smythe, 1981, pp. 233–242).

Among less powerful countries, Canada has played an influential role. Nations trying to protect their own domestic music have studied CanCon regulations for radio (Straw, 2000, p. 176). After Canada managed to secure a cultural exemption during negotiations for the 1988 Free Trade Agreement with the United States, France and the European Union tried but failed to secure a cultural exemption under the General Agreement on Trade in Services. Along with France, Canada has also led the attempt to establish an international agreement upholding the right of governments to support and promote the diversity of cultural expression (Azzi, 2005, pp. 766–768).

This agreement on cultural diversity was drafted as a formal convention through the United Nations Educational, Scientific and Cultural Organization (UNESCO). In a vote held by UNESCO members during October 2005, 148 countries approved the convention, while 2 countries opposed it (including the United States) and 4 countries abstained from voting (Coalition for Cultural Diversity, 2005a). It was noted at the time that the convention would have to be ratified by as many countries as possible in order to become an effective counterweight against American pressure for free trade in culture. In November 2005, Canada became the first country to ratify the convention (Coalition for Cultural Diversity, 2005b). Since then, the convention has been ratified by 117 countries and the European Union (Coalition for Cultural Diversity, 2011).

The emergence of an international agreement has been supported by Canada's Coalition for Cultural Diversity, which includes the CIMA and SOCAN, additional bodies connected to Canadian music, and various cultural organizations or trade unions (Coalition for Cultural Diversity, 2011). The coalition noted that the massive vote in favour of the convention shows that "the right to have cultural policies (domestic content quotas, subsidies, tax credits, foreign ownership rules, etc.) is now recognized as a priority by countries all over the world" (Coalition for Cultural Diversity, 2005a). Since many countries are engaged in a struggle to protect their culture, and since Canada has taken a leadership role in this struggle, any movement toward reducing or abandoning CanCon regulations will be a step in the wrong direction.

CONCLUSION

CanCon regulations have been fundamental to the promotion and support of Canadian music. Evidence suggests that CanCon has been effective in many ways, despite the efforts of private radio broadcasters to undermine the regulations. The economic interests of these broadcasters, combined with the worrying implications of neoliberalism, demonstrate a need to maintain and strengthen existing Canadian content requirements. CanCon regulations are an example of what the eminent Canadian communications scholar Dallas Smythe (1981) referred to as "cultural screens." Smythe warned that if the notion of cultural screens and the need for them ever seemed "novel or strange," this would indicate how successfully the screens had been dismantled by "modern capitalism" in "its ceaseless quest for profits" (p. 232). Such a situation should not be allowed to exist, and it is up to Canadian citizens to ensure that this does not happen.

References

Adams, B. (1992, February 8). "Real talent will always win out," Adams says. *Toronto Star*, p. J1.

Audley, P. (1983). *Canada's cultural industries: Broadcasting, publishing, records and film*. Ottawa: Canadian Institute for Economic Policy.

Azzi, S. (2005). Negotiating cultural space in the global economy: The United States, UNESCO, and the Convention on Cultural Diversity. *International Journal, 60*(3), 765–784.

Breithaupt, D. (1999, May 8). Second-class stars no more. *National Post*, p. 5.

Canadian Radio-television Commission. (1971). *Annual report, '70–'71*. Ottawa: Information Canada.

Canadian Radio-television and Telecommunications Commission. (2006, December 15). Broadcasting Public Notice CRTC 2006-158 (Commercial Radio Policy 2006). Retrieved from http://www.crtc.gc.ca/eng/archive/2006/pb2006-158.htm

Canadian Radio-television and Telecommunications Commission. (2009, October 8). The MAPL system. Retrieved from http://www.crtc.gc.ca/eng/info_sht/r1.htm

Cloonan, M. (1999). Pop and the nation-state: Towards a theorisation. *Popular Music, 18*(2), 193–207.

Coalition for Cultural Diversity. (2005a, October 21). Coalitions for Cultural Diversity hail adoption of UNESCO Convention on Cultural Diversity; urge countries to ratify on urgent basis [News release]. Retrieved from http://www.cdc-ccd.org/Anglais/Liensenanglais/nouveautes_eng/framenouveautes_eng.htm

Coalition for Cultural Diversity. (2005b, November 23). Canada's action to become first country to ratify UNESCO Convention on Cultural Diversity applauded by Canada's cultural sector [News release]. Retrieved from http://www.cdc-ccd.org/Anglais/Liensenanglais/nouveautes_eng/framenouveautes_eng.htm

Coalition for Cultural Diversity. (2011). UNESCO convention. Retrieved from http://www.cdc-ccd.org/Convention-UNESCO?lang=en

Dafoe, C. (1991, September 24). It's time to fine tune a sound principle, Chris Dafoe argues. *The Globe and Mail*, p. C1.

Department of Canadian Heritage. (2010). *The Canadian music industry 2008 economic profile*. Ottawa: Author.

Everett-Green, R. (2001, March 1). Why Nelly became a radio star. *The Globe and Mail*, pp. R1, R3.

Haysom, I. (1996, March 8). Do we still need CanCon after 25 years? *The Hamilton Spectator*, pp. F1, F4.

Hoy, C. (1998, May 11). Media applauds CRTC's assault on broadcast freedom. *The Hill Times*. Retrieved from Proquest, McMaster University, Hamilton, ON: http://search.proquest.com.libaccess.lib.mcmaster.ca/cbcacurrent/docview/208533380/1337D8CF7E4FF51C56/1?accountid=12347

Jones, C. (1996, April). Review of CanCon regs urged. *Words & Music*, 16.

Lanthier, N. (1989, May–June). The CanCon ghetto. *The Music Scene*, 2–3.

Leary, J. (2003, July 7). Bachman: Rocker says increase in Canadian content good for radio. *The Vancouver Sun*. Retrieved from Friends of Canadian Broadcasting: http://www.friends.ca/news-item/4075

McCabe, M. (2001, March 29). Our stars in their stripes. *The Globe and Mail*, pp. R1, R11.

McLean, S. (1996, March 11). Indies getting skinned on CanCon spins. *The Record*, 1, 13, 14.

McPhail, B. M. (1986). Canadian content regulations and the Canadian Charter of Rights and Freedoms. *Canadian Journal of Communication, 12*(1), 41–53.

Naiman, J. (2000). *How societies work: Class, power, and change in a Canadian context* (2nd ed.). Toronto: Irwin.

Shecter, B. (2006, March 16). Ease content rules, CRTC told. *National Post*, p. FP4.

Smythe, D. W. (1981). *Dependency road: Communications, capitalism, consciousness, and Canada.* Norwood, NJ: Ablex.

Spurgeon, P. (1992, May). Why we need Canadian content regulations. *SOCAN Probe*, 2.

Stanbury, W. T. (1998, August). Canadian Content regulations: The intrusive state at work. *Fraser Forum*, 5–90.

Straw, W. (1993). The English Canadian recording industry since 1970. In T. Bennett, S. Frith, L. Grossberg, J. Shepherd, & G. Turner (Eds.), *Rock and popular music: Politics, policies, institutions* (pp. 52–65). London: Routledge.

Straw, W. (2000). In and around Canadian music. *Journal of Canadian Studies, 35*(3), 173–183.

Sutherland, R. (2002, June). Canadian content at 32. *Canadian Issues*, 13.

Sutherland, A. (2011, February 20). Drake and Bieber boosting Canadian artists. *Humber Et Cetera*. Retrieved from http://humberetc.com/2011/02/20/drake-and-bieber-boosting-canadian-artists/

Taras, D. (2001). *Power and betrayal in the Canadian media* (updated ed.). Peterborough, ON: Broadview.

Wright, R. A. (1987–88). "Dream, comfort, memory, despair": Canadian popular musicians and the dilemma of nationalism, 1968–1972. *Journal of Canadian Studies, 22*(4), 27–43.

Young, D. (2004). The promotional state and Canada's Juno Awards. *Popular Music, 23*(3), 271–289.

ISSUE 2

Music matters: Are CanCon regulations necessary to promote Canadian music?

✗ NO

The B Side: Why Canadian Content Isn't Necessary for the Survival of Canadian Music
Ira Wagman

Ira Wagman is an associate professor of communication studies at Carleton University. He researches and writes in the areas of cultural policy, postwar media history, and digital media. He is the co-editor (with Will Straw and Sandra Gabriele) of *Intersections of Media and Communications* (2011).

There is something dramatic about the idea that Canadian content regulations, or CanCon, are necessary for the survival of Canadian music. It conjures up images of innocent victims, nefarious characters, and superheroes arriving just in time to save the day. Here, the innocent victims are Canadian musicians struggling to eke out a living, while the nefarious characters are money-hungry commercial radio broadcasters playing the stylized music produced by multinational corporations over the airwaves. These forces conspire to divert the aural attention of Canadians away from the music of their fellow citizens, slowly corroding the nation's cultural fabric. As for the superheroes? They are officials from the CRTC, Canada's broadcast regulator. Their main weapon against the villains of Canadian music, the content regulation, ensures the survival of an entire nation's musical expression by forcing broadcasters to play a certain amount of material certified as "Canadian."

For a country not known for its heroic narratives, the story of how CanCon protects Canadian culture is a notable exception. In fact, it is repeated so often that it seems commonsensical. One can find it in newspaper columns, like that of *Ottawa Citizen* columnist Charles Gordon, which argue that Canadian content rules are necessary because "no one else in the world is going to protect and encourage our artists" (Gordon, 1998, p. A13). One can also find it in the rhetoric used by music industry associations, like the Canadian Music Publishers Association, which states that their members "would be mortally handicapped" without content regulations (CMPA, 2005). Everywhere one looks, it is easy to find examples of arguments articulating how Canadian content saved Canadian music.

However, simply repeating a story doesn't make it true. By relying on a simplistic explanation about the role of government regulations on Canada's music sector, we continue to lack a solid understanding of the relationships among Canadian musicians, record companies, and listening audiences. Indeed, to believe the story about CanCon saving Canadian music, one needs to accept that Canadian music was on the brink of extinction and that an artist's citizenship is more important than musical skill or talent. There is little evidence to suggest that Canadians were on the verge of losing their abilities to express themselves musically, and there is even less evidence that an artist's passport determines listening behaviour or musical acuity.

Once we set aside these myths, what can be said about Canadian content regulations? First, CanCon regulations have very little to do with music. There are examples of Canadian content regulations in a number of industrial sectors; this model has been transposed onto the sound recording industry. As a number of case studies will illustrate, CanCon regulations actually worked against some of the country's most successful artists. Second, the argument for Canadian content saving Canadian music stands only if we fail to examine the elaborate networks, agencies, institutions, and social formations that play a key role in the ways Canadians experience and engage with music. Studying these "pathways of cultural movement" (Straw, 2005) shows that musical success or failure has little to do with content regulations.

ANYTHING BUT MUSIC: CANADIAN CONTENT AS INDUSTRIAL DEVELOPMENT STRATEGY

The most popular component of the triumphalist narrative about CanCon equates the invention of content regulations with the development of Canada's music industry. As the story goes, Canada's music industry barely existed before 1970. During this time, one rarely heard Canadian acts on domestic radio stations. In addition to the relative silence over the air, few federal initiatives were offered to support the development of the Canadian sound recording industry (Audley, 1983, p. 236). Then, thanks to the lobbying efforts of music industry representatives, the CRTC instituted CanCon regulations requiring Canadian radio broadcasters to air specific amounts of Canadian music. This was a measure that had already been applied to television a decade earlier, and it offered to stimulate the development of Canada's sound recording industry. To determine exactly what constitutes a "Canadian song," the CRTC created the MAPL system. If two of the following components of a song—musician, lyricists, producer, and label—are Canadian, or if the piece of music has been performed or recorded in Canada, it is considered to be Canadian.

The impact of these regulations on the music industry is easy to grasp. A rule that required radio stations to air specific types of material produced by specific categories of people naturally resulted in the creation of an industry able to satisfy these rules. This would happen in any industry. If the government required the Banana Republic chain of stores to ensure that 35 percent of its inventory came from Canadian clothing manufacturers, or if it required Starbucks to ensure that 40 percent of its coffee sales came from beans produced by Canadian roasters, then producers would spring forth to satisfy these regulations. This is precisely what happened in the music industry, with independent record labels and the Canadian arms of multinational corporations being created, producing content to meet the new demand.

As an industrial strategy offering protection and market stability, Canadian content regulations didn't actually begin in the cultural sector, but existed in a variety of industrial sectors before they were applied to solve the problems of the music industry. One of the first to get CanCon regulations was the country's automotive sector. As a way of fending off the effects of the Great Depression in the 1930s, the government of the day proposed to stimulate automobile production in Canada by dropping high tariffs on the import of American engines if the final automobile contained a certain percentage of "Canadian content" measured parts and labour. This arrangement existed well into the twentieth century as part of the Canada–U.S. Auto Pact (see Anastakis, 2005). A similar dynamic occurs in the Canadian Football League, where an "import quota" exists preventing teams from stocking their lineups with too many "foreign" players.

For a music industry whose size and shape are directly related to CanCon regulations, satisfying these criteria is serious business. Even the slightest alteration to the rules—raising or lowering Canadian content regulations by 5 percent, for example—prompts both excitement and hand-wringing not about the future of *Canadian music,* but about the future of the *Canadian music industry.* Michel Filion reveals this reaction when he explains that, in Canada, "cultural and industrial objectives are closely interrelated" (1996, p. 112).

Since the 1980s, the government has unveiled several measures to assist Canada's sound recording industry. For example, the Canada Music Fund and the Radio Starmaker Fund assist musicians to develop their musical and entrepreneurial skills, and assist record companies to produce music from Canadian artists. VideoFact is a program that gives grants to artists to produce music videos, while PromoFact helps record companies develop promotional materials. Seeing that CanCon is just one of many measures targeting the sound recording industry, it is unreasonable to conclude that its elimination would contribute to the disappearance of Canadian music.

Considering both its history and the affinities it has developed over time, CanCon carries important and deep-seated consequences. The first is the issue of regulatory compliance; just because the government requires an industry to act in a certain way does not mean either that it will fully cooperate or that customers of that industry will adopt the appropriate behaviour pattern. To the question of listener compliance, the answer is that exposure does not equal consumption. Those who listen to radio may prefer to listen to non-Canadian acts, to purchase non-Canadian CDs, to see non-Canadian musicians in concert, or may pay little attention to the nationality of the music they enjoy. In other words, while governments can manage industry behaviour, they cannot manage audience tastes. One might argue that this has always been the purpose of Canadian content: produce the conditions that stimulate the production of content and leave the question of audience demand constrained to the most limited of abstractions. A phrase like "Canadians want access to their own stories" has always been an effective feature of nationalist rhetoric, particularly as a means of propping up the importance of content regulations. Who wouldn't want access, for example?

It is also unclear whether even with numerous methods of surveillance, the CRTC can truly manage the behaviour of radio stations themselves. Through its policies, the CRTC has come close to telling broadcasters what to broadcast but not exactly to the point of telling them exactly *whom* to broadcast and *when.* The gap between the making of rules and the inability to truly enforce them has contributed to a long-standing cat-and-mouse game, since broadcasters view CanCon regulations as obstacles to achieving their commercial objectives, even if those objectives are themselves a result of policies that limit competition in the marketplace. For many years, critics of CanCon have pointed to the fact that in response to the CRTC's regulations, radio stations have come up with constructive ways to keep the Canadian material from interfering with their primary musical content, such as by playing a small number of Canadian artists repeatedly over the course of the broadcast day (Belanger, 2006, pp. 134–135).

A recent example from French-language radio serves as a case in point. Many French-language stations play a compilation of a series of songs that are called "montages" (Wyatt, 2011). Imagine six or seven songs strung together in which only a portion of the overall song itself is played. Until a recent CRTC intervention against a number of radio stations, including CKOI-FM in Montreal, this compilation counted as one song. One can easily imagine how playing six or seven songs from non-Francophone artists that counts as only one song in the content regulations allows the network the chance to play more of what its listeners want (American or English-language music) and less of what the government wants them to play (Canadian or French-language music).

There are also a number of well-known examples in which content regulations appear to work against the efforts of Canadian musicians. Two have acquired legendary status in policy circles. Consider the case of Bryan Adams, widely acknowledged to be a Canadian performer. In 1992 his song "Everything I Do (I Do for You)" failed to qualify as Canadian because it was recorded in another country and co-written with a non-Canadian. At around the same time, however, songs by American singer Bonnie Raitt and British rocker Rod Stewart *did* qualify as Canadian because they had been written and composed by Canadians.

By now you might be asking, what separates Bryan Adams from Rod Stewart? The answer to that question is that in using a Canadian writer and composer, Rod Stewart worked with more Canadians than Bryan Adams. Therefore, in the eyes of those enforcing Canadian content regulations, Rod Stewart is "more Canadian" than Bryan Adams. Here one sees how Canadian content regulations privilege quantitative, industrial factors over qualitative, individual, or artistic factors. Should it matter if Adams decides that the best way to enact his artistic vision is to work with non-Canadians? Is the artistic vision more important than the extent to which the artist contributes to larger job creation? While such a question may apply when talking about the automotive industry, the **cultural industries** are supposed to operate according to a logic that is different than that applied to the mass production of cars.

This makes claims about Canadian content's cultural components highly questionable, unless those claims are considered according to broad economic objectives and crude nationalist ideology. What I mean here is that if Canadian content regulations were about Canadian musicians, Adams and others like him would not have been punished for their individual artistic achievements or been subjected to questions about the citizenship of their artistic work. However, since Canadian content regulations are about industrial development through a rhetoric of cultural nationalism, those who do not put enough Canadians to work on their songs don't count and—even worse—are not "Canadian enough." If one argued, on the other hand, that artists who work with record labels in Britain or prominent American performers do not need CanCon regulations to get their material on the air, the result is the further stigmatization of Canadian music as forced upon Canadian citizens by the state, devoid of any artistic merit because of its function as "content." Furthermore, if such work manages to elude the negative stigma, it must endure a tiresome aesthetic discussion about the extent to which the song—and its artists—exude an artistic sensibility that is inherently Canadian.

Two recent examples involving the American band the Black Eyed Peas serve as contemporary cases of Canadian content's ugly side. In the last few years, the band performed in the Grey Cup's halftime show and during the Juno Awards honouring Canada's music industry. The presence of the Peas during these events attracted editorials in some newspapers wondering why an American band was appearing at a venue honouring Canadians. The editors of the *Regina Leader-Post* put it this way: "At the risk of seeming chauvinistic, this is Canada's biggest sporting event, why not feature Canadians?" ("Who Gives a Rap?" 2005, p. B7). For the editors of *The Globe and Mail*, a similar theme emerged: "You don't have to be a wild-eyed cultural nationalist to wonder why the Canadian Football League could not have found a Canadian group for this all-Canadian event" ("Imported Peas," 2005, p. A20). Similar language followed the band in the lead-up to their next major performance at the Juno Awards. An article in the *Edmonton Journal* focused on the fact that many industry representatives were "uncomfortable with the international line-up, arguing that home-grown artists should be the focus" (Pacienza, 2006, p. C3).

The backlash over the Black Eyed Peas reveals once again that the industrial components of CanCon appear even in places where content regulations do not apply. First, the notion that only someone approved by the Canadian music industry, or someone who "qualifies" as a Canadian musician, should perform at "real Canadian" events like the Grey Cup and the Juno Awards is the extension of an industrial argument to other zones of cultural activity. Since there are so few major "Canadian" events, allowing the Black Eyed Peas to perform squeezes out opportunities for Canadian musicians. If the Americans dominate the rest of the airwaves and awards shows, the critics maintain, why should they also be present on *our stages*?

The answer to this question is that, like most concerts, the musical act was booked based on the idea that the audience would enjoy the performance, not as an extension of citizenship or as sponsorship of Canada's music industry. The unease over the Black Eyed Peas expresses the long-standing discomfort with the impact of American culture on Canada, and assumes that the audience's musical preferences should always be calculated based on how their enjoyment contributes to industrial development. Having the Black Eyed Peas at the Junos alongside Canadian artists actually demonstrates that Canadians possess musical tastes that are both sophisticated in nature and international in scope. This is a compliment. Since CanCon regulations do not to recognize audience behaviour except to frame it around nationalist themes, commentaries on the Black Eyed Peas are oblivious to this fact.

The point of these examples is to show that CanCon has very little to do with music making as an artistic form. Instead, CanCon measures are part of an *industrial* strategy that can be applied to any economic activity for which music happens to be a convenient location. A specifically *cultural* strategy might look very different but would also require that we ask some clear-minded questions about the place of music in Canadian society and how those components operate in an industrial context, rather than the naive and brutish questions that now surround the regulation of music in Canada.

EVERYWHERE BUT RADIO: THE OTHER SPACES OF CANADIAN MUSIC

Perhaps the most compelling argument against CanCon regulations is that the overwhelming focus on the effectiveness of these regulations overlooks the numerous venues in which Canadians experience music in the course of their daily lives. Radio has always been only one venue for musical exposure; it has always offered a limited number of formats to listeners, based primarily on the different ways in which stations cut up their local advertising market. The proliferation of stations offering "Jack" or "easy listening" formats is just the latest in a long line of formats stretching back to the invention of top-40 that have effectively limited musical diversity on the radio dial. As a result, many musical styles, ranging from punk to opera, have found it difficult to gain airplay on Canadian radio, particularly on stations located outside big cities.

Since many types of music do not receive regular airplay, the question that remains is exactly what the relationship is between radio exposure and the purchase of Canadian recordings. For Richard Sutherland, radio airplay has an "intrinsic impact on record sales" (2002, p. 15). However, a report submitted by the Canadian Association of Broadcasters (CAB) to the CRTC argued—with citations from record company executives—that radio airplay had a "waning impact" on overall sales (Leblanc, 2006). Some have observed that radio has exercised a declining influence on record sales, particularly for younger listeners, for some time, owing largely to the fact that station playlists became more and more conservative by the end of the 1970s (Lopes, 1992, pp. 67–69). The emergence of music video channels like MTV and MuchMusic have offered artists new opportunities for exposure beyond radio and have captured the interest of younger music fans (Wagman, 2001). In addition, the proliferation of technologies to make recorded works portable, from the tape deck in cars to the Walkman, and from MP3 players to iPods, has served as effective competition to radio for the listening time of many Canadians.

What neither Sutherland nor the CAB recognized is that understanding why Canadians consume the music they do is complicated. Many Canadians learn about domestic musical acts by seeing them in local surroundings, such as in bars or at events like Ottawa's Blues Festival or the Montreal Jazz Festival. Bands also emerge out of local music scenes in which there happens to be an explosion of new musical talent, abundant performance spaces, and local support from fans who buy CDs, attend concerts, and tell friends in other cities about their favourite bands or DJs. This is a major reason for the success of Montreal's music scene, which has produced acts such as Wolf Parade, the Stills, and Arcade Fire.

In some measure, the popularity of these bands took off through exposure in American media circles, articles in U.S. magazines, Internet radio stations, websites such as Pitchfork or PopMatters, and social networking sites like MySpace that provide music samples, band information, and fan feedback. Services from Amazon to iTunes offer people the chance to sample music before paying to download it and provide examples of user playlists built around themes such as "I Love Canadian Music," available on amazon.ca, and "Canada Now" or "Toronto 20," available on iTunes. Sites such as YouTube and Google Video now allow people to stream music videos and concert footage. Finally, there are numerous websites and now blogs offering reviews of music and featuring sound clips.

These relatively new musical spaces are significant for a couple of reasons. First, they provide effective means of reaching audiences both domestically and internationally in ways that were previously restricted to musical acts signed to major record labels. Second, they fall outside the CRTC's jurisdiction, as the regulator has chosen wisely not to regulate Internet activity. By the time bands like Arcade Fire began appearing on mainstream Canadian radio stations, they had already achieved a significant level of success. Justin Bieber has YouTube to thank for giving him his big break, a site that does not have content regulations. In other words, if some artists are helped by content regulations, for others, those same measures are the last link in the promotional chain, if they serve any purpose at all, after the band has been exposed in these other windows.

We must therefore remember that Canadians experience music in a variety of ways and through an elaborate web of social networks, media forms, and, government policy measures. As Will Straw explains, "Cultural citizenship is less about residing in culture than about the necessity of moving within it, and the negotiations and transformations which that movement entails" (2005, p. 183). The interpretation that equates Canadian content with the survival of Canadian music only perpetuates our romance with CanCon, and the apparent one-to-one relationship between a policy measure and an industry's survival. Such thinking, despite the assurances it provides to us, simply cannot capture the complexity that lies at the heart of the Canadian cultural experience.

As most of us know, such a discussion means something very different in the age of the Internet, whether we're talking about websites like MySpace and Facebook, illegal downloading of music on BitTorrent, and of course iTunes, which has become the primary platform for the consumption and distribution of music for many Canadians. Of course, these are hardly the only places where that consumption circulates online. Accessing iTunes from a Canadian IP address frequently yields spotlights on Canadian artists, as well as separate sections or playlists featuring Canadian talent. Given its prominence, should iTunes be subjected to Canadian content regulations? What about Facebook? The social networking site now distributes more music to more people than radio stations could ever dream of accessing. If we feel uneasy about the prospects of CanCon regulating iTunes or Facebook, we should be equally uneasy about the essential ideas that underlie the existence of CanCon regulations in what we now clumsily refer to as "conventional broadcasting."

CONCLUSION

When Canadian content regulations appeared over thirty-five years ago, issues surrounding the success or failure of the cultural industries dealt with ensuring place over scarce airwaves. Radio frequencies were in short supply, and concerns were raised that without various forms of government intervention, Canadians would be denied access to their own performers, and Canada's sound recording industry would never leave the ground. Even if we accept the argument that Canadian content regulations have assisted in developing the sound recording industry, it is extremely unlikely that Canadian music would have died out if the measures had never been put in place. While the industry would look significantly different than it does today, this does not mean that Canadians would have been unable to carve out their own musical niches in other ways, with music reaching local and national audiences through different distribution pathways.

If scarcity served as the prominent feature driving cultural policies such as Canadian content for the better half of the twentieth century, abundance is now the dominant motif for the digital age. While conventional radio and television frequencies are limited, channels for music distribution are numerous. While a number of broadcasters can determine what is and isn't heard on AM and FM stations, such an argument is impotent in a world where musical materials flow through the Internet relatively effortlessly. It is in this environment that Canadian music is thriving, in a zone of cultural activity free of content regulations. While CanCon rules represent a handy resource for some musical acts and serve as a powerful form of nationalist rhetoric, they are hardly necessary for Canadian music to succeed, in spite of the stories we tell.

The uncomfortable fact remains that just because Canadian content regulations helped to create the music industry does not mean that a music industry would not have emerged in the absence of this form of regulation. Even if we wanted to accept the faultiness of its logic, the argument that a particular kind of music industry in Canada emerged as a result of Canadian content regulations should strike us not as incisive but as obvious. Our refusal to explore the question of what kind of industry would have emerged in its absence—or indeed, to consider the very *possibility* that one would have emerged—speaks volumes about the ways that Canadians privilege views of culture as a *political* problem in need of *regulatory* solutions above other ways of making sense of artistic achievements.

References

Anastakis, D. (2005). *Auto pact: Creating a borderless North American auto industry, 1960–1971.* Toronto: University of Toronto Press.

Audley, P. (1983). *Canada's cultural industries.* Toronto: James Lorimer & Co.

Belanger, P. (2006). Radio in Canada: An industry in transition. In P. Attallah & L. R. Shade (Eds.), *Mediascapes: New patterns in Canadian communication* (2nd ed., pp. 130–147). Toronto: Thomson Nelson.

Canadian Music Publishers Association. (2005, March 1). Position paper. Retrieved from http://www.musicpublishercanada.ca/userUploads/industry.CMPA-Position-CanCon.pdf

Filion, M. (1996). Radio. In M. Dorland (Ed.), *The cultural industries in Canada* (pp. 118–141). Toronto: James Lorimer & Co.

Gordon, C. (1998, May 7). A home grown philosophy of Canadian content. *Ottawa Citizen,* p. A13.

Imported Peas [Editorial]. (2005, November 29). *The Globe and Mail,* p. A20.

Leblanc, L. (2006). *Music distribution in Canada.* Report prepared for the Canadian Association of Broadcasters. Retrieved from http://www.cab-acr.ca/english/research/06/sub_mar1506_app_h.pdf

Lopes, P. (1992). Innovation and diversity in the popular music industry, 1969–1990. *American Sociological Review, 57,* 56–71.

Pacienza, A. (2006, March 21). Homegrown acts miffed at Junos' international line-up. *Edmonton Journal,* p. C3.

Straw, W. (2005). Pathways of cultural movement. In C. Andrew, M. Gattinger, S. Jeannotte, & W. Straw (Eds.), *Accounting for culture: Thinking through cultural citizenship* (pp. 183–197). Ottawa: University of Ottawa Press.

Sutherland, R. (2002, June). Canadian content at 32. *Canadian Issues/Thèmes canadiens,* 13–17.

Wagman, I. (2001). Rock the nation: MuchMusic, cultural policy and the development of English-language music video programming. *Canadian Journal of Communication, 26*(4), 503–518.

Who gives a rap? (2005, November 29). *Regina Leader-Post,* p. B7.

Wyatt, N. (2011, November 24). CRTC tells Francophone radio broadcasters to limit use of musical montages. *Canadian Business.* Retrieved from http://www.canadianbusiness.com/article/58748--crtc-tells-francophone-radio-broadcasters-to-limit-use-of-musical-montages

Discussion Questions

1. In addition to radio airplay, where else do you consume music?

2. In your opinion, what would happen if Canadian content rules were somehow phased out of existence?

3. If we live in an environment of "media abundance," what is the purpose of cultural policy in the twenty-first century?

4. Review the findings of the Decima Research survey conducted for the Department of Canadian Heritage. How do your preferences compare to those of the survey respondents? Through what media do you spend most of your time listening to music? How do you typically discover new music?

5. What do you think about Bryan Adams's controversial position on CanCon regulations? Do you agree or disagree with him?

6. Is it important to protect Canada from globalizing and Americanizing cultural influences? Why or why not?

ISSUE 3

Speakers cornered:
Should Canada regulate around issues of taste?

✔ YES

Should Canada Censor Shock Jocks, Talk Show Hosts, and Televangelists?
Ronald I. Cohen

Ronald I. Cohen is a senior fellow of the Faculty of Public Affairs of Carleton University. Having served as national chair of the Canadian Broadcast Standards Council for almost two decades, he has written many articles on the subject of the council, broadcast standards, and self-regulation. As the author of the definitive three-volume *Bibliography of the Writings of Sir Winston Churchill* and numerous articles on the subject, he is also one of the leading authorities on the British prime minister and regularly answers queries from around the world on Churchillian bibliographical issues. He is currently the president of the Sir Winston Churchill Society of Ottawa, past president of Friends of Library and Archives Canada, and a member of the Quebec Bar Association. He was also the founding chair of the Academy of Canadian Cinema and Television, a professor at the McGill University Faculty of Law, senior counsel to the Quebec Inquiry into Organized Crime, producer of motion pictures for a decade, and the author of the following books: *Quebec Votes: An Analysis of Quebec Voting Patterns in Federal Elections*; *The Regulation of Misleading Advertising: A Comparative Approach*; and *The Constitutional Validity of a Trade Practices Law for Canada*, and numerous articles in newspapers, magazines, and journals.

Censor? The word begins in such a dialogue on the negative side of the ledger. It implies externally mandated restriction. Imposition rather than self-control. Orwellian Big Brotherism rather than self-measured judgment. It is a provocative term to describe what might reasonably be characterized as the societal comfort of the preservation of values and order on the airwaves. Could the question not equally have been framed "Should shock jocks, talk show hosts, and televangelists be free to say whatever they wish on Canadian airwaves?"

Using such an unpalatable word as "censor" implies that, in the competition between an offending speaker and the "offendee" in a modern democracy, the former ought always to win. Should that be the case? I know of no reason why it should. In the clash of societal values in the twenty-first century, it cannot make sense that freedom of expression is the *only* value worth preserving, the one that *must* trump all others.

The point is that freedom of expression must take its place with other societal rights, those that, essentially, entitle audiences to be free from certain broadcast matter. Not *all* nasty, disagreeable, insulting, violent, coarse, sexually explicit, or otherwise offensive content that is broadcast need be protectively cocooned in order for us to be confident that the state will survive. Is the concern that any restriction of broadcast content will somehow threaten our polity? It seems fair to ask whether *all* broadcast content is created *equal*, and should be given equal airtime.

As a concomitant issue, if freedom of expression is not the ace of trumps, someone must decide which rights will triumph in the event of a conflict. Someone must, in other words, weigh the contending rights. Who that is, what rules should be applied, and when are all relevant issues. What one *calls* the process is of minor import. Whatever word or phrase is used—whether censor or restriction—we need to balance society's rights, values, and concerns. As this chapter will argue, that will inevitably and justifiably lead to restrictions on broadcast fare.

AN AGE OF ACCESS

We live in an age of access, indeed, an age of *two-way* access. There is, of course, access *by* us to content on an increasing number of platforms, but also growing access *to* us by content providers. Our ability to pick and choose the speech, information, or entertainment we will consume differs significantly from that available to individuals in the era when the fundamental principle protecting the right of the speaker was enshrined. In what we might describe as the pre–Bill of Rights era, when suppression by authority could put the speaker's right to expound at risk, it was critical to the underlying principle of democracy itself that the preservation of that right would be safeguarded. Moreover, the concern was greatest when it was uncertain that the expression of political perspectives, particularly policy dissidence, might not otherwise be assured.

Today, the access issue is different, at least in the normal broadcast environment. When we turn on our radios or televisions, they deliver the full content gamut of the published offerings of all stations, networks, and services licensed by the regulator: news and public affairs (including information, magazine format, documentary, political commentary, and other forms); news-like programming (often sharply opinionated or with a religious "righteousness" bent); talk or call-in programs; drama in its manifold guises, including weekly series of many genres, soap operas, and movies (whether live action or animation); children's programming; comedy (whether stand-up, sketch, or fictional); music (from classical, jazz, and oldies to rap and hip-hop); reality programming; sports; and so on. And almost any of those genres may include content that is potentially offensive to someone, whether on the basis of coarse language, abusive comment, violence, nudity, sexual content, other adult themes, bad taste, the forceful expression of a political point of view, or religious proselytizing. The question is, should any of those categories of content be overseen by a third party, that is, anyone other than the individual viewer or listener?

To those who would argue that no such oversight should exist, I would ask whether the audiences of our licensed broadcasters are better off being the recipients of just *any* commentary, even if abusive. Are our audiences *advantaged* in any way by talk show hosts or televangelists spewing nasty or abusive comments about, say, homosexuality or Islam (to choose two more common present-day targets)? Surely not. If anything, such comments only fuel negative sentiments about such vulnerable groups by legitimizing such perspectives to their proponents and desensitizing fence-sitters about the use of such terminology. Who is served by characterizing gays and lesbians as aberrant, deviant, or dysfunctional? And who is served by describing all Muslims as terrorists?

The American system "protects" its citizenry against an errant, briefly exposed nipple or buttocks,[1] or a fleeting expletive (as in a one-time use of the F-word in a live televised awards show),[2] but not against homophobic or religious diatribes. In Canada, our concerns are the reverse. The Canadian Broadcast Standards Council (CBSC), which administers the various codes that are the regulatory basis for evaluating all complaints about content aired on private broadcast stations, networks, and services, has decided on numerous occasions that nudity will not injure audiences (no matter what time of day it is broadcast), while abusive or unduly discriminatory comment based on skin colour, nationality, religion, gender, and sexual orientation may have such an unwanted effect.

Some might argue that it is enough that broadcasting, like all other activities in Canada, is subject to the public laws enacted by the federal and provincial legislatures (including laws relating to slander, public incitement of hatred, the federal *Broadcasting Act*, and so on). Surely, in this age of access, though, those rules, designed for other purposes, cannot suffice. In the first place, the airwaves are publicly owned. Second, while important spectrum is no longer as scarce as once it was (before the digital era), the access to individual markets is limited. Third, the industry is regulated; it makes no sense that simply anyone should be able to access a licence without regard to rules and conditions of relevance to the state. And the state and its inhabitants have values and concerns. Are those values and concerns not entitled to respect?

SOME CONSTITUTIONAL COMPARISONS

What we in Canada refer to as "freedom of expression" is termed "free speech" in the United States. It may indeed be that the root of that American right, familiarly known as the First Amendment, is the single best-known legislative provision in the world. It dates from 1792, while its Canadian equivalent (in the *Canadian Charter of Rights and Freedoms*) is from 1982. One might say that Canada went to school on its American statutory forebear.

The First Amendment provides that "Congress shall make no law … abridging the freedom of speech, or of the press." Section 2(*b*) of the Canadian *Charter* is framed differently. It protects "freedom of thought, belief, opinion and expression, including freedom of the press and other media of communication."

The American principle is more absolute—"Congress shall make no law …"—while our equivalent appears far more, well, Canadian. It does not even *appear* absolute. It feels balanced. It is legally subject "to such reasonable limits … as can be demonstrably justified in a free and democratic society." It feels like it can and should be weighed against something else. It generally is by the CBSC and the CRTC, as well as, to some extent at least, the Federal Court of Appeal. In a 2005 appeal by a broadcaster of a CRTC decision refusing a licence renewal to a Quebec City broadcaster that had aired abusive comments about persons on the basis of their skin colour and mental incapacity, Mr. Justice Létourneau was quite explicit on the boundaries of freedom of expression:

> The appellant makes much of the guarantee of freedom of expression in paragraph 2(*b*) of the *Charter* and seems to want to treat it as unqualified, something that the courts have never recognized. I do not think I am mistaken in saying that freedom of expression, freedom of opinion and freedom of speech do not mean freedom of defamation, freedom of oppression and freedom of opprobrium.[3]

The point really is that, whatever either constitutional provision sounds like, free speech is not totally free in either the United States or Canada. "Free" is in the end a relative term, reflecting the values and concerns of each country, and that is as it should be.

SPEECH WORTH PROTECTING

The CBSC has over the past two decades drawn a clear line between comments dealing with political issues, government policies, religious practices, and the like, and all other comment. In 1993 a CBSC panel ruled that "nothing can be more fundamental to the principle of freedom of speech enshrined in the *Charter* than the entitlement of an individual to express a differing view on a matter of public concern, including government policy."[4]

The consistent application of the principle was tested in the first of the Howard Stern decisions (1997), tested in the sense that the challenged comments by the American shock jock were largely racist, sexist, sexual, and inappropriate for children. For example, the host referred (on the first day of his broadcasts on Canadian stations) to the French by using the following expressions: "peckerheads," "pussy-assed jack-offs," "scumbags," "pussies," "Frig the French," and "Screw the French." He also referred to women with the following words: "pieces of ass," "horny cow," "dumb broads," "dikes" (referring to women with even moderately feminist views), and "sluts."

During the challenged programs, he also expressed views on the state of radio in Canada, the use of English in Quebec, the value of French culture, Canada as an appendage of the United States, the role of the vanquished French in Vichy France, the issues relating to separatism, and so on. The CBSC found that the insulting words and expressions targeting identifiable groups breached the codified standards, while the comments relating to the political or historical environment in Canada and France were only the host's opinions and were, "unless utterly and irresponsibly uninformed, … his to espouse."

In a 2010 decision dealing with comments by Canadian televangelist Charles McVety about gays and lesbians, the CBSC summarized the distinction between acceptable and unacceptable commentary on that subject.

> In previous decisions interpreting discriminatory comments about gays and lesbians, the CBSC has explained that religious programs (indeed, all programs) breach no standard by merely objecting to homosexuality. Furthermore, Panels have found no fault with broadcasters characterizing homosexuality as a sin. Nor have Panels found any breach of standards when program participants have criticized policies that involve sexual orientation issues, such as same-sex marriage, gay adoption, representation of LGBT issues on school curricula, and government funding for LGBT events. Even the criticism of homosexual activists on the basis of their political actions, but not their sexual orientation alone, has been found acceptable under the Human Rights Clause. Where, however, programs include extremely negative, insulting, nasty generalizations about the group of persons on the basis of their sexual orientation, the comments will be found to violate the Human Rights clauses of the *CAB Code of Ethics* and the *CAB Equitable Portrayal Code.*[5]

SPEECH WORTH PROTECTING?

Where, however, the expression has no such *inherent* redeeming value as that described in the preceding section, the CBSC panels will not stretch to defend it. Consider, for example, the nonhistorical/nonpolitical comments Howard Stern made in the challenged episodes of his program in 1997. In addition to the juvenile locker-room banter about women's breasts and sexual activities, there was, in one of the broadcast bits, a dash of violence added to his sarcastic comments about actress Kim Basinger.

> **Howard Stern**: Oh, I just wanna take that piece of ass body, put tape over her mouth, and do things to her. [Playing sound effects of a woman in a sexual encounter throughout the following passage.] And have her lay by my pool in a bikini and have her come out and service me. […] Oh. And then I break her legs and position them in the back of her head so that she's sitting, and they're permanently fixed like that. We let them knit and mend.[6]

All in all, the panels found the comments to be sexist and in breach of the broadcasting code of ethics. They expressed their position in the following terms:

> Stern *consistently* uses degrading and irrelevant commentary in dealing either with guests or callers. The CBSC understands, by his demeanour and laughter, that *he* … find[s] such comments amusing. It may well be the case that many in his audience find such comments entertaining. This sort of adolescent humour … is thoroughly in breach of Canadian codified broadcast standards. Women in this country are entitled to the respect which their intellectual, emotional, personal and artistic qualities merit. No more than men. No less than men. But every bit as much as men.

Since the World Trade Center attack in 2001, the Muslim community and Islam itself have been the subject of discussion and even the butt of humour. One example of offending humour ran on a Calgary station as a parody "quiz" segment, during which callers were asked a few multiple-choice questions that they had to answer with the third choice, "c," which was in each case predictably the most provocative of all three possible choices. One segment went as follows:

> **Forbes:** Okay. Muslims around the world continue to travel to Mecca on the weekend to celebrate: a) a celebration of forgiveness; b) homage to Allah; or c) just a way to build up some frequent flyer miles so you don't have to pay the next time you want to ram an airplane in the stronghold of the Western civilization.[7]

The Prairie Regional Panel (1997) concluded,

> Society is frequently ready to find a scapegoat for segments of its ills, perhaps as a catharsis for their resolution. It is perhaps when such solutions come most easily that society ought to be most vigilant.… The humour in this broadcast was singularly unacceptable. The implication that all Muslims (how else could one interpret the words "Muslims around the world"?) might travel to their *holiest* city in order to fund terrorist activities is outrageous. To put it in perspective, the failure to distinguish between the Muslim community and terrorists is no more acceptable or justifiable than a failure to distinguish between (to choose one of many possible examples) white persons and the Ku Klux Klan. The Muslim community bears no more responsibility for persons within its ranks who break the laws than all white persons bear responsibility for the illegal actions of Klan members.[8]

COMMENTARY ON THE CUSP

There are also the undeniably right-wing, quasi-religious observations of commentators like Laura Schlessinger, Jimmy Swaggart, R. W. Schambach, John Hagee, James Dobson, Charles McVety, and others opposed to homosexuality and same-sex marriage. Should there, for example, be a distinction made between Laura Schlessinger's comments characterizing the sexuality of gays and lesbians as "abnormal," "aberrant," "deviant," "disordered," "dysfunctional," and "an error," and dialogue between politicians on the policy of same-sex marriage? For that matter, do the following comments of televangelist Jimmy Swaggart on that subject deserve protection or condemnation?

> This utter, absolute, asinine, idiotic stupidity [...] of men marrying men [sounds of agreement from audience]. I've never seen a man in my life I wanted to marry [Swaggart laughs; audience applauds]. And I'm gonna be blunt and plain; if one ever looks at me like that, I'm gonna kill him and tell God he died.[9]

In the 2010 Ontario decision referred to above, numerous comments by host Charles McVety, including his accusation that the human rights tribunals of Alberta and Ontario have a "one hundred per cent conviction rate" on issues relating to sexual orientation, his assertion that "it is now a crime to speak against homosexuality" (under the Criminal Code of Canada), the characterization of the revised Ontario school curriculum as one designed to *teach* homosexuality, and the accusation that gays prey on young, underage boys and girls were found by the panel to be purposefully misleading or "excessive, inappropriate, disparaging, and abusive," all in breach of various code provisions.

The various CBSC panels called upon to deal with aggressive comments by the above individuals have been careful to distinguish the nature and extent of the comments. The more extreme comments, such as those of Jimmy Swaggart, have been found in breach of the human rights clause of the Canadian Association of Broadcasters (CAB) code of ethics. More balanced comments, such as those of James Dobson in *Focus on the Family*, have been protected, the distinction being drawn as follows:

> Where, in other words, the challenged comments are "not directed to the *group* of persons *on the basis of* their sexual orientation," where there is no offending characterization of the group, where the comments are limited to a moral or religious assessment of *practices* alone, the comments will be unlikely to be viewed as abusively or unduly discriminatory.[10]

THE CANADIAN SOLUTION

There are other examples of programming that has interfered with different kinds of public rights, including the right to be free from gratuitously violent programming, misleading news, improper comment, unduly coarse language and unduly sexually explicit programming (these relate to time of broadcast), and so on. Canada's private broadcasters, however, have applied a common solution to these public rights and to human rights. In these and other areas, they have codified the standards by which they consider they and the public would be well served. And these are administered by the CBSC.

It goes without saying that the CRTC is the regulatory authority with ultimate jurisdiction in all aspects of broadcasting, but, as a general rule, it limits its interventions in content issues to public broadcasters and those few private broadcasters that are not members of the CBSC.

It is worth noting, on a comparative basis, that the United States limits its content differently. Its Federal Communications Commission has been primarily concerned with indecency. Bare breasts, butts, or penises, the F-word or its derivatives, sexual commentary—*these* are the American issues. The fleeting glimpse of Janet Jackson's right breast cost the CBS affiliates who ran the 2004 Super Bowl $550 000 (U.S.).[11] In Canada, we received fewer than 200 complaints on the matter and, it should be added, found no breach. Presumably due to its nudity, coarse language, and sexual content, the organized crime series *The Sopranos* could run only on pay cable south of the border, while in Canada, the series was aired on both pay and conventional television, although only after the 9 p.m. watershed.

CONCLUSION

The bottom line is that both Canada and the United States feel constrained to restrict broadcast content, although the substance of the impositions on freedom of expression differ in both jurisdictions. In Canada, our concerns relate more to comments of the shock jock variety, the opinions heard on talk radio, or the homophobic and right-wing religious commentary of some televangelists. While, in an age of access, it is clear that freedom of speech is a precious right, this does not mean that Canadian audiences should be subject to absolutely *any* form of speech. Because the Canadian system does not permit excessive violence during children's programming; because it does not allow abusive comments on the basis of people's religion, sexual orientation, or skin colour; because it does not allow imbalance in the portrayal of men and women does not mean that our free speech is unduly restrained or that the Canadian social and political fabric is thereby weakened.

Notes

[1] During the telecast of the 2004 Super Bowl halftime show, a move by Justin Timberlake revealed Janet Jackson's nipple for a fraction of a second, later alleged to have been a "wardrobe malfunction." Some 550 000 complaints were filed with the FCC; they resulted in a significant financial penalty. In Canada, the matter generated only 200 complaints, which were summarily dismissed by a CBSC Summary Decision.

[2] The FCC dealt with fleeting expletives used by Cher during the 2002 Fox Billboard Awards, Nicole Richie during the 2003 Billboard Awards, and Bono during the 2003 Golden Globe Awards.

[3] See *Genex Communications v. Canada*, 2006 [2 F.C.R.] 199, p. 221.

[4] All CBSC decisions can be searched on its website, at http://www.cbsc.ca/english/decisions/about.htm.

[5] CITS-TV re *Word.ca* and *Word TV* (CBSC Decision 08/09-2142 & 09/10-0383+, June 22, 2010).

[6] Transcript provided in Appendix B of CBSC decisions 97/98-0001+ and 97/98-0015+ (see http://www.cbsc.ca/english/decisions/about.htm).

[7] Transcript provided in CBSC Decision 02/03-0638, "The Facts" (see http://www.cbsc.ca/english/decisions/about.htm).

[8] CJAY-FM re *Forbes and Friends (multiple choice "quiz")* (CBSC Decision 02/03-0638, December 15, 2003).

[9] Transcript provided in CBSC Decision 04/05-0097, "The Facts" (see http://www.cbsc.ca/english/decisions/about.htm).

[10] CFYI-AM re *Focus on the Family* (CBSC Decision 99/00-0724, June 28, 2001).

[11] The decisions of the FCC in the cases of the Billboard Music Awards shows of 2002 and 2003, and the Golden Globes Awards of 2003 involving indecency (including fleeting expletives) were, at the time of writing, at various stages of reconsideration in the American courts as the result of decisions by the Second and Third Circuit Courts of Appeal and the Supreme Court of the United States. In June 2012, the Supreme Court vacated the original FCC decisions on *fleeting* expletives on the basis of unconstitutional vagueness and absence of due process rather than free speech issues. The Court did, however, leave the FCC room to define its rules more clearly to deal with such fleeting matters in future broadcasts.

ISSUE 3

Speakers cornered:
Should Canada regulate around issues of taste?

✗ NO

Free Expression and Censorship of Shock Jocks in Canada
Josh Paterson

Josh Paterson is a lawyer who previously served as director of the Freedom of Expression Project at the Canadian Civil Liberties Association in Toronto, advocating and coordinating litigation on free speech and human rights issues. He holds law and master's degrees from the University of Toronto. He currently practices in First Nations and environmental law at West Coast Environmental Law in Vancouver, a non-profit legal organization. He is involved in civil liberties and urban issues through his work with the Vancouver Public Space Network.

On a radio talk show, the host is discussing psychiatric hospitals. Discussing a particular patient, the host asks, "Why don't they just pull the plug on him? He doesn't deserve to live. The guy's a freaking burden on society. What I think they should do in [the psychiatric wing of the hospital] is fill up the rooms, and then there'd be a switch, and once every four months, they press the button and just a little bit of gas comes out, and then you go in and pick it all up and put it in bags" (*Broadcasting Decision CRTC 2004-271*, 2004, para. 49). When listeners complained, the radio station said that the comments were just a joke during a debate on the controversial social issue of euthanasia. Most people would probably find these remarks offensive. Plenty of people, disabled and able alike, might find this "joke" to be hurtful. Yet, this is an actual example of something said by a shock jock on a Canadian radio station.

For a number of years in Canada, controversy has simmered about whether shock jocks should be allowed on the airwaves. Shock jocks are radio personalities whose shows aim to entertain—often by saying offensive things. Many people, even some who are periodically offended, think that shock jock radio shows are funny, entertaining, and even politically subversive. The shows' huge audiences attest to that. Sometimes shock jocks' remarks come across as racist. Often they are perceived as sexist and as disrespectful of women. Almost always, they are controversial. Should something be done about them? Should this expression be censored?

Attempts to regulate what people are allowed to say on air may be well intentioned; usually, regulation is aimed at promoting equality by banning statements that offend, poke fun at, or attack people based on their race, culture, religion, or gender. While the promotion of equality is an important goal in a democracy, censorship is a clumsy tool that can do a lot more harm than good. It restricts freedom of expression, a vital feature of democratic society. Furthermore, censoring offensive opinions and humour has not been shown to help promote understanding and equality. There is no evidence that censoring such messages leads to less discrimination and greater intercultural understanding. It can, however, hide prejudicial views and ensure that nobody is able to challenge them—because nobody is allowed to hear them.

Radio stations operate under licences from the federal government. The CRTC decides who is allowed to operate a radio or television station in Canada. Its mission is to regulate radio, television, and telecommunications in the public interest. Its powers apply only to radio and television media, and not to other media such as print or the Internet.[1] The CRTC doesn't have the power to tell broadcasters what they can and cannot put on the air, other than specifying Canadian content regulations.[2] The CRTC requires broadcasters to comply with its regulations. Since the broadcast licences aren't permanent and need to be renewed every few years, the CRTC can rescind a radio station's permission to be on the air when it breaches these standards. The CRTC is not meant to act as a board of censors with a power of **prior restraint**, which prohibits material from being heard or seen at all. Prior restraint censorship is ordinarily not permitted in Canadian law. The Supreme Court of Canada has stated that censoring material before the fact is a severe restriction on freedom of expression (*Little Sisters Book & Art Emporium v. Canada*, 2000, p. 1154).

The refusal to renew a licence can be based on the broadcaster's failure to comply with the broadcasting industry's self-imposed code of ethics or with the CRTC's morality-based regulations. This is what happened to Quebec City's CHOI-FM, the radio station that carried the comments about psychiatric patients by host Jeff Fillion in May 2003. The CRTC received numerous complaints about the station's "shock jock" broadcasts from listeners who felt that the material they heard was sexist, racist, and otherwise offensive. These included Fillion's numerous remarks about a female television host's sexual attributes, in particular, the size of her breasts, and host André Arthur's criticism of the number of African and Muslim foreign students at Laval University. In November 2003, Arthur claimed the students were mostly the "children of the most disgusting political leaders in the world, people who are sucking their countries dry, people who kill to gain power and torture to keep it. People we call cannibals, people who are extremely cruel." CHOI-FM argued that the comments were in the public interest and were meant as an exaggeration so listeners would think about whether the children of dictators were attending Quebec universities. The CRTC disagreed, and in 2004, because of repeated complaints (and in spite of the public demonstrations of thousands of the station's supporters), the CRTC refused to renew the station's licence. It found that the broadcasts violated the law because they "did not constitute programming that reflects Canadian values" and did not reflect the right to equality (*Broadcasting Decision CRTC 2004-271*, 2004, para. 54). Instead, it concluded that the broadcasts were likely to expose persons with mental disabilities, and black or Muslim students at Laval, to hatred or contempt. The CRTC also found that the remarks about the female television host were abusive and exposed her, and women in general, to contempt on the basis of sex. Moreover, it concluded that the remarks did not "safeguard, enrich or strengthen the social fabric of Canada, nor do they reflect the status and aspirations of women." It stated that programming that substantially undermines the value of equality between women and men "runs counter to the objectives of broadcasting policy for Canada and is not worthy of broadcast on the public airwaves." As a result, the CRTC ordered CHOI-FM to shut down. That unprecedented decision was even challenged at the Supreme Court of Canada. Jeff Fillion has since left broadcasting, and André Arthur was elected as an independent member of Parliament in the January 2006 federal election.

In effect, the CRTC's power to revoke a broadcast licence because of program content that is being aired by a radio station amounts to a power of prior restraint. While the CRTC wasn't able to pre-empt the broadcast of the offensive material that precipitated the refusal to renew, it made sure that the station will never again broadcast offensive material—or any material at all. The station was permanently shut down.

Even when the CRTC does not go so far as to actually refuse a licence renewal, it can threaten to do so, or issue fines, if stations continue to broadcast objectionable material. The threat to cancel a licence, in effect, is a form of prior restraint in disguise. It can impose a chilling effect on expression that is much broader than the censorship of a particular segment of a particular broadcast. It can stop the broadcaster from putting *anything* on the air that could even come close to violating CRTC rules. A wide range of speech that doesn't violate the rules can effectively be prevented from getting to air simply by the CRTC's threatening termination.

What rules does the CRTC use in making these kinds of determinations? The *Radio Regulations* of 1986 state that "a licensee shall not broadcast ... any abusive comment that, when taken in context, tends to or is likely to expose an individual or a group or class of individuals to hatred or contempt on the basis of race, national or ethnic origin, colour, religion, sex, sexual orientation, age or mental or physical disability" (s. 3). The *Broadcasting Act* sets out that the Canadian broadcasting system should "safeguard, enrich and strengthen the cultural, political, social and economic fabric of Canada" and requires programming to be "of high standard" (s. 3). The CRTC also bases its decisions on the code of ethics of the Canadian Association of Broadcasters, which prohibits the broadcast on radio of all content that is "unduly sexually explicit."[3] The CRTC has agreed on standards in cooperation with the broadcasting industry, which is largely responsible for self-regulation. However, when a radio station does not appear to be adequately regulating its content, the CRTC is able to warn and to shut down the station. This is what happened in the CHOI-FM case.

Let's look at the government's rationale for the CRTC's powers over broadcasting content. The four basic reasons are the scarcity of the broadcast spectrum, the "public trust" of the airwaves, the desire to protect children, and the pervasive and inescapable nature of the broadcast media.

1. SCARCITY OF THE RADIO BROADCAST SPECTRUM

The principal justification for government regulation of the airwaves relates to two propositions: that the bandwidth available for broadcast media is limited, or scarce, and that the few available frequencies should be used in the public interest (Antonoff, 2005, p. 273). Radio spectrum scarcity implies that there is competition for free-to-air broadcasting. This means that if one station is using a particular frequency, another station is deprived of the ability to use the same frequency. If any broadcaster were free to use any frequency that it chose, then in most crowded urban markets it would be impossible to listen to the radio at all—there would be too much interference caused by overlapping frequencies. This is why radio and television broadcasters require licences, while other media such as newspapers do not. Anyone who wishes to print a newspaper or start a webpage may do so, assuming they have the necessary financial resources, as there is currently no effective limit on the amount of newsprint or web space available (Varona, 2006, pp. 167–168).

Some commentators, and notably, some judges in the United States, reject the scarcity argument. They respond that the supply of resources used in other kinds of media, such as newsprint, is also limited. They note that scarcity is an obsolete idea in the era of 600-channel cable subscriptions, satellite television, the Internet, and the ability to cram more signals onto the broadcast spectrum than ever before (Varona, 2006, p. 153).

Because technology has provided a great abundance of ways for media messages to be disseminated, the idea that broadcast resources are scarce is simply outdated. However, the fact is that many more potential broadcasters apply for radio licences in major markets than there are frequencies to allot to them. This is not the case for websites, newspapers, and many other media. It remains the case that television and radio are still, by far, the media that most consumers use to get their information and entertainment (Varona, 2006, p. 153).

Scarcity, then, is a notion that effectively applies uniquely to those media using the airwaves, not to the media across the board. However, even if we accept that a limited number of signals are available, does this necessarily justify content regulation and censorship? Does it make any difference? Scarcity alone doesn't seem to be enough to justify censorship.

2. "PUBLIC TRUST" OF THE AIRWAVES

Closely connected to the idea of scarcity is the idea that the airwaves are publicly owned. Since signals are limited in number, and since it is in the public interest that broadcast signals be used clearly, without interference, for public communication, the government created the legal fiction that the airwaves are a public trust. It is a fiction because it is impossible for anyone to have *actual* possession of the broadcast spectrum; it is difficult to possess something that cannot be seen or touched. Nonetheless, the concept of public ownership of the airwaves allows the government to set up a system in which it grants a licence to a broadcaster in exchange for a promise that the broadcaster will act as a trustee over the public resource of broadcast bandwidth, using it in the public interest (Brown & Candeub, 2005, p. 1479). The broadcaster, of course, stands to profit a great deal from the revenues that a radio or television station can bring.

The new broadcast technologies are not regulated in the same way. In both the United States and Canada, broadcast regulators have decided against regulating the Internet.[4] The U.S. regulator, the FCC, decided that there should be no Internet regulation, even for the purpose of protecting children, if this would place an "undue burden" on the communication of material between adults (Antonoff, 2005, p. 272). The CRTC's 1999 *New Media* decision not to regulate the Internet cited the fact that technologies now develop so quickly that the lag time for the CRTC to develop regulations and a licensing scheme for new media might effectively stifle the industry's growth. As a result of this decision, different broadcasting standards are being applied, depending on which form of media is used to communicate a message. This double standard is hard to justify and will only become more problematic as technologies advance and other media proliferate (see Antonoff, 2005, p. 274).

Given that the government must have a very compelling reason to justify a restriction on free expression under Canada's *Charter of Rights and Freedoms*, the seeming arbitrariness of the distinction between radio and other media puts the CRTC's content regulation on a shaky footing.

3. PROTECTION OF CHILDREN

Most people agree that the government has an important responsibility to ensure the protection of children. Supporters of broadcast censorship, not least lawmakers and courts, often justify censorship by saying that it is needed to protect children from hearing age-inappropriate things on the radio, or seeing them on television. They argue that the broadcast media are uniquely accessible to children, and that children are not as likely to gain access to inappropriate material (either accidentally or on purpose) through other media. The U.S. Supreme Court has even said that it is less likely that children will encounter this material on the Internet than in broadcast media, because they have to take more affirmative steps to see sexually explicit or indecent content on the unregulated Internet than they do in the broadcast media (Rooder, 2005, p. 896).

Anyone who knows a twelve-year-old knows that this view is out of touch with reality. If one were to imagine that there was no regulation of content on the radio or TV at all, then it is easy to picture children accidentally stumbling across inappropriate material in their channel surfing. But while children might be marginally less likely to *accidentally* run across explicit content on the Internet than on unregulated broadcasting, it is clearly very easy for them to gain access to a world of sexual material on the Internet never contemplated on TV or the radio. The child who seeks it out will be exposed to reams of sexual material in seconds, and even children who don't seek it out may accidentally happen across it with some frequency, depending on the terms they use in their Internet searching.

A justification for censorship that is based on broadcasting's easy accessibility by children is fairly shaky, because in reality, broadcasting is not significantly more accessible by children than are other forms of media. It also has the problematic result of preventing adults from hearing the material deemed to be unfit for children (Rooder, 2005, p. 895). Some believe that, in fact, this is exactly the point. A famous U.S. court decision involving indecency in broadcasting stemmed from a comedy routine by George Carlin in which he used a great number of "swear words." The case, *FCC v. Pacifica Foundation* (1977), generated a list of seven words that the court decided should be illegal to say in broadcasting. While protecting children was a major theme in the decision, some think that this might be, in part, a cover for the fact that the court actually wanted to protect unwilling *adults* from hearing such material, even for the few seconds that it would take to change the channel (Greene et al., 2005, pp. 1127–1128).

The right of adults to listen to a wide range of material, part of *their* freedom of expression, is constricted by protections ostensibly aimed at children. These rules might be worthwhile if children were actually protected by the censorship. But technology and indeed popular culture have progressed to the point that, in spite of government regulations, children can gain access to inappropriate content with unprecedented freedom. Not only the Internet, but also movies and music (granted, with the ratings system and parental advisory labels) contain all sorts of material that was relatively unknown in popular media thirty years ago, before some of the major court decisions (Marino, 2005, pp. 160–161). As much as it may be a worthy goal, censoring broadcast media does not effectively protect children from undesirable influences (Rooder, 2005, p. 906). In light of this, the cost of radio censorship in terms of freedom of expression, and the freedom to listen, is too great to justify. We are paying a high price in freedom for very feeble, even nonexistent results.

4. PERVASIVENESS OF BROADCAST MEDIA

The concern about the risk of coming across inappropriate content is not limited to children. In the debate over shock jocks, the concern has been less about what children might hear than about what adults will be exposed to, and the harm that the messages could create. Some of the discussion about shock jocks has suggested that (prior to moving his show to satellite radio), a listener could come across the most outspoken American shock jock Howard Stern, doing a monologue on anal sex just by using the seek key on your radio (Garry, 2005, p. 554). There is disagreement over whether the strategy of just hitting the seek key again, changing the channel, or averting one's eyes is an adequate solution to the problem of offensive content in broadcasting (Garry, 2005, pp. 557–558).

Many, including some court decisions, support a "marketplace" model in which content will be regulated simply by whether or not people choose to listen. If too many people are offended, they will stop listening and even complain to advertisers. Advertisers will pull their support from stations and shows that have smaller audiences, and eventually broadcasters will be forced to switch to content that is in line with community standards.

Others argue that the broadcast media work hard to ensure that viewers and listeners become habituated to their programming, and that they shape people's media consumption tastes deliberately to support that programming which will generate the most revenue. According to this view, individual agency and choice by rational consumers are, in effect, supplanted by the seduction of the media. Here, broadcasting is unlike the speaker on the street or the pamphleteer; the aim is not to persuade but to hook the listener (Garry, 2005, pp. 557–560). As a result, it may make less sense to rely on the individual choices of media consumers to regulate the industry. Collective action through government regulation is seen as necessary to balance the relationship between broadcasters and the public (see Garry, 2005, pp. 560–561). This argument supposes that because the media work hard to shape individual consumers' choices, consumer choice ought to be taken away by the government. This idea can also be framed in terms of listeners' rights: consumers shouldn't need to spend the effort to change the channel or turn off their TVs in order to avoid sexual or violent content (Garry, 2005, p. 560). This view sees controversial content as an imposition or an invasion on consumers' private enjoyment of broadcasting.

To stave off the risk of such brief exposures of the unwilling listener to unwanted material, the law has created a remedy that dramatically constrains freedom of expression. The fines imposed on broadcasters in the United States are problematic enough, but in Canada, the CRTC goes so far as to completely pull the plug on a radio station. Although Canada already has laws against the promotion of hatred against identifiable groups, the Canadian government has additionally reserved for itself the power to silence voices that simply offend rather than break the law. In the American *Pacifica* case, one of the justices of the Supreme Court wrote in dissent that "whatever the minimal discomfort suffered by a listener who inadvertently tunes into a program he finds offensive during the brief interval before he can simply extend his arm and switch stations, or flick the 'off' button, it surely is worth [it] to preserve the broadcaster's right to send, and the right of those interested to receive, a message entitled" to full constitutional protection (*FCC v. Pacifica*, 1977, p. 766).

Arguably, the criminal law's prohibitions against **hate speech** and obscenity that are already in place, and the anti-hate provision of the *Canadian Human Rights Act*, are enough to deal with expression that is thought to be truly harmful. While these laws are themselves the subject of much debate, and are opposed by many proponents of civil liberties as excessive and dangerous to free speech, there is certainly no need to supplement them with CRTC censorship.

CONCLUSION

In spite of the waning relevance of the CRTC and FCC brought about by technological developments, or perhaps because of it, content regulators have stepped up their enforcement of obscenity rules. In the United States, former President George W. Bush signed an Act that saw a tenfold increase in fines for radio and television content that violates decency standards, including extensive profanity or sexual conduct.[5] This was seen as a move by Congress to shore up ebbing support in the conservative Republican base. Even before this law, the FCC had been stepping up its enforcement, sending a shockwave of self-censorship through the industry. CBS Radio announced a zero tolerance policy for indecency on the air, and Clear Channel fired its shock jocks, including Howard Stern, who moved to satellite radio, which is unregulated in the United States. In April 2007, long-time shock jock Don Imus had his show cancelled by CBS for negative remarks he made about black women athletes on a university basketball team, prompting a firestorm of debate over free speech and the airwaves in the United States. When Bono used the "F-word" in excitement at receiving a Golden Globe Award on NBC in 2003, the FCC ruled in March 2004 that his statements were indecent and profane. After the Super Bowl halftime show featuring Janet Jackson's "wardrobe malfunction" on February 1, 2004,[6] there was a political firestorm in the United States and a push to "clean up the airwaves" (Fallow, 2004, p. 25). The same month, the Grammys on CBS aired with a five-second delay for the first time in history and removed Janet Jackson from its roster of presenters (although not Justin Timberlake, who was the other performer involved in the incident). The Oscars on ABC followed with a five-second delay, also for the first time in its history (Fallow, 2004, p. 26). Two years after the Janet Jackson incident, ABC adopted a five-second delay for the Super Bowl itself (CBC, 2006). Many broadcasters may even curtail live broadcasting segments, including news, because of the difficulty in predicting whether or not the program will violate the rules (see Cohen, 2005, p. 138). The FCC is using a vague standard for indecency that says, essentially, they can't tell you in advance what is indecent, but they'll know it when they see it. But how can such a body truly determine what is offensive and what is not for 300 million Americans? How can the CRTC do it for Canada?

If you ask a hundred different people what is offensive, you are liable to get a hundred different answers (Patel, 2004, p. 12). Does this mean that people should be able to say anything they want on the air? Maybe not, but the restrictions on freedom of expression (on air and elsewhere) have to be both narrowly defined and constitutionally justifiable. The CRTC's overly broad and nebulous prohibition of "abusive" language on air cuts a wide swath through freedom of expression, and imposes a chill on free speech that is out of proportion to any public interest that the government relies on to justify it.

Notes

[1] The CRTC also regulates telecommunications and telephone services, in addition to all forms of broadcasting, including radio and television (free-to-air, cable, and satellite).

[2] Forcing radio stations to broadcast certain material, such as Canadian musical content, also has implications on freedom of expression. I am unable to address the issue of Canadian content within this chapter, but it has been noted that while the government's public ownership of the airwaves may not justify censorship, it probably justifies government regulations that force broadcasters to carry certain material. The government can require the addition of content on air, but it cannot prohibit content from being broadcast (see Greene et al., 2005, pp. 1127–1128).

[3] The "Human Rights" clause of the Canadian Association of Broadcasters' code of ethics states, "Recognizing that every person has the right to full and equal recognition and to enjoy certain fundamental rights and freedoms, broadcasters shall ensure that their programming contains no abusive or unduly discriminatory material or comment which is based on matters of race, national or ethnic origin, colour, religion, age, sex, sexual orientation, marital status or physical or mental disability" (2002).

[4] In the United States, the FCC does not regulate the content of any fee-based media, including satellite radio and cable television, although it does issue broadcast licences and has allocated satellite bandwidth between different service providers. There is currently some pressure in Congress to extend the FCC's content oversight to pay television and radio services. See PBS, "Revolutions in Radio," at http://www.pbs.org/newshour/media/radio/comparison.html.

[5] President Bush signed the *Broadcast Decency Enforcement Act* on June 15, 2006.

[6] The "wardrobe malfunction" occurred when Janet Jackson's breast was exposed during a live television performance with Justin Timberlake for the Super Bowl halftime show in 2004. The FCC fined CBS $550 000 on February 21, 2006, for broadcasting indecent material (see *FCC Forfeiture Order*, 2006).

References

Antonoff, Ian J. 2005. You don't like it … change the (expletive deleted) channel! An analysis of the constitutional issues that plague FCC enforcement actions and a proposal for deregulation in favor of direct consumer control. *Seton Hall Journal of Sports and Entertainment Law, 15,* 253–274.

Brown, K., & Candeub, A. (2005). The law and economics of wardrobe malfunction. *Brigham Young University Law Review, 2005*(6), 1463–1513.

Canadian Association of Broadcasters. (2002). *Code of ethics.* Retrieved from http://www.cab-acr.ca/english/social/codes/ethics.shtm

Canadian Radio-television and Telecommunications Commission. (1999). *Broadcasting Public Notice CRTC 1999-84/Telecom Public Notice CRTC 99-14—New Media.* Retrieved from http://www.crtc.gc.ca/archive/ENG/Notices/1999/PB99-84.htm

CBC. (2006, February 4). Nervous ABC keeps delay on Super Bowl signal. Retrieved from http://www.cbc.ca/arts/story/2006/02/04/abc-delay.html

Cohen, M. J. (2005). Have you no sense of decency? An examination of the effect of traditional values and family-oriented organizations on twenty-first century broadcast indecency standards. *Seton Hall Legislative Journal, 20,* 113–143.

Fallow, K. A. (2004). The big chill? Congress and the FCC crack down on indecency. *Communications Lawyer, 22*(1), 25–32.

Garry, P. M. (2005). Confronting the changed circumstances of free speech in a media society. *Capital University Law Review, 33,* 551–565.

Greene, A., Davenport, W., Hoeh, J., Baker, E. E., McGeady, P. J., & Fiorini, J., III (2005). Panel III: Indecent exposure? The FCC's recent enforcement of obscenity laws. *Fordham Intellectual Property, Media and Entertainment Law Journal, 15,* 1087–1142.

Marino, J. L. (2005). More "filthy words" but no "free passes" for the "cost of doing business": New legislation is the best regulation for broadcast indecency. *Seton Hall Journal of Sports and Entertainment Law, 15,* 135–172.

Patel, S. I. (2004). An indecent proposal. *New Jersey Lawyer, 231,* 10–14.

Rooder, B. J. (2005). Broadcast indecency regulation in the era of the "wardrobe malfunction": Has the FCC grown too big for its britches? *Fordham Law Review, 74,* 871–907.

Varona, A. E. (2006). Out of thin air: Using First Amendment public forum analysis to redeem American broadcasting regulation. *University of Michigan Journal of Law Reform, 39,* 149–198.

Cases

Broadcasting Decision CRTC 2004-271. (2004, July 13). Retrieved from http://www.crtc.gc.ca/archive/eng/decisions/2004/db2004-271.htm

FCC Forfeiture Order—Complaints against various television licensees concerning their February 1, 2004, broadcast of the Super Bowl XXXVIII halftime show (FCC 06-19). (2006, March 15). Retrieved from http://www.fcc.gov/eb/Orders/2006/FCC-06-19A1.html

FCC v. Pacifica Foundation (1977), 438 U.S. 726.

Little Sisters Book & Art Emporium v. Canada, [2000] 2 S.C.R. 1120.

Legislation

Broadcasting Act, 1991. c. B-9.01. Available from http://www.crtc.gc.ca/eng/LEGAL/BROAD.htm

Radio Regulations, 1986, S.O.R./86–982. Available from http://www.crtc.gc.ca/eng/LEGAL/Radioreg.htm

Discussion Questions

1. What are some of the differences between Canada's "freedom of expression" and the United States' "free speech"?

2. Discuss the role that the CBSC played during the Howard Stern decisions in 1997.

3. Should offensive speech on radio programs be censored? If so, whose determination of offensiveness should be used for this purpose (radio station management, government, etc.)?

4. Should there be government guidelines for public expression?

5. Should broadcasters be required to have a government-issued licence? If so, for what purpose, and will licensing broadcasters achieve this purpose? What are some other effects you can think of that might result from a licensing requirement?

6. Aside from government directives, how can we protect children from seeing or hearing inappropriate expressions of opinions, ideas, arguments, and values on public media?

ISSUE 4

Sharing sounds:
Does file sharing harm the music industry?

✔ YES

The Economics of File Sharing, Its Harm to the Music Industry, and the Case for Stronger Copyright Laws
George R. Barker

George Barker is director of the Centre for Law and Economics at the Australian National University, and past president of the Australian Law and Economics Association. He gained a D.Phil. in Economics from Oxford University 1992, and holds both a bachelor of laws and master of economics. He was awarded the Olin Fellowship in Law and Economics at Cornell University in 2000, was visiting fellow at Oxford University Law School in 2008, and is currently a visiting fellow at the Centre for Law and Economics, University College London, and at the British Institute of International and Comparative Law London. He was elected a fellow of the Law and Economics Association of New Zealand in 2009. He is on the editorial board of the *European Journal of Law and Economics* and is the editor of *Asia Pacific Law and Economics Review*. He has authored books and articles, and has given expert testimony on a wide range of matters involving the economic analysis of law, including intellectual property, communications, Internet and media law, competition law, and cultural capital. Dr. Barker has testified in the Asia Pacific Region before Australian, U.S., Canadian, Hong Kong, Korean, Vietnamese, and New Zealand ministers, courts, and regulatory agencies.

INTRODUCTION

File sharing significantly harms the music industry. As I outline in this chapter, economic theory clearly predicts this, overwhelming empirical evidence confirms it, and it is also common sense. Pirated music is a close substitute for legitimate purchases for many consumers, so it is little wonder that some consumers have stopped paying for music that they can pirate for free. It is estimated that around 21 percent of the Canadian population engages in file sharing, costing the music industry hundreds of millions of dollars in stolen product (Barker, 2011, 2012).

In what follows, I will first outline the nature of file sharing and how those responsible for organizing file sharing make money from their illegal services (e.g., BitTorrent websites). Second, I will outline why users download illegal files, and how this creates harm. Third, I will summarize the empirical literature that clearly confirms that considerable harm is being created. Finally, I will outline the economic rationale for copyright law that makes unauthorized copying of music files illegal and explain why it is in society's interest that file sharing is illegal.

WHAT IS FILE SHARING?

File sharing first came to attention when Napster began operations in mid-1999. Its purpose was to allow music files to be copied and shared among strangers for free. Napster worked by storing music files on a central server and allowing people access to copy or download them for free and in breach of the owner's copyright. Napster quickly grew until it was shut down by a preliminary injunction granted to the recording industry in February 2001.[1] With Napster's closure, numerous other file-sharing programs emerged, particularly in a new form called peer-to-peer (P2P) file sharing. Unlike Napster, P2P file sharing was not based on a central server and instead allowed one computer on the Internet to search for and access files on the hard drives of other computers that were connected to the Internet. Successful lawsuits against companies engaging in P2P file sharing around the world (including Grokster, StreamCast,[2] and Kazaa[3]) established they could be sued for inducing copyright infringement. Kazaa, for example, settled with the music industry in 2006 and is now understood to be running under licence as a legal music subscription service by Atrinsic.

BitTorrent websites use a more sophisticated technology that makes it easier for users to find and download large files such as movies. BitTorrent sites, such as Vancouver-based isoHunt, collect, categorize, index, and make available BitTorrent files for download. In December 2009, a U.S. federal district court found isoHunt liable for massive copyright infringement. The court cited unrebutted evidence that 95 percent of the files traded through isoHunt's sites are likely infringing. In his judgment, United States District Court Judge Stephen Wilson explains that these new sites are no different than those P2P file-sharing sites previously mentioned: "Defendants' technology is nothing more than old wine in a new bottle. Instead of logging into a proprietary network in order to download files from each others' computers, Defendants' users access Defendants' generally-accessible website to download those files" (Colombia Pictures Indus., Inc. v. Fung, 2009, at 9).

The companies engaged in file sharing make millions of dollars by selling advertising. They often use incentives to encourage users to upload the most popular files to their sites in order to increase traffic and create better value for advertisers.[4] Furthermore, they do not pay the artists for the creative content they are giving away for free. The fact is that the pirates are making a lot of money at the expense of musicians. For example, whose music they give away is clear from the fact that Kazaa's owners were able to settle their legal issues by paying $100 million in reparations as well as agreeing to close down the pirate file-sharing service.

Any individual on a file-sharing network can make available any file on his or her hard drive to all other members of the file-sharing network. Stan Liebowitz noted:

> The term "file sharing" is actually something of a misnomer, however. Individuals do not "share" the files that move back and forth on the Internet. They do not experience these files together nor are they likely to ever meet or even know one another. Nor do they lend or trade the files among one another, since the files are not borrowed or given back. A more appropriate term might be "anonymous file copying," since that reflects what actually occurs. The end result of file sharing is that individuals who do not own and have not purchased a particular song or movie can nevertheless obtain that song or movie from unknown third parties. (2006, p. 5)

Because music files are easily compressed, relatively small, and very popular, they have been the most common creative content to be the subject of file sharing. However, with new technologies, like the BitTorrents described above, and as Internet transmission speeds increase, file sharing is now also affecting full-length movies, e-books, and computer programs.

WHY DO PEOPLE DO IT, AND WHAT IS THE HARM?

As noted, the pirated music obtained through file sharing is a close substitute for legitimate purchases for many consumers. It's not surprising that some consumers stop paying for music they can pirate for free. Music pirates engaged in file sharing respond to incentives. Why pay for music when you can get it for free? The incentive for some to free ride on the investment of artists and their distributors, who make up the music industry, and shoplift online, often from the safety and seeming anonymity of their own home, is clearly strong. **Free riders** use or benefit from copyright material without paying for it.

Such music piracy or free riding creates harm. The empirical work outlined below on the impact of unauthorized file sharing and music sales generally indicates that free riding has serious negative effects. Free riding, or **piracy** by file sharing, reduces legitimate sales and harms the music sector. It reduces the ability of the copyright owner and others engaged in the industry to earn an adequate return on their investment, and ultimately acts as a disincentive for the creation and dissemination of further original material. As we shall see, economists view copyright of music as a useful mechanism for changing incentives and reducing the adverse consequences of free riding by file sharing.

THE EMPIRICAL EVIDENCE

Empirical studies by Bounie, Bourreaus, and Waelbroack (2005), Peitz and Waelbroeck (2004), and Liebowitz, Zentner, Rob, and Waldfogel (Waldfogel, 2011) all find that music sales are significantly reduced by unauthorized file sharing. Professor Liebowitz succinctly summed up the academic literature in the *Journal of Law and Economics*:

> The current findings from almost all econometric studies that have been undertaken to date, including those in this issue—[indicate that] file sharing has brought significant harm to the recording industry.... [This] conclusion ... should not be much of a surprise. Common sense is, or should be, the handmaiden of economic analysis. When given the choice of free and convenient high-quality copies versus purchased originals, is it really a surprise that a significant number of individuals will choose to substitute the free copy for the purchase? The conditions needed to override this basic intuition are demanding and seemingly not met in the case of file sharing. (2006, p. 24)

Similarly, Waldfogel comments:

> Most observers agree that file sharing is responsible for much if not most of the reduction in revenue to the recorded music industry. To put this another way, most observers agree that technological change has sharply reduced the effective degree of protection that copyright affords since 1999. (2011)

The evidence then is clear that P2P file sharing harms the music sector, which employs hundreds of thousands of artists, musicians, songwriters, engineers, producers, marketing specialists, talent managers, and others. Nothing like the facts to end a good debate!

Only two studies have claimed the opposite. Both of these studies, however, have been discredited and/or shown to be inherently unreliable. The first study, by Andersen and Frenz, was published on Industry Canada's website in 2007, and revised and republished in 2010. The second is the 2007 publication by Oberholzer-Gee and Strumpf published in the *Journal of Political Economy.*

The Andersen and Frenz study is a Canadian one, and perhaps the most unreliable. In this 2007 publication, the authors claimed that file sharing increased music sales. The authors' 2010 report, however, recanted and disproved this original proposition using the same data. The 2010 study finds instead "no association between the number of P2P files downloaded and CD album sales," (p. 374) claiming nevertheless that "this paper show [*sic*] that P2P file-sharing is not to blame for the decline in CD markets" (p. 375). Both the Andersen and Frenz study analyzed data from a 2006 survey commissioned by Industry Canada (IC). This survey was commissioned "to inform IC's policy development work"[5] by measuring the extent to which P2P file-sharing activities act as substitutes or complements to music purchases. On reviewing the survey data, however, I discovered a key section from the survey that was overlooked by Andersen and Frenz. I therefore conducted new analysis of the survey data (Barker, 2011, 2012). This analysis clearly refuted the 2007 and 2010 claims made by Andersen and Frenz. Even though only a minority of the Canadian population were engaged in illegal P2P file sharing (21 percent), my research confirmed that the availability of P2P file sharing is reducing music sales by hundreds of millions of dollars each year and, therefore, is reducing artists' incomes, music industry revenues, and government tax revenues. My analysis of the survey further revealed that actions to strengthen copyright law and reduce the availability of illegal files on P2P networks will have a positive impact on the economy and, in particular, the music sector.

My analysis of the IC survey directly contradicts and discredits not only the 2007 and 2010 conclusions of Andersen and Frenz, but also the 2007 study of Oberholzer-Gee and Strumpf, who claimed that while downloads occur on a vast scale, most users are likely individuals who in the absence of file sharing would not have bought the music they downloaded. This assertion is refuted by my analysis of the IC survey, which showed three out of four people who download some or all of their music using P2P say they would purchase music through legal means if P2P was not available. Even *hardcore* downloaders in the IC survey, or those who access music only through P2P downloading, say they would legally purchase one-third of their music if P2P was not available. This adds up to hundreds of millions of dollars in lost revenue to the music industry.

Professor Stan Liebowitz of the University of Texas has also published a number of in-depth critiques of the Oberholzer-Gee and Strumpf's 2007 study showing why they study could never have provided useful information about the impact of file sharing on record sales (Liebowitz, 2007a, 2007b, 2010). Oberholzer-Gee and Strumpf themselves in their latest paper have also concluded: "The majority of studies find that file sharing reduces sales, with estimated displacement rates ranging from 3.5% for movies (Rob and Waldfogel, 2007) to rates as high as 30% for music (Zentner, 2006).… A typical estimate is a displacement rate of about 20%" (2009, p. 35). However, again Liebowitz takes issue with even this latest analysis (2011, p. 6).

WHY HAVE COPYRIGHT IN CREATIVE OUTPUT LIKE MUSIC?

The evidence that file sharing harms the music industry strengthens the case for copyright law. Clearly, the ability to freely copy another person's creation or invention without permission encourages those who may benefit from it to free ride on the creator's effort and copy the work without paying for it. This undermines the ability of a creator or inventor to earn a living through voluntary exchange or sale. Artists cannot compete with freely distributed copies of their own work. By limiting the reward of creators and inventors, free riding weakens their incentive and ability to create in the first instance, and is therefore likely to lead to less creative and inventive work over time. Copyright law is a mechanism for changing incentives and reducing the adverse consequences of free riding by file sharing, not only for music, but also for e-books, software, film, video, and other digital creations.

The mainstream economics view that the enforcement of copyright law has significant economic benefits by counteracting free riding has been around for at least 250 years. In 1762 Adam Smith, the acknowledged founder of modern economics, commented on both copyright and patents that "these two privileges can do no harm and may do some good" (1762/1978, p. 83). The support of leading mainstream economists for copyright protection continued through time. Jeremy Bentham, writing in the early nineteenth century, clarified that copyright solves the so-called free rider problem that can lead to the underproduction of creative works[6] (1843). John Stuart Mill in 1848 concurred with Smith and Bentham in his *Principles of Economics*, noting that granting exclusive rights to creators and inventors was better than any real-world alternatives (1848/1909, p. 563). Sidgwick (1887), another famous economist of the late 19th century, shared the view of Smith, Bentham, and Mill that copyright created benefits and no harm[7] (Sidgwick, 1887, p. 434). The same was true of John Bates Clark, the famous American economist of the early twentieth century[8] (1907, p. 360). Although in the early twentieth century concern was expressed about the potential monopoly costs of copyright and patent (Plant, 1934a, 1934b), in more recent times, the benefit from intellectual property rights including copyright has been articulated through the work of a number of influential economists, including Nobel Prize–winning economists. The work of Kenneth J. Arrow, writing on the economic nature of invention and creativity as a process[9] (1962); George J. Stigler, writing on the economic nature of information (1961); and Ronald Coase, writing on the role of law and property rights in the economic system (1960) contributed to the appreciation of the important economic role of intellectual property rights (including copyright, patents, and trademarks). This culminated in the work of Harold Demsetz (1967, 1969, 1970), which was advanced in later applied work on copyright law, including that of William Landes and Richard Posner (1989). Together, all of these works established a coherent and integrated view of the economics of intellectual property rights. Economic historian and Nobel laureate Douglas North has further elaborated the important general role property rights play in economic growth and development through their effect in limiting the free rider problem (1981).

A key feature of the new economic analysis of copyright law is its comparative institutional analysis, or its focus on the role and both the costs *and* benefits of such personal property rights, compared to any alternative solutions[10] (Barker, 1996). Ultimately, at issue is the efficiency, or economic consequences, of copyright in one form, compared to the efficiency, or economic consequences, of feasible alternative means of promoting creative and inventive activity. In this regard, if one compares the economic consequences of letting free riders have the right to copy creative works versus allocating the right to creators, one finds there will be less creative output under the "free rider" regime. Copyright serves to alleviate scarcity by creating property rights, thereby facilitating investment and exchange, and overcoming the so-called free-rider problem. It serves to promote creative and inventive activity. Without the enforcement of laws allocating property rights and supporting contracts, free riders will rule; theft of creative output will prevail; and investment, exchange, and cooperation will suffer to the detriment of the cultural, economic, and social development of society. In the same way that farmers gave up investing in their land when their property rights to the harvest were not protected from marauding Vikings (North, 1981), so too with creative investments. Copyright law in this way does not involve a tradeoff or exacerbate scarcity as some suggest,[11] but rather alleviates it, bringing forth more and new information and creative goods to meet the expanding demand for them.[12]

CONCLUSION

File sharing significantly harms the music industry. Economic theory clearly predicts this, empirical evidence confirms it, and it is also common sense. Pirated music is a close substitute for legitimate purchases for many consumers, leading them to stop paying for music that they can pirate for free. The estimated 21 percent of the Canadian population engaged in file sharing is costing the music industry hundreds of millions of dollars in stolen product. To the extent that many engaged in file sharing are young, they may not understand or appreciate the harmful effects of their actions, in which case this is the benefit of educating people as to the social costs or harm caused by file sharing—it may encourage them to change their behaviour. It seems a simple and wonderful thing to be able to access great music for free through file sharing. Who could possibly be harmed? The answer is that the hundreds of thousands of artists, musicians, songwriters, engineers, producers, marketing specialists, and talent managers employed in the music sector across the country, and their families, can be harmed. Ultimately, however, music lovers are harmed too as the quality and quantity of music over time will be less than it would be without music file sharing. If people paid the relatively small market price for legal downloads, rather than engaging in file sharing, those employed in the music industry would be better rewarded, there would be more of them, and they would have a greater incentive and ability to invest in more creative activity, improving the flow of creative material, and the vibrancy of our culture and economy over time.

Notes

[1] See *A&M Records v. Napster, Inc.*, 239 F.3d 1004 (9th Cir.) 2001.

[2] See *MGM Studios, Inc. v. Grokster, Ltd.* 545 U.S. 913 (2005), a United States Supreme Court decision in which the court unanimously held that defendant P2P file-sharing companies Grokster and StreamCast (maker of Morpheus file-sharing software) could be sued for inducing copyright infringement for acts taken in the course of marketing file-sharing software. The plaintiffs were a consortium of twenty-eight of the largest entertainment companies (led by Metro-Goldwyn-Mayer studios).

[3] See *Universal Music Australia Pty Ltd v. Sharman License Holdings Ltd* [2005] FCA 1242 (5 September 2005), available at http://www.austlii.edu.au/au/cases/cth/federal_ct/2005/1242.html.

[4] See isoHunt decision.

[5] Quote from project description on Industry Canada's website at http://www.ic.gc.ca/eic/site/ic1.nsf/eng/01464.html.

[6] "But that which one man has invented, all the world can imitate. Without the assistance of the laws, the inventor would almost always be driven out of the market by his rival, who finding himself, without any expense, in possession of a discovery which has cost the inventor much time and expense, would be able to deprive him of all his deserved advantages, by selling at a lower price" (Bentham, 1843, Chapter 3, "Of Wealth").

[7] Commenting, "So far as at least as protection is limited to the results which persons other than the author protected could not conceivably have produced by independent effort—as mainly the case with copyright" (Sidgwick, 1887, p. 434).

[8] Clark commented that the exclusive rights offered the creator can cause no harm as "the man is allowed to have an exclusive control of something which otherwise might not, and often would not have come into existence at all" (1907, p. 360).

[9] Arrow noted, "In the absence of special legal protection, the owner cannot, however, simply sell information on the open market." The solution Arrow pointed to was simple. "With suitable legal measures, information may become an appropriable commodity" (Arrow, 1962, p. 615).

[10] For a detailed elaboration of the comparative institutional method, see Barker (1996).

[11] For example, see Lemley (2005), who comments, "Intellectual property, then, is not a response to allocative distortions resulting from scarcity, as real property law is. Rather, it is a conscious decision to create scarcity in a type of good in which it is ordinarily absent" (p. 1055). See also footnoted references therein, including Lessig (2005).

[12] See Landes and Posner (2003), who argue that "information is a scarce good, just like land" (p. 374).

References

Andersen, B., & Frenz, M. (2007). *The impact of and P2P file-sharing on the purchase of music: A study for Industry Canada*. Retrieved from http://www.ic.gc.ca/eic/site/ippd-dppi.nsf/eng/h_ip01456.html

Andersen, B., &Frenz, M. (2010). Don't blame the P2P file-sharers: The impact of free music downloads on the purchase of music CDs in Canada. *Journal of Evolutionary Economics, 20*(5), 715–740.

Arrow, K. J. (1962). Economic welfare and the allocation of resources for invention. In National Bureau of Economic Research, *The rate and direction of inventive activity: Economic and social factors* (p. 615). Princeton, NJ: Princeton University Press.

Barker, G. R. (1996). Comparative institutional analysis of law and legal institutions *Victoria University Law Review, 26*(1), p. 109.

Barker, G. R. (2000). *Cultural capital and policy*. Canberra, Australia: Centre for Law and Economics, Australian National University.

Barker, G. R. (2011). *The true price of peer to peer file-sharing*. Report prepared for the Canadian Intellectual Property Council. Retrieved from http://www.ipcouncil.ca/uploads/The%20True%20Price%20of%20Peer%20to%20Peer%20File%20Sharing.pdf

Barker, G. R. (2012). *Assessing the economic impact of copyright law: Evidence of the effect of free music downloads on the purchase of music CDs*. Retrieved from http://papers.ssrn.com/sol3/papers.cfm?abstract_id=1990153

Barker, G. R., Fuss, M., & Waverman, L. (2008). The contribution of ICT to productivity in Australia. Working Paper 3, Centre for Law and Economics, Australia National University.Retrieved from http://law.anu.edu.au/cle/Papers/The_Impact_of_ICT_on_Productivity.pdf

Bentham, J. (1843). *The works of Jeremy Bentham / now first collection; under the superintendence of his executor, John Bowring. Vol. 3. A manual of political economy*. Edinburgh: W. Tait.

Bentham, J. (1843). *The Works of Jeremy Bentham, published under the superintendence of his executor, John Bowring. Vol. 3. A manual of political economy*. (11 Vols., 1838–1843). Edinburgh: William Tait.

Retrieved from http://oll.libertyfund.org/index.php?option=com_staticxt&staticfile=show.php%3Ftitle=1922&Itemid=27

Bounie, D., Bourreaus, M., & Waelbroeck, P. (2005). *Pirate or explorers? Analysis of music consumption in French Graduate Schools.* Paper presented at the Annual Congress of the Society for Economic Research on Copyright Issues, Montreal.

Clark, J. B. (1907). *Essentials of economic theory.* New York: Macmillan.

Coase, R. (1960). The problem of social cost. *Journal of Law and Economics, 3*(1), 1–44.

Columbia Pictures Indus., Inc. v. Fung, 2009 WL 6355911 (C.D. Cal. Dec. 21, 2009).

Demsetz, H. (1967, May). Toward a theory of property rights. *The American Economic Review, 57*(2), Papers and Proceedings of the Seventy-ninth Annual Meeting of the American Economic Association, 347–359.

Demsetz, H. (1969, April). Information and efficiency: Another viewpoint. *Journal of Law and Economics, 12*(1), 1–22.

Demsetz, H. (1970). The private production of public goods. *Journal of Law and Economics, 13,* 293–306.

Landes, W. M., & Posner, R. A. (1989). An economic analysis of copyright law. *Journal of Legal Studies, 18*(2), 325–363.

Landes, W. M., & Posner, R. A. (2003). The economic structure of intellectual property law. Cambridge, MA: Harvard University Press.

Lemley, M. A. (2005). Property, intellectual property, and free riding. *Texas Law Review, 83,* 1031, 2004–2005.

Lessig, L. (2004). *Free culture: How big media uses technology and the law to lock down culture and control creativity.* New York: Penguin.

Liebowitz, S. J. (2006). File-sharing: Creative destruction or just plain destruction? *Journal of Law and Economics, 49,* 1–28.

Liebowitz, S. J. (2007a). A comment on Oberholzer-Gee and Strumpf paper on file-sharing? Retrieved from http://ssrn.com/abstract=1017418

Liebowitz, S. J. (2007b). How reliable is the Oberholzer-Gee and Strumpf paper on file-sharing? Retrieved from http://ssrn.com/abstract=1014399

Liebowitz, S. J. (2010, May 1). The Oberholzer-Gee/Strumpf file-sharing instrument fails the laugh test. Retrieved from http://ssrn.com/abstract=1598037 and http://dx.doi.org/10.2139/ssrn.1598037

Liebowitz, S. J. (2011). *The metric is the message: How much of the decline in sound recording sales is due to file-sharing?* Centre for the Analysis of Property Rights and Innovation Publication 11-02. Retrieved from http://jindal.utdallas.edu/files/filesharing-metrics-11-2.pdf

Mill, J. S. (1909). *Principles of political economy with some of their applications to social philosophy* (7th ed.). London: Longmans, Green. (Original work published 1848). Retrieved from http://www.econlib.org/library/Mill/mlPCover.html

North, D. C. (1981). Structure and change in economic history. New York: Norton.

Oberholzer-Gee, F., & Strumpf, K. (2007). The effect of file sharing on record sales: An empirical analysis. *Journal of Political Economy, 115*(1), 1–42.

Oberholzer-Gee, F., & Strumpf, K. (2009). File sharing and copyright. In J. Lerner & S. Stern (Eds.), *NBER's Innovation Policy and the Economy Series,* Vol. 10. Chicago: University of Chicago Press.

Peitz, M., & Waelbroeck, P. (2004). The effect of Internet piracy on music sales: Cross-section evidence. *Review on Economic Research on Copyright Issues, 1*(2), 71–79.

Plant, A. (1934a, February). The economic theory concerning patents for inventions. *Economica, New Series, 1*(1), 30–51.

Plant, A. (1934b, May). The economic aspects of copyright in books. *Economica, New Series, 1*(2), 167–195.

Rob, R., & Waldfogel, J. (2007, September). Piracy on the silver screen. *The Journal of Industrial Economics, 55,* 379–393.

Sidgwick, H. (1887). *The principles of political economy*. London: MacMillan and Co.

Smith, A. (1978). *Lectures on jurisprudence* (R. L. Meek, D. D. Raphael, & P. G. Stein, Eds.). London: Clarendon Press. (Original work published 1762)

Stigler, G. J. (1961). The economics of information. *Journal of Political Economy, 69*, 213.

Waldfogel, J. (2011, March). Bye, Bye, Miss American Pie? The supply of new recorded music since Napster. NBER Working Paper No. w16882. Retrieved from http://papers.ssrn.com/sol3/papers.cfm?abstract_id=1789463

Zentner, A. (2006). Measuring the effect of music downloads on music purchases. *Journal of Law and Economics, 49*(1), 63–90.

ISSUE 4

Sharing sounds:
Does file sharing harm the music industry?

✗ NO

Four File Sharing Fallacies
John Shiga

John Shiga is an assistant professor in the School of Professional Communication at Ryerson University. He received his Ph.D. in communication at Carleton University and was a postdoctoral fellow in the Department of Art History and Communication at McGill University. His research and teaching focus on the areas of media regulation, digital culture, and sound studies.

Since the rise of Napster in 1999, music industry organizations such as the International Federation of the Phonographic Industry (IFPI), the Recording Industry Association of America (RIAA), and Music Canada (formerly the Canadian Recording Industry Association, or CRIA), and their many counterparts in countries around the world, have claimed that peer-to-peer (P2P) file sharing will destroy the industry, weaken economies, and undermine musical creativity. According to CRIA, the widespread use of unpaid downloads means "fewer artists get the chance to make their mark, and the labels are less likely to take a risk with more experimental music or niche genres. Consumers of 'free music' may get a short-term benefit, but at the long-term cost of hurting the artists they most admire, and new talent" (quoted in Leman-Langlois, 2005, p. 145). In response to the file sharing threat, the major record companies sued tens of thousands of alleged file sharers,[1] deployed technologies that monitor and constrain the use of digital music content,[2] and pressured governments around the world to grant copyright owners unprecedented control over online communication.[3] However, the academic literature and economic data related to file sharing suggest that the industry's claims regarding the harmfulness of file sharing rests on a series of fallacies. This chapter discusses four of these fallacies and argues that they divert attention from the contexts that shape file sharing's uses and effects.

FALLACY 1. THE MUSIC INDUSTRY IS ON THE BRINK OF COLLAPSE

In 2001 the IFPI claimed, "Music piracy poses a greater threat to the international music industry than at any other time in its history" and that piracy (including file sharing) "stunts the growth of the information-based economy [and] erodes innovation and cultural creativity" (2001, p. 2). Yet, according to the IFPI's data, the value of the worldwide digital music market grew by 1000 percent to $4.6 billion from 2004 to 2010 (IFPI, 2011, p. 5). Despite this spectacular growth, Frances Moore, the CEO of IFPI, claimed in 2011 that the industry should still be very worried about the danger of file sharing: "Digital piracy, and the lack of adequate legal tools to fight it, remains the biggest threat to the future of creative industries" (IFPI, 2011, p. 3). The report goes on to suggest that combating file sharing with more severe penalties for noncommercial copying is not an option but "an economic necessity" (p. 18).

There are at least two good reasons to be skeptical of such claims. First, many scholars have demonstrated that industry organizations construct file sharing as a threat in order to deflect attention from problematic practices and conditions in the music industry, to discourage artists from experimenting with network media's capacity to bypass the industry's monopoly of distribution, and to shore up public support for legislative changes that extend the market dominance of the major record companies to the Internet (Gillespie, 2009; Klimis & Wallis, 2009; Leman-Langlois, 2005; Logie, 2006; McCourt & Burkart, 2003; Yar, 2005). Second, media history is rife with similar claims about the negative impact of copy technologies. In previous episodes of the "piracy wars," copyright owners claimed that piano rolls, film, radio, cable television, VCRs, and cassette tapes, among other technologies, would ruin the cultural industries (Lessig, 2004). In each case, copy technologies strengthened rather than harmed those industries.

Have industry revenues actually declined? For industry organizations, the answer is yes. In a section of its report devoted to digital piracy, the IFPI includes a graph that shows a 77 percent decline in global debut album sales between 2003 and 2010 (2011, p. 16). As with many of the industry's claims about declining sales and revenues, this figure reflects sales of sound recordings, which refers to sales of digital downloads (such as iTunes audio files) and physical copies (such as CDs). In Canada, revenue from sales of sound recordings did indeed decline by 22 percent from $489 million in 2007 to $380 million in 2009 (Statistics Canada, 2009, p. 14). However, industry organizations often understate the importance of revenue from performance rights,[4] music and music video for mobile devices,[5] live music,[6] and artist-related merchandise,[7] all of which are growing but are usually excluded from the category of record sales.[8]

In order to squeeze profit from these growing segments of the music industry, record labels have rewritten contracts with artists. The use of file sharing by artists to bypass the industry's monopoly of music distribution is potentially a much greater threat to the dominance of the major record companies than the use of file sharing by consumers to avoid paying for music (Jones, 2002, p. 220). Labels have responded to this threat with so-called **360 deals**, which promise artists an array of complementary services such as merchandising deals but which also lock artists into a dependent relationship with the label for those services (Curien & Moreau, 2009, p. 111; Klimis & Wallis, 2009, p. 280; Leyshon, Webb, French, Thrift, & Crewe, 2005, p. 199). As Matt Stahl (2011) explains, whereas traditional recording contracts allow the record company to acquire revenue from licensing and sales of the artist's recordings, the expanded-rights contracts in 360 deals enable "the company to 'participate' in virtually all artist activities and revenue streams, including such formerly off-limits areas as merchandise and touring" (p. 669). The widespread use of expanded-rights contracts undermines the renewed sense of independence and entrepreneurialism among artists inspired by file sharing and other network media, and buffers labels against the threat of declining record sales by allowing them to control revenue from concerts, merchandising, and other artist activities.

Dwayne Winseck (2011) points out that by including revenue streams from concerts, merchandising, ring tones, and other music-related products in the calculation of the music industry's total revenue, it becomes clear that music industry revenue in Canada is growing, not declining (para. 6). Between 1998 and 2011 (the period in which the IFPI claims that file sharing began to decimate industry revenues), the value of the Canadian music industry increased from $1.26 to $1.4 billion (para. 8). By focusing exclusively on sound recording sales and downplaying the growth of revenue streams that have been opened up by new technologies, expanded-rights contracts, and royalties from new sources such as web radio and social media, music industry organizations paint a portrait of an industry on the brink of ruin. In fact, the music industry is thriving, not withering, and record companies have successfully contained the threat of file sharing by extending their reach into revenue streams formerly controlled by artists.

FALLACY 2. SUBSTITUTION IS THE ONLY SIGNIFICANT EFFECT OF FILE SHARING ON RECORD SALES

The claim that file sharing is harmful stems from a narrow focus on one type of effect that file sharing might have on sales. Known as the **substitution effect**, the hypothesis is that unpaid P2P downloads substitute for or displace copies that would have been purchased through stores or online retailers (Connolly & Krueger, 2006, p. 710). Key elements of the industry's campaign against file sharing—metaphors of theft, estimates of the cost of piracy, and causal links between file sharing and declining record sales—are based on the assumption that P2P downloads substitute for purchases and are thus "lost sales."[9]

To what extent does file sharing substitute for purchased downloads and CDs? In an oft-cited analysis of industry sales data, Stan Liebowitz (2003) tested various explanations for the decline in record sales and determined that the substitution effect does indeed cause "significant harm to the record industry" (p. 29). Several subsequent studies produced similar results, although many of these studies are based on consumer surveys and thus lack detailed information about activity in file sharing networks (e.g., Rob & Waldfogel, 2004; Zentner, 2006). In one of the few studies of file sharing that does not rely on survey data, Felix Oberholzer-Gee and Koleman Strumpf (2007) examined server logs and tracked files transferred by P2P network users in the United States over a four-month period and compared these data with sales data provided by Nielsen SoundScan. Although billions of files were downloaded from P2P networks in 2002 (the year of the study), Oberholzer and Strumpf found that "file sharing has only had a limited effect on record sales.... This estimated effect is statistically indistinguishable from zero" (p. 3).[10] Using Canadian survey data, Birgitte Andersen and Marion Frenz's (2007) study, commissioned by Industry Canada, found "a positive and statistically significant relationship between the number of music tracks downloaded via P2P networks and the number of CDs purchased" (p. 27). The studies by Andersen and Frenz and by Oberholzer-Gee and Strumpf suggest that file sharing's effects vary according to the context in which people use file sharing networks, and many of those effects conflict with the substitution hypothesis.

At least five other uses of file sharing networks can help offset or decrease the impact of substitution. Consumers frequently use file sharing networks to "taste test" music prior to purchasing it, which can generate a *sampling effect* where consumers purchase more music because they are confident that they will like what they buy (Cenite, Wang, Peiwen, & Shimin Chan, 2009, p. 212; Connolly & Krueger, 2006, p. 710).[11] Consumers also use file sharing networks to explore and learn about music, which can lead to an *exposure effect* by introducing users to artists and expanding the potential market for products associated with those artists (Blackburn, 2006, p. 9;

Gopal, Bhattacharjee, & Sanders, 2006, p. 1530). By circulating recordings quickly and widely, file sharing might generate a *network effect,* increasing the value of paid downloads and related music products by expanding the "network" (community, scene, or fan base) in which those products are meaningful (Blackburn, 2006, p. 10; Liebowitz, 2006, p. 18).[12] File sharing networks are also important tools for *collecting* recordings that are difficult to find because they are no longer commercially available; such recordings acquire what Lawrence Lessig (2004) calls a "second life" by means of their circulation in file sharing networks.[13] Finally, file sharing networks have important *non-infringing* uses, enabling, for example, the sharing of works that are in the public domain, works to which the copyright has expired, or works that copyright owners want to give away (Lessig, 2004, p. 69).

The claim that file sharing negatively affects record sales obscures the diverse uses that have a positive effect or no effect on sales. Of the six uses—substitution, sampling, exposure, network effects, collecting, and non-infringing uses—only substitution has a potentially negative effect on sales.

FALLACY 3. FILE SHARING IS THE ONLY SERIOUS CHALLENGE FACING THE MUSIC INDUSTRY

While industry organizations link the popularity of file sharing to the decline in record sales, one might just as easily point to the rise in DVD sales, which occurs at roughly the same time as the glut in record sales (Geist, 2005, para. 10; Oberholzer-Gee & Strumpf, 2007, p. 39). In Canada, sales of video game hardware and software also increased from $423 million in 2001 to $1.7 billion in 2010 (PricewaterhouseCoopers, 2006, p. 27; Secor, 2011, p. 6). Liebowitz (2005) notes that CD sales may be affected by a process called time-substitution, whereby consumers spend more time watching DVDs and playing video games, for example, and thus have less time for listening to CDs. According to Liebowitz, time-substitution may account for up to half of the drop in CD sales between 1999 and 2003 (p. 459).[14]

Decisions made by the music industry's largest firms may have also contributed to the decline in record sales. One such decision was the shift to mass merchant retailing for CD distribution. In the 1990s, record companies became increasingly reliant on big-box store chains like Best Buy and Wal-Mart for CD distribution (Blackburn, 2006, p. 8; Oberholzer-Gee & Strumpf, 2007, p. 39). Mass merchant retailers charge consumers less for CDs than music stores and they carry a few thousand titles rather than the tens of thousands of titles that music store chains like HMV and Tower Records once carried (Geist, 2005, para. 12–14). This reliance on big-box chains in physical distribution has led to reduced shipments of CDs to stores, less store space devoted to CDs, a decline in the amount and variety of CDs on shelves, and lower record label revenue from CD sales.[15]

Consolidation in the music industry also reduced revenues. The majority of the decline in 2005, for example, was due to losses incurred during the merger of Sony-BMG (Oberholzer-Gee & Strumpf, 2007, p. 39). Consolidation in music distribution put a stranglehold on smaller labels, which have been forced to develop alternatives to record sales such as live performance (Ontario Media Development Fund, 2011, p. 6). Concentrated ownership also set the conditions for CD prices to rise, which may have had an adverse effect on sales. In the 1990s, the "big five" music labels allegedly inflated the price of CDs through a price-fixing arrangement with the largest

American music retailers beginning in 1995 (McCourt & Burkart, 2003, p. 335). The price of CDs increased from $12 to $15 during the period in which the labels were allegedly colluding to inflate prices (Peitz & Waelbroeck, 2004, p. 6).

High prices for official or licit copies have been particularly harmful to sales in low-income countries. As Joe Karaganis (2011) argues, in emerging economies, the vast majority of musical works are obtained illicitly; in Mexico, for example, 82 percent of music is pirated (p. i). The consumption of unauthorized recordings will likely increase in developing countries as laptops connected to mobile data connections enable access to P2P networks (Sandvine, 2011, p. 8). While music industry organizations claim that these high levels of piracy are due to outdated and poorly enforced copyright laws, Karaganis notes that prices of licit CDs and other cultural goods are so high in emerging economies that they have become luxury items. Prices are deliberately kept high in developing countries, despite dismal sales, in order to maintain high prices in developed countries. In other words, record companies and other media firms sacrifice sales in low-income countries in order to maximize profit across the global market. The surge in media piracy in developing countries is not a law enforcement problem but a "pricing problem," Karaganis argues, since the demand for illicit copies is largely a result of pricing problems in the licit market (p. iii).

Industry reports typically ignore sales data prior to 1999, which gives the impression that the current slump in record sales is the first of its kind in the history of the music industry. In fact, record sales declined in the late 1970s and early 1980s, in part due to economic recession (Connolly & Krueger, 2006, p. 710). Liebowitz (2003) points out that U.S. music sales plummeted during the Great Depression from 74.8 million units in 1929 to 5.5 million units in 1932 (p. 14). But the recession of the early 2000s was, according to Liebowitz (2005), "far too mild" to have any significant impact on sales (p. 455). However, it is unlikely that record industry revenues have been immune to the global financial crisis now that the scale and severity of this recession have become clear.

Perhaps the most significant challenges facing the industry stem from the unintended consequences of the industry's expansion into online licensing and sales. As Marie Connolly and Alan Krueger (2006) suggest, "Perhaps what has occurred is not just substitution of CDs for MP3 files, but a shift in leisure activities brought about by the new technologies. Internet and computers could have created a change in how people spend their time, possibly reducing the demand for pre-recorded music" (p. 711). These shifts are particularly evident among teenagers, whose consumption habits are shifting away from file sharing, paid downloads, and CDs (both purchased and shared) and toward cloud-based streaming and social media listening services (NPD Group, 2009, March 31). As Jeremy Morris (2011) argues, underlying these technological and industrial trends is a crisis regarding "the place of music in social life" as consumption practices and musical experiences become integrated into a "series of interfaces and formats" controlled by software and telecommunications firms (para. 39). The IFPI's representation of file sharing as the industry's primary problem overestimates the economic impact of file sharing and underestimates the complexity of the challenges stemming from the industry's transition to network media.

FALLACY 4. FILE SHARING AFFECTS EVERYONE IN THE MUSIC BUSINESS IN THE SAME WAY

Industry organizations often give the impression that most artists are opposed to file sharing. However, over half of the artists surveyed in a 2004 Pew study identified their position as "not too concerned" or "not concerned at all" about file sharing (Madden, 2004, p. 21). The survey points to significant variations in artists' perceptions of file sharing. While certain high-profile artists periodically denounce file sharing in their media appearances, many other artists claim that long-standing problems within the music industry, such as recording contracts that favour labels over creators, pose a much greater threat to artists' rights and livelihoods than file sharing and other forms of unauthorized copying.[16]

Just as perceptions of file sharing vary between artists, the financial impact of file sharing on artists varies due to differences in the sources of artists' income (some artists depend on record sales while others, including many "top earners," rely almost entirely on sales of concert tickets) and uneven distributions of royalties, promotional services, and other resources in the music business.[17] In his analysis of file sharing activity and U.S. sales data, David Blackburn (2006) argued that file sharing benefits emerging artists by increasing awareness of those artists and expanding their potential market, whereas stars have little to gain from file sharing's exposure effect since they are already extensively promoted by their record labels and the media.[18] According to Blackburn, "The effects of file sharing on sales of recorded music are extremely unlikely to be consistent across artists, and therefore it is vital to identify these differences to get an accurate representation of the effects" (p. 6). Despite the efforts of researchers to highlight the heterogeneity of file sharing's effects, the industry continues to promote the view that the effects of file sharing are homogeneous.

In each country, file sharing's effects are also mediated by a *regime of copying*, which refers to the institutions, rules, technologies, and practices that regulate copying. In the 1990s, many governments changed their regimes of copying in response to digital media. Some countries, such as the United States, focused on preventing piracy through the development of copy control technologies that encrypt and monitor digital content. Other countries, such as Canada, emphasized **alternative compensation systems** for unauthorized copying. Alternative compensation systems are based on the notion that some degree of unauthorized copying is inevitable and that individuals in democratic societies should be able to make copies privately without being monitored by governmental or corporate institutions. In this view, governments should focus on developing systems that offset losses associated with unauthorized copying rather than using public funds in a perpetual attempt to prevent or eliminate unauthorized copying (Condry, 2004, pp. 344–345). In 1997 the Parliament of Canada amended the *Copyright Act* to allow individuals to copy sound recordings for personal use and created an alternative compensation system through the blank media levy. Manufacturers and importers of CD-Rs and other recordable media are required to pay the levy to the Canadian Private Copying Collective (CPCC), which distributes private copying royalties to artists and labels through their royalty collection organizations. As Michael Geist (2005) notes, "The evidence suggests that Canadian artists have scarcely been harmed by the reduced sales [of sound recordings] from 1999 to 2004 since royalty losses are fully compensated through the private copying levy" (para. 17). By 2010, the CPCC had distributed over $212 million to Canadian artists, record labels, and other copyright owners (Canadian Private Copying Collective, 2011, p. 1).

File sharing's economic impact in countries like Canada, where artists and labels are compensated for private copying, is considerably different from file sharing's impact in countries where alternative compensation systems are either absent or ineffective. In her study of twenty-one independent music labels in Montreal, Tina Piper (2011) found that these labels generate the majority of their revenue from grants and other forms of government funding (rather than from record sales and licensing) and that the owners of these labels were less concerned about piracy than other issues in the industry. This suggests that Canada's alternative compensation system, along with other forms of federal and provincial support for music production, to some extent insulates smaller labels from the effects of file sharing and other shifts in consumer technology, and allows those labels to distance themselves from the obsessive focus on piracy characteristic of transnational music firms operating in Canada.

CONCLUSION

Through the IFPI and other industry organizations, the major record companies are in the process of persuading policymakers in Canada and many other countries to create anti-piracy rules that would grant copyright owners and other private institutions tremendous control over online communication, including the ability to block websites and terminate alleged infringers' Internet access. The industry argues that these wide-reaching anti-piracy laws and international agreements are necessary to reduce the harm caused by file sharing and other forms of piracy. However, the claim that file sharing is harmful is not based on a consensus among researchers; it primarily reflects the assumptions of large copyright owners about the effects of file sharing technologies on the behaviour of audiences. Few other proposed legal reforms that affect so many communicative activities are based on such scant evidence of harm. As a result of the industry's intensive and ongoing intervention in uses and perceptions of file sharing, file sharing remains largely untapped as a source of alternative modes of circulating and communicating music.

Notes

[1] Since 2003, the major record companies have filed over 30 000 copyright infringement lawsuits against individual file sharers in the United States (Anderson, 2009). The major labels' "shock and awe"–style litigation campaign was extended to Canada in February 2004 when CRIA sued twenty-nine Canadian users of the Kazaa file sharing network, but the Federal Court of Canada ruled that CRIA had not established a prima facie case of infringement (Canadian Internet Policy and Public Interest Clinic, 2005). In April 2005, the IFPI announced that it was coordinating at "new wave of lawsuits" across Europe and Asia (IFPI, 2005).

[2] The music industry pressured Apple and other electronics firms and online music retailers to implement technological protection measures (TPMs) and digital rights management (DRM) systems, which are designed to make copying more difficult. Whereas copyright law enables owners to take legal action after infringement has occurred, the music industry has adopted technologies that are designed to prevent unauthorized copying altogether. Scholars have criticized these copy control technologies on the grounds that they contribute to monopolization in the media and cultural industries, undermine freedom of expression and privacy, and restrict forms of copying that are permitted and even encouraged by copyright laws (Cameron, 2009; Radin, 2004; Sharpe & Arewa, 2007).

[3] As Ariel Katz (2005) notes, in the 1990s, the music industry's lobbying efforts "yielded significant achievements in the form of new international treaties, such as the TRIPS Agreement and the WIPO Copyright Treaty; new legislation at the national level (such as the *Digital Millennium Copyright Act* in the United States); and increased government spending on enhanced public enforcement of copyright laws" (pp. 155–156). Music industry organizations are currently focusing their efforts on the development of more effective means of enforcing copyright online, such as "graduated response" systems whereby warnings are sent to alleged infringers, followed by the termination of the users' Internet access. In this way, copyright owners

are bypassing the legal system and using other private institutions such as Internet service providers to identify and punish alleged infringers. Graduated response rules have been signed into law in the U.K., France, and South Korea, and were incorporated into the proposed Anti-Counterfeiting Trade Agreement, to which Canada is a signatory. The proposed *Stop Online Piracy Act* in the United States goes a step further and would enable foreign websites suspected of infringement to be blocked.

[4] Worldwide in 2010, "performance-rights distributions to record companies totaled US$868 million, up 9.2% compared with US$794.6 million in 2009," according to Music & Copyright, a music industry research service (2011, para. 3). In the United States, performance rights grew more rapidly than the global average. Citing the IFPI's data, *Billboard* reported that revenue from performance rights increased by 28 percent, from $70 million in 2009 to $90 million in 2010 (Billboard, 2011, para. 6). The proliferation of mobile and online music services that pay royalties to the labels and the development of more effective royalty collection systems are largely responsible for this increase in performance rights revenue.

[5] According to the Warner Music Group, global industry revenue from mobile music was $1.6 billion (U.S.) and Warner expects that mobile revenues will continue to increase: "While revenues from ringtones initially drove the mobile music business, new mobile phones equipped with new capabilities are increasingly offering the capability for full-track downloads and streaming audio and video" (Warner Music Group, 2010, p. 19). One recent success story in the mobile music market comes from U.S.-based mobile provider Cricket, which claims that its Muve Music plan (which bundles unlimited music downloads with its monthly mobile plans) acquired 500 000 subscribers in 2011, its first year of operation (Steinberg, 2012).

[6] Although the number of concert tickets sold in the United States has declined since 2000, revenue from ticket sales has grown because the price of tickets has increased (Connolly & Krueger, 2006, p. 682).

[7] Revenue from merchandising has increased due to reduced costs and the use of expanded-rights contracts, which allow record labels to acquire a share of merchandising revenue.

[8] Since the 1980s, record companies have increasingly focused on the exploitation of intellectual property rights in musical works across different media rather than relying on the more traditional understanding of profit in terms of "moving products" or selling records (Jones, 2002, p. 218). The transition to digital media and online distribution is intensifying this trend toward cross-media rights exploitation.

[9] Various trade organizations calculate the cost of piracy by estimating the number of pirated goods consumed in a given market and using retail prices to gauge the monetary value of those goods. The figures produced in this manner are rather alarming and are thus useful for constructing piracy as an urgent policy problem. For instance, the Canadian Intellectual Property Council (2009) suggests that, in Canada, the cost of "piracy" (everything from counterfeit Viagra pills to P2P downloads) is approximately $22 billion "in lost tax revenue, investment and innovation" (p. 14). These estimates assume that all P2P downloads substitute for purchased recordings even. No economic study of file sharing that I am aware of demonstrates such far-reaching and encompassing substitution effects. Unlike estimates of the cost of piracy, links between increases in file sharing and decreases in record sales have the merit of focusing on actual historical trends. While there are some indications in the economics literature of a correlation between the popularization of file sharing and declining record sales, industry organizations often mistake this correlation for causality.

[10] According to the authors' estimates, "While file sharers downloaded billions of files in 2002, the consequences for the industry amounted to no more than 0.7 percent of sales" (Oberholzer-Gee & Strumpf, 2007, p. 39).

[11] Andersen and Frenz (2007) found that substitution effects were offset by file sharers who use file sharing in order to sample and who tend to buy more CDs as a result (pp. 28–29).

[12] Such effects have been observed in the software industry, where publishers deliberately leave their products open to piracy in order to achieve faster and wider distribution than competitors (Katz, 2005, p. 157). Some economists have suggested that business models in the music industry could be adapted so that rightsholders would be able to charge more for official copies when file sharing begins to generate a network effect (Gayer & Shy, 2005, p. 477).

[13] Mark Cenite and co-authors (2009) found that some file sharers use P2P networks as a kind of archive in which music that is difficult to find can be heard once again. See also Markus Giesler and Mali Pohlmann (2003) for an extended discussion of the use of file sharing in practices of music collecting.

[14] Liebowitz (2003, 2006) rejected the idea that competing products, such as DVDs, had a significant impact on music industry revenues. In his view, CD and DVD purchasing complement rather than displace each other.

[15] The Warner Music Group notes that these trends in physical distribution and retailing have had a significant impact on record sales: "Retailers still account for the majority of sales of our physical product; however, as the number of physical music retailers has declined significantly, there is increased competition for available display space. This has led to a decrease in the amount and variety of physical product on display" (Warner Music Group, 2011, p. 51).

[16] In the U.K., Annie Lennox, Ed O'Brien (Radiohead), Dave Rowntree (Blur), and others formed the Featured Artists Coalition (FAC), which advocates for artists' rights in the negotiation of record contracts and in intellectual property reforms and other areas of law and policy (Featured Artists Coalition, n.d.). Rather than seeking increased legal restrictions on file sharing networks, FAC encourages the development of strategies and policies that enable artists to "monetize" file sharing and other forms of unauthorized reproduction and distribution.

[17] Artists have traditionally enjoyed 100 percent of merchandise sales at their concerts and 50 percent of ticket sales, whereas in record contracts, the artist's share of royalties was often so low that "only the most popular artists earn substantial revenue from record sales" (Connolly & Krueger, 2006, p. 674). The industry practice of allocating the vast majority of revenue from record sales to the label forces many artists to seek alternative sources of income, such as increased touring.

[18] Although many pro-file sharing commentators cite Blackburn's study as evidence of the positive effects of file sharing, Blackburn (2006) notes that the long-term effects depend on the way record companies respond to the perceived effect of file sharing on sales (p. 38). If record companies stop investing in new artists owing to the fear that file sharing will reduce the probability that new acts will achieve stardom, this decline in investment would have a negative effect in the long term.

References

Andersen, B., & Frenz, M. (2007). *The impact of music downloads and P2P file-sharing on the purchase of music: A study report for Industry Canada.* Retrieved from http://www.ic.gc.ca/eic/site/ippd-dppi.nsf/vwapj/IndustryCanadaPaperMay4_2007_en.pdf/$FILE/IndustryCanadaPaperMay4_2007_en.pdf

Anderson, N. (2009). Has the RIAA sued 18,000 people or 35,000? *Ars Technica.* Retrieved from http://arstechnica.com/tech-policy/news/2009/07/has-the-riaa-sued-18000-people-or-35000.ars

Billboard. (2011, March 30). IFPI 2011 report: Global recorded music sales fall 8.4%. Retrieved from http://www.billboard.biz/bbbiz/industry/global/ifpi-2011-report-global-recorded-music-sales-1005100902.story

Blackburn, D. (2006). The heterogeneous effects of copying: The case of recorded music. Harvard University Working Paper. Retrieved from http://davidjhblackburn.com/papers/blackburn_fs.pdf

Cameron, A. (2009). Learning from data protection law at the nexus of copyright and privacy. In I. Kerr (Ed.), *Lessons from the identity trail: Anonymity, privacy and identity in a networked society* (pp. 43–63). Oxford: Oxford University Press.

Canadian Intellectual Property Council. (2009). *A time for change: Toward a new era for intellectual property rights in Canada.* Retrieved from http://www.ipcouncil.ca/uploads/ATimeForChange.pdf

Canadian Internet Policy and Public Interest Clinic. (2005, November 9). CRIA file-sharing lawsuits. Retrieved from http://www.cippic.ca/file-sharing-lawsuits/

Canadian Private Copying Collective. (2011). Financial highlights. Retrieved from http://www.cpcc.ca/en/wp-content/uploads/2011/12/CPCC-Financial-Highlights-2010-En.pdf

Cenite, M., Wang, M. W., Peiwen, C., & Shimin Chan, G. S. (2009). More than just free content: Motivations of peer-to-peer file sharers. *Journal of Communication Inquiry, 33*(3), 206–221.

Condry, I. (2004). Cultures of music piracy: An ethnographic comparison of the US and Japan. *International Journal of Cultural Studies, 7*(3), 343–363.

Connolly, M., & Krueger, A. B. (2006). Rockonomics: The economics of popular music. In V. A. Ginsburgh & D. Throsby (Eds.), *Handbook of the economics of art and culture* (pp. 667–719). Amsterdam, Netherlands: Elsevier.

Curien, N., & Moreau, F. (2009). The music industry in the digital era: Toward new contracts. *Journal of Media Economics, 22,* 102–113.

Featured Artists Coalition. (n.d.). Who we are. Retrieved from http://www.featuredartistscoalition.com/about/

Gayer, A., & Shy, O. (2005). Copyright enforcement in the digital era. *CESifo Economic Studies, 51,* 477–489.

Geist, M. (2005). Piercing the peer-to-peer myths: An examination of the Canadian experience. *First Monday, 10*(4). Retrieved from http://firstmonday.org/htbin/cgiwrap/bin/ojs/index.php/fm/article/viewArticle/1217/1137

Giesler, M., & Pohlmann, M. (2003). The anthropology of file sharing: Consuming Napster as a gift. *Advances in Consumer Research, 30,* 273–279.

Gillespie, T. (2009). Characterizing copyright in the classroom: The cultural work of antipiracy campaigns. *Communication, Culture & Critique, 2*(3), 274–318.

Gopal, R. D., Bhattacharjee, S., & Sanders, G. L. (2006). Do artists benefit from online music sharing? *The Journal of Business, 79*(3), 1503–1533.

IFPI. (2001). IFPI music piracy report. Retrieved from http://www.ifpi.org/content/library/Piracy2001.pdf

IFPI. (2005, April 12). Music file-sharers face biggest round of legal actions yet. Retrieved from http://www.ifpi.org/content/section_news/20050412.html

IFPI. (2011). IFPI digital music report 2011. Retrieved from http://www.ifpi.org/content/library/DMR2011.pdf

Jones, S. (2002). Music that moves: Popular music, distribution and network technologies. *Cultural Studies, 16*(2), 213–223.

Karaganis, J. (2011). Rethinking piracy. In J. Karaganis (Ed.), *Media piracy in emerging economies* (pp. 1–74). Social Science Research Council. Retrieved from http://piracy.ssrc.org/wp-content/uploads/2011/06/MPEE-PDF-1.0.4.pdf

Katz, A. (2005). A network effects perspective on software piracy. *University of Toronto Law Journal, 55*(2), 155–216.

Klimis, G. M., & Wallis, R. (2009). Copyright and entrepreneurship: Catalyst or barrier? *Information, Communication & Society, 12*(2), 267–286.

Leman-Langlois, S. (2005). Theft in the information age: Music, technology, crime, and claims-making. *Knowledge, Technology & Policy, 17*(3–4), 140–163.

Lessig, L. (2004). *Free culture: How big media uses technology and the law to lock down culture and control creativity.* The Penguin Press. Retrieved from http://www.free-culture.cc/freeculture.pdf

Leyshon, A., Webb, P., French, S., Thrift, N., & Crewe, L. (2005). On the reproduction of the musical economy after the Internet. *Media, Culture & Society, 27*(2), 177–209.

Liebowitz, S. (2003). *Will MP3 downloads annihilate the record industry? The evidence so far.* Retrieved from http://www.utdallas.edu/~liebowit/intprop/records.pdf

Liebowitz, S. (2005). Pitfalls in measuring the impact of file-sharing. *CESifo Economic Studies, 51*(23), 439–477.

Liebowitz, S. (2006). File-sharing: Creative destruction of just plain destruction? *Journal of Law & Economics, 49*(1), 1–28.

Logie, J. (2006). *Peers, pirates, and persuasion: Rhetoric in the peer-to-peer debates.* West Lafayette, IN: Parlor Press.

Madden, M. (2004). *Artists, musicians and the Internet.* Pew Internet & American Life Project. Retrieved from http://pewinternet.org/~/media//Files/Reports/2004/PIP_Artists.Musicians_Report.pdf.pdf

McCourt, T., & Burkart, P. (2003). When creators, corporations and consumers collide: Napster and the development of on-line music distribution. *Media, Culture & Society, 25*(3), 333–350.

Morris, J. (2011). Sounds in the cloud: Cloud computing and the digital music commodity. *First Monday, 16*(5). Retrieved from http://firstmonday.org/htbin/cgiwrap/bin/ojs/index.php/fm/article/viewArticle/3391/2917

Music & Copyright. (2011, October 19). SoundExchange takes the crown as the world's biggest performance-rights society. Retrieved from http://musicandcopyright.wordpress.com/2011/10/19/soundexchange-takes-the-crown-as-the-world%E2%80%99s-biggest-performance-rights-society/#more-614

NPD Group. (2009, March 31). Always a bellwether for the music industry, teens are changing how they interact with music. Retrieved from https://www.npd.com/wps/portal/npd/us/news/pressreleases/pr_090331a/!ut/p/c5/04_SB8K8xLLM9MSSzPy8xBz9CP0os3g3b1NTS98QY0OLwGBDA09Ld8tQcwt_Q1MPc_1I_SjjeBc3Sw8PN28TQ4sgSwsDT1d_QxfPoAAjC0sj_YLsQEUAwcXNUQ!!/

Oberholzer-Gee, F., & Strumpf, K. (2007). The effect of file-sharing on record sales: An empirical analysis. *Journal of Political Economy, 115*(1), 1–42.

Ontario Media Development Fund. (2011). *Industry profile: Music.* Retrieved from http://www.omdc.on.ca/AssetFactory.aspx?did=6566

Peitz, M., & Waelbroeck, M. (2004). An economist's guide to digital music. CESifo Working Paper No. 1333. Retrieved from http://www.sfbtr15.de/dipa/32.pdf

Piper, T. (2011, October 21). The independence of copyright's labels. Paper presented at the Conference of the Canadian Initiative in Law, Culture and Humanities, Ottawa, Ontario.

PricewaterhouseCoopers. (2006). *Global entertainment and media outlook 2006–2010.* Retrieved from http://www.cenacine.com.br/wp-content/uploads/globaloverviewweb.pdf

Radin, M. J. (2004). Regulation by contract, regulation by machine. *Journal of Institutional and Theoretical Economics, 160*(1), 142–156.

Rob, R., & Waldfogel, J. (2004). Piracy on the high C's: Music downloading, sales displacement, and social welfare in a sample of college students. National Bureau of Economic Research Working Paper 10874. Retrieved from http://www.econ.yale.edu/seminars/apmicro/am04/waldfogel-041021.pdf

Sandvine. (2011). *Global Internet phenomena report: Spring 2011.* Retrieved from http://www.wired.com/images_blogs/epicenter/2011/05/SandvineGlobalInternetSpringReport2011.pdf

Secor. (2011). *Canada's entertainment software industry in 2011.* Report prepared for the Entertainment Software Association of Canada. Retrieved from http://www.theesa.ca/wp-content/uploads/2011/08/SECOR_ESAC_report_eng_2011.pdf

Sharpe, N. F., & Arewa, O. B. (2007). Is Apple playing fair? Navigating the iPod FairPlay DRM controversy. *Northwestern Journal of Technology and Intellectual Property, 5*(2), 332–350.

Stahl, M. (2011). From seven years to 360 degrees: Primitive accumulation, recording contracts, and the means of making a (musical) living. *Triple C, 9*(2), 668–688.

Statistics Canada. (2009). *Sound recording and music publishing.* Catalogue no. 87F0008X. Retrieved from http://www.statcan.gc.ca/pub/87f0008x/87f0008x2011001-eng.pdf

Steinberg, S. (2012, January 9). Muve Music nets 500,000 subscribers in one year. *Rolling Stone.* Retrieved from http://www.rollingstone.com/culture/blogs/gear-up/muve-music-nets-500-000-subscribers-in-one-year-20120109

Warner Music Group. (2010). *Annual report 2009.* Retrieved from http://phx.corporate-ir.net/phoenix.zhtml?c=182480&p=irol-reportsannual

Warner Music Group. (2011). *Annual report 2010.* Retrieved from http://phx.corporate-ir.net/phoenix.zhtml?c=182480&p=irol-reportsannual

Winseck, D. (2011, May 17). Restrictive copyright plays into music industry myths. *The Globe and Mail.* Retrieved from http://www.theglobeandmail.com/news/technology/digital-culture/dwayne-winseck/restrictive-copyright-plays-into-music-industry-myths/article2023845/singlepage/

Yar, M. (2005). The global "epidemic" of movie "piracy": Crime-wave or social construction? *Media, Culture & Society, 27*(5), 677–696.

Zentner, A. (2006). Measuring the effect of music downloads on music purchases. *Journal of Law & Economics, 49*(1), 63–90.

Discussion Questions

1. When did the issue of file sharing begin to gain attention? What were some of the first considerations raised?

2. Explain how P2P file sharing harms the music sector.

3. What role do free riders play in the harm being done to the music sector?

4. This chapter discussed six uses of file sharing networks: substitution, sampling, exposure, network effects, collecting, and non-infringing. Based on your own experience with file sharing networks, burned CDs, or other music-sharing media, do you agree with the major labels that substitution is the only significant use of these media? Or do you use music-sharing media for other reasons as well?

5. File sharing played an important role in the shift from tangible music formats towards network media in which recorded music acquires the characteristics of software: intangible, customizable, portable, remotely-accessible, and ubiquitous. In your view, are these characteristics of music in the network media environment having a positive or negative impact on the way people consume and experience music?

6. In the early days of file sharing, digital media theorists such as Steve Jones suggested that file sharing's most significant threat to record labels is not the manner in which consumers use file sharing to obtain free downloads but rather artists' uses of file sharing (and other network media) as alternative means of promoting and distributing their own works. Do you agree with Jones? Why or why not?

PART 5 Entertainment and Popular Culture

ISSUE 1   **Trash television: Is reality television harmful to society?**

ISSUE 2   **Informed comedy: Do mock news shows make for a more informed public?**

ISSUE 3   **Social networks and privacy: Should government be more interventionist in protecting personal privacy?**

ISSUE 4   **Entertaining politics: Is it all about image?**

Entertainment is a substantial component of both interpersonal and mass communication. Popular entertainment, in many respects, operates as the lingua franca of contemporary society—we connect with others through a shared interest in (or dislike of) popular television shows, musical genres, movies, Internet sites, and celebrity fandom. Yet the question arises: what is the relationship between popular entertainment and personal perspective? If entertainment is a powerful backdrop to our culture, how does what we consume for entertainment influence our broader understanding and view of the world?

Such queries are particularly relevant to our personal, political, and social lives. This section explores how popular television genres, including reality television and mock news shows, have implications that extend beyond the thirty- or sixty-minute time slot. Sometimes these implications have to do with degree, that is, exploring the extent to which mock news shows influence political awareness and engagement. Sometimes they have to do with questions resting at the heart of our democracy, as is the case with the media pushing the concept of politics as entertainment. Does representing politics as entertainment really advance our democracy? (Some have argued that

laughter is good when you cannot change anything, but laughing at situations that you have the power to change things—as we do as citizens—is deeply problematic.) Every debate in this section speaks to the question of whether such "entertainment" has gone too far.

Opening with a focus on reality television, Fiona Whittington-Walsh frames its "entertaining spectacle" as a dangerous pastime. Reality television, she argues, is not merely inexpensive programming. Rather, it works to depoliticize, disconnect individuals from one another, and foster commodity capitalism. Whittington-Walsh asserts that viewers of reality television act as armchair flâneurs. They complacently view the outside world from the comfort of the home and the problem, she says, is that these audiences act simply as gawkers. Reality television shows do not encourage people to develop empathy for others, or work to create communal experiences that can foster positive change in society.

Derek Foster disagrees with the view of reality television as destructive. Starting from the premise that "one person's trash is another one's treasure," Foster urges us to consider the possibility that reality television can do some good if it can also do harm. The good can be found in the way that trashy

TV narratives provide stories that not only keep us entertained, but also provide a celebration of ordinary life. Foster observes that even disagreeable content can be valuable for providing a trigger for debate and discussion around controversial issues, dominant ideologies, or unquestioned norms.

To view these shows as harmful is also to overlook the ways that these shows may generate positive social action by virtue of the very ire that they raise. "Most objectionable programming," he argues, is more productive than "least objectionable programming" because it inspires people to talk, to mock the show, to write outraged letters or rants on blog sites and Facebook. All of this constitutes a form of active participation. To suggest that viewers mindlessly accept the messages they find in these shows is deeply wrong-headed.

Reality television is not the only genre embroiled in controversy. The second debate pivots on whether popular mock news shows (such as *The Daily Show* and *The Colbert Report*) make for a more informed public. When comedian Stephen Colbert makes *Time* magazine's 2012 "100 Most Influential People in the World" list and Jon Stewart is cited in a 2009 *Time* magazine poll as one of America's most trusted newscasters, it is important to take a serious look at comedic discourse. This is particularly important given that these fake news shows have become the primary news sources for the younger demographic (eighteen- to twenty-nine-year-olds). Does news parody play a positive role in citizen engagement and civic culture?

Ian Reilly argues that it does. Satirical news is positive for democracy because it functions as a type of watchdog to the mainstream media itself. Such media critique, which interrogates and challenges the narratives and practices of mainstream journalism, constitutes the *fifth estate*. It is a type of journalism *about* journalism, a metadiscursive critique, which expands the "audience's capacity to think critically about the news and information it consumes." This can only be good for civic culture.

Mary Francoli contests this. While it is wonderful to laugh at life, she affirms that it is troubling to view mock news as a source of information and/or means

of education. By probing the concepts of substance, framing, audience, and purpose, Francoli asks us to consider how approaching news with the view to being entertained works to trivialize serious policy issues. Mock news presents an epidermal treatment of news because that is what it aims to do. Mock news is not news. As Francoli concludes, "it does little to inform and we shouldn't expect it to."

Moving from comedy to privacy, Leslie Shade examines the world's largest social network site, Facebook, to unveil how the sharing of photos, quotes, wall posts, and pokes is equally bound up with issues of personal security and privacy. Shade details the manifold "Facebook follies" that makes users' private information available to advertisers and others, and critiques its "capricious take on our personal privacy." Her call to action is for a radical transparency applied to our personal privacy.

Boyd Neil agrees that personal privacy on social networks should be tightly guarded. However, Neil rejects the notion that governments should intervene to advance this right to privacy. Observing that government regimes frequently threaten individual privacy themselves (with legislation that supports surveillance for their own purposes), Neil places the responsibility for moderating between the sale of personal data and the right to privacy on social network platforms and marketers. In the final analysis, Neil finds that the bigger threat resides in the government, not social networks or corporations, seeking our personal information without our consent.

The final debate moves from the personal to the political, tackling the question of whether contemporary Canadian politics is "all about image." Bernie Gauthier argues that it is, but also that image can provide critical insight into the person making the promises. Image is a powerful system of communication: it is about appearance, articulation, and actions, which Canadians observe and actively use to decide whether or not to support a politician. Image, in brief, provides an efficient snapshot for voters who are striving to assess a politician's potential effectiveness, integrity, and competency. People need to use all communication channels available to them in order to evaluate the messages we receive from politicians.

Echoing Gauthier, Jennifer Ditchburn agrees that "packaging politics" is a central component of modern democracy. However, she equally affirms that political success "is much more complex than the properly scuffed shoe or the impromptu piano performance." Leadership material, avers Ditchburn, "isn't made of denim." Other circumstances, including the stumbles made by political rivals and the ability to target voters strategically, factor strongly in the end result. Image has nothing to do with the internal leadership rules that allow candidates to win the top position in their party's leadership races, nor is image really about the type of "savvy" required to win a political election. Much more is required for political success. Image without ideas simply does not work, and any victory stems from a much more complicated interplay of factors.

ISSUE 1

Trash television:
Is reality television harmful to society?

✔ YES

Reality Television and the Armchair Flâneur
Fiona Whittington-Walsh

Fiona Whittington-Walsh received her Ph.D. in sociology at York University in 2010. Her research focuses on the areas of community–academic research partnerships, the cultural industries, disability issues, and the everyday experiences of women and body image. She has published in the areas of disability and health, disability and cinematic representation, beauty and women with disabilities, and women and cosmetic surgery. Her current research is exploring the history of disability representations in mainstream film. She currently teaches at Kwantlen Polytechnic University, Surrey, British Columbia.

Empathy is the nature of the intoxication to which the flâneur abandons himself in the crowd. [quoting Charles Baudelaire:] "[He] enjoys the incomparable privilege of being himself and someone else as he sees fit. Like a roving soul in search of a body, he enters another person whenever he wishes. For him alone, all is open...."[1]

—Walter Benjamin (1973, p. 55)

THE REALITY

The promise of reality television is to provide a connection for the audience. Derek Foster (2008) draws a division between "good" reality television, such as shows that offer audience participation in determining outcomes, and the (presumably bad) reality shows that "rely on the shock of the real" (p. 274). What constitutes the foundation of reality television that breaks free of shock value, according to Foster, is that the narratives are non-scripted and outcomes are unplanned. Murray and Ouellett (2004) maintain that certain important distinctions exist between what is considered real broadcasting and reality television. The "real" is the type of broadcasting that is based on news, documentary, and other informational formats and has its foundation in the tradition of public service. Reality television, on the other hand, is based on a construction of everyday life but is "presented in the name of dramatic, uncertainty, voyeurism, and popular pleasure" (p. 2). While "real" broadcasting purports to advance the public good, reality television takes the public's entertainment as its primary focus.

The reality television genre encompasses many formats including the following:

- Documentary—MTV: *The Real World* (1992–present) and *16 and Pregnant* and *Teen Mom* (2009–present); A&E: *Hoarders* (2009–present)

- Historical re-creations—Canada's History Television: *Pioneer Quest: A Year in the Real West* (2000)

- Science—The Discovery Channel: *Mythbusters* (2003)

- Dating—ABC: *The Bachelor* (2002–present); Fox Reality Channel: *Seducing Cindy* (2010)

- Game show—CBS: *Survivor* (2000–present)

- Talent—Fox: *American Idol* (2002–present); CTV: *Canadian Idol* (2008–present)

- Law enforcement—Fox: *Cops* (1990–present); A&E: *Steven Seagal: Lawman* (2009–2010)

- Transformation and lifestyle change—ABC: *Extreme Makeover* (2002–2007) and *Extreme Makeover Home Edition* (2003–present); Bravo: *Queer Eye for the Straight Guy* (2003–2007), ABC: *Supernanny* (2005); MTV: *I Used to Be Fat* (2010–present)

- Celebrity cult—MTV: *The Osbournes (2002–2005)*; A&E: *Gene Simmons Family Jewels* (2006–present); E!: *Keeping up with the Kardashians* (2007–present)

In this article I discuss the role that the audience plays while "participating" in watching reality television shows.[2] I will use as my foundation for analysis a brief[3] discussion of MTV's *16 and Pregnant* and *Teen Mom*. Drawing on the philosopher Walter Benjamin,[4] I argue that reality television is just another process produced by the cultural industries that facilitates depoliticization, alienates the viewer from appreciating authentic human experiences, and undermines the ability of a democratic medium to emerge.[5]

STORYTELLING

Benjamin was interested in images and how the mediated world of the cultural industries distorts those images in order to draw the audience into the fantasy word of capitalism. In this dream world, visual pleasure has surfaced as the primary sense and has become mediated more and more by the commodification of social life. Entertainment has become manifested in viewing the enormous numbers of consumer goods available and presented in the city centres. Key to this dream state is to keep the audience from feeling empathy and therefore a connection to the images and to one another. We are only to feel a connection to the consumer goods that demand our attention at every turn.

In his book *Charles Baudelaire: A Lyric Poet in the Era of High Capitalism*, Benjamin (1973) quotes the German sociologist Georg Simmel, who discusses the disembodying nature of the city centre under capitalism:

> Someone who sees without hearing is much more uneasy than someone who hears without seeing. In this there is something characteristic of the sociology of the big city. Interpersonal relationships in big cities are distinguished by a marked preponderance of the activity of the eye over the activity of the ear. (pp. 37–38)

We can use Benjamin's analysis of the character the flâneur to critically analyze the principles of viewing reality television. The famous literary figure, the flâneur, floats like a partially seen ghost through the city, listening and watching life as it bustles by. In metaphorical terms, the flâneur is a window shopper of life, both a part of and separate from the crowd. The flâneur is always active, moving through the streets, listening, hearing, smelling, and in some instances feeling or sensing the crowds. Roaming the city streets, the outside world becomes the flâneur's interior.

I draw on Benjamin's notion of the flâneur because the sense of floating through the city, at once detached and connected, a participant and a voyeur, is a useful way of critically thinking about how audiences watch reality TV. The endless choices of reality programs are presented to us as a city labyrinth, never ending and always leading into another. However, as the outside world becomes the flâneur's interior world, through the lens of reality TV we explore the outside world while remaining within the confines of our own interior. We become complacent in the comfort of our armchair, never fostering empathy or becoming one with the crowd. To *not* possess empathy with the crowds whom we watch is symptomatic of the alienating and individuated social world. We become a *badaud*—a gawker—an "impersonal creature" who becomes intoxicated by spectacle and is "no longer a human being" (Benjamin, 1973, p. 69).[6] This is the **commodity self** (Ewan, 1988), where one's relationships cease to be between each other but between individuals and things. We become alienated from what makes us social, and our very sense of identity is intrinsically linked up with the commodities that surround us and are repeatedly marketed to us, and which we consume.

When we are watching reality TV we become the *baduad*—an armchair flâneur—positioned to be inactive, even if we have the ability to participate by nominating offenders (for example, *Style by Jury*[7]) or choosing a winner (*Canadian Idol*). We become mere spectators unable to feel empathy for those whose stories we are watching. This is a key allure of reality television: the idea of storytelling. Benjamin (1968) maintains that with the advancement of mass produced culture, and in particular the commodified publishing industry, the art of storytelling started to die and thus the desire to communicate one's actual lived *communal* experiences also declined. This is all symptomatic of an ever-alienating social world under advanced capitalism. Through the advancement of technology we have become alienated from oral storytelling and have resorted to absorbing "information" rather than experiencing it.

As C. Wright Mills (1999) maintained, one of the key principles of using one's sociological imagination is the ability to connect one's own experiences to the wider social world. According to Mills, "The sociological imagination enables us to grasp history and biography and the relations between the two within society. That is its task and its promise" (pp. 11–12). While Benjamin does not directly reflect on the principals involved in utilizing one's sociological imagination, his main propositions regarding the dream world of capitalism are interestingly similar. Benjamin maintains that in order to shatter the dream state that is produced by the mediated images, we need to be able to make Mill's connection and in particular make the web of stories by feeling empathy with the crowds. This is what creates the social world: a web of communal experiences. This web is also connected to the wider social forces that help shape our very experiences. Reality television creates an opportunity to watch people's lives and to listen to their stories *without* feeling empathy and *without* constructing a web of stories. While in some cases we may feel a wide variety of emotions toward the participants of reality TV, empathy is generally not one of them. Most often, as in the case of *16 and Pregnant* and *Teen Mom*, we are positioned to feel *pity* for the subjects, which is not the same as being able to see ourselves in what we are watching. In order to feel empathy and to become one with the crowd as the flâneur does, we need to not only see ourselves in the reflection but also connect our web of stories to the material conditions that affect all of our lives.

One of the reasons for the success of the reality television genre (other than the low production costs and high revenues) is the fact that with a few exceptions[8] we are not "flies on the wall." In fact, our presence is known while we remain anonymous and completely unseen. In some shows (such as *16 and Pregnant*, *Teen Mom*, and *I Used to Be Fat*) the characters directly speak to us in preambles that set up the context of their prepackaged stories. For example, each episode on MTV's[9] hits, *16 and Pregnant* and *Teen Mom*, is presented to us as if the teen is writing in her diary. The artwork that frames every episode and each subsequent scene change reinforces this as it resembles a lined notebook complete with dreamy doodles representing what we are watching. We are surveying the private realm of the teenage girl and are given access to personal thoughts, feelings, and fantasies.

> Hey—my name is Maci. I'm sixteen, I live in Chattanooga, Tennessee, and I'm a total overachiever. I get good grades, I play softball, and I'm even on the cheerleading squad. But don't let that fool you—I do have a wild side. I'm all about dirt bikes. My boyfriend, Ryan, started chasing me when I was a sophomore. I wasn't into him at first because he rides four wheelers—which to me are not cool. But eventually he swept me off my feet. He even put a ring on my finger. All my friends are psyched for senior year but I'm graduating early and moving in with Ryan because [long pause] I'm pregnant.[10]

Despite the initial contact between Maci and the audience, we resort to assuming the *badaud* role and become comfortable being voyeurs who are merely watching (and judging) her. Anonymity as produced through the reality television genre does not offer a web of stories that helps maintain and foster communal experience so central to what makes us social beings. Creating a safe distance between what we are surveying and our own lives keeps us symbolically in the comfort of the armchair and destroys any ability for igniting our capacity to wish for and actively seek change.

Further and most significant to Benjamin's propositions regarding the dream wish world and the depoliticization of the crowds is the fact that through the corporate filter all connections to the wider social world, including social institutions and structural inequality, are removed. For example, while many of the teens on *16 and Pregnant* and *Teen Mom* have conversations about money, jobs, and worry about being able to support their babies, the stark reality portrayed in the 2009 film *Precious*[11] is nowhere to be found. There are no sixteen and pregnant youth living in busy, crowded urban settings in Viacom's pastoralized world. There are no babies living with grungy walls, cockroaches, or abusively drunk parents, at least not while the cameras are rolling.[12] On reality TV shows, the majority of the expecting or new teen moms drive cars, some even have SUVs, and most live in sanitized suburbia.

Key to this pastoralized image of middle-class family life is the idealized notions of what constitutes a good mother. For example, Maci is represented as being a "good" mother, and her family's social capital helps reinforce this. When we first meet her, she is living with her fiancé, Ryan, in a two-storey brick duplex. After splitting up with Ryan, Maci returns to her family home, comfortably situated in a middle-class neighbourhood complete with sprawling lawns and large single-family homes. By the time her son, Bentley, turns two, Maci has moved again to live closer to her new boyfriend, Kyle, in Nashville. She rents a small, clean, two-storey home with new stylish furnishings. Maci, Ryan, and Kyle enjoy leisure activities involving off-road vehicles, and Bentley has his own three-wheeled off-road vehicle by the time he is two.

In contrast, Amber[13] comes closest to a typical working-class reality because her cultural background is significantly different from Maci's and she is represented as being a bad mother. She is from Anderson, Indiana, and when she introduces herself to us she is shown lighting firecrackers beside cars in a crowded parking lot. Amber lives on and off again with boyfriend and father to her daughter, Gary. When their daughter, Leah, is born they live in a small two-bedroom upper-level apartment in an old house. Their apartment is always in a state of disarray, a metaphor of their conflictual and contemptuous relationship.

While Amber and Gary do discuss financial worries, Amber's story is focused on her own personal problems. With the birth of their daughter, Leah, Amber and Gary's relationship deteriorates. They fight in front of Leah, and Gary has to remind Amber on many occasions to stop swearing and yelling in front of the baby. Everything climaxes in season two of *Teen Mom*, when Amber physically assaults Gary, punching him several times in the head. Season three sees Amber dating a young man she met in a Wal-Mart parking lot; soon afterwards, she allows him to temporarily move in with her and Leah. She is also arrested and charged in the assault on Gary. Most significantly, Leah is temporarily removed from her care.

Amber's story is perhaps the closest reality of life for the average teen parent. However, for Amber and the all the other teen moms in MTV's sanitized world, reality is short-lived and replaced with corporate filters that prevent connection and empathy. Despite all of her controversy, at the end of season three of *Teen Mom*, Amber moves into a beautiful two-storey single-family home just before Christmas and regains custody of Leah. Her personal problems have momentarily vanished and have been replaced with all the dream images of capitalism. She is now a good mother.

CONCLUSION

While reality television can be an entertaining spectacle, we need to be cognizant of the fact that it is not without problems. As students and scholars of communication and media studies, we need to use our sociological imaginations and understand the deeply encoded messages that are part of the spectacle. The "reality" on reality programming is that structural inequalities (such as poverty, gender inequality, violence, racism, and ableism) are packaged up as personal problems, and personal problems can be solved in the dream wish world of commodity consumption. Far from awakening our capacity to feel empathy and to try to change undesirable social conditions, reality television turns us into inactive flâneurs who are more content being comfortable in our armchairs, watching and judging anonymously at a distance. Reality television replaces communal experiences with stories mediated by commercial media entities and subsequently helps construct us as good consumers, ultimately depoliticizing us in the process.

Notes

[1] For both Benjamin and Baudelaire, the flâneur is a male revolutionary hero. A thorough discussion of the flâneur and gender is beyond the scope of this chapter. For such a discussion, see Gleber, 1997.

[2] See Whittington-Walsh (2008, 2010) for an analysis of the makeover reality formula.

[3] A thorough discussion and analysis of both shows is beyond the scope of this article.

[4] While the work of Walter Benjamin and his contentions about technology facilitating revolutionary experiences have been linked to the idea of new digital media, including the Internet and social networking

sites (Kang, 2009) and digital art (Betancourt, 2006; Nichols, 1988), very little connection has been made between his work and reality television. One study that makes the connection between Benjamin's work and reality television is Arild Fetveit's 1999 article, "Reality TV in the Digital Era: A Paradox in Visual Culture?" However, Fetveit does not discuss the flâneur. He focuses on Benjamin's *Short History of Photography* in connection to television shows that depict "authentic recordings of dramatic events" such as a plane crash (p. 794), to which we can now add the events of 9/11.

5 Benjamin is using propositions put forth by his friend and mentor, German playwright Bertolt Brecht. Brecht was interested in developing a democratic medium through performing arts, which would document real people's lives without any kind of corporate control or filter.

6 Benjamin (1973, p. 69) is quoting nineteenth-century journalist Victor Fournel (1829–1894).

7 For a thorough analysis of *Style by Jury*, see Whittington-Walsh, 2008.

8 For example, the *Candid Camera* format where people nominate their friends and family to be unknown contestants. See Couldry, 2004.

9 MTV is a division of Viacom Inc., the world's fourth-largest media conglomerate with assets totalling over $22 billion (U.S.) in 2011. Its foundation as a commercial media outlet and reason for the billions in revenues and assets is our active participation as consumers. According to their own publicity, *16 and Pregnant* and *Teen Mom* have both helped secure MTV's spot as the number-one cable network for the age demographic twelve to thirty-four. Interestingly, in March 2007 Viacom was involved in a $1 billion (U.S.) lawsuit against YouTube for violating copyright laws, claiming that the online video-sharing website made approximately 160 000 of Viacom's videos/films available for downloading (VerSteeg, 2007). It could be argued that YouTube comes closest to Benjamin's propositions being discussed in this article. A thorough discussion is beyond the scope of this article.

10 *16 and Pregnant*, season one, episode one, 2009.

11 *Precious* (2009) is the story of a young teenage girl who lives in Harlem on welfare with her unemployed, physically and emotionally abusive mother. Precious also suffered from long-term sexual abuse by her father, who impregnated her twice.

12 Recently a lot of media attention has been paid to two stars of *Teen Mom Three*, who were found living on a military base in filthy conditions ("*16 and Pregnant*," 2011). Their circumstances were not shown on the show.

13 *16 and Pregnant*, season one, episode three, and *Teen Mom* (2010), seasons one and two.

References

Benjamin, W. (1968). The storyteller. In H. Arendt (Ed.), *Illuminations: Essays and reflections* (pp. 83–110). New York: Schocken Books.

Benjamin, W. (1973). *Charles Baudelaire: A lyric poet in the era of high capitalism.* London: Verso.

Betancourt, M. (2006, September 5). The aura of the digital. *1000 days of theory.* Retrieved from http://www.ctheory.net/articles.aspx?id=519

Couldry, N. (2004). Teaching us to fake it: The ritualized norms of television's "reality" games. In S. Murray & L. Ouellette (Eds.), *Reality TV: Remaking television culture* (pp. 57–74). New York: New York University Press.

Ewan, S. (1988). *Consuming images: The politics of style in contemporary culture.* New York: Basic Books.

Fetveit, A. (1999). Reality TV in the digital era: A paradox in visual culture? *Media, Culture & Society, 21*(6), 787–804.

Foster, D. (2008). Extremely real: How we can learn from reality television? In J. Greenberg & C. Elliot (Eds.), *Communication in question: Competing perspectives on controversial issues in communication studies* (pp. 283–290). Toronto: Thomson Nelson.

Gleber, A. (1997). Female flanerie and the symphony of the city. In K. Ankum (Ed.), *Women in the metropolis: Gender and modernity in Weimar culture.* Berkeley: University of California Press.

Kang, J.-H. (2009). The ur-history of media space: Walter Benjamin and the information industry in nineteenth-century Paris. *International Journal of Politics, Culture, & Society, 22,* 231–248.

Mills, W. C. (1999). *The sociological imagination.* New York: Oxford University Press.

Murray, S., & Ouellette, L. (2004). Introduction. In S. Murray & L. Ouellette (Eds.), *Reality TV: Remaking television culture.* New York: New York University Press.

Nichols, B. (1988, Winter). The work of culture in the age of cybernetic systems. *Screen, 21*(1), 22–47.

16 and Pregnant couple arrested for child endangerment. (2011, September 23). *News Online.* Retrieved from http://newsone.com/entertainment/associatedpress3/16-and-pregnant-couple-arrested-for-child-endangerment/

VerSteeg, R. (2007). Viacom vs. YouTube: Preliminary observations. *North Carolina Journal of Law & Technology, 9*(1), 43–68.

Whittington-Walsh, F. (2008). Guilty by assumption: *Style by Jury* and makeover reality TV. In J. Greenberg & C. Elliott (Eds.), *Communications in question: Canadian perspectives on controversial issues in communication studies* (pp. 273–282). Toronto: Thomson Nelson.

Whittington-Walsh, F. (2010). Beautiful ever after: "Extreme Makeover" and the spectacle of rebirth. In M. Pomerance & J. Sakeris (Eds.), *Popping culture* (6th ed., pp. 179–190). Boston: Pearson Education.

ISSUE 1

Trash television:
Is reality television harmful to society?

✘ NO

One Person's Trash Is Another One's Treasure: Why Reality TV Can Do Just as Much Good as Harm
Derek Foster

Derek Foster is an associate professor in the Department of Communication, Popular Culture and Film at Brock University in St. Catharines, Ontario. His research focuses on visual rhetoric and popular media in the public sphere. He has numerous publications studying discourses of reality television and the rhetoric of other forms of visual and material culture. His current research combines these foci and investigates the visual and material rhetoric of television-based memorials and commemorative exercises.

Reality television is not harmful to society. You know what is harmful, though? Making such broad statements and dismissing one of the most popular forms of contemporary entertainment. I'll admit that some viewers do classify some reality television as offensive. As damnation goes, though, this is mighty underwhelming. Still, the obverse of the statement "you can't please all the people all the time" is the acknowledgment that you're likely to displease some of the people all the time and maybe even all the people some of the time. But, as the old saying goes, one person's trash is another one's treasure. So, let us resuscitate the reputation of reality TV and some of its trashiest elements. Let's put a stake in priggish TV criticism. Let us not make any assumptions about universal values and remain open to the possibility that reality television can do some good if it can also do harm. And, let's not preclude the learning of lessons from some programming that ostensibly has no educational content.

Let's be reasonable too. A lot of reality television is unlikeable and even more of it is disposable. It is easy to lament and critique its baleful effects. But because this knee-jerk reaction seems so natural, we must guard ourselves against it. A level-headed rejoinder against such naysaying depends upon a number of assumptions: Trash TV cannot be (only or always) harmful because TV as a whole is not harmful. Trash TV is, in some ways, the essence of TV. Even better, trashy tales are at the foundation of how we as a society understand who we are (and television seems to be one of the major media for circulating such stories today). While not all reality TV is "trash TV," not all trashy reality TV is harmful either. Trash is, in general, noxious, but the content of these shows that at first glance appears quite offensive may not actually be bad for us. Finally, we must look beyond the content. We ought to appraise this programming on the basis of what we as a society do with it and how audiences respond rather than presume negative effects based upon negative content. Let's now deal with these assumptions in greater detail.

TRASHY (TV) TALES ARE HOW WE KNOW WHO WE ARE

In the film *Network*, newsman Howard Beale declares TV to be "a travelling troupe of acrobats, storytellers, dancers, singers, jugglers, sideshow freaks, lion tamers, and football players." It has always been thus. Entertainment is the modus operandi and outrageousness sells. In fact, some shows like *Trailer Park Boys* are critically lauded even though they celebrate the **carnivalesque** lives and lifestyle of the petty criminal lower classes. Here, life at the bottom of the social ladder is presented as excessive, absurd, and comical. Often, much of the content on television presents a less-than-flattering portrait of human nature. So-called reality TV merely makes this take on human nature abundantly obvious.

The sideshow freaks have become some of our culture's most noteworthy storytellers. But this is not any more harmful to society than the trashy novels we read, the trashy movies we flock to, or the trashy lyrics that drive some of the most popular songs today. Of course, the trashy subset of the larger genres of reality TV (or TV itself), publishing, films, and music do not compose the universe of content available to audiences. There is still plenty of edifying content to consume. In fact, compared to other media, trashy TV makes up a smaller percentage of the most popular fare to which audiences flock. A quick look at random bestseller lists, Hollywood box office revenues, and Billboard ratings is often likely to show that readers, moviegoers, and music listeners aren't always motivated by good taste. The dreck and the contrived often become blockbusters.

But while critics find an easy target in reality television, there is nothing particularly new about the fears that circulate around the medium. Societies have always depended on debasing or dehumanizing distractions for their collective entertainment. To wit, "of all the contributions made by Roman thought and imagery to what would later become the mass society outlook, probably the most important was the belief that the multitude must be fed bread and cheap entertainment if it was to be kept quiet, submissive and loyal to the powers that be" (Giner, 1976, p. 23). Reality TV is but the most recent iteration of these entertainments.

It is important to note that there is nothing trivial about these entertainments. "Popular cultural texts and practices are important because they provide much of the wool from which the social tapestry is knit" (Hermes, 2005, p. 11). The material that is the lingua franca of all reality television— "real" people whose interactions are unscripted, and are at least "keeping it real" even if acting in "unreal" situations—is powerful because of its resonance with our everyday realities. Viewers often relate to trashy reality TV, too, since television has always depended on these types of narrative, as have all media before it. "It is in the nature of myth and storytelling to explore the edges of a society's accepted beliefs and conventions.... So when we see the popular culture exploring behavior that many see as morally bankrupt, we need to remind ourselves that deviating from an ethical norm is not just an old story. In a real sense, it's where stories begin" (Johnson, 2006, p. 189). It should not come as a surprise, then, that some reality television pushes so provocatively at the boundaries of acceptable moral values or that such efforts are met with such popularity among some audiences.

THE CONTENT OF TRASHY REALITY TV MAY ACTUALLY BE GOOD FOR US

TV has been widely known as the "boob tube," the "idiot box," a "plug-in drug," and a "vast wasteland." It's understandable that many would accuse reality TV of continuing (and emphasizing) this tradition. However, this critique is too short-sighted. "*The Apprentice* may not be the smartest show in the history of television, but it nonetheless forces you to think while you watch it, to work through the social logic of the universe it creates on the screen. And compared with *The Price Is Right* or *Webster*, it's an intellectual masterpiece" (Johnson, 2006, p. 99). The shows that represent the antithesis of high-brow content are perhaps the most interesting. These shows are contentious, and they fuel debates over whether they exploit participants and insult audiences or provide a public forum for a broad range of characters and behaviour that otherwise would not be featured so prominently in the public sphere.

It is easy to despise reality TV; it offers a celebration of ordinary (and sometimes hyperreal, extra-ordinary) life. Yet even disagreeable content is not entirely unredeemable. The very vapidness of some programming sows the seeds for its use-value. Cultures need not celebrate noxious elements but can use them to clarify (and yes, sometimes re-evaluate) boundaries of good and bad, appropriateness and inappropriateness, morality and immorality, and so on. Some content is simply sensational—which isn't to suggest that it is great, but rather, it causes a sensation. As a culture, we can't help but pay attention. It's like traffic slowing down to catch a glimpse of a tragic car wreck. Trashy reality TV is that car wreck. Some get captivated by the spectacle. But everyone else ends up hearing about it on the news. In addition, social media ensure that the conversations that once took place around the "water cooler" the next day happen immediately and are far more widespread. Even if you don't watch programming that you consider offensive or beneath you, you're likely to know about it because those who do watch also share their reactions; video excerpts go viral, appearing on Facebook, and Twitter tells you what's trending. And maybe, just maybe, we might learn something from this exercise in collective navel-gazing and rubbernecking.

By pushing boundaries, TV can create new conversations about those boundaries, destabilizing judgments and problematizing previously unquestioned (or undiscussed) norms. For instance, the 1994 cast of *The Real World* featured "an openly gay Hispanic man with AIDS who used the platform of the popular show to educate viewers about the stigmatized disease shortly before his death" (Mittell, 2010, pp. 347–348). From this point of view, reality TV does more than show the literal "real." Reality TV can show the bizarre and the outlandish and ultimately shift our notions of what constitutes the real. To be honest, wide-scale or in-depth questioning of cultural norms and mores may be as rare as unthinking acceptance of disempowering ideologies of trashy programming. Most viewers don't tune into *The Bachelorette* or *A Shot at Love with Tila Tequila* in order to challenge dominant ideologies and question **heteronormativity**. But we must admit, "television entertainment can prove a key tool in both the reification of others' power over the public, or the public's power over itself" (Gray, 2008, p. 155).

IT'S NOT THE STUPID CONTENT THAT MATTERS, IT'S WHAT WE DO WITH THE CONTENT, STUPID

Television, even its most staggeringly inane examples, can provide forms of cultural engagement and civic participation. As Dahlgren asserts, "Television is a tricky medium and can do many things, including, perhaps—given the right circumstances—generating societal involvement and conveying a sense of citizenship" (1998, p. 93). Hartley has made a similar argument about the possibility for "cross-demographic communication" (2008, p. 119). Voting for one's favourite contestant on shows such as *American Idol* is one (admittedly shallow) version of this. Also, the continual discursive contests over who we see ourselves as and what we want to see on our screens are a clear way that we negotiate this sense of mediated citizenship. I have made this argument elsewhere, suggesting that "bad" reality TV can still further the public interest in the context of informing debates about Canadian nationalism (see Foster, 2012).

If content is judged to be trashy (or even because it is so appraised), it tends to enliven public discussion. Trashy reality television is not enervating television; instead of weakening or draining the energy of viewers, it regularly inspires great ire. It provokes resentment rather than resignation. It gets under people's skin and prompts action in the form of angry letters to the editor, blog posts, commentary on YouTube, tweets, and Facebook status updates. Why is it, then, that the qualities of "high culture" are praised as important while the drivel of televised debauchery and douchbagginess is viewed with disgust? "Most objectionable programming" is more productive than "least objectionable programming." It gets people to pay attention and starts them talking. It gets them involved in debates over standards of quality and how to police them. In essence, it performs a civic function by creating a lightning rod for public discussion of the things we value and the values we hold dear.

So, the **cultural wasteland** of trashy television might, in fact, not prefigure widespread cultural demise. It might, instead, also be important and culturally necessary. Trashy content inspires active viewers and their interactive connections with both the reality TV text and other viewers. If TV can augur antisocial behaviour, it must also have the capacity for pro-social behavior. Indeed, if TV is critiqued for provoking violence or encouraging passivity, it must also be acknowledged that with new technologies, genres like reality TV are at the vanguard of showing how participatory popular programming can be.

> E-mail conversations or Web-based analyses of *The Apprentice* are not the same as literary novels, of course, but they are equally text-driven. While they suffer from a lack of narrative depth compared to novels, many online interactions do have the benefit of being genuinely two-way conversations; you're putting words together yourself, and not just digesting someone else's. Part of the compensation for reading less is the fact that we're writing more. (Johnson, 2006, p. 183)

The substance of this online engagement goes deeper than fanatical fawning and devotion. Too often, we think that the content of reality TV narcotizes its viewers. But many viewers see themselves as a type of anti-fan, seeking to co-opt the message of a show rather than ideologically cooperate with it. The website votefortheworst.com is a clear example of how many fans of reality television avoid mindless consumption of these shows' meanings through mocking and subverting them. Similarly, fraternities on college campuses throw *Jersey Shore*–inspired parties not because of a desire to be like the "stars" of that show but precisely because they recognize the portrayals on the series as farcical stereotypes. They only want to replicate their behaviour in a limited, temporary, and knowingly tongue-in-cheek fashion.

And while it's easy to bemoan the popularity of trashy TV, we might also take comfort with the fact that a lot of trashy TV never finds an audience. The reality show *H8R* exemplifies this. Broadcast briefly in 2011, this series featured Mario Lopez brokering meetings between TV celebrities and their "haters." Reality stars such as Snooki from *Jersey Shore* and Kim Kardashian met (and generally won over) viewers who had expressed a severe antipathy toward them. The moral of the show, such as it was, instructed viewers to not trust everything they see on (reality) TV. The irony was that it was reality TV that was telling viewers this. Yet in the end, audiences hated *H8R* and the series was cancelled after airing just four episodes. So, we ought to have some faith in the collective intelligence of viewers. Sometimes, the thing that audiences want to do most of all is turn away.

CONCLUSION

Obviously, what is represented on reality TV is not unimportant, but it is not as significant as what audiences choose to do with these representations. "It would be a stretch to view reality television primarily as a vehicle for social uplift or creative expression, but it is just as extreme to view it solely as a tool for profitability and consumerist degradation" (Mittell, 2010, p. 96). Today, some watch *The Ultimate Fighter* just as many in the past flocked to Roman circuses and coliseums in which gladiators fought for their lives. We might suggest that both the distractions of then and now insinuate values that degrade civilized life, but we can also hold out hope that lessons can be learned.

Ultimately, reality TV is not to blame for the societal ills we're sad to acknowledge and loath to confront. Reality TV is like all TV. We would be wise to recognize that we don't only learn how to be buffoons and boors by watching examples of this type of behaviour. Nor do we become brainless consumers of such imagery, populating a dreamworld of unachievable expectations where the very poor either try to emulate the very rich or are kept happy watching them. TV viewers today are more sophisticated than ever before; while we still seek our entertainment in cheap pleasures, frequently audiences are "in on the joke." Some of us revel in the unreality of reality TV, recognizing the ridiculousness of it all while enjoying it too. Meanwhile, those who don't enjoy the genre and its baser elements reject these vulgar spectacles and probably make up the majority of society. Clearly, it is too simplistic to suggest that society as a whole is brainwashed by banality or seduced by the siren call of salacious content.

Some reality TV is trashy, highlighting incivility and breaches of decorum, sometimes celebrating decadence and barbaric behaviour. But these need not be seen as indisputable evidence that something is out of order with modern Western civilization. Instead, these representations should be understood as revealing the cracks and fissures in our civilized society. Accordingly, we ought not to be worried about such content appearing on our screens, but instead should consider what the content actually reflects. While some people's actions on reality TV may seem ridiculous, such conduct is common among some elements of society. While many viewers might consider some of the behaviour on *Toddlers and Tiaras* akin to child abuse, or the polygamy on *Sister Wives* to be offensive, these series are unscripted and nonfiction. They may seem larger-than-life, but they are slices of life. After all, the producers of *Jersey Shore* didn't build incredibly intricate sets for their series; while the cameras reveal the most unflattering moments and the casting encourages caricatures, the bars and the beaches were popular attractions before the series shone a light on them. We might not like certain representations, but it is more accurate to say that they reflect a reality rather than create one.

Sometimes seduced by fantasies, sometimes disgusted enough to be motivated to action, audiences will continue to be divided by the enthralling spectacle of trashy reality TV. Yes, reality

TV could be bad for society. But it could also be good for it. I'm inclined to emphasize more of the latter and less of the former. Anything can be bad, placed in the wrong hands or put to the wrong uses. Reality TV can be quite entertaining. Even its trashiest examples can be a good thing for society. Of course, it's true that you can get too much of a good thing.

References

Dahlgren, P. (1998). Enhancing the civic ideal in television journalism. In K. Brants, J. Hermes, & L. van Zoonen (Eds.), *The media in question: Popular cultures and public interests* (pp. 89–100). London: Sage.

Foster, D. (2012). How even American reality TV can perform a public service on Canadian television. In M. Bredin, S. Henderson, & S. A. Matheson (Eds.), *Canadian television: Text and context* (pp. 135–152). Waterloo, ON: Wilfrid Laurier University Press.

Giner, S. (1976). *Mass society.* New York: Academic.

Gray, J. (2008). *Television entertainment.* New York: Routledge.

Hartley, J. (2008). *Television truths.* Malden, MA: Blackwell.

Hermes, J. (2005). *Re-reading popular culture: Rethinking gender, television and popular media audiences.* London: Blackwell.

Johnson, S. (2006). *Everything bad is good for you: How today's popular culture is actually making us smarter.* New York: Riverhead Books.

Mittell, J. (2010). *Television and American culture.* New York: Oxford University Press.

Discussion Questions

1. Why do you think reality television, such as MTV's *16 and Pregnant* and *Teen Mom*, are so popular with both producers and audiences?

2. Watch one episode of a reality television show and reflect on how the show "frames" the participants of the show. Do you feel empathy, as stipulated by Walter Benjamin's flâneur by understanding their social-political "reality," and therefore make a connection with them?

3. Discuss ways in which the reality television genre depoliticizes audiences.

4. Is there anything new to criticize about reality television that hasn't already been said about generations and genres of TV that have come before? Isn't everything old new again?

5. Foster argues that the things that are said and done on trashy reality TV are less important than the things viewers and culturally-savvy citizens say and do when responding to and evaluating this programming. Do you find this to be a compelling argument? Why or why not? Think of your own experience when answering.

6. Can reality TV generate social involvement (either in the series or with fellow viewers or with fellow members of the media-informed public)? If so, what is the nature of that citizen engagement? Can this programming really have social value and serve the public interest?

ISSUE 2

Informed comedy:
Do mock news shows make for a more informed public?

✔ YES

New(s) Parodies, New(s) Alternatives
Ian Reilly

Ian Reilly is an Assistant Professor in the Communication Studies Department at Concordia University. He received his Ph.D. in literary studies from the University of Guelph. His research explores the intersections of politics, humour, civic engagement, and media activism. He teaches courses on mass media, Internet politics, media subcultures, telecommunications policy, and media history. He is currently at work on a book about—and in collaboration with—media activists the Yes Men.

Media studies scholarship has produced conflicting perspectives on the role news parody plays within the realm of civic culture. Due in large part to the growing ubiquity and influence of news parody in North America, numerous studies, surveys, and scholarly articles have speculated on the role this cultural form plays in citizen engagement and civic culture. Scholars continue to grapple with the overall impact these narratives have on public discourse, examining the form's capacity to influence political discourse (Baym, 2005; Jones, 2005), social change (Boler, 2006), agenda setting in news media (Kowalewski, 2009), political values and ideologies (LaMarre, Landreville, & Beam, 2009), audience perception (Becker, Xenos, & Waisanen, 2010), activism (Day, 2011), civic engagement (Hoffman & Thomson, 2009), and political participation (Hoffman & Young, 2011). A 2007 report conducted by the Pew Research Center for People and the Press has shown that satirical news programs like *The Daily Show* (*TDS*) and *The Colbert Report* (*TCR*) have not only become the primary news sources for the younger (eighteen to twenty-nine) demographic, but have also yielded the most well-informed demographic of news consumers.[1] It seems that young people's turn to news parody as a source of political information has increased viewers' political knowledge. Yet while previous studies have shown that audiences are among the most well informed, other scholarship suggests that so-called gains in political knowledge are, at best, modest (Baek & Wojcieszak, 2009).[2] However modest, establishing a firm correlation between young people's consumption of news parody as the primary (and in some cases the only) news source and their participation in and contribution to civic culture remains a contentious issue.

In this chapter, I argue that news parody creates a more informed public by interrogating the official, authoritative discourses that dominate the flow of public discussion as framed by dominant news media outlets. By attacking ready-made truths through its deployment of humour and satire, news parody pushes the logic of news discourse to (il)logical extremes and re-presents them to reveal their limitations and shortcomings. In most instances, the satirist merely uses "the words of those in power against them, revealing 'truth' by a simple reformulation of their statements" (Jones, 2010, p. 113). Thus, the satirist serves as a "comedic interrogator" implicated in an act of "dialogical interaction," that is, of "cross-examining the rhetoric both of public figures and of standard news discourse" (Day, 2011, p. 74). In this regard, satire's questioning mode of critique helps reveal two things: its capacity to "subvert hierarchies of value" (Weisenburger, 1995, p. 3) and modes of meaning-making, as well as its ability to make visible the often mystified construction of everyday news narratives. As the discussion below makes explicit, this parodic and pedagogical cultural form prepares the way for a more informed and self-reflexive engagement with contemporary journalism—how it functions, what its shortcomings and limitations may be, and what its future might hold.

NEWS PARODY AND JOURNALISM IN CONTEXT

Over the past decade news parody has incited a much-needed re-evaluation of journalism's relationship to politics and civic culture. As Jeffrey P. Jones (2005) observes in *Entertaining Politics: New Political Television and Civic Culture*, critical discussions of emergent forms of satire like "fake news" (Jones's terminology) have appeared in large part due to "a fundamental change in political communication in America" (p. 7). Whereas entertainment television has traditionally shied away from the "serious" realm of politics (only occasionally exploring political themes and subjects), politics now forms an integral part of entertainment programming. This shift, Jones argues, has been instrumental in blurring the boundaries between serious and entertaining discourse(s), placing politics squarely (and perhaps uncomfortably) at the centre of new debates surrounding the function and value of entertainment in civic culture.

According to a recent Pew (2007) study of public opinion toward news media, "the public continues to fault news organizations for a number of perceived failures, with solid majorities criticizing them for political bias, inaccuracy and failing to acknowledge mistakes." The study reflects a significant increase in public dissatisfaction with news media over a twenty-two-year period (1985–2007); nonetheless, it also importantly reveals that "public support for the news media's role as political watchdog has endured." Indeed, journalism's watchdog function to serve as a critical check on governments and the power elite has never been more crucial to the preservation of democracy and the public sphere (Jones, 2000; Kovach & Rosenstiel, 2007). Mainstream news media's failure to fulfill this role (Herman & Chomsky, 1988; McChesney, 1999), however, has bolstered a burgeoning culture of alternative and independent media that monitors, critiques, and reframes the discourses and practices of mainstream journalism. Political communication and media scholars have labelled this burgeoning culture of media critique the *fifth estate* (Collins, 2009; Dutton, 2009; Hayes, 2008; Reilly, 2010); this scholarship identifies citizen journalists, bloggers, press critics, and, of particular relevance to the present discussion, political satirists as the culture's key practitioners.

Indeed, within the context of popular media criticism, political satirists play an important role in the circulation of discourse that often escapes the notice and/or scrutiny of mainstream news media. "Aided by an existing cultural predilection and a media system hungry for anything with entertainment value" (Day, 2008), parody and satire have become particularly attractive modes for the circulation of political speech and discourse. More than this, parody and satire serve a crucial critical function in today's expansive media system precisely because practitioners express a broader concern for the improvement of public discourse *and* journalistic practices. By its very nature, news parody enacts a metadiscursive critique (a kind of journalism *about* journalism); it also contributes its own form of meta-critique through sustained attacks against accepted values, ideologies, modes, and conventions. As the two brief case studies below reveal, news parody is an important vehicle for critiquing news form and content in the interests of revealing the inner workings of the genre, and expanding the audience's capacity to think critically about the news and information it consumes.

HOW TO CRITIQUE AND DEMYSTIFY THE NEWS: DIEBOLD'S STOLEN ELECTION

Our first case study dramatizes persistent anxieties regarding the overall integrity and trustworthiness of electronic voting machines. In February 2008, the satirical weekly *The Onion* depicted the dystopian fantasy of mass election fraud in the video segment "Diebold Accidentally Leaks Results of 2008 Election Early." One of many parodic news reports to air during the Onion News Network's (ONN) coverage of the 2008 election, the segment tackled the question of election fraud to shed light on some problems a shift toward digital voting might precipitate. The story depicts the Diebold Corporation (a major player in the development, delivery, and implementation of electronic voting machines in the United States), accidentally releasing the results of the 2008 presidential election—*ten months before election day*. As the ONN news anchor remarks, Diebold's mistake "marks the first time the nation's leader has been revealed prematurely." Attempting to downplay the severity of the situation, Diebold PR spokesperson Ernie Kenilworth states that despite his company's recklessness in spoiling the election, the citizenry would still have the opportunity to vote in the November ballet. Although Senator John McCain's fictitious victory would hold (the front-running Republican slated to win 48 percent of the popular vote), Kenilworth also noted that Diebold would still uphold its duties of pretending to count votes on election night. Lastly, rather than formally apologizing to the American public for destroying the integrity of one of democracy's most sacred rituals, Kenilworth reserved his final apology for the "shadowy puppet masters" of the electoral process, signalling these backstage actors as the real motors of American democracy. The parodic news story brings into sharper relief the potential threat electronic voting poses to fundamental democratic processes. The story's use of artifice, moreover, reveals the layers of PR rhetoric and journalistic posturing that would arguably emerge following such a spectacular debacle. Far from merely using parody to play out ill-defined anxieties surrounding electronic voter fraud, *The Onion* draws heavily on contemporary events (both real and imagined) to broaden the frame of discussion on an issue that is all too often pushed to the margins of mainstream news reportage.

Indeed, *The Onion*'s critique of electronic voting was not without measure, as concerns over the implementation and use of the machines had grown steadily since the 2004 election. In 2004, for example, California lawmakers banned four counties from using electronic voting machines and ordered ten other counties to improve security and reliability features before an upcoming November election. Secretary of State Kevin Shelley announced the ban, citing Diebold's "reprehensible" and illegal conduct as the key rationale behind the legal ruling (Lucas, 2004). Two years later, a Princeton study of the Diebold AccuVote-TS voting machine concluded that the devices were vulnerable to external tampering, making election fraud virtually undetectable through the implementation of voting machine viruses (Feldman, Halderman, & Felten, 2006). Similarly, in 2008, electronic touch-screen voting machines were just as easily manipulated and were susceptible to undetectable voter fraud (Nelson, 2008). The story's broader function is twofold: first, to incite discussion on the future impact electronic voting machines may have on the democratic process; and second, to critique news media's sensationalist entertainment-style reportage (what *Onion* writers might readily call the dominant register of election coverage).

The segment begins with all the hallmarks of a contemporary television news broadcast: dramatic music, an ONN network logo (a parody of the CNN logo), and the ever-present American flag; what is more, the story's opening credits are punctuated by the inclusion of spectacular graphics (explosions, flames, and fighter jets soaring above an engulfed White House). These features, however outlandish they may appear, do not assume as much hyperbolic resonance next to their more traditional journalistic counterparts; as such, these examples of pastiche establish a much-needed framework for evaluating and critiquing the original. In its recurring "War for the White House" segment, ONN readily channels all the bombast and production values of other well-known televisual precursors, namely, Fox News' "War on Terror" coverage and CNN's "Attack on America" reportage. The seamlessness of the production values (graphics, tickers) and the calculated seriousness of the news anchors and interviewees prepare the way for critical reflection.

In reproducing these highly stylized, grossly mediated news reports, "War for the White House" uses pastiche[3] (in a near replication of the original) to call attention to news media's overblown emphasis on entertainment values.[4] The evaluative distance generated by the pastiche creates moments for the audience to discern the major networks' reliance on entertainment-style news reportage at the expense of delivering valuable election analysis and commentary. As *The Onion*'s Diebold story emphasizes, McCain's win is treated as nothing more than "a big election spoiler"; any attempts to question or interrogate major breaches in the democratic process are easily glossed over in the interests of preserving the story's spectacular arc. In the end, ONN election coverage deploys critique in productive ways, in that it subtly amplifies and makes ridiculous the ways in which news organizations shape, produce, and package content. In dramatizing a compelling scenario of electronic voter fraud, *The Onion* proves successful in bringing the question of electoral fraud to the foreground of public discourse. While revealing the flawed inner machinations of media spectacle constitutes an important part of news parody's larger critical project of informing audiences, our next case study illustrates how the form not only prepares the way for reframing public discourse, but also for reimagining the future of news.

PRESENTING NEW(S) ALTERNATIVES: THE YES MEN'S FAKE *NEW YORK TIMES*

On the heels of Barack Obama's rise to the U.S. presidency, media activist collective the Yes Men presented a different kind of news parody through the careful appropriation of America's newspaper of record—*The New York Times* (*NYT*). On November 12, 2008, the Yes Men distributed a "special edition" of the newspaper to an estimated 1.2 million urban dwellers in major American cities (*The New York Times Special Edition*, 2008). The special issue's headline boldly proclaimed the end of an era: "Iraq War Ends: Troops to Return Immediately." As (real) *NYT* reporter Sewell Chan (2008) observed, the fake newspaper reported stories on America's national health care system, "a rebuilt economy, progressive taxation, a national oil fund to study climate change, and other progressive politics." The issue also included stories on the implementation of a maximum-wage law that would create salary caps for CEOs, the closing of Guantánamo Bay and other detention camps, the inauguration of a United Nations–sanctioned weapons ban, the passing of the National Health Insurance Act, and a soon-to-be-passed bill that would eliminate tuition fees at public universities. In a compelling editorial note, editors of the special issue expressed an optimistic agenda for the future: "We can begin to make the news in this paper the news in every paper." Before engaging in any analysis of the newspaper, it is worth noting that the fake *NYT* puts forward a different kind of parodic critique: whereas satirical fake news outlets like *The Onion* and *TDS* often deliver stories using humour and irreverence to challenge dominant journalistic forms and conventions, the *NYT* parody uses an interesting mix of humour, irony, and sincerity as a vehicle for communicating critique.

For citizens accustomed to reading about war, famine, civil unrest, environmental disaster, political corruption, and global economic crises—ever-present problems often presented without solutions—the paper strikes a sincere (if utopian) note, reporting stories in a register rarely deployed in journalistic coverage. Whereas a conventional news story might deliver information according to a prescribed set of instantly recognizable journalistic standards (decorum, seriousness, and professed objectivity), news parody enjoys far greater leverage to tell a story in a variety of ways. Without any obligations to respect the codes and ethics of traditional journalism, the Yes Men freely deploy humour, wit, and ironic posturing to depict the staging of symbolic victories over dominant institutions, to question existing government policies, to scrutinize the activities of corporations, and to reveal the discrepancies between an imagined progressive future and the fateful present. For example, in "Corporate Personhood Gets Real," the reader learns that legislation will soon abolish the notion of "limited liability" for corporations, making shareholders liable for the crimes their corporations commit; in "All Public Universities to Be Free," Congress is poised to pass a bill that would eliminate tuition fees at public universities, an initiative meant to improve access to education in the country; and finally, in "Nation Sets Its Sights on Building Sane Economy," the passing of the SANE Act effectively caps CEO salaries, breaks up financial conglomerates, stabilizes mortgages, and invests in public housing, in a bill that constitutes a significant sea change in the country's financial makeup. Here the interplay between fantasy and reality serves a crucial satirical function: to reimagine contemporary issues and debates and to frame them constructively, so as to lay the groundwork for social and political change. Importantly, satire of this kind also asks the reader to imagine what other forms and practices of journalism are possible within the context of the ongoing shift between politics and entertainment.

Rather than merely presenting the shortcomings of newsmakers, the fake *NYT* presents a utopian vision of contemporary journalism and politics as practised in the not-so-distant future. The fake edition delivers its critique through a careful dramatization of a future in which the citizenry holds its elected officials and news organizations accountable for the work that they do. It is in this capacity that the citizenry can be seen to accomplish two vital tasks: to goad then president-elect Barack Obama to uphold his campaign promises, and to pressure traditional news media (of which the *NYT* represents but one outlet) to fulfill their broader role as civic watchdog. In numerous instances, the Yes Men put forward an explicit critique of the news organization's editorial policies, its newsgathering practices, its political punditry, and its business philosophy.

In each instance, the Yes Men assume a strong critical stance toward the news organization, all the while providing insightful suggestions as to the direction the *NYT* might make to correct its shortcomings. Importantly, the Yes Men perform a timely diagnostic critique of an elite news media in the interests of not only reforming their institutional practices, but also presenting new alternatives to producing and disseminating news. Here the reader is both privy to the power of critique and presented with a powerful alternative to existing *ways of doing journalism*. As Baym (2005) suggests, news parody has emerged as an alternative model of journalism, "one that uses satire to interrogate power, parody to critique contemporary news, and dialogue to enact a model of deliberative democracy" (p. 261). More than simply satirizing current affairs, *The Onion* and the Yes Men use parody to reframe important civic issues within a critical context generally ill afforded in today's corporatized and often information-poor twenty-four-hour news cycle.[5]

ENGAGING SERIOUS AND ENTERTAINING DISCOURSE

This chapter has situated news parody as an important actor in the transmission of news media critique. I have argued that news parody constitutes a useful pedagogical tool in the demystification of journalistic conventions and in the examination of news discourse. The satirical interventions of both *The Onion* and the Yes Men invite (and incite) critical thinking and self-reflexive analysis of news content in the consumption of entertaining information. In terms of engaging a more informed public, I argue that news parody creates a tangible framework for building interpretive skills and capacities, for expanding media (and genre) literacy, and for bolstering critical thinking. News parody creates the conditions necessary for creating informed, media-literate audiences that can readily grapple with and scrutinize a wide range of news content. Thus, the proliferation of these satirical news narratives makes different modes of journalistic expression possible, ensuring in the process that being informed hinges on one's tempered engagement with both entertaining and serious forms of news. Lastly, given news parody's growing influence and popularity among young people, the form will continue to serve as a useful tool for teaching media literacy skills and for expanding one's understanding of journalism, satire, and public discourse.

Notes

[1] These findings are also in step with earlier studies conducted by Pew (2004) and the University of Pennsylvania's National Annenberg Election Survey ("Daily Show Viewers," 2004). In noting the results of the Annenberg survey, senior analyst Dannagal Goldthwaite Young identifies "*Daily Show* viewers [as having] higher campaign knowledge than national news viewers and newspaper readers—even when education, party identification, following politics, watching cable news, receiving campaign information online, age, and gender are taken into consideration" ("O'Reilly," 2006).

[2] While most scholars have embraced these findings as contextual markers for future discussions of satirical fake news, Jones cautions against accepting these statistics at face value. Statistics of this kind, he argues, have enabled journalists and scholars alike to develop a "full-blown myth" about young people's news consumption without properly discerning the report's findings. As Jones puts it, these findings reveal two things: "that comedians mine current affairs for humorous content, and that different programming types differ in their popularity among different demographic groups" (2010, p. 170). What Jones's study suggests, however, is that a comparative analysis of *TDS* with CNN reveals that satirical fake news programming can provide "quality information that citizens can use in making informed choices about electoral politics" (p. 181).

[3] Pastiche refers to a special kind of imitation, one that is meant to be deciphered by the audience. As Dyer (2007) suggests, pastiche is perhaps best understood as a form of imitation that has both an evaluative and a critical attitude toward the object of imitation (p. 35).

4 *The Onion*'s critique of television news' production values finds its most perfect expression in a passage in Neil Postman's *Amusing Ourselves to Death* (1985), in which he bemoans the use of music:

> All television news programs begin, end, and are somewhere in between punctuated with music. I have found very few Americans who regard this custom as peculiar, which fact I have taken as evidence for the dissolution of lines of demarcation between serious public discourse and entertainment. What has music to do with the news? Why is it there? It is there, I assume, for the same reason music is used in the theater and films—to create a mood and provide a leitmotif for the entertainment. (p. 102)

5 Nowhere is this notion more aptly described than in McChesney (1999), in which the author delineates the consequences of media conglomeration in the realm of journalism and civic culture:

> The corporate media cement a system whereby the wealthy and powerful few make the most important decisions with virtually no informed public participation. Crucial political issues are barely covered by the corporate media, or else are warped to fit the confines of elite debate, stripping ordinary citizens of the tools they need to be informed, active participants in a democracy. (p. 281)

References

Baek, Y. M., & Wojcieszak, M. E. (2009). Don't expect too much! Learning from late-night comedy and knowledge item difficulty. *Communication Research, 36*(6), 783–809.

Baym, G. (2005). *The Daily Show*: Discursive integration and the reinvention of political journalism. *Political Communication, 22*(3), 259–276.

Becker, A. B., Xenos, M. A., & Waisanen, D. J. (2010). Sizing up *The Daily Show*: Audience perceptions of political comedy programming. *Atlantic Journal of Communication, 18*(3), 144–157.

Boler, M. (2006). The transmission of political critique after 9/11: "A new form of desperation"? *M/C Journal, 9*(1). Retrieved from http://journal.media-culture.org.au/0603/11-boler.php

Chan, S. (2008, November 12). Liberal pranksters hand out times spoof. *The New York Times*. Retrieved from http://cityroom.blogs.nytimes.com/2008/11/12/pranksters-spoof-the-times

Collins, R. (2009). Trust and trustworthiness in the fourth and fifth estates. *International Journal of Communication, 3*, 61–86.

Daily Show viewers knowledgeable about presidential campaign. (2004). *National Annenberg Election Survey*. Retrieved from http://www.naes04.org

Day, A. (2008). Are they for real? Activism and ironic identities. *The Electronic Journal of Communication, 18*(2, 3, 4). Retrieved from http://www.cios.org/www/ejc/EJCPUBLIC/018/2/01846.html

Day, A. (2011). *Satire and dissent: Interventions in contemporary political debate*. Bloomington: Indiana University Press.

Diebold accidentally leaks results of 2008 election early [Video]. (2008). *The Onion*. Retrieved from http://www.theonion.com/video/diebold-accidentally-leaks-results-of-2008-electio,14214

Dutton, W. H. (2009). The fifth estate emerging through the network of networks. *Prometheus, 27*(1), 15.

Dyer, R. (2007). *Pastiche*. London and New York: Routledge.

Feldman, A. J., Halderman, A., & Felten, E. W. (2006). *Security analysis of the Diebold AccuVote-TS voting machine*. Retrieved from http://www.usenix.org/events/evt07/tech/full_papers/feldman/feldman_html

Hayes, A. S. (2008). *Press critics are the fifth estate: Media watchdogs in America.* Westport, CT: Praeger.

Herman, E. S., & Chomsky, N. (1988). *Manufacturing consent: The political economy of the mass media.* New York: Pantheon Books.

Hoffman, L. H., & Thomson, T. L. (2009). The effect of television viewing on adolescents' civic participation: Political efficacy as a mediating mechanism. *Journal of Broadcasting & Electronic Media, 53*(1), 3–21.

Hoffman, L. H., & Young, D. G. (2011). Satire, punch lines, and the nightly news: Untangling media effects on political participation. *Communication Research Reports, 28*(2), 159–168.

Jones, P. (2000). Democratic norms and means of communication: Public sphere, fourth estate, freedom of communication. *Critical Horizons, 1*(2), 307–339.

Jones, J. P. (2005). *Entertaining politics: New political television and civic culture.* Lanham, MD: Rowman & Littlefield.

Jones, J. P. (2010). *Entertaining politics: Satiric television and political engagement* (2nd ed.). Lanham, MD: Rowman & Littlefield.

Kovach, B., & Rosenstiel, T. (2007). *The elements of journalism: What newspeople should know and the public should expect.* New York: Three Rivers Press.

Kowalewski, J. (2009). *Does humor matter? An analysis of how hard news versus entertainment news styles influence agenda-setting and priming effects* (Unpublished doctoral dissertation). University of North Carolina at Chapel Hill.

LaMarre, H. L., Landreville, K. D., & Beam, M. A. (2009). The irony of satire: Political ideology and the motivation to see what you want to see in *The Colbert Report. The International Journal of Press/Politics, 14*(2), 212–231.

Lucas, G. (2004, May 1). State bans electronic balloting in 4 counties. *The San Francisco Chronicle.* Retrieved from http://articles.sfgate.com/2004-05-01/news/17425285_1_touch-screen-voting-electronic-voting-disabled-voters

McChesney, R. W. (1999). *Rich media, poor democracy: Communication politics in dubious times.* Urbana: University of Illinois Press.

Nelson, B. (2008). Class voting hacks prompt call for better audits. msnbc.com. Retrieved from http://www.msnbc.msn.com/id/27205654

O'Reilly: Young Americans "have no idea what's going on" because they "get their news from Jon Stewart." (2006, May 25). *Media Matters.* Retrieved from http://mediamatters.org/research/200605250003

Pew Research Center for People and the Press. (2004, January 11). *Cable and Internet loom large in fragmented political new universe.* Retrieved from http://people-press.org/report/200/cable-and-internet-loom-large-in-fragmented-political-news-universe

Pew Research Center for People and the Press. (2007, August 9). *Internet news audience highly critical of news organizations.* Retrieved from http://pewresearch.org/pubs/564/internet-news-audience

Postman, N. (1985). *Amusing ourselves to death: Public discourse in the age of show business.* New York: Viking.

Reilly, I. (2010). *Satirical fake news and the politics of the fifth estate* (Unpublished doctoral dissertation). University of Guelph, Ontario.

The New York Times Special Edition. (2008, November 12). Retrieved from http://nytimes-se.com

Weisenburger, S. (1995). *Fables of subversion: Satire and the American novel, 1930–1980.* Athens: University of Georgia Press.

ISSUE 2

Informed comedy:
Do mock news shows make for a more informed public?

✖ NO

Informed Comedy or Impotent Politics?
Mary Francoli

Mary Francoli is an assistant professor at Carleton University's School of Journalism and Communication. She received her Ph.D. in political science from the University of Western Ontario. She was the Leverhulme Visiting Fellow in New Media and Internet Politics at Royal Holloway, University of London, in 2006/2007.

People love comedy. A cursory look at ratings shows that **mock news**—political satire that parodies "real" or "hard" news by mimicking its content and structure—is particularly popular. In May 2011 alone, *The Daily Show* with Jon Stewart—the quintessential mock news show—averaged 2.3 million viewers (Easley, 2011). *The Colbert Report* showed similarly high ratings. Our desire to laugh at life, politics, and current affairs is not new. The widespread popularity of puppetry like Punch and Judy, which included political satire, is a testament to the longevity of our love affair with comedy and politics. On the face of it, this relationship is harmless. There's nothing wrong with wanting, and in some cases even needing, to laugh at the world. It can be therapeutic. However, the idea that people might be using mock news for informing and educating (and not just entertainment) is cause for concern.

Even more worrying is evidence that mock news is being used as a replacement for conventional news programming. In 2004 *The Daily Show* was awarded the Television Critics Award for Outstanding Achievement in News and Information. It was selected for the award from a pool of shows that included more traditional hard news programming, such as CBS's *60 Minutes* and NBC's *Meet the Press* (Warner, 2010, p. 43). In 2009 a poll released by the Pew Research Center for the People and the Press found that 21 percent of people aged eighteen to twenty-nine cited *The Daily Show* and *Saturday Night Live* as a place where they regularly learned presidential campaign news ("Young Get News," 2009). Later that year, *Time* magazine conducted an online poll to determine the identity of America's most trusted newscaster. Jon Stewart, host of *The Daily Show*, won with a surprising 44 percent majority of votes (Hitchens, 2009). More conventional newscaster Brian Williams trailed with 29 percent, Charles Gibson with 19 percent, and Katie Couric with 7 percent (Hitchens, 2009). Setting aside questions regarding methods of polling and data collection, these polls draw attention to two interesting phenomena. First, some people might be viewing hosts of mock news shows (comedians like Jon Stewart) in the same light as traditional network newscasters. Second, some people believe that they are informed and educated by mock news. These observations point to a convergence between traditional news and mock or satirical news, and raise an interesting question: Does mock news make for a more informed public? After all, an "enlightened citizenry remains one of the foundations of a successful and thriving democracy" (Hollander, 2005, p. 403). This chapter starts to explore this question by identifying some of the main arguments supporting the idea that mock news informs. These assertions, and the underlying idea that there is value in mock news beyond fulfilling a desire to be entertained, are challenged through a discussion of substance, **framing**, audience, and purpose. The chapter draws heavily on mock news shows, such as those referenced above, but the conclusions and arguments are applicable to mock news more generally.

SUBSTANCE

The popular answer to the question of whether mock news makes for an informed public is yes. Scholars such as Matthew Baum (2002, 2011) and Christopher Cooper and Mandi Bates Baily (2008) argue that the apolitical might be more willing to pay attention when political issues are packaged and presented in an entertaining fashion. According to Baum, such packaging "dramatically reduces the cognitive costs of paying attention" (2011, p. 115). This argument relies on incidental attention. The idea is that some substantive political information can be attached, or "piggybacked," with information meant purely for entertainment purposes. Here "political information might thus become a free bonus, or incidental by-product, of paying attention to entertainment oriented information" (Baum, 2011, p. 117). However, because political news and the provision of information is not the priority under this model, it is devalued for the viewer. And, as Baum himself notes, the **incidental by-product model** has the potential to work only when the political information being piggybacked is dramatic in nature, which significantly limits the scope and ability of mock news to inform.

Baum (2011) also observes that mock news has a democratizing effect. Interviews in mock news that resemble interviews with traditional media have become a means through which political leaders communicate with the public and reach an audience who may not consume traditional hard news. At first glance, this would certainly seem to be the case. Political leaders and political hopefuls have increasingly gravitated toward mock news venues. They have become a vital part of the public relations toolbox. *The Daily Show*, as just one example, has had an impressive lineup of political guests including President Barack Obama, Bill Clinton, Tony Blair, and Vincente Fox. *The Mercer Report* in Canada, which contains elements of mock news, has included interviews with the leaders of major political parties and numerous members of Parliament. It is clear that leaders and candidates are drawn to mock news. There is a common perception that such venues "help candidates seem more ordinary and amiable to scores of often hard-to-reach voters" (Parkin, 2010, p. 3). However, in trying to appeal to voters, the potential for such political appearances to inform is often minimized, or lost, along with substance.

Political interviews on mock news shows tend to be much more informal than interviews occurring with mainstream news media. Policy as substance tends to fall to the wayside as mock news hosts focus on lighter, more personal topics of conversation. As Mason (2004) states, these "cozy gab sessions increasingly serve as a substitute for more substantive exchanges" (p. 14). Similarly, in commenting on the 2008 U.S. presidential election, Gold (2007) found that "John and Elizabeth Edwards got substantially gentler treatment from Leno on *The Tonight Show* than they did from Katie Couric on *60 Minutes*." In this case, not only does mock news not adequately inform, but it also has the potential to reduce voters' critical assessment of candidates as it might prompt the politically unaware to base their votes on a candidate's likeability. Image will be favoured above policy positions (Kolbert, 2004).

FRAMING

Similar criticisms regarding lack of depth or substance can also be made of mock news segments more generally. In parodying traditional hard news, mock news emphasizes jokes and entertainment value over the imparting of information. Information that is presented is very selective. It rarely gives viewers an appreciation of the diversity found in traditional news. Moreover, to maximize comedic appeal and popularity, mock news shows engage in a range of techniques and practices that have the potential to mislead or misinform viewers. For example, editing allows mock news to frame information in a way it deems entertaining. As Wiesman notes, "*The Daily Show* uses the structural framing power of video editing to ensure that the only material included is that which will support its Comic Frame" (2011, p. 173). Here, footage from traditional newscasts is cut, manipulated, and presented in ways that may not be reflective of reality. This is not meant to be a criticism of mock news. It does not bear the responsibility or goal of accuracy or educating. This is the role of traditional political news. However, it is useful to think about framing when considering the value of mock news.

Some argue that framing to support the underlying goal of comedy allows mock news to effectively draw our attention to inaccuracies and problems related to mainstream news (Wiesman, 2011). In this sense, mock news allows us to think critically about the information with which media presents us. However, the opposite corollary may also be true. Framing with the goal of comedic effect, as mock news does, has the potential to misinform and mislead. Stephen Colbert's infamous "report" on the concept of "wikiality" in which he manipulates Wikipedia pages to reflect untruths is an entertaining example. Practices where mock news shows play a clip of a journalist posing a question to a politician at a news conference where the politician's answer is drawn from footage taken from a separate event also highlights this point. Here, the importance of the comic frame to the success of mock news is recognized. However, framing prompts us to reconsider and question its impact beyond entertainment.

AUDIENCE

Given its epidermal treatment of news and the way that framing is used to create satire, it can be argued that mock news does not inform, but is meant to entertain those who are already informed. The comedic value of mock news cannot be fully appreciated by an audience who lacks prior knowledge of political and public affairs. As Moy, Xenos, and Hess (2005) note, audience members must have some degree of political sophistication and context in order to "get the joke." There is also evidence that mock news audiences are particularly attentive to traditional news and have some degree of knowledge of political and public affairs (Feldman & Young, 2008). As Hess (2011) stresses in looking at *The Daily Show*, "For viewers to simultaneously get their news and 'get' the jokes from *The Daily Show*, the intertextual reference must be understood via both its original and parodic reference. In other words, to watch and understand *The Daily Show*, audiences must be aware of current affairs" (p. 203). This underscores the value and continued importance of hard news as a venue for informing and mock news as a vehicles for, if anything beyond entertainment, reifying certain information and knowledge captured from traditional news.

Studies seeking to measure the political knowledge of those who rely on mock news as a source of information have not found a solid, concrete correlation between the two. Using survey data, Prior (2003) attempts to measure the impact of soft news, which includes mock news, on political knowledge. Ultimately, he found that there was very little evidence to support the claim that soft news increases political knowledge. Only around the most scandalous issues was there a trace of evidence for heightened knowledge. This finding poses serious problems for the claims of Baum and others. As Prior (2003) says, "If the effect of soft news is restricted to the most scandalous of the soft news topics, it becomes hard to defend it on the grounds that it informs people about politics" (p. 160).

PURPOSE

The tenuous evidence connecting mock news with the function of informing viewers is perhaps not surprising if we consider the motive of audiences consuming mock news and the broader purpose of mock news itself. Studies have shown that the primary goal of those consuming mock news is to be entertained (Baum, 2002; Brewer & Cao, 2006; Prior, 2003). They are not looking for news. This purpose might affect their retention of any incidental knowledge (Brewer & Cao, 2006). Similarly, if the goal of the audience is to be entertained, the purpose of mock news is to provide satirical amusement. Satire is a very specific art form. It "seeks to persuade an audience that something or someone is reprehensible or ridiculous" (Griffin, 1994, p. 1). It does this through attack and the use of exaggeration. And, as Griffin (1994) notes, its victims come from the "real world." According to Wiesman (2011), the identification of comedy as a goal or purpose "determines that all other political, critical or social agendas attributed to the show are secondary" (p. 165).

Comedians reinforce entertainment as the intended purpose or goal of mock news, answering the question of whether mock news informs with a somewhat horrified and emphatic *no*. Jon Stewart articulated this carefully in a lengthy November 11, 2010, interview on the *Rachel Maddow Show*, stating, "I feel more of a kinship to Jerry Seinfeld than I do to what you guys [journalists] do, or what CNN does.… If you were to look at our process—he [Seinfeld] is much more our process than the news is.… Because we are parodying a news organization we have to have the logistics and mechanics of one, but the process that the material goes through is not a news process." When pushed further about *The Daily Show* and its branding as "fake news," Stewart replied, "Fake news is wrong. It's glib. It's not news anything." In spite of Maddow's relentless push to draw a parallel between traditional news and mock news, Stewart stood his ground, maintaining the distinct goals, processes, and raison d'être of each profession:

> You're in a better game than I am. You're on the playing field and I'm in the stands yelling things and criticizing. What satire does best is articulate an intangible feeling that people are having, bring it into focus … it might be a positive feeling … but it's impotent…. There is no honour in what I do, but I do it as honourably as I can…. There is a high-mindedness to news and journalism. I do have liberties that you don't have.

Stewart isn't alone in pointing out the distinction between comedy and satire. Woody Allen once said, "Comedy just pokes at problems, rarely confronts them squarely" (Benayoun, 1987, p. 41). This is a fundamentally different approach from conventional news media, whose role as the fourth estate is one inherently linked to democracy and citizenship.

Stewart's point regarding the liberties and freedom of mock news—or "glib," as he calls it—is significant. Those involved in traditional journalistic practice follow, or are supposed to follow, a set of widely understood guidelines. Lance Bennett (2001) outlines six distinct journalistic practices: (1) maintaining political neutrality, (2) observing prevailing standards of decency and good taste, (3) using documentary reporting practices that rely on evidence, (4) using standardized formats to package the news, (5) training journalists as generalists instead of specialists, and (6) using editorial review to enforce these methods. Mock news, given its mandate for satire and to entertain as opposed to informing, is not bound by, nor does it employ, such methods and standards; these are the liberties Stewart refers to in the quotation above.

Somewhere along the way there has been a disjuncture between how comedians and those involved in the creation of mock news see themselves and how a growing percentage of the population sees them. This disjuncture is cause for concern. While mock news might make politics and public affairs more entertaining to some, there is little concrete evidence that it allows for a comprehensive understanding of policy and government. The minimal evidence that does demonstrate a correlation between mock news and the informing of its audience appears to indicate that the imparting of information occurs in only the narrowest of cases, primarily around events or issues that are particularly scandalous, such as the amorous indiscretions of those in positions of power. If anything, mock news reifies information and knowledge already attained elsewhere by its audience. Moreover, the framing of mock news to maximize comedic appeal—its intended purpose—is cause to critically consider its value in terms of informing its audience. In this sense, to parrot the words of Jon Stewart, mock news is impotent. It does little to inform and we shouldn't expect it to. It is not news. Satire would be a more appropriate term. As satire it entertains and pokes fun at the "real world."

References

Baum, M. (2002). Sex, lies, and war: How soft news brings foreign policy to the inattentive public. *American Political Science Review, 96*, 91–110.

Baum, M. (2011). How soft news brings policy issues to the inattentive public. In D. Graber (Ed.), *Media power in politics* (pp. 113–128). Washington, DC: CQ Press.

Benayoun, R. (1987). *The films of Woody Allen.* New York: Harmony Books.

Bennett, L. (2001). *News: The politics of illusion* (4th ed.). New York: Addison Wesley Longman.

Brewer, P., & Cao, X. (2006). Candidate appearances on soft news shows and public knowledge about primary campaigns. *Journal of Broadcasting and Electronic Media, 50*(1), 18–35.

Cooper, C., & Bates Baily, M. (2008). Entertainment media and political knowledge: Do people get any truth out of truthiness? In J. Foy (Ed.), *Homer Simpson goes to Washington: American politics through popular culture* (pp. 133–150). Lexington: University Press of Kentucky.

Easley, J. (2011). Jon Stewart's ratings are now higher than all of Fox News. *PoliticusUSA.* Retrieved from http://www.politicususa.com/en/jon-stewart-fox-ratings

Feldman, L., & Young, D. (2008). Late-night comedy as a gateway to traditional news: An analysis of time trends in news attention among late-night comedy viewers during the 2004 presidential primaries. *Political Communication, 25*(4), 401–422.

Gold, M. (2007, September 29). Candidates embrace the chat: Daytime gabfests and late night comedy TV become essential stops on the presidential trail to reach "regular folks." *Los Angeles Times*. Retrieved from http://articles.latimes.com/2007/sep/29/entertainment/et-poltalk29

Griffin, D. (1994). *Satire: A critical reintroduction*. Lexington: The University Press of Kentucky.

Hess, A. (2011). Breaking news: A postmodern rhetorical analysis of *The Daily Show*. In T. Goodnow (Ed.), *The Daily Show and rhetoric: Arguments, issues and strategies* (pp. 168–186). Lanham, MD: Lexington Books.

Hitchens, C. (2009, October). Cheap laughs: The smug satire of liberal humorists debases our comedy—and our national conversation. *The Atlantic*. Retrieved from http://www.theatlantic.com/magazine/archive/2009/10/cheap-laughs/7650/

Hollander, B. (2005). Late-night learning: Do entertainment programs increase political campaign knowledge for young viewers? *Journal of Broadcasting and Electronic Media, 49*(4), 402–415.

Kolbert, E. (2004, April 15). Stooping to conquer: Why candidates need to make fun of themselves. *The New Yorker*. Retrieved from http://www.newyorker.com/archive/2004/04/19/040419fa_fact1

Mason, J. (2004, September 22). Kerry makes TV rounds to aid image; more candidates seeking advantages of popular shows. *Houston Chronicle*, p. A14.

Moy, P., Xenos, M. A., & Hess, V. K. (2005, Summer). Priming effects of late-night comedy. *International Journal of Public Opinion Research, 18*(2), 198–210.

Parkin, M. (2010). Taking late night comedy seriously: How candidate appearances on late night television can engage viewers. *Political Research Quarterly, 63*(1), 3–15.

Prior, M. (2003). Any good news in soft news? The impact of soft news preference on political knowledge. *Political Communication, 20*(2), 149–171.

The Rachel Maddow Show. (2010, November 11). Season three, episode 534. Retrieved from msnbc.msn.com

Warner, J. (2010). *The Daily Show* and the politics of truth. In T. M. Dale & J. J. Foy (Eds.), *Homer Simpson marches on Washington: Dissent through American popular culture* (pp. 37–58). Lexington: University Press of Kentucky.

Wiesman, P. (2011). We frame to please: A preliminary examination of *The Daily Show*'s use of frame. In T. Goodnow (Ed.), The Daily Show *and rhetoric: Arguments, issues and strategies* (pp. 144–167). Lanham, MD: Lexington Books.

Young get news from Comedy Central. (2009). *CBS News*. Retrieved from http://www.cbsnews.com/2100-207_162-603270.html

Discussion Questions

1. Why have comedians, satirists, and activists turned to journalism as a medium or channel for communicating critique?

2. How useful is parody as a strategy for communicating information? To what extent does news parody create a better informed audience or public?

3. The Yes Men perform alternative *ways of doing* journalism. What impact will these alternative forms have on contemporary journalists and traditional news media?

4. Why might the incidental by-product model be considered problematic?

5. Political leaders and candidates are increasingly using mock news shows as part of their public relations toolbox. What problems and benefits might be associated with this practice?

6. Compare and contrast the purpose and approaches taken by mock news and conventional news.

ISSUE 3

Social networks and privacy: Should government be more interventionist in protecting personal privacy?

✔ YES

Whose Radical Transparency? Why Privacy Rights Are Necessary for the Facebook Generation
Leslie Regan Shade

Leslie Regan Shade is an associate professor at the University of Toronto in the Faculty of Information. Her research focus since the mid-1990s has been on the social, policy, and ethical aspects of information and communication technologies (ICTs), particularly issues of gender, globalization, and political economy.

A short video appearing on YouTube purporting to be a movie trailer of a sequel to the widely acclaimed and feted Hollywood film *The Social Network* (produced by David Fincher and released in the fall of 2010) parodies our complicit reliance on the popular social network site Facebook.

In the trailer, we learn that twenty-something Jeremy Hewitt, "the most gifted Facebook user in the world," did not see foresee the day when Facebook would go down. He sees his neighbours packing up their car. "Zuckerberg deleted Facebook ... and then he killed himself ... forever," they say to him, ominously. Thereafter everyday life mimics Facebook sociability. Hewitt's doorbell rings. A dweebish man appears: "We had seventh grade math together.... I'd like to request you to be my friend." A strange bearded man rifles through the postcards and pictures on his refrigerator. "How did you get into my home?" Hewitt gasps. "You haven't updated your privacy settings," the strange man replies, with a malicious chuckle.

Quick scenes mimic Facebook activities: a woman complains that her ex-boyfriend is stalking her—in real life; a man stands on a busy street corner entreating everyone to look at his dog: "Isn't she adorable?!"; another man whimpers, "I can't remember anyone's birthdate!" "Here comes another summer album!" a woman exudes, giddily tossing a pile of photos at the camera; young people scamper away from writing on the walls of a living room. The trailer ends with Hewitt in a basement meeting. Pulling down his grey hoodie, he resolutely proclaims: "We can't live like this anymore.... We're taking back Facebook" (Gasienica & Silverman, 2011).

We laugh knowingly at this clever video parody of Hollywood teen thrillers and its wry commentary on the ubiquity of Facebook in our everyday lives—for maintaining routine social connections, for lifelogging, and for branding ourselves. But often, popular culture parodies can also imitate real life.

Two weeks after the video was posted on YouTube, a headline on photo site Imgur read: "It's time to fix those security flaws Facebook." Members of a body-building forum had posted fourteen private pictures of Facebook CEO Mark Zuckerberg engaged in routine domestic activities (cooking with his fiancée, playing with his puppy), hacked from his private feed, in order to illustrate a bug in Facebook's system that inadvertently displayed private photos. Facebook quickly acknowledged the mistake and corrected it ("Facebook Bug," 2011).

These two examples illustrate a cascading array of public discourse on the impact of Facebook on the social realities and cultural imagination of citizens all over the world. With over 901 million monthly users worldwide ("Company Profiles," 2012), Facebook is the world's largest social network site. Thirty billion pieces of content are posted on Facebook *every month*, according to McKinsey Global Institute, and they further add that "if Facebook were a country, it would have the third-largest population in the world" (Manyika et al., 2011, p. 21).

But despite this popularity and profligacy, the mishaps and notoriety of Facebook, particularly related to management of users' personal privacy, is contested terrain. Governments and privacy advocates have admonished Facebook for their cavalier attitude toward privacy, with rebukes and policies designed to stem the tide of Zuckerberg's ethos of "radical transparency"—the company's credo that creating more open and transparent identities creates a healthier society (Kirkpatrick, 2010).

This article argues that governments have a constructive and necessary role to play in regulating and monitoring social network sites, and uses the social media company Facebook Inc. and its ever-evolving predicaments with privacy as a case study. The "friending" culture that Facebook cultivates—implicit pokes and wall posts for sharing personal tidbits, images, videos, important news, and public events with friends, family, and colleagues—has also exposed our personal information to third-party marketers zealous to monetize this data, or even to governments, law officials, and potential employers, eager to compile a dossier of our activities without our knowledge and consent. The architecture and terms of service on Facebook have a significant impact on the security and privacy of our personal information related to data collection, retention, distribution, and control.

In what follows, recent actions by the Office of the Privacy Commissioner of Canada (OPC) and the Federal Trade Commission (FTC) in the United States requiring Facebook's compliance with privacy legislation and the creation of transparent privacy settings and options for their users will be discussed. At stake are our privacy rights as consumers and citizens on social network sites.

FACEBOOK MEETS THE OPC

In 2008 five University of Ottawa law students, with the support of the Canadian Internet Policy and Public Interest Clinic (CIPPIC), filed a complaint with the Office of the Privacy Commissioner (OPC), alleging twenty-two separate violations of Canadian privacy laws by Facebook under the *Personal Information Protection and Electronic Documents Act* (PIPEDA, 2000). *PIPEDA* applies to the federally regulated private sector with respect to the collection, use, and disclosure of personal information for the transaction of commercial activities. *PIPEDA* is concerned with fair information practices and affirms that personal information should be collected, used, and disclosed only with an individual's consent.

The Office of the Privacy Commissioner, an arm of the federal government, regulates *PIPEDA* alongside the other piece of federal privacy legislation—the *Privacy Act* (1982), which places limitations on the collection, use, disclosure, and disposal of personal information held by the federal government and federal agencies. The OPC can investigate complaints, conduct audits, and pursue court action on public and private sector organizations that handle personal data. The OPC also engages in public education about privacy, and under the leadership of Commissioner Jennifer Stoddart has emerged as a major advocate for protecting the privacy of users in social media milieus, working with global data commissioners and privacy advocacy groups.

The complaint argued three main points: (1) Facebook should be open with users about its use of their personal information, (2) Facebook should obtain express permission to share its users' personal information, and (3) Facebook should limit the personal information that it shares to what is necessary. The complaint alleged infractions under *PIPEDA* Principles 4.2 (Identifying Purposes), 4.3 (Consent), 4.4 (Limiting Collection), 4.5 (Limiting Use, Disclosure and Retention), 4.7 (Safeguards), and 4.8 (Openness) (CIPPIC, 2008). In the complaint, CIPPIC noted that many Facebook users are high school and junior high students, and some are even under age thirteen. They pointed out the difficulty in comprehending the extensive legal language in Facebook's privacy policy, particularly related to the sharing of personal information and the operations of social ads that target the interests and profile data of users. Lisa Feinberg, one of the law students who filed the complaint, further argued that the impact of Facebook's terms of service and privacy policy, particularly for young people, was in the creation of a permanent evidentiary record wherein intimate contents could be leaked to employers, teachers, identity thieves, or cyberstalkers. As Feinberg wrote,

> Privacy is integral to maturity—we need a safe space to grow into ourselves. It is important for us to be able to recognize when a space is not safe—when there are unwanted listeners. It is also important for us to know that we have rights: we cannot be bound by illegal terms of service. We should be taught to challenge the questionable practices of these online social networking sites. As customers of these commercial websites, we have a voice. (2008, p. 78)

A yearlong investigation ensued, and in July 2009 the OPC released their findings. Stating that the central issues revolved around knowledge and consent, their investigation concentrated "on whether Facebook was providing a sufficient knowledge basis for meaningful consent by documenting purposes for collecting, using, or disclosing personal information and bringing such purposes to individuals' attention in a reasonably direct and transparent way" (Denham, 2009). They ruled that of CIPPIC's twelve major complaints, four were unfounded, four well-founded and resolved, and four well-founded with issues unresolved. The following table outlines the decision.

Facebook acknowledged that changes made in response to the OPC recommendations would apply to Facebook users worldwide, and stated that they were in dialogue with other international privacy regulators (Delacourt, 2009). However, ten months later, in May 2010, many Facebook users threatened to abandon the site because of discontent with mechanisms that "aggressively pushed to make more of its users' personal information public in an effort to make the site more alluring to deep-pocketed advertisers that are seeking to pinpoint their marketing campaigns to specific demographic groups" (El Akkad & McNish, 2010). CEO Zuckerberg admitted that Facebook needed to tighten its privacy controls. The OPC was not placated, citing concerns that the

TABLE 3.1	OPC Report on Facebook Complaint Filed by CIPPIC	
UNFOUNDED	**WELL-FOUNDED AND RESOLVED**	**WELL-FOUNDED AND UNRESOLVED**
That Facebook was not notifying users of new purposes for the collection, use, or disclosure of their personal information.	Collection of date of birth. Facebook was asked to clarify to users when registering why birth dates are required, and how they may be used.	Account deactivation and deletion—concern was that there was no account deletion option. Facebook agreed to provide information about account deletion in the privacy statement, but declined to create a retention policy for deactivated accounts.
That they were collecting personal information from sources outside of Facebook.	Precision on default privacy settings. Facebook was asked to make user profiles inaccessible through search engines by default; provide a link to the privacy setting when registering; and allow users to choose gradations of privacy settings (high/medium/low) and per-object privacy for items such as photos and status updates.	Accounts of deceased users—concern was that memorialization was only included in terms of use rather than the privacy policy, thus depriving users of meaningful consent for use of their personal information. Facebook declined to explain this process in their privacy policy.
That there were inadequate privacy safeguards on Facebook Mobile.	Advertising—Facebook was asked to clarify advertising and how their profile information is used for targeted advertising in their privacy policy.	Personal information of non-users—concern was that Facebook was not obtaining consent from non-users by allowing users to post personal information about non-users in their profiles, news feed, and wall, and allowing image tagging of non-users in photos and videos. Facebook declined to make changes to the invitation feature or implement a time limit on the retention of non-users' email addresses after being invited to Facebook.

UNFOUNDED	WELL-FOUNDED AND RESOLVED	WELL-FOUNDED AND UNRESOLVED
That Facebook was intentionally deceiving or misrepresenting itself by claiming to be solely a social networking site when it also engages in third-party applications and marketing.	Monitoring for anomalous activity such as voluminous friend requests that could be construed as harassment, spam, or abuse by scammers.	Third-party applications—concern was that Facebook was not informing users of the purposes for disclosing personal information to third-party application developers, that third-party developers were provided with personal information of users, and that Facebook was not adequately safeguarding users' personal information. Facebook did not agree to implement technological measures limiting application developers' access to user information or provide users with informed notice of the use and intent of applications.

Source: Appendix A of the Report of Findings into the Complaint Filed by the Canadian Internet Policy and Public Interest Clinic (CIPPIC) against Facebook Inc. under the Personal Information Protection and Electronic Documents Act by Elizabeth Denham, Assistant Privacy Commissioner of Canada, 2009.

new privacy settings revealed more personal information, including "names, profile information, pictures, gender and networks to the broader Internet" (McNish & El Akkad, 2010, n.p.). Indeed, Facebook's 2010 privacy policy was a verbal gargantuan: it was longer than any other social media privacy policy at 5830 words—longer, critics tittered, than the United States Constitution at 4543 words (Bilton, 2010).

In September 2010 the OPC announced the closure of their follow-up review, as Facebook clarified both default privacy settings (allowing for customization and easier configuration, providing a privacy guide and a more readable privacy policy) and privacy from third-party application developers (requiring express consent for each category of personal information requested) (OPC, 2010).

FACEBOOK MEETS THE FTC

In late November 2011 Zuckerberg posted a lengthy note to the Facebook blog: "Facebook has always been committed to being transparent about the information you have stored with us—

and we have led the internet in building tools to give people the ability to see and control what they share. But we can also always do better. I'm committed to making Facebook the leader in transparency and control around privacy" (Zuckerberg, 2011).

In this frank admission, Zuckerberg was reacting to a proposed settlement released by the Federal Trade Commission (FTC) that obliges the company to obtain users' consent before making any changes to their privacy settings, and subjects them to biannual independent privacy audits for the next twenty years. The FTC is a United States federal agency whose mandate is to ensure consumer protection and competitive jurisdiction across the economic spectrum through the development of policy, research tools, workshops, and law enforcement; in particular, it examines and regulates "unfair and deceptive acts or practices" (FTC, 2011a).

The settlement arose from a complaint filed in 2009 to the FTC by public interest groups, including the Electronic Privacy Information Center (EPIC), the American Library Association (ALA), the Center for Digital Democracy, the Consumer Federation of America, Privacy Activism, and the Privacy Rights Clearinghouse. In their complaint, the groups alleged that changes in Facebook's privacy settings "violate user expectations, diminish user privacy, and contradict Facebook's own representation" (EPIC et al., 2009, p. 1). Specifically, the complaint asked for the restoration of privacy settings that allowed users to choose the public disclosure of personally identifiable information (name, current city, friends) and to opt out of revealing personal information to third-party developers. The complainants also asked Facebook to make their data collection practices more transparent, as well as to allow users "meaningful control" over personal information given to third-party marketers and developers.

Jon Leibowitz, chairman of the FTC, stated, "Facebook's innovation does not have to come at the expense of consumer privacy" (FTC, 2011b). To this end, they issued eight complaints against the company and in their settlement required them to cease from making misrepresentations about the privacy and security of users' personal information; obtain "affirmative express consent" before making any changes to privacy preferences; establish and maintain a privacy program; prevent the access of any user's material more than thirty days after the user has deleted an account; and require biannual independent third-party privacy audits "certifying that it has a privacy program in place that meets or exceeds the requirements of the FTC order, and to ensure that the privacy of consumers' information is protected" (FTC, 2011b). Will the FTC order have any noticeable impact for Facebook users? Most likely not, according to EPIC executive director Marc Rotenberg, who commented that the FTC ruling does not require Facebook to adhere to pre-2009 default privacy settings (McCullagh, 2011).

FACEBOOK'S FOLLIES CONTINUE

Facebook has faced the ire of privacy advocates, consumer rights organizations, devoted users, and governments for its capricious take on our personal privacy. Facebook, with ad revenues predicted to be in excess of $4 billion for 2011 alone, is at the forefront of social media advertising innovation, a system Jeff Chester of the Center for Digital Democracy characterizes as comprising "a stunning infrastructure of commercial surveillance throughout the digital world" (Chester, 2011, p. 2). Facebook's widely anticipated IPO (initial public offering—the first sale of private company stock to the public) in May 2012 raised $16 billion and valued the company at a staggering $104 billion— higher than McDonald's, Amazon.com, and Citigroup, with Zuckerberg's worth alone estimated to be

$20 billion. In order to placate new shareholders Facebook will need to effectively turn users' personal information into data for advertising (Sengupta, 2012). Commodification processes are resilient and ever more pervasive in social network sites. Targeted ads, social marketing, and **behavioural advertising** (acquisition of empirical data on users through monitoring their online actions) are constitutive of what Vincent Mosco calls "**immanent commodification**": the processes wherein the social network user is him- or herself a commodity who in turn produces new media commodities— our content is monetized and captured to tailor and streamline new products that allegedly match our consumer preferences. In the process, immanent commodification "creates powerful surveillance tools that threaten privacy" (Mosco, 2009, p. 143). The managing director of Facebook's Canadian operations, Jordan Banks, argues that this "radical digital shift" in marketing demands that companies leverage social networks to promote their brand, calling this strategy "social by design": "We think ads can be more effective when seen through the social context of your friends" (Doyle, 2011).

The OPC has continued their research on the privacy implications of social media, and their 2011 report detailed the impact and resiliency of *PIPEDA* on online tracking, profiling, and targeting in social media. Applying *PIPEDA* to rapid changes and consumer uptake in social media is challenging, they noted, particularly in "defining what is (or is not) personal information, determining the appropriate form of consent, limiting the use of personal information, implementing reasonable safeguards, providing access and correction to online information, and ensuring accountability" (OPC, 2011a). Because these practices remain largely invisible to the average consumer, and especially for young people, transparency "is needed for the benefit of individuals and to ensure innovation" (OPC, 2011a).

Several months after the release of this report (and concomitant with the FTC decision), the OPC issued guidelines for behavioural advertising related to meaningful consent, appropriate collection, and retention. These stipulate that opt-out consent is reasonable if users are made aware of the purposes and practices at or before the time of collection, and with knowledge of the parties involved in behavioural advertising; if the information collected is of a nonsensitive manner, and is used and destroyed as soon as possible or de-identified; if uses are made transparent and obvious and not buried in a privacy policy; if users can easily opt out at or before the time of collection; and if such opting out takes effect immediately and is persistent. And, at no time should children be subjected to behavioural marketing because they cannot provide meaningful consent (OPC, 2011b).

There is an escalating social and economic necessity to engage with social media in our many roles as students, friends, employees, job seekers, and cultural creators, and it is thus difficult to opt out of these services. Indeed, the complexity of the technical platforms of social media and the often arcane business models that undergird their operations can render our ability to comprehend our rights as users difficult. But given the strong condemnations and guidelines issued from regulatory bodies in Canada and the United States, instigated by public interest and privacy advocates, it is clear that government oversight of Facebook related to the personal privacy of its users is necessary. As users of social media, we must demand and expect "radical transparency" of our personal privacy from these corporations.

Note

This paper benefited from the generous funding from the Social Sciences and Humanities Research Council for the research project "Young Canadians, Participatory Digital Culture and Policy Literacy."

References

Bilton, N. (2010, May 12). Price of Facebook privacy? Start clicking. *The New York Times.* Retrieved from http://www.nytimes.com/2010/05/13/technology/personaltech/13basics.html

Canadian Internet Policy and Public Interest Clinic. (2008, May 30). *PIPEDA complaint to the Office of the Privacy Commissioner.* Ottawa: Author. Retrieved from http://www.cippic.ca/uploads/CIPPICFacebook Complaint_29May08.pdf

Chester, J. (2011). Social media marketing and surveillance of teens: Curating the conversation on food and beverage products linked to the obesity epidemic. Washington, DC: Center for Digital Democracy. Retrieved from http://www.centerfordigitaldemocracy.org/sites/default/files/ChesterSocialMediaPaper-1.pdf

Company profiles: Facebook Inc. (2012, May 22). *The New York Times.* http://topics.nytimes.com/top/news/ business/companies/facebook_inc/index.html

Delacourt, S. (2009, July 17). Facebook gets poked by Canada over privacy. *The Toronto Star.* Retrieved from http://www.thestar.com/news/canada/article/667700

Denham, E. (2009, July). *PIPEDA case summary #2009-008. Report of findings into the complaint filed by the Canadian Internet Policy and Public Interest Clinic (CIPPIC) against Facebook Inc., under the* Personal Information Protection and Electronic Documents Act. Ottawa: Office of the Privacy Commissioner of Canada. Retrieved from http://www.priv.gc.ca/cf-dc/2009/2009_008_0716_e.cfm

Doyle, S. (2011, December). Facebook urges companies to "go social." *The Wire Report, 5,* 9.

El Akkad, O., & McNish, J. (2010, May 25). Facebook backs down on privacy. *The Globe and Mail.* Retrieved from http://www.theglobeandmail.com/technology/facebook-backs-down-on-privacy/article561205/

Electronic Privacy Information Center et al. (2009). *Submission to the Federal Trade Commission in the matter of Facebook, Inc. complaint, request for investigation, injunction, and other relief.* Retrieved from http://epic. org/privacy/inrefacebook/EPIC-FacebookComplaint.pdf

Facebook bug sees Zuckerberg pictures posted online. (2011, December 7). *BBC News.* Retrieved from http:// www.bbc.co.uk/news/technology-16067383

Federal Trade Commission. (2011a). About us. Retrieved from http://www.ftc.gov/ftc/about.shtm

Federal Trade Commission. (2011b, November 29). Facebook settles FTC charges that it deceived consumers by failing to keep privacy promises [Press release]. Retrieved from http://www.ftc.gov/opa/2011/11/ privacysettlement.shtm

Feinberg, L. (2008, Summer). Facebook: Beyond friends. *Our Schools/Our Selves, 75–80.* Retrieved from http://www.policyalternatives.ca/sites/default/files/uploads/publications/Our_Schools_Ourselve/9_ Feinburg_facebook_beyond_friends.pdf

Fincher, D. (Director), & Sorkin, A. (Screenwriter). (2010). *The social network.* Retrieved from http://www. thesocialnetwork-movie.com/

Gasienica, J., & Silverman, B. (Producers). (2011, November 21). *The social network 2 (official trailer).* Nice Piece Productions. Available from http://www.youtube.com/watch?v=95N3EV4jAoE&feature=player_embedded

Kirkpatrick, D. (2010). *The Facebook effect: The inside story of the company that is connecting the world.* New York: Simon & Schuster.

Manyika, J., Chui, M., Brown, B., Bughin, J., Dobbs, R., Roxburgh, C., & Hung Byers, A. (2011). *Big data: The next frontier for innovation, competition, and productivity.* McKinsey Global Institute. Retrieved from http://www.mckinsey.com/Insights/MGI/Research/Technology_and_Innovation/Big_data_The_next_ frontier_for_innovation

McCullagh, D. (2011, November 29). Facebook's FTC settlement won't change much, if anything. *CNET News.* Retrieved from http://news.cnet.com/8301-31921_3-57333398-281/facebooks-ftc-settlement- wont-change-much-if-anything/

McNish, J., & El Akkad, O. (2010, May 26). Facebook warned it's not in compliance. *The Globe and Mail.* Retrieved from http://www.theglobeandmail.com/news/technology/facebook-warned-its-not-in- compliance/article1582155/?cmpid=nl-tech1

Mosco, V. (2009). *The political economy of communication* (2nd ed.). Thousand Oaks, CA: Sage P.

Office of the Privacy Commissioner of Canada. (2010, September 22). *Backgrounder: Facebook investigation follow-up complete.* Ottawa: Author. Retrieved from http://www.priv.gc.ca/media/nr-c/2010/bg_100922_e.cfm

Office of the Privacy Commissioner of Canada. (2011a, May). *Report on the 2010 Office of the Privacy Commissioner of Canada's consultations on online tracking, profiling and targeting, and cloud computing.* Ottawa: Author. Retrieved from http://www.priv.gc.ca/resource/consultations/report_201105_e.cfm

Office of the Privacy Commissioner of Canada. (2011b, December). *Privacy and online behavioural advertising: Guidelines.* Retrieved from http://www.priv.gc.ca/information/guide/2011/gl_ba_1112_e.cfm#contenttop

Sengupta, S. (2012, May 14). Facebook's prospects may rest on treasure trove of data. *The New York Times.* Retrieved from http://www.nytimes.com/2012/05/15/technology/facebook-needs-to-turn-data-trove-into-investor-gold.html?pagewanted=1&hp

Zuckerberg, M. (2011, November 29). Our commitment to the Facebook community [Blog post]. Retrieved from https://blog.facebook.com/blog.php?post=10150378701937131

Statutes

Personal Information Protection and Electronic Documents Act, S.C. 2000, c.5. Retrieved from http://laws.justice.gc.ca/en/P-8.6/index.html

The Privacy Act, R.S., 1985, c. P-21. Retrieved from http://laws.justice.gc.ca/en/p-21/index.html

ISSUE 3

Social networks and privacy:
Should government be more interventionist
in protecting personal privacy?

✘ NO

Social Media and Privacy Protection: A Public Issue,
an Individual Responsibility
Boyd Neil

A former magazine journalist, Boyd Neil has more than thirty years of experience in the public and private sectors as a communication strategist providing senior-level counsel to clients in the oil and gas, financial services, mining, and packaged goods industries, among others. As national practice leader of the social media and digital communications practice at a large Canadian communications consultancy, Boyd guides a team of social media consultants in providing clients with creative solutions to their reputation challenges. Boyd has M.A. and M.B.A. degrees from the University of Toronto.

The question of whether government should be more interventionist in protecting personal privacy on social networks contains two entirely different questions:

1. Should personal privacy be protected on social networks?
2. Should the government be more interventionist to assist in this?

The answer to the first is yes; to the second, no.

Let's explore each one: first, the question of whether or not personal privacy should be (and needs to be) protected on social networks.

The extraordinary phenomenon of the last ten years is not so much the new Web 2.0 technologies that facilitated the interoperability of social platforms, as well as user-generated content, but what the resulting **social networks** have brought about in terms of how democracy is practised, revolutions birthed and nurtured, relationships begun and ended, information and ideas shared and debated, and products devised and sold. For some it is difficult to imagine a world in which people could only talk on the phone or go to parties and meetings (often organized by phone calls) as a way to do all these things.

Ubiquitous social networks have also brought into much sharper relief questions of privacy. People have surrendered—sometimes unconsciously or at least tacitly—various levels of personal data to social networks and other web-based applications. A billion or so people globally have relinquished their privacy on social networks like Facebook, Ren-Ren (Chinese), Badoo, Twitter, YouTube, Flickr, and Google+ for the benefit of having a platform on which they can connect to friends, causes, products, and services.

Although not by any means alone, Facebook has been the focus of much of the concern about privacy leakage. Recently, the social network once again stepped on privacy toes by offering brands what were originally called "sponsored stories," later changed to "featured" stories (a language change that, interestingly, seems to hide the fact that the stories are paid ads).

Featured stories allow brands to create ads that target users based on when they "like" a product or brand. The ad identifies that your friends have "liked" the product or brand and includes their pictures and names in the ad. The featured stories appear in your Facebook news feed automatically, and next to the time stamp is a little note that explains that the ad is appearing because you or perhaps your friends have liked the brand previously. The concern, of course, is that the brand "like" content has been taken from your friends' pages without their consent.

At the end of 2011, the appropriateness of this intrusive use of personal data was still before the U.S. courts. Twitter also collects personally identifiable information and sells it to third parties who can target users with advertising as a result. The microblogging service has been the subject of a Federal Trade Commission prosecution for a variety of security breaches, including a hacker accessing a Twitter administrator's account—a doorway into private information of any Twitter user (Gonsalves, 2010).

Google's challenge to Facebook—Google+—also came under criticism in early 2012 by the Electronic Privacy Information Center (EPIC), which expressed concern about privacy issues arising out of "a new feature, called 'Search Plus Your World', that blends information such as comments and photos posted on its Google+ social network into users' search results" (Rushe, 2012).

The infographic below from allfacebook.com gives some idea about what, in general terms, Facebook and Google do with privacy (with the allfacebooks.com site's own evaluation of the items in the list).

But admittedly, Facebook and Twitter in particular have worked very hard over the last couple of years to meet users' privacy concerns while trying to monetize (they are businesses, after all) the valuable data they have on the one billion or so people who use these social networks. In August 2011, for example, before the sponsored ads misstep, Facebook made the most sweeping changes to privacy controls in its short history. It embedded privacy controls on users' profile pages rather than forcing them to find them through a privacy settings page. And the process of tagging people's names in photos and posts and noting their whereabouts through location-based services was made safer by giving users more control over who tags them and how the tags appear on their profile pages, as well as making it clearer how to "untag" themselves from posts by others.

In general, though, social network natives, millennials in particular, have accepted that by giving up personal information, they leave themselves open to possible abuse by marketers, stalkers, and identity thieves and to surveillance by teachers, employers, parents, boyfriends, girlfriends, husbands, and wives. Perhaps it is no different for them than accepting the risk that when you drive a car you are at the mercy of drunk drivers.

However, accepting a certain amount of privacy risk can't be assumed to mean that people are offering unrestricted use of the information. In fact, in an interview, Jeffrey Cole, director of the Center for the Digital Future at the USC Annenberg School for Communication and Journalism, warned that Americans in particular are worried about their loss of privacy:

> Perhaps the biggest price that Americans pay for Internet use is the loss of their personal privacy—in particular, as a result of the growing trend of information-gathering about online behavior.
>
> "The issue of privacy is simple—if you go online for anything at all, your privacy is gone," said Cole. "Americans love that they can buy online, look for information online, and join social communities online. But the price we pay is that we are monitored constantly; private organizations know everything there is to know about us: our interests, our buying preferences, our behavior, and our beliefs.
>
> "Americans are clearly concerned about this," Cole said. "Our latest Digital Future study found that almost half of users age 16 and older are worried about companies checking what they do online; by comparison, 38 percent said that the government checking on them is a concern." ("Is America," 2011)

Granting reasonable and approved (no matter how casually) access is not the same as allowing carte blanche for search, investigation, and sale of that personal data, either by government for what it perceives to be security or criminal investigation purposes, or by marketers who use software to become "nimble online stalkers" and follow customers from site to site (Houpt, 2011).

Governments and marketers shouldn't divine in someone's allowing limited access to a small amount of personal data so that he or she can exchange images, information, pictures, and quips with friends that he or she is therefore permitting these marketers and authorities to venture into that data to test patriotism or slyly pitch products. "In fact, trusting that your private data will remain private could be a key requirement for everyday, mainstream users to be willing to input all the more of their personal data into systems that would build value on top of that data," says Marshall Kirkpatrick (2010) in a post on *ReadWriteWeb*.

So, yes, personal privacy should be guarded on social networks, and today privacy on social networks needs to be protected more than ever. Who should do it, though?

The social network platforms themselves should be responsible for balancing the selling of personal data against the need to protect personal privacy. Marketers, too, may have to learn that consumer trust, if threatened by overzealous manipulation of the huge global database that is social networks, can easily be withdrawn. And as consumers and users of social networks, we should all be vigilant—and critical—when companies like Facebook and Google+ push the boundaries of fair use of the information we give them.

Marketers and social platforms have to allow for **meaningful consent** with respect to the information we let them have in exchange for access to social networks like Facebook and Twitter. We should ask that they build choice and opt in and out privileges with respect to data exposure at every decision step in online transactions, and hold them to account—through online social action (by withdrawal of commerce, among other things)—if they play free and loose with those data, our online friendships, and our images. And we should urge them to limit the types of profile information collected and the length of time it is stored. This is a good starting point for legitimate protection of privacy on social networks.

But government intervening to protect privacy on social networks? Now that's a different question.

Let's start with a basic premise: intervention by government should always make us nervous. Elected officials are motivated as much by political expediency as they are by the common good. And when expediency and pressure are involved it's the wrong time to make decisions about anything, never mind sensitive issues like privacy protection, freedom of expression, authorization to access, or piracy prevention.

There is a legitimate role for governments to play in ensuring that companies behind social networks recognize and act on legislated standards with respect to privacy. Since the Ontario Court of Appeal affirmed in *Jones v. Tsige1* that there is a tort of invasion of privacy in Ontario at least and that "Charter jurisprudence recognizes privacy as a fundamental value in our law and specifically identifies, as worthy of protection, a right to informational privacy that is distinct from personal and territorial privacy" ("Ontario Recognizes," 2012), it is fair to assume that government and the courts should be providing guidance to corporations about when, how, and if their actions step over legal boundaries for protecting privacy. This may pose something of a challenge to consumer sovereignty over its relationship with private business. But it is marginally better than relying solely on the alternative that would see consumer activism—which often comes late and after the damage is done—as the recourse when companies stray.

Certainly, arm's length government agencies such as the Office of the Privacy Commissioner in Canada can help educate us about our responsibilities for safeguarding our own personal data and the risks of moving more and more of those data online. The OPC has—and should continue to—call out Facebook, Twitter, Google, and other digital media corporations when they act in breach of Canada's privacy legislation and *Charter* jurisprudence on privacy issues.

But let's add another observation: privacy discussions globally have taken on a dramatic new urgency as authoritarian and democratic governments alike attempt to rein in what they see as the digital anarchy occasioned by the anonymity of web sharing. In terms of governments and privacy protection on social networks and other web destinations, the concern today should be not so much with how governments can help protect our privacy on social networks through legislation and regulation, but how they are threatening individual privacy with legislation that supports— without personal consent or court-backed approval—surveillance by police and security forces. It is a trope of authoritarian regimes—like those in China—that restriction on use and access to data, and official scrutiny of online sharing and discussion are necessary to prevent criminals and terrorists from using social networks to organize themselves for evil.

However, now some democracies, including the United States and Canada, have tabled legislation that threatens Internet privacy under the guise of giving "law enforcement agencies the ability to address organized crime and terrorism activities" (Greenberg, 2011) or, in the case of the United States, to prevent piracy of movies and music. The U.S. *Stop Online Piracy Act*, which was sidelined after widespread and effective online activism (including twenty-four-hour blackouts on Wikipedia and Reddit) in early January 2012, could have forced Internet service providers to block websites suspected of violating copyright or trademark legislation. While the U.S. measures were targeted at Internet piracy, to many they smacked of a government incursion into freedom of expression and unwarranted treading on the privacy of online exchange and sharing.

In Canada, something more meddlesome is being considered.

> In a series of legislative moves relating to overhauling the Criminal Code (Bills C-50, C-51, C-52), the Conservative government will require Internet Service Providers to hand over personal information about Canadians to the police without warrant, to retool their networks in ways that enable live monitoring of consumer online activities, and to assist police in the testing of online surveillance capabilities. (Valiquet & Simonds, 2011)

Or, as the OpenMedia advocacy group puts it, "**The government is trying to push through a set of electronic surveillance laws that will invade your privacy and cost you money.** The plan is to force every phone and Internet provider to allow 'authorities' to collect the private information of any Canadian, at any time, without a warrant" ("Stop Online Spying," n.d.).

Now this is not the place to argue the philosophy of the "private mind" or the Lockian idea of which of people's natural rights they are willing to exchange for protection in a society governed by common law. Suffice it to say that Internet users might have as much to fear from overprotective legislation as they do dodgy marketing practices or religious or political zealots, depending on how the legislation in both countries finally looks.

Certainly, the Canadian federal privacy commissioner thinks Canadians have something to be concerned about. In a letter to Minister of Public Safety Vic Toews, the Privacy Commissioner of Canada, Jennifer Stoddart, seems to have it right:

> Read together, the provisions of the lawful access bills from the last session of Parliament (C-50, C-51, and C-52) would have had a significant impact on our privacy rights. By expanding the legal tools of the state to conduct surveillance and access private information, and by reducing the depth of judicial scrutiny, the previous bills would have allowed government to subject more individuals to surveillance and scrutiny. In brief, these bills went far beyond simply maintaining investigative capacity or modernizing search powers. Rather, they added significant

new capabilities for investigators to track, and search and seize digital information about individuals. (2011)

What is striking about these efforts by governments to wrangle to the ground what they seem to think is Internet mayhem is how insensitive they are to what truly troubles ordinary citizens about privacy issues. We want to be protected from our own ignorance (no, I don't read those terms of service descriptions either), but not in a way that sets up frighteningly loose protections to freedom or puts unchecked authorities in charge of online surveillance. We want social network platforms to prevent third-party applications from combining our information with other sources of data to steal our identities. We want to express our affection for a brand without that expression being used to sell us more, at least without our express consent. Most of all, we—or at least certainly I—don't want governments to confuse shielding private data or sheltering intellectual property with granting law enforcement access to our private information.

The answer to the question, "Should government be more interventionist in protecting personal privacy on social networks?" is an equivocal no. There is a place for governments and arm's-length agencies like the OPC in leading an open dialogue with business about better protection of personal data online. There is a job for government and the courts in going after companies that breach their own codes, *Charter* rights, or legal precedent.

But at the end of the day the larger threat is in government requiring Internet service providers to collect and release to it user data, and with government providing law enforcement unsupervised access to our personal information even when parts of it are unwittingly surrendered. This is what we need to be vigilant of, and as digital citizens we need to be willing to fight back both online and off when that threat rears its subtle head.

Note

[1] See *Jones v. Tsige*, 2012 ONCA 32 (CanLII), at http://www.canlii.org/en/on/onca/doc/2012/2012onca32/2012onca32.html.

References

Gonsalves, A. (2010, June 25). Twitter, Feds, settle security charges. *InformationWeek Security*. Retrieved from http://www.informationweek.com/news/security/privacy/225701450?subSection=Privacy

Greenberg, J. (2011, October 29). The Janus-face of the Conservative government and new technology: Digital democracy and the information state. *The Ideas Lab—Reflections on Communication, Politics & Culture* [Blog]. Retrieved from http://theideaslab.wordpress.com/2011/10/29/the-janus-face-of-the-conservative-government-and-digital-media/

Houpt, S. (2011, December 6). Privacy watchdog takes aim at online consumer "profiling." *The Globe and Mail*. Retrieved from http://www.theglobeandmail.com/report-on-business/industry-news/marketing/adhocracy/privacy-watchdog-takes-aim-at-online-consumer-profiling/article2262372/

Is America at a digital turning point? (2011, December 14). *USC Annenberg News*. Retrieved from http://annenberg.usc.edu/News%20and%20Events/News/111214CDF.aspx

Kirkpatrick, M. (2010, January 28). Privacy, Facebook and the future of the Internet. *ReadWriteWeb* [Blog]. Retrieved from http://www.readwriteweb.com/archives/privacy_facebook_and_the_future_of_the_internet.php

Ontario recognizes tort of invasion of privacy. (2012, January 18). *Canadian Privacy Law Blog*. Retrieved from http://blog.privacylawyer.ca/2012/01/ontario-recognizes-tort-of-invasion-of.html

Rushe, D. (2012, January 12). Epic to FTC: Google Search+ is violating users' privacy. *The Guardian*. Retrieved from http://www.guardian.co.uk/technology/2012/jan/12/epic-ftc-google-search-plus-privacy

Stoddart, J. (2011, October 26). Letter to Minister of Public Safety Vic Toews. Office of the Privacy Commissioner of Canada. Retrieved from http://www.priv.gc.ca/media/nr-c/2011/let_111027_e.cfm#contenttop

Stop online spying (n.d.). OpenMedia.ca. Retrieved from http://stopspying.ca/

Valiquet, D., & Simonds, K. (2011, February 3). *Legislative summary of* Bill C-51: Investigative Powers for the 21st Century Act. Publication No. 40-3-C51-E. Ottawa, ON: Library of Parliament. Retrieved from http://www.parl.gc.ca/About/Parliament/LegislativeSummaries/bills_ls.asp?ls=c51&source=library_prb&Parl=40&Ses=3&Language=E

Discussion Questions

1. What has been the impact of new social media channels on the role of image in politics? Do Twitter, Facebook, and YouTube focus voters more on image or more on issues? How so?

2. Think of a politician you feel strongly about, and search for videos and photos of him or her in action. Deconstruct their performance, taking into account the audio, kinesthetic, proxemic, tactile, and clothing channels. What works in the politician's performance? What doesn't work? Which of these channels do you pay attention to most, and why?

3. Would democratic elections become more or less democratic if politicians went without image consultants? Why is that?

4. Who should be principally responsible for balancing the selling of personal data against the need to protect personal privacy; individuals, governments, or the social network platforms themselves?

5. Should social networks take greater responsibility for demonstrating to individuals the amount of personal information they are making available when they use these platforms, as well as its possible uses by them for marketing purposes?

6. Are governments threatening individual privacy when they introduce legislation that allows police services to access private data without warrants in the context of investigating alleged criminal activity?

ISSUE 4

Entertaining politics:
Is it all about image?

✔ YES

Image Is Everything in Politics
Bernard Gauthier

Bernard Gauthier is a consultant in a leading public relations agency in Ottawa. With more than twenty-five years of experience in the field, he has counselled and trained dozens of leaders in business, the nonprofit sector, and government on how to communicate more effectively using words, body language, and clothing. He is a regular commentator on political communication and image with some of the country's leading media outlets, including CTV, CBC Radio, and *The Globe and Mail*. Bernard is also a professor in the bachelor of public relations program at Conestoga College. He is currently completing a Ph.D. in communication at Carleton University. His principal areas of interest include intercultural communication, the culture of professionalism, political communication, and advertising history.

If, in the era of FDR, or even Kennedy, economists, intellectuals and engineers constituted the requisite "brain trust," today's inner circle is made up of pollsters and image consultants.... Advertising and public rezlations experts, pollsters and spin doctors, political consultants and cosmeticians were now beginning to script the political process itself. (Ewen & Ewen, 1992, p. 212).

Stuart and Elizabeth Ewen are among the many communication scholars who have noted and criticized the growing role of image in politics.[1] They are joined by a host of news reporters who lament how "appearances by cabinet ministers—whether it's a speech or an interview—are carefully staged, starting with a 'message event proposal' vetted by the Privy Council Office" (Campion-Smith, 2008). If politics is all about carefully controlled image, so the argument goes, then democracy is weakened because voters are no longer assessing the policies of the candidates. Instead of debating the issues, we're comparing suits and falling for carefully rehearsed speeches and photo opportunities. Television, being a popular and effective way to transmit images, often gets much of the blame.[2]

This chapter will argue that modern politics is indeed largely about image. Unlike many critics, however, I won't point a finger at PR professionals, nor sound the alarm bells for the political process. Instead, I'll take a close look at the 2011 federal election in Canada and argue that image matters in politics because it's much more than just image. Rather than being overwhelmed or duped, voters make full use of what they learn by assessing a **candidate's image**. They base their votes not only on promises and policies but also on an assessment of the person behind the promises and policies. That assessment is based on qualities like body movement, clothing, speaking style, and more.

Before moving to the argument, however, it's important to define exactly what is meant by "image" in politics. Dan Nimmo and Robert Savage (1976) offer up a concise definition that emphasizes how a candidate's image is subjective; it resides in each individual voter's mind: "The candidate's image consists of how he is perceived by voters, based on both the subjective knowledge possessed by voters and the messages projected by the candidate" (1976, p. 9).

How we perceive a politician interacts with the messages that individual communicates to create image. Linda Lee Kaid and Mike Chanslor (2004) offer a definition that puts more emphasis on the role of a candidate's appearance. For them, image is composed of a combination of "appearance dimensions and candidate characteristics" (p. 134). Image, then, is based partly on what a candidate says and does during an election campaign, and partly on how the candidate looks in the process.

MORE THAN JUST IMAGE

Kaid and Chanslor also argue that by considering both what is said and how, voters are able to assess a politician's competence, integrity, reliability, and charisma. This is a key point. As voters, we assess much more than politicians' appearance and speaking skills when we construct their image. We are able to accomplish this because the speaking style, clothing choices, and body language that many people dismiss as just image actually constitute a complex and powerful system of communication. Ray L. Birdwhistell, a pioneering communication scholar[3] in the field of body motion and meaning, felt strongly that the communication that happens when one person utters words and others listen is important but is only part of a complex system. He wrote in the introduction to his book *Kinesics and Context* that "whatever 'meaning' is, it is not merely conventional understandings boxed in *words*" (italics added, 1970, p. xii). For Birdwhistell, communication[4] between people is made possible by a layered and continuous system that includes numerous channels operating at once: an "audio" channel that transmits words, a "kinesthetic" channel, and a "tactile" or touch channel, among others (1970, p. 70). To this list of channels, I will also suggest we add a "clothing" channel.

The audio channel carries the words and sentences we speak, the tone of voice and silences we create. This complete package of sounds and silences (what Birdwhistell calls the "speech behaviour") works to create meaning (1970, p. 27). This is why, for example, finishing a sentence (e.g., The country's economy is strong) with a rising voice changes it from a declarative statement to a question.

Kathleen Hall Jamieson studied the speech behaviour of politicians and explored how modern communication technology has profoundly changed this channel in her book *Eloquence in an Electronic Age: The Transformation of Political Speechmaking* (1988). Jamieson laments the passing of traditional speech behaviour or rhetoric from political speechmaking and describes the new qualities that ensure the success of modern politicians who communicate using the audio channel. In particular, she notes how successful politicians now use a more conversational style of delivery better suited for the close up and intimate space of the radio or television in the home. She suggests that success comes with a speaking style that is intimate and reveals the autobiographical details of the individual. Jamieson also demonstrates how the use of memorable phrases and memorable images is essential if a politician wants to make an impact in the media. These phrases and images become "the capsules in which television viewers store the event" (1988, p. 91). In the federal election of 2011, NDP leader Jack Layton demonstrated all of these qualities. He revealed the intimate details of his battle with cancer and never hid the walking stick he needed after hip surgery, providing the most memorable images of the campaign.

Timothy Stephen, Teresa M. Harrison, William Husson, and David Albert (2004) also studied how modern politicians use the audio channel and reached many of the same conclusions as Jamieson. Using statistics rather than historical analysis, they studied the impact of voters' perceptions of the interpersonal communications styles of candidates. The authors found that the winning candidates in each of three U.S. presidential elections (1984, 1988, and 1992) were more likely to be described as "self-contained, secure, relaxed and interpersonally functional" in their speaking style. On the other hand, the losing candidates in each election were more likely to be described by survey respondents as "overbearing, tense, contentious, histrionic and serious" (2004, p. 185).[5] Their findings are well illustrated by Prime Minister Stephen Harper's performance in the 2012 election debates. Despite the efforts of three competitors to upset him, Harper maintained his composure and consistently used a voice that was self-contained, secure, and relaxed. The image he created was that of a leader and statesman.

The channel on which Birdwhistell focused his research—the kinesthetic channel—carries all the body movements we use to express ourselves, from head movements to hand gestures and the way we plant our feet. For Birdwhistell, a seemingly simple gesture like a smile is actually a complex combination of movement in the lips, the cheeks, the muscles around the eyes, the forehead, the head, the shoulders, arms, hips, legs, and feet. Here again, the complete package on the kinesthetic channel is what helps us determine the meaning of the original movement of the lips—whether the politician's smile for the cameras signals happiness, embarrassment, or fear.

Subtle differences in the kinesthetic channel can be magnified by TV cameras, making this a very powerful channel in modern politics. For example, pointing a finger at an opponent during a televised debate contributes to an angry and aggressive image. The very same gesture done holding a pen softens the image considerably. Even the way a candidate looks at others can create meaning. Michael Argyle, in his essay "The Syntaxes of Bodily Communication" (1975), discusses how the way we make eye contact (or not) with the person to whom we are speaking carries meaning. The gaze can help us communicate to others that we are paying attention and that we want to engage them. That's why skilled political debaters look directly at the television camera instead of at their opponent during a political debate. They reserve the gaze for the people at home and capture our attention.

Birdwhistell's third channel—the tactile channel—is both powerful and delicate. Edward T. Hall studied this tactile channel closely and expanded the concept to include not only touch but also the distance people keep between them when they communicate—what he dubbed "proxemics." In his book, *The Silent Language* (1959), Hall wrote that "space communicates" (p. 190) and showed how the meaning created by standing very close and touching or standing far apart varies greatly from one culture to another. Politicians want to demonstrate that they are warm and approachable, which is why they never miss an opportunity to hug babies and shake hands with supporters. The 2011 federal election provided an interesting contrast in this respect. The Conservative Party kept crowds and reporters far away from Stephen Harper during their media events; he was often isolated at his podium, perhaps backed by a group of supporters but rarely touching or interacting with them. The NDP events, on the other hand, often featured walks through the crowd by Jack Layton, as supporters shook hands or patted him on the back. The image of both party leaders was in many ways shaped by these very different uses of the tactile channel.

To Birdwhistell's audio, kinesthetic, and tactile channels, I propose that we could also add a clothing channel. In his book *Fashion, Culture and Identity* (1992), Fred Davis argues that clothes speak by allowing people to communicate some things about themselves, their status, and their lifestyle, as well as their "attributes and attitudes about themselves" (p. 16). Unlike spoken language, the meanings evoked by combinations of fabric, texture, colour, pattern, volume, and silhouette are forever shifting and "in process" (p. 5). The codes are clearer with formal uniforms, of course, but the meaning of a blue business suit or a cowboy hat can vary widely based on the occasion (e.g., a speech to the United Nations or a pancake breakfast at the Calgary Stampede) and the social group in whose midst the politician happens to be (e.g., banking executives or university students).

The 2011 campaign often revealed the importance of the clothing channel. Jack Layton selected a range of outfits that included a casual wool sweater, a classic Montreal Canadiens jersey, unbuttoned blue shirts, and, of course, traditional suits. Each was carefully selected to send the right message to a particular audience in a particular setting. Stephen Harper was more limited in the messages he sent through the clothing channel, preferring a navy blazer, white shirts, and perhaps a tie (depending on the event). He did stray from this more restrained message to wear a Team Canada Olympic jacket and a Team Canada Olympic hockey jersey. In all of these cases, the intended meaning was clear.

INFORMATION PUT TO WORK

So far, I've argued that politics is all about image because image is more than just window dressing—it's communication. Of course, if this communication was largely ignored by voters, then politics would not be all about image. Voters, however, do pay attention and use what they learn by assessing a candidate's image to help make a choice on election day.

Samuel Popkin argued in his book *The Reasoning Voter: Communication and Persuasion in Presidential Campaigns* (1991) that voters who are increasingly busy and deluged with information need to be very strategic in how they gather and use information during an election. Far from a pessimist who sees modern voters as overwhelmed, Popkin writes that voters find efficient ways to arrive at reasoned choices—what he calls "**low information rationality**" (p. 41). Popkin describes many shortcuts to reasoned choices, such as seeking the opinions of others around us, taking cues from the political party to which the candidate belongs, and assessing the candidate's overall competence rather than the specifics of the candidate's stance on a particular issue. Rather than learn the candidate's specific position on a long list of issues, voters base their choice of candidates on "a measure of ability to handle a job, an assessment of how effective the candidate will be in office, of whether he or she can 'get things done'" (p. 61). And where do voters get the information with which they can assess the candidate's competence? They look to those qualities that critics are quick to dismiss as mere image. Consider, for example, Popkin's description of how voters assess a candidate's performance during a political convention:

> The campaign exposes the candidate to voters in complex and fast-breaking situations. As they watch the candidate handle crowds, speeches, press conferences,

> reporters and squabbles, they can obtain information with which they imagine how he or she would be likely to behave in office. (1991, p. 62)

As we watch candidates in these moments, the audio, kinesthetic, tactile, and clothing channels are operating fully. This is precisely when image is formed, candidates are assessed, and voters decide.

Popkin also draws attention to how voters focus on assessing the personal qualities of candidates along with their overall competence. When voters consider a candidate's stated position on a particular issue, for example, they also question how sincere the candidate's stance is. As Popkin writes, "We care more about sincerity and character when we are uncertain what someone will do" (1991, p. 65). The process is more subtle than the simple comparison of where candidates stand on issues. Here, voters are searching for clues about values, empathy, emotions, bonds, caring, and morality. Positions on issues are perfectly suited to words on the audio channel, but, it seems to me, voters look beyond the words and consider the myriad other ways candidates communicate as they assess personal qualities.

WHY THE SPIN?

So if we agree that modern politics is all about image, the next question is why does it have to be managed so carefully? The answer has much to do with the way these more subtle communication channels work. Birdwhistell argues that, unlike the words and sentences we use, we are often not aware of the meaning of the messages we send through the nonverbal channels. The language of speaking style, **kinesics,** and proxemics is not as precise, and we haven't all been formally schooled in these since the age of five. Similarly, Fred Davis describes how we give meaning to clothing "allusively, ambiguously and inchoately" (1992, p. 5). Sending the right message with these channels is difficult and the risk of inadvertently sending the wrong message is high. Early in his career as prime minister, Stephen Harper chose the wrong outfits for events, including a leather vest and cowboy hat that neither fit him nor the Calgary Stampede event he was attending. The Conservative Party learned from these mistakes and hired a personal stylist for the prime minister—someone who is well versed in the complex codes of clothing and appearance.

Adding to the importance of managing what is said through these channels is the fact that the flow of messages through them is continuous. Though the channels are not always operating simultaneously, Birdwhistell argues that one or more of them are always on. The audio channel matters most whenever politicians step up to the microphone, of course, but the other channels do most of the communicating whenever the candidate is seen but not heard. Kathleen Hall Jamieson (1988) argued that, in the age of television, candidates are seen more often and heard less, as speeches are reduced to sound bites and sixty-second advertisements. In the sixteen years since she made her observation, the visual impact of television has been supplanted by photos and video on the Internet, as well as ever more colourful newspapers and glossy magazines.

Of course, adding to the need for careful attention to the messages sent through all channels is the very nature of election campaigns. Politicians, like most of us, simply change when they're under pressure. They stiffen up, their eyes dart nervously, their skin pales, and their brow sweats— with disastrous results, as Richard Nixon found out in his first televised debate against a tanned and more relaxed John F. Kennedy.[6] The glare of camera lights and the threat of every mistake being broadcast to millions and aired dozens of times only add to the tension. In these conditions, the risk of inadvertently sending the wrong message is high. The decision to hire people who can help a politician communicate effectively using all channels makes sense.

CONCLUSION

So where does this leave us? Is politics all about image? Should it be? I would argue the answer is yes to the first question and no to the second.

Yes, image matters a great deal in politics. The way candidates move, use personal space, look at others, dress, and use speaking style communicates a great deal to voters and helps them better understand the meaning of what candidates say. What's more, voters actively use what they learn from this communication to assess the overall competence of candidates and determine their personal qualities. For voters who feel the issues of an election are not pertinent to them, the candidate's image becomes all the more essential.[7]

That being said, there is also and should also be an important place for genuine discussion of important issues in modern politics. Many Canadian federal elections, for example, have been focused on important issues (e.g., free trade in 1988, accountability in 2006) and, at the end of the day, the choices we make as a country on those important issues will in large part determine the kind of future we have collectively. Even the most focused discussion of issues, however, can be rendered moot if matters of image are ignored and voters are left to misunderstand, distrust, forget, or ignore the debate. Image helps voters connect with candidates and connect to the issues those candidates are discussing. While I don't believe the debate about image versus issues in politics is simply an either-or proposition,[8] I do think that in an environment that features so many competing messages and so many complex channels, image plays a determining role.

The lesson for voters is to make the effort to get beyond negative candidate images and pay attention to the debate on important issues. Democracy needs engaged voters who make the effort to listen actively, even when much of what is coming across on various nonverbal channels is distracting or confusing. The lesson for candidates is to work hard to meet voter expectations of image and get their message across. Voters need candidates who reach out, communicate effectively through multiple channels, and provide information voters can use to engage in the political process and make informed decisions.

Notes

[1] See also the conclusion to Graeme Turner's *Understanding Celebrity* for a critique of "celebrity, politics and spin" (2004, p. 130).

[2] Though she longs for the logic and clarity of classical rhetoric, Kathleen Hall Jamieson recognizes the essential role that image necessarily plays in "this age of electronic advocacy … when you must get your message across in twenty-eight-second cellular morsels" (1988, p. 248).

[3] Though Birdwhistell is among the first communications scholars to look seriously at the meaning we create with our bodies, he is by no means the first to explore the topic. As early as 1873, Charles Darwin wrote *The Expressions of the Emotions in Man and Animals* and explored the links between verbal and visible behaviour of different mammals and certain emotional states.

[4] Birdwhistell later offers a very concise yet broad definition of communication that is helpful to remember as you consider image in politics: "a structural system of significant symbols (from all the sensorily based modalities) which permit ordered human interaction" (1970, p. 95).

[5] Further analysis by the authors revealed five qualities or "factors" of interpersonal communication style that are particularly effective in predicting the outcome of elections. Winners are more likely to be those rated highly by voters for the five following factors: (1) attentive, thoughtful, considerate, egalitarian; (2) good natured, convivial, laughing, smiling; (3) self-confident, assertive; (4) able to mount aggressive verbal attacks; and (5) speaking with great volume, force, compelling gestures (2004, p. 187).

[6] The 1960 debate was the first televised presidential debate in the United States and remains the subject of some controversy among scholars. A poll immediately after the debate found that those who watched the debate on TV were more likely to declare Kennedy the winner, as compared to those who listened to the debate on the radio. Kraus offers a thorough review of the debate and concludes that "Kennedy won on television, while Nixon won on radio" (1996, p. 94).

[7] Samuel Popkin argues that busy voters are increasingly selective about the issues to which they pay attention, favouring those that are personally relevant and visible. For each issue, a community of concerned voters will emerge; the rest of the public will only pay limited attention. The result, according to Popkin, is that "there are few, if any, national policy debates that the mass public can follow in their entirety" (1991, p. 35).

[8] Indeed, Kenneth L. Hacker, editor of *Presidential Candidate Images* (2004), argues that the hard line between image and issues is artificial and overemphasized by both those who feel elections are all about issues and those who feel elections are all about image. Instead of this artificial duality, Hacker calls for a "consolidative dual processing model" (2004, p. 124) by which information on issues and information on candidate character traits are processed at the same time, as each influences the other. Hacker describes his model as "a complex process involving many possible causal directions among many cognitive elements" (2004, p. 129).

References

Argyle, M. (1975). The syntaxes of bodily communication. In J. Benthall & T. Polhemus (Eds.), *The body as a medium of communication* (pp. 143–161). London: Allen Lane.

Birdwhistell, R. L. (1970). *Kinesics and context: Essays on body motion communication.* Philadelphia: University of Pennsylvania Press.

Campion-Smith, B. (2008, May). How Harper controls the spin. *Toronto Star*, p. A1.

Davis, F. (1992). *Fashion, culture and identity.* Chicago: University of Chicago Press.

Ewen, S., & Ewen, E. (1992). *Channels of desire: Mass images and the shaping of American consciousness.* Minneapolis: University of Minnesota Press.

Hacker, K. L. (2004). A dual processing perspective of candidate image formation. In K. L. Hacker (Ed.), *Presidential candidate images* (pp. 105–132). Toronto: Rowan and Littlefield.

Hall, E. T. (1959). *The silent language.* Garden City, NY: Doubleday & Company.

Jamieson, K. H. (1988). *Eloquence in an electronic age: The transformation of political speechmaking.* New York: Oxford University Press.

Kaid, L. L., & Chanslor, M. (2004). The effects of political advertising on candidate images. In K. L. Hacker (Ed.), *Presidential candidate images* (pp. 133–150). Toronto: Rowan and Littlefield.

Kraus, S. (1996). Winners of the first 1960 televised presidential debate between Kennedy and Nixon. *Journal of Communication, 46*(4), 78–96.

Nimmo, D., & Savage, R. (1976). *Candidates and their images.* Pacific Palisades, CA: Goodyear.

Popkin, S. L. (1991). *The reasoning voter: Communication and persuasion in presidential campaigns.* Chicago: University of Chicago Press.

Stephen, T., Harrison, T. M., Husson, W., & Albert, D. (2004). Interpersonal communication styles of political candidates: Predicting winning and losing candidates in three U.S. presidential elections. In K. L. Hacker (Ed.), *Presidential candidate images* (pp. 177–196). Toronto: Rowan and Littlefield.

Turner, G. (2004). *Understanding celebrity.* Thousand Oaks, CA: Sage.

ISSUE 4

Entertaining politics:
Is it all about image?

✗ NO

Leadership Material Isn't Made of Denim
Jennifer Ditchburn

Jennifer Ditchburn has been a parliamentary correspondent since 1997, with a focus on Conservative politics (the Progressive Conservatives, the Canadian Alliance, and the Conservative Party of Canada). For most of her time on Parliament Hill, Ditchburn has worked for the Canadian Press, but she also spent five years as a national reporter with CBC Television. She won a 2010 National Newspaper Award in the politics category for her work on the elimination of the long-form census. The native Montrealer appears regularly as a political commentator on TV and radio. She worked previously for the Canadian Press in Montreal, Toronto, and Edmonton between 1995 and 1997. She is currently a master's student at Carleton University's School of Journalism and Communication.

In the 2011 Hollywood drama *The Adjustment Bureau*, the hunky congressional candidate earnestly played by Matt Damon takes his shoe off in the middle of a concession speech to lament the cult of image in politics:

> Shiny shoes we associate with high-priced lawyers and bankers. If you want to get a working man's vote you have to scuff up your shoes a little bit, but you can't scuff them up so much that you alienate the lawyers and the bankers because you need them to pay the [image] specialists.... So what is the proper scuffing amount? You know we paid a consultant $7,300 ... to tell us that *this* is the perfect amount of scuffing? (Nolfi, 2011)

His popular rejection of the PR team that flapped and pecked around him seems to catapult him into the next Senate race, as he relies more on his authentic voice and abandons artifice. Little does he know (and please excuse the semi-spoiler here) that a higher power has been plotting his political failures and successes, including the life experiences that made him leadership material.

I'm obviously not going to argue that God is what really matters in politics (although some politicians probably think so), nor am I going to suggest that candidates don't benefit from proper framing by public relations professionals, but being successful in politics is much more complex than the properly scuffed shoe or the impromptu piano performance or catching a football correctly in front of the cameras.[1] "Packaging politics," as Robert Franklin has put it (2004), has become a key part of our contemporary democracy. But there are other markers of success in the game. There are critical elements that are both outside of the politician's control—acts of God if you like—and factors that are entirely within his or her control, such as fundraising, tactics, and party rules. Finally, there are more fundamental qualities that centre around a particular candidate's own judgment, instinct, experience, and background, and which speak to his or her own leadership abilities. Image can enhance any of these criteria, but it cannot be the sole or most important reason for success.

Much has been made of Jean Chrétien's own version of a scuffed shoe—the famous denim shirt of the 1993 general election campaign. In campaign posters, Chrétien is seen smiling broadly, his arms casually crossed. The denim shirt seemed to encapsulate the image that his team had been trying to transmit to the public—here was a down-home, friendly leader, the so-called little guy from Shawinigan. Never mind that Chrétien had become a millionaire, wore designer suits, and had spent decades already as part of the political and legal establishment—his particular brand of plainspeaking, anti-intelligentsia populism won the hearts of Canadian voters.

But to ascribe Chrétien's success to a smart image campaign is to ignore completely the unique set of circumstances—those acts of God, the luck, or destiny, take your pick—that were lining up to deliver him an impressive victory. His main rival, Progressive Conservative Leader Kim Campbell, was quickly sinking in the polls following a lacklustre campaign and finally a disastrous advertising move at the end of the writ period that seemed to ridicule Chrétien's physical image.[2] The implosion of the Tory party was not completely Campbell's fault—she had been left to pick up the pieces left by predecessor Brian Mulroney, who had become fabulously unpopular. Mulroney had alienated groups of Progressive Conservatives in both Quebec and Western Canada, giving rise to both the Reform and Bloc Québécois parties. What this meant for Chrétien was a sharply divided political landscape, particularly in Ontario, that allowed him to scoop up large tracts of seats. In one of the first wire stories about Chrétien's victory on the evening of October 25, 1993, Canadian Press reporter Warren Caragata baldly wrote, "When Chrétien moves into the prime minister's residence at 24 Sussex Drive, he should invite Conservative Leader Kim Campbell to the housewarming. For it was the pratfalls and mistakes of the Tory campaign, and the legacy of nine Tory years, that handed the Liberals victory."

Circumstances also played into Stephen Harper's success in the 2006 campaign. Political author Lawrence Martin describes a "striking run of fortune" (2010, p. 8) starting in 2002 that propelled Harper to power. If we look only at the 2006 campaign and Harper's first electoral victory, again it's clear that the circumstances of the day had much to do with the win. The Liberals under Paul Martin were dealing with the aftermath of the scandal around the sponsorship program, including an inquiry that Martin himself had called. The public was already feeling wary of the Liberals, and the RCMP seemed to deliver Martin a decisive blow and hand Harper an incredible gift. Midway through the campaign, the Mounties revealed that they had begun investigating the Liberals to root out the source of leaked information on income trusts. "Destiny was on his side," as Lawrence Martin put it (2010, p. 18).

Bland and brittle Stephen Harper is perhaps a perfect example of the limitations of image when evaluating political success. To say that Harper has completely disregarded the importance of image is untrue—this was a leader who employed a personal stylist for several years and does not appear before television cameras without a good powdering. But overall, Harper's staying power has had much more to do with the control that he and others have exerted on the political processes available to them. Harper has actually done more to alienate the national media than endear himself to them, basically the opposite of what one would expect of an image-conscious leader.

So what has been the key to Harper's success, besides a list of fortuitous events on the political scene? Harper and his team have proven to be masterful manipulators of some of the more subterranean levers of political power. For example, the Conservatives began putting into place an elaborate **voter identification system** in 2004 that helped them store data on the Canadians they came into contact with as party volunteers and candidates went door to door (Flanagan, 2007). The Constituency Information Management System (CIMS) has been envied by other political parties, who see exactly how knowing who is out there can help with the all-important getting out of the vote. Knowing where potential supporters were located helped the Tories figure out where to devote resources and the leader's time during campaigns.

Working hand in hand with knowing where potential pockets of support existed was knowing what kinds of policies they could be sold on. As Tom Flanagan detailed in his book about Harper's path to 24 Sussex, the party began to put together a platform and ad campaign that responded directly and strategically to those pockets of support that could help deliver a win—the Tim Hortons crowd instead of the Starbucks crowd. The end result was a set of clearly understood policies that appealed to the right kind of people in crucial ridings (Flanagan, 2007).

And Harper's party has been incredibly adept at one of the essential tools of modern politics, fundraising. Using both CIMS and the party's own membership database, the Conservative Fund of Canada has used hot political issues to leverage millions from Canadians. That cash has in turn been used to put Harper at an advantage over his rivals even in pre-writ periods. Two Liberal leaders in a row, Stéphane Dion and Michael Ignatieff, suffered the consequences of having the Conservatives define their images for them through negative advertising. Dion was "Not a Leader," a sort of weak-kneed bumbler who would likely cripple the economy. Ignatieff was "Just Visiting," an arrogant dilettante who had spent most of his adult life away from Canada. Dion and Ignatieff became only the second and third Liberal leaders not to ascend to the prime minister's job.

Another way that success comes to political actors is by manipulating, or simply being a captive to, internal **leadership rules**. Few might have anticipated that former prime minister Joe Clark, Liberal Leader Stéphane Dion, or, more recently, Alberta Premier Alison Redford would have nabbed their positions without prevailing over the peculiarities of their own leadership races. In each of these cases, the person who won was not the first choice of most of the delegates at a leadership convention. Rather, it was the result of other, weaker candidates shifting camps and choosing to back former rivals that put them over the top. In the case of the Alberta PC leadership, a preferential ballot meant that the second choice of delegates became a powerful force.

In more extreme cases, leadership rules are more actively manipulated to favour a particular candidate. Paul Martin's team was ingenious at slowly moulding the party's rules and stacking its executive and different tentacles, including campus clubs, to ensure an easy victory. Well before Chrétien had announced he was stepping down as leader, Martin's people in the provincial wings of the party had an iron grip on how membership forms were given out, putting other potential contenders at a clear disadvantage. In the end, there was no real race, and Martin was crowned leader. His camp was the "juggernaut" of Susan Delacourt's book of the same title (2003).

Finally, there is a critical element to success in politics that is often confused with image but has much more to do with qualities that are difficult to put your finger on. In reporting, we rely on words and phrases such as "royal jelly," "savvy," "political smarts," "good judgment," and "strategic thinking." If we drill down even more, we can see some of the components of the elusive royal jelly: work and political experience, intelligence, self-confidence, and analytical skills. In Richard Ben Cramer's chronicling of the 1988 U.S. election and its candidates, *What It Takes* (1992), he provides some spectacularly detailed insight into how a candidate like George H. W. Bush could have possibly won the election. Bush had been pilloried in the media as a wimp, a milquetoast, a shill for Reagan with no real voice of his own. But behind that negative image was still somebody skilled in the art of accommodation, networking, personal discipline, and raw determination. All of those qualities, as well as his deficiencies, were tied up in his upbringing and personal experience—from growing up wealthy yet humble, to bobbing in the South Pacific for two hours after his plane was shot down in World War II. "*They* shouldn't be President.… This was *his* time—he was ready for this game, like no one else," Cramer wrote of Bush's mindset mid-campaign (1992, p. 928).

The flipside of that is a lack of judgment, problems with one's background, and generally being too green for whatever stage a candidate is trying to climb onto. That was certainly the case for Canadian Alliance Leader Stockwell Day, whose short time at the helm was characterized by one political gaffe after another. Although Day had been a successful provincial politician in Alberta, and was initially thought of as an attractive candidate because of his looks, his experience as a minister, his energy, and his bilingualism, the image he tried to put forward eventually became transparent. His controversial positions on social issues were brought up almost immediately by the Liberals and were used to sow uncertainty among the electorate. Once he came to Ottawa, he made bizarre decisions, such as demanding unsuccessfully that journalists meet him at a basement Parliament Hill press room to ask questions rather than the usual scrums in the foyer of the House of Commons.[3] He dared Chrétien to call an election—which the Liberal leader of course did, only a few months after Day had arrived on the federal scene. After the bumpy election campaign, things got even worse, with Day confirming and then denying he had hired a private investigator to get information about the Liberals. Then there was the tale of Lorne Goddard, an Alberta lawyer who had been defending a man against child pornography possession charges. Goddard sued for libel in connection with a critical newspaper piece Day had penned while he was still a provincial minister. Scott Anderson wrote in *NOW* magazine that year (2000) that the issue revealed "the former Alberta treasurer to have a perilously immature concept of how the justice system works, and raising questions about whether he has the sophistication for national leadership." It was only after Day had become a cabinet minister in the Harper government, appearing more seasoned and competent than his peers, that Day's reputation was finally rehabilitated and even earned.

Returning to the example of Jean Chrétien, it would be easy to say that he was a master at portraying the image of a **folksy** get-tough leader, reeling in the supporters with his photo ops capturing him waterskiing, cycling through the streets of China, or bounding up the stairs outside the House of Commons to his office. But Chrétien came to the game with decades of experience in the trenches, toiling away in different portfolios. He took to the campaign trail in 1993 like a fish to water, endearing himself to many voters in the same way that late NDP leader Jack Layton suddenly seemed to catch fire with voters in the 2011 general election. Chrétien in 1993 was no longer the "yesterday's man" that his rivals had made him out to be. Layton in 2011 had shaken loose of the third-place contender label, displaying more gravitas and more authenticity than in any campaign before. Both men had had their share of failures, but at a certain point in their careers were self-assured, well versed in the issues of the day, and more than experienced in the cut and thrust of party and parliamentary life.

There's no question that in a political milieu obsessed with strategic communications, tailoring an image can be an important component of a political campaign or a government's survival. But is it possible that we in the media have given too much credit to the importance of the visual in politics? Michael Schudson in *The Power of News* (1995) talks of a "telemythology," a sort of folklore built up around big events that occurred on television that ascribes to them a much bigger societal punch than they merit. He goes on to dissect the Reagan years, and how the media collectively manufactured the legend of a TV president with enormous popularity—something that was not borne out in any of the polls at the beginning of his presidency. "The power of the media resides in the perception of experts and decision makers that the general public is influenced by the mass media, not in the direct influence of the mass media on the general public" (Schudson, 1995, p. 121).

Media scholar and Rutgers University professor David Greenberg has touched on some of that "telemythology" himself, punching holes in what is the sacred cow of the image crowd: the Kennedy–Nixon debate of 1960. That first televised presidential debate spawned a whole school of thought around the power of television, and how Kennedy's appearance propelled him to power. Greenberg and others have found the claim that Kennedy won solely based on good looks and presentation to be largely unsubstantiated. The oft-repeated "fact" that radio listeners believed Nixon had won the debate was not supported by the evidence. "I think there was a lot about Kennedy's presentation, including his poise and intelligence and command of the issues, that impressed people and dispelled the kind of lightweight playboy image that bothered a lot of people of Kennedy. So I think to chalk it all up to image, as say Daniel Boorstin did in *The Image* and millions have done since, is not quite right," Greenberg told the *Toronto Star* (Pevere, 2010).

Each time there is a leaders' debate in Canada, media pundits build up the moment with every ounce of hyperbole they've got. Perhaps it's because they occur mid-campaign and there's a pent-up desire for drama, or because we've been conditioned to puff up scheduled political events to draw in viewers to the networks. But the fact of the matter is there has been only a smattering of notable moments in Canadian federal debates. Most debates are dull affairs that slip the mind almost immediately after they're finished. All that planning over image—the right tie and the right haircut and the right way to look into the camera—seems far less important than it has been billed. Ultimately, nothing as facile as a debate performance or an appearance on *Tout le monde en parle* is enough to secure a win.[4] Image isn't everything. The reality is that victory is a complex series of hits and misses, the right chess moves within a party and out in the field, and the right sort of leadership qualities. Image can enhance all these things, but in the end it's what the leader brings to the scuffed shoe rather than what the scuffed shoe brings to the leader.

Notes

[1] Prime Minister Stephen Harper garnered positive coverage in 2009 when he took to the National Arts Centre stage to play a few Beatles tunes on the piano. In 1974 a front-page photo of former Conservative leader Bob Stanfield fumbling a football was believed to have seriously hurt him during the campaign.

[2] The Tory campaign ad featured unflattering close-ups of Chrétien's face, and asked the question, "Is this a prime minister?" Chrétien responded by saying he had a physical defect since childhood that he had risen above.

[3] Reporters, including me, found this ploy irritating and inefficient. Soon after he instituted the press conferences in the Charles Lynch room, the number of journalists showing up slowed to a trickle.

[4] *Tout le monde en parle* is a widely watched current affairs chat TV show on Radio-Canada. It features a pair of hosts who interview politicians, artists, activists, and other celebrities from the Quebec cultural milieu in an informal setting. It has been known to bring in more than two million viewers on a Sunday night. Jack Layton's appearance in the 2011 campaign was hailed by some pundits as a huge success and another part of the story of how he managed to sweep Quebec.

References

Anderson, S. (2008, November 16–18). Stockwell Day ruined my life: Shocking comments about respected defence laywer Lorne Goodard raise questions about Alliance leader's fitness for office. *NOW*. Retrieved from http://www.nowtoronto.com

Caragata, W. (1993, October 25). CP newsmaker: Jean Chrétien. *The Canadian Press Newswire*. Retrieved from http://www.fpinfomart.ca

Cramer, R. B. (1992). *What it takes.* New York: Random House.

Delacourt, S. (2003). *Juggernaut: Paul Martin's campaign for Jean Chrétien's crown.* Toronto: McLelland & Stewart.

Flanagan, T. (2007). *Harper's tam: Behind the scenes in the Conservative rise to power.* Montreal: McGill University Press.

Franklin, R. (2004). *Packaging politics* (2nd ed.). London: Arnold.

Martin, L. (2010). *Harperland: The politics of control.* Toronto: Penguin.

Nolfi, G. (Director, Adapted Screenplay Writer). (2011). *The adjustment bureau* [Motion picture]. United States: Universal Pictures.

Schudson, M. (1995). *The power of news.* Cambridge: Harvard University Press.

Pevere, G. (2010, September 24). Kennedy-Nixon: Reign of image politics turns 50. *Toronto Star*. Retrieved from http://www.thestar.com

Discussion Questions

1. Can you think of a particular set of circumstances or a series of events that either helped to bring a leader to power or seriously hurt his or her chances?

2. How important do you think a person's background and experience is to success in politics? Can a person with no charisma and poor TV skills, but lots of experience in politics, become leader or prime minister?

3. Is there more attention paid to image depending on a politician's gender? Is it harder for women to grab hold of the party levers that the author says are part of the path to power?

ABUSIVE SEXTING: The nonconsensual production, transmission, and/or reception of sexually explicit digital images or text, such as forwarding a private image without permission or sending an image to someone who did not want to receive it. (p. 162)

ADMINISTRATIVE COMMUNICATION RESEARCH: Research that pursues questions useful to governments and media corporations on the ways in which citizens use and interact with media. An example would be the work of Paul Lazarsfeld and his colleagues at the Princeton Office of Radio Research and Columbia University's Bureau of Applied Social Research. (p. 54)

ADMINISTRATIVE THEORY: An approach to the study of communication that favours measurement, empiricism, and objective results rather than qualitative opinion or critique. It is often used to buttress critique in policy or professional circles. Administrative research is the backbone of professional communication practice, providing both a knowledge base and a list of best practices. It is often criticized by critical theorists for being neutral vis-à-vis social justice issues and thus supporting the status quo. (p. 50)

AGENCY: In the context of communication technology, the premise that human beings—individually and in groups—have the power to make decisions that go beyond the "tendencies" of the devices they are using, or use them in new and possibly unexpected ways. (p. 140)

AGGRESSION: Definitions vary, but in general aggression is defined broadly as behaviour that intends to harm another person who has reason to avoid the harm inflicted. There are many types of aggression, including physical aggression (intentional physical injury to another person), verbal aggression (harm to another person inflicted by hurtful or threatening speech), and relational aggression (intentional damage to others' friendships and other personal relationships). (p. 97)

ALTERNATIVE COMPENSATION SYSTEM: An alternative compensation system places a levy or tax on recordable media in order to compensate artists for copies made using those media. Canadian policymakers chose this system because it is considered to be a realistic and cost-effective solution to unauthorized copying, since it does not expend public funds on arguably endless and ineffective monitoring and preventing of copying and instead raises funds through a tax on copy equipment to generate a new and significant source of revenue for artists. (p. 257)

ALTERNATIVE MEDIA: Media that provide a range of perspectives and stories not covered in the profit-oriented corporate mainstream media and that are not owned or operated in the same manner as corporate mainstream media. (p. 126)

ANARCHIST PHILOSOPHY: An approach that rejects the authoritarian power of the state and espouses autonomous, self-organized, and federated societies based on guiding principles of freedom and equality in order to develop each human being's innate capacities and talents for the benefit of all. (p. 185)

ANTI-SEMITISM: Discrimination or prejudice against Jews or Judaism. (p. 119)

ASYNCHRONOUS COMMUNICATION: The intermittent transmission of information that does not require an immediate response to complete the communication. Text messaging is one example. (p. 169)

AUTEUR: French for "author," this word is usually used in film criticism to designate certain consistently artful and powerful film directors as the "authors" of their films. (p. 202)

BEHAVIOURAL ADVERTISING: Acquiring personal information and details on an Internet user's online transactions (including search queries, social network site content, web pages visited, email content, and mobile phone location). Content is analyzed to create targeted advertising. (p. 301)

CANCON GHETTO: A term used to describe the practice, common at some radio stations in the 1980s and 1990s, of meeting Canadian content regulations by playing many Canadian songs in the middle of the night or at other low listening times. (p. 224)

CANDIDATE IMAGE: A subjective summary of what an individual knows and feels about a politician, based on both the knowledge possessed by voters and the messages projected by the candidate. Candidate image is constantly being reshaped by new information about the politician; at the same time, the politician's image helps shape the way voters receive and interpret new messages. (p. 316)

CARNIVALESQUE: A carnival-like atmosphere in which typical rules of comportment get turned upside down or temporarily suspended. People mock or challenge authority and traditional hierarchies by showing their bodies at play and putting their trash on display through excessive, rowdy, over-the-top behaviour. (p. 276)

CAUSE MARKETING: In traditional cause marketing a business partners with a charity or nonprofit to help promote a product and to direct some of the proceeds from product sales to advancing a cause or combating a particular societal problem. Crucial to understanding this concept is recognizing the connection between the company's stated "core values" and the cause that it is supporting. (p. 106)

CHECKS AND BALANCES: Democracies are built on a series of checks and balances that are designed to prevent tyranny. Checks and balances are built into constitutional and political systems, and the media also act as a "watchdog" preventing the abuse of power. (p. 6)

CIVIL SOCIETY: Refers to all social relations that spring spontaneously from interpersonal contact and are not governed or managed by the state or political authority. Such relations can range from family picnics to bowling leagues to social protest movements. Civil society is the source of public opinion to which the state and political authorities must usually respond. (p. 17)

COMMODITY SELF: A term created by Stuart Ewan (1988) that describes how under modern capitalism, relationships between people, which make up the social world, are transformed and distorted into relationships between people and commodities. (p. 270)

CONSENSUAL SEXTING: The willing production, transmission, and reception of sexually explicit digital images or text. (p. 159)

CORPORATE PHILANTHROPY: Refers to corporations making direct donations to social causes that do not in any way reflect the business focus of the company. (p. 105)

CRITICAL COMMUNICATION RESEARCH: Research that focuses on questions of communication and social power, seeking to produce knowledge that can assist in social transformation and individual and collective emancipation. An example would be the work of Michael Geist to mobilize Canadians around their intellectual property rights. (p. 58)

CRITICAL THEORY: An approach to the study of communication that favours qualitative methods, opinion and critique over measurement, empiricism, and objective results. It is the theoretical approach most often adopted in Canadian communications departments. It is focused on illuminating differences of power and influence among members of a population, with the direct aim of fighting oppression and inequality. Critical theory understands social power as hierarchically organized and seeks to change existing power relations. Historically this has meant theories critical of fascism and capitalism—notably the Frankfurt School and Marxist thought—however, it now includes a range of post-structuralist, critical race, feminist, queer, post-colonial, diaspora, social movement theories, and more. (p. 50)

CULTURAL IMPERIALISM: Also known as information imperialism, media imperialism, and electronic colonialism, the phrase is intended to capture the domination of one culture by another through systems of communication. The suggestion is that as a nation—most particularly the United States—exports cultural products such as news, movies, and television programs, it also exports its values and priorities. Recipient nations are not only denied the opportunity to develop their own domestic film and television, but come to adopt the values and perspective of the nation that has colonized their media. (p. 29)

CULTURAL INDUSTRIES: A phrase used to describe the industries that have a cultural role—such as creating, producing, and commercializing contents. The cultural industries include advertising, architecture, crafts, fashion clothing, film, printing, publishing and multimedia, audio-visual and cinematic productions, and so forth. The contents produced can take the form of goods or services. (p. 220)

CULTURAL SOVEREIGNTY: The flip side of the concept of cultural imperialism, cultural sovereignty became a concern in Canada in the 1960s and onwards. It was coined to capture the idea that a nation could have sovereign dominion over its territory, its laws, and its government, and yet still be subordinate to another nation in the realm of culture and ideas. Given the prominence of American information and entertainment products in Canada, there was a call to reclaim Canadian cultural sovereignty by reinvigorating domestic cultural production—hence Canadian content regulations in radio and television. (p. 26)

CULTURAL WASTELAND: A metaphor to describe the vacuous nature of much of commercial television programming. It references a 1961 speech by Federal Communications Commission chairman Newton Minow where he described "bad" television as a vast wasteland, "populated by a procession of game shows … unbelievable families, blood and thunder, mayhem … and most of all, boredom." (p. 278)

CYBERNETICS: A branch of information theory concerned with the use of communication to control, through feedback, the actions of systems. (p. 7)

DATA DOUBLE: One's virtual identity located in a networked database. Created by the multiple forms of surveillance users experience online, it is a new form of individual, one made up of pure information. (p. 184)

DEREGULATION (MEDIA): The practice of removing regulatory restrictions and/or public interest responsibilities to which media corporations must adhere. Deregulation is often promoted as a means for stimulating competition. However, it might be better defined as a form of re-regulation in the service of corporate interests. (p. 43)

FACEBOOK ACTIVISM: Various forms of social media activism that, critics argue, have little political impact. Whether it's signing online petitions, donating to causes online, or joining online groups identified with political causes, it is seen as low-risk activism. (p. 153)

FILE SHARING: When digital files (e.g., music) are copied and shared among strangers for free. Peer-to-peer file sharing occurs when participants use software that connects to a peer-to-peer network to search for shared files on the computers of other users (i.e., peers) connected to the network. (p. 243)

FLÂNEUR: A nineteenth-century literary figure who strolls through the newly organized modern city streets and observes life as a mediated spectacle of commodity consumption. The flâneur is both part of and separate from the crowds that inhabit the city and, because of this relationship, feels empathy toward the crowd and understands their relationship to commodity capitalism and the alienation it produces. (p. 265)

FOLKSY: A term often used by journalists to describe a politician's down-to-earth, populist style. A folksy politician chooses to speak in plain language and tries hard not to come off as overly serious or intellectual. (p. 321)

FRAMING: Techniques and practices, such as editing and the selective use of information, employed to create a desired message. (p. 290)

FREE RIDER: Someone who consumes a resource without paying for it, or pays less than the full cost. (p. 245)

HATE SPEECH: A contested term that can mean any expression that denigrates persons on the basis of their race or ethnic origin, religion, gender, age, physical condition, disability, or sexual orientation. It could also be more narrowly defined as persecutory, hateful, or degrading speech communicating messages of inferiority directed at historically oppressed groups. (p. 239)

HETERONORMATIVITY: An ideology that promotes conventional social arrangements such as heterosexuality, traditional gender roles, and conventional family arrangements and defines them as normal. (p. 277)

IMMANENT COMMODIFICATION: The development of intensive measurement and surveillance technologies that produce detailed demographic portraits of social network users. (p. 301)

INCIDENTAL BY-PRODUCT MODEL: A model whereby political knowledge is ascertained through information that is entertainment oriented. (p. 290)

ISLAMOPHOBIA: Hostility toward and/or fear of Muslims or Islam. (p. 119)

KINESICS: Coined by Ray Birdwhistell, a language-like system of meaning we use when we move our body to communicate, including facial gestures, how we move our head, how we move our hand, and how we plant our feet. (p. 315)

LEADERSHIP RULES: All political parties have internal rules that govern how their leaders are chosen. Some parties have a one-member, one-vote system, others elect delegates to send to conventions, and others have a combination of the two. There are also rules around how memberships are sold and for how long. The way the rules are set can be considered more or less advantageous to particular candidates. (p. 320)

LOW INFORMATION RATIONALITY: A term used by Samuel Popkin to describe the many shortcuts people use to make reasoned choices in a limited amount of time. In an election, these could include asking the opinions of others around us, taking the advice of the news media or other opinion leaders, and taking cues from the political party to which the politician belongs. Assessing a candidate's image during an election to draw assumptions about how that candidate will perform once in power is also a form of low information rationality. (p. 314)

MEANINGFUL CONSENT: The giving of consent in which the person possess and understands all the essential information needed to give valid agreement. (p. 307)

MEDIA CONCENTRATION: The degree of concentrated ownership both within and across various media sectors. Critics fear that more heavily concentrated ownership reduces diversity of information, limits access to marginalized groups, and reduces accountability of media owners to the public. Others argue that increased capital of media owners increases competitiveness and allows for more differentiated products that will appeal to niche audiences. (p. 36)

MEDIA PANICS: Apprehension about the uses of new media technologies and their cultural implications where the media act as both the source and object of concern. Adopted by Kirsten Drotner from Stanley Cohen's notion of moral panics. (p. 170)

MOBILIZATION: A key stage in social movement organizing where shared interests of people are converted into collective action for social or political change. Effective mobilization requires a sense of shared purpose and identity. (p. 154)

MOCK NEWS: Political satire that parodies "real" or "hard" news by mimicking its content and structure. (p. 289)

NEOLIBERALISM: A political-economic and regulatory ideology characterized by the privatization of public services, a reduction in the size and scope of government, and the removal of regulations that supposedly limit the freedom of players in a global market. (p. 42)

NEW MEDIA DISPOSITION: Changes in broadcasting technology and audiences associated with the shift from the classical period (1950s–1980s), when a few large networks dominated the airwaves and manufactured content in their own studios for widespread dissemination according to fixed schedules, to a newer period (1970s–present). This period is marked by the introduction of cable and then VCRs, DVDs, video games, the Internet, etc., which allow audiences to watch what they want when they want and to even produce or distribute content. (p. 18)

NEW WORLD INFORMATION AND COMMUNICATION ORDER (NWICO): An initiative spearheaded by UNESCO in the 1980s, first to draw attention to U.S. domination of the global information flow, and second to redress this imbalance. Fiercely resisted by U.S. and allied interests, the initative faltered. Elements of the argument have recently been revived on the international stage, but on economic rather than cultural grounds. The new objection to U.S. media exports is not that they threaten national identities but that they unfairly inhibit the development of profitable national media production, especially in the film and television industries. (p. 25)

NUTRITIONISM: A term coined by Gyorgy Scrinis to refer to what has become our culture's standard means of evaluating food—by focusing strictly on its nutrient profile the level of its nutrients. Nutritionism has become a powerful means of marketing products in the current food environment. (p. 83)

NUTRI-WASHING: When food manufacturers use health-themed marketing to sell processed food. A good example would be the claim of "all natural" or "low fat" on items like potato chips. (p. 84)

OBESOGENIC ENVIRONMENT: The influence that our surroundings, or cultural environment, have on promoting obesity in individuals or populations. Aspects that play into this environment can be *physical* (e.g., availability of bike trails, walking paths, grocery stores, fast-food outlets), *political* (e.g., food regulations/policy), *economic* (e.g., family income, food taxes), and *socio-cultural* (e.g., food marketing and promotion, consumer attitudes). (p. 82)

OLIGOPOLY: A situation wherein a small number of large corporations dominate the marketplace for a particular product or service. Especially in media industries, these corporations often maintain market control through horizontal and vertical mergers or acquisitions. (p. 85)

OPEN SOURCE ORGANIZING: A new form of social movement organizing modelled on the open source software development method, where the source code is transparent and freely available. During the Toronto G20, activists used corporate social media tools and the Internet to openly organize protests with little concern for privacy protection, security culture, or police surveillance, on the premise that they were doing nothing wrong and therefore had nothing to hide. (p. 181)

PANOPTIC SURVEILLANCE: Surveillance that entails one party watching over other subjects, without the subjects ever being certain that they are being watched. The potentiality of observation causes subjects to feel inhibited and incline their choices toward the mainstream. (p. 178)

PIPEDA: The *Personal Information Protection and Electronic Documents Act* or *PIPEDA* (2000) is federal privacy legislation governing private sector enterprises regulated by the federal government, such as banks, airlines, retail companies, and law firms. It requires private sector organizations to protect users' privacy in their collection, use, and disclosure of personal information. (p. 296)

PIRACY (INTERNET): When digital files (e.g., music) are compressed, posted, and transmitted globally via the Internet without permission of the rights holders. (p. 245)

PRIOR RESTRAINT CENSORSHIP: A particularly severe form of restriction on freedom of expression that requires government approval before material can be published, broadcast, or exhibited. Courts in Canada, the United Kingdom, and the United States have been historically reluctant to approve of prior restraints on speech, although they have been tolerated in a number of situations—publication bans on court proceedings and prohibition of certain "obscene" materials are forms of prior restraint censorship. (p. 235)

PROFESSIONAL COMMUNICATION: An interdisciplinary field that exists at the convergence of the areas of public relations/public affairs, communication and opinion measurement, journalism, and communications management. It is rapidly growing area of both academic scholarship and professional practice. (p. 51)

PROMOTIONAL STATE: A form of state that intervenes to support domestic music through means such as public broadcasting, government funding, and content regulations. (p. 211)

PUBLIC SERVICE BROADCASTING: These broadcasters are supported by either government or public funding and differ from private broadcasters in that they have a mandate to pursue the public interest and address their audiences as citizens rather than as consumers. (p. 7)

RACIALIZATION: The process of imposing a racial character on individuals or groups of people. (p. 117)

REPRESSIVE POLITENESS: Being overly polite as a reactionary means to repress a strong desire by performing its opposite. While Canadians are generally proud of their reputation for being extremely polite, this good behaviour might actually hide overpowering feelings of hostility and rage. (p. 199)

SCOPOPHILIA: Defined as "the love of looking," scopophilia entails stripping subjects of their inherent human dignities and transforming them into mere objects to be observed. (p. 179)

SEXTING: The practice of producing, sending, and/or receiving sexually explicit photo, video, or text messages through cellphones or via Internet applications. (p. 159)

SOCIAL CAPITAL: Refers to the degree to which citizens are involved in the lives of their communities by volunteering, joining, voting, and participating. Communities that are rich in social capital tend to be healthier and more prosperous. (p. 7)

SOCIAL MARKETING: The 'products' of social marketing campaigns can be a material good (e.g. food item), a practice (e.g. exercise regimen), a service (e.g. breastfeeding support group) or an idea (e.g. sustainability). Unlike traditional marketing campaigns, which principally benefit the company or organization, social marketing campaigns are designed by and for consumers, and are often developed following consumer input. (p. 106)

SOCIAL MEDIA: A range of Web 2.0 applications characterized by user-generated content and interactive capacity. The six types of social media classified by Kaplan and Haenlein (2010) are social networking sites, content communities, blogs, collaborative projects, virtual game worlds, and virtual social worlds. (p. 144)

SOCIAL NETWORK: An online platform that allows individuals to connect with each other to exchange text, images, and links. (p. 304)

STEREOTYPES: Generalized, frequently simplistic, belittling, hurtful, or prejudicial ideas, often widely held, that are unreflective of the complexity of the group of people being stereotyped. (p. 118)

SUBSTITUTION EFFECT: The use of file-sharing networks to obtain free copies of music that would have otherwise been purchased. Industry organizations tend to assume that the effects of file sharing are homogeneous (all uses of file sharing can be characterized as substitution), when in fact the evidence suggests that the effects of file sharing are differential or heterogeneous because the relationship between file sharing, music purchasing, and artist and label revenue is much more complex and varied than labels suggest. (p. 254)

SURVEY RESEARCH: A form of research used to identify correlations between two or more variables using questionnaires with a large group of respondents, either measured at only one point in time or over a period of months or years. (p. 99)

SYNOPTIC SURVEILLANCE: Surveillance where all individuals watch all other individuals. This mutual watching "democratizes" surveillance, insofar as it removes hierarchical power relations (i.e., the one or few watching the many) that are presumed in panoptic surveillance. (p. 178)

TAGGING: The process of attaching keyword descriptions to identify images or text within a social network, blog, or website. (p. 306)

TAUTOLOGY: A circular argument such as "Canadian films have these qualities and therefore films with these qualities are Canadian." (p. 208)

TECHNOLOGICAL DETERMINISM: A theoretical position that suggests technologies have the power to shape human behaviour, social structures, and cultural norms. (p. 168)

360 DEAL: Emerging in the early 2000s, these now-standard agreements between a label and an artist are based on an expanded-rights contract, which allows the label to access revenue from nearly all of the artist's activities. 360 deals help offset the effects of file sharing by allowing labels to profit from activities other than record sales and by discouraging artists from using file sharing to promote and distribute their own works. (p. 253)

VOTER IDENTIFICATION SYSTEM: Computer-based software used pervasively by political parties in countries such as Canada, the United States, and Australia to collect and store data about voters. Each entry can include information on the voter's political views, as well as details such as the individual's address and number of children. (p. 320)